Data Structures, Computer Graphics, and Pattern Recognition

Academic Press Rapid Manuscript Reproduction

Data Structures, Computer Graphics, and Pattern Recognition

Edited by

A. Klinger

University of California
Computer Science Department
Los Angeles, California

K. S. Fu

Purdue University
Department of Electrical Engineering
Lafayette, Indiana

T. L. Kunii

University of Tokyo
Department of Information Science
Hongo Bunkyo, Tokyo

Academic Press, Inc.

NEW YORK   SAN FRANCISCO   LONDON   1977

A Subsidiary of Harcourt Brace Jovanovich, Publishers

ACADEMIC PRESS, INC.
111 Fifth Avenue, New York, New York 10003

United Kingdom Edition published by
ACADEMIC PRESS, INC. (LONDON) LTD.
24/28 Oval Road, London NW1

Library of Congress Cataloging in Publication Data

Main entry under title:

Data structures, computer graphics, and pattern
        recognition.

        Consists of papers, many of which evolved from
presentations given at the IEEE Computer Society con-
ference held in Los Angeles, May 1975.
        Includes bibliographies and index.
        1.   Data structures (Computer science)—Addresses,
essays, lectures.   2.   Computer graphics—Addresses,
essays, lectures.   3.   Pattern recognition systems—
Addresses, essays, lectures.   I.   Klinger, Allen,
Date   II.   Fu, King Sun,   Date   III.   Kunii,
Toshiyasu.
QA76.9.D35D37   001.6'4   77-1598
ISBN 0−12−415050−0

PRINTED IN THE UNITED STATES OF AMERICA
79 80 81 82   9 8 7 6 5 4 3 2

Contents

Organizing Data in Computer Graphics Applications
Robin Williams

a. A Survey of Data Structures for Computer Graphics Systems
Robin Williams

b. On the Application of Relational Data Structures in Computer Graphics
Robin Williams

c. Data Structures in Computer Graphics
Robin Williams, Gary M. Giddings, Warren D. Little, W. Gerald Moorhead, and Daniel L. Weller

Some Observations on Linguistics for Scene Analysis
T. Kasvand

PART II: DESIGN DECISIONS

Data Management and Pattern Recognition
Carl V. Page

The Design of Satellite Graphics Systems
James D. Foley

Automatic Detection of Suspicious Abnormalities in Breast Radiographs
Carolyn Kimme, Bernard J. O'Loughlin, and Jack Sklansky

Error-Correcting Parsing for Syntactic Pattern Recognition
K. S. Fu

List of Contributors

Numbers in parentheses indicate pages on which authors' contributions begin.

R. E. Barnhill (413),* University of Utah, Department of Mathematics, Salt Lake City, Utah 84112

Charles M. Eastman (31), Carnegie-Mellon University, School of Urban & Public Affairs, Schenley Park, Pittsburgh, Pennsylvania 15213

James D. Foley (239), Bureau of the Census, Graphics Software Branch, Washington, D.C. 20233

K. S. Fu (449), Purdue University, Department of Electrical Engineering, West Lafayette, Indiana 47907

Marilyn L. Griffith (309), Information Sciences, Electronics Research Division, Rockwell International, 3370 Miraloma Avenue, P.O. Box 3105, Anaheim, California 92803

R. A. Jarvis (273), The Australian National University, Department of Computer Science, Canberra, A.C.T. 2600, Australia

T. Kasvand (179), National Research Council of Canada, Computer Graphics Section, Radio & Electrical Engineering, Ottawa, Ontario, K1A OR8 Canada

Carolyn Kimme (427),* University of California, School of Engineering and Department of Radiological Sciences, Irvine, California 92664

Allen Klinger (385), University of California, Computer Science Department, 3531 Boelter Hall, Los Angeles, California 90024

Bernard J. O'Loughlin (427), University of California, School of Engineering and Department of Radiological Sciences, Irvine, California 92664

*Indicates first author

Carl V. Page (213), Michigan State University, Computer Science Department, East Lansing, Michigan 48824

Michael L. Rhodes (385),* University of California, Computer Science Department, 3531 Boelter Hall, Los Angeles, California 90024

R. F. Riesenfeld (413), University of Utah, Computer Science Department, Salt Lake City, Utah 84112

John P. Riganati (309),* Information Sciences, Electronics Research Division, Rockwell International, 3370 Miraloma Avenue, P.O. Box 3105, Anaheim, California 92803

Jack Sklansky (427), University of California, School of Engineering and Department of Radiological Sciences, Irvine, California 92664

Frank W. Tompa (3), Department of Computer Science, University of Waterloo, Waterloo, Ontario, Canada

Robin Williams (103, 105, 153, 167),* International Business Machines, Monterey and Cottle Roads, San Jose, California 95193

Charles T. Zahn, Jr. (59), Stanford Linear Accelerator Center, Computation Research Group, Stanford, California 94305

*Indicates first author

Preface

Many researchers have seen the close connection between computer graphics and pattern recognition and the central role of data structures in those fields. Data structures are themselves an important subject of study in computer science. Many data structure types and application areas use the special properties of them to facilitate computing algorithms. Among the main structuring techniques are linear lists, trees, and binary trees. Distinctions between sequential and linked allocation of storage, the number and types of pointers, and the modes of data organization (e.g., stacks, queues, trees, and lists) are all important in planning software. This book focuses on the computer graphics and pattern recognition applications of data structures methodology. It presents design related principles and research aspects of the computer graphics, system design, data management, and pattern recognition tasks.

Computer graphics and pattern recognition, respectively, stand for synthetic and analytic aspects of processing patterned data. In both computer graphics and pattern recognition, there is a core of dependence upon data structures and this is the central subject of this book. In all programs written to do patterned data processing, the data structure is a formal basis for organizing quantities that are to be processed. Hence, the data structure is actually a common medium, one that can join these two special research areas. Data structure design, selecting the data's memory representation, is central to programs for creating graphics console displays. Data structures serve as "transformers" between complex data relationships and serial processing systems, since they are links between a complex pattern that humans may perceive in an input stream of patterned data and the programs that will process that data.

Recent developments in computer technology have made available small machines with graphic display capability. This has increased the tendency to present the pattern recognition task as an interactive process where the computer partially serves man as a reformatting tool. Since data structures theory contributes to programming in the small memory context, this technological change has also highlighted the need for using a common representation medium for the display and analysis aspects of problems.

Rapid development of the pattern recognition and computer graphics technical fields and their common use of data structure principles in organizing sophisticated processing routines has led to an increasing awareness in the research community of the close relationship among these three topics. A conference held in May 1975 in Los Angeles, in participation with the IEEE Computer Society, brought together researchers working on all these themes. Over three hundred scientists attended, and *The Proceedings of the Conference on Computer Graphics, Pattern Recognition, and Data Structure* (IEEE, New York, 75 CHO 981-1C) includes ninety technical papers. While this conference was being organized, the three editors conceived the need for a book that would focus on the conference theme in a format allowing more extensive presentation of expository material. The intent, to provide a starting point for researchers interested in the intersection of the three fields, is realized by this volume. Many of the papers included here evolved from papers presented at the 1975 conference, and from discussions at the time of the conference between the editors jointly, and with individual authors.

The material presented here will be of interest to practitioners in data structures, particularly those who are applying real computer systems to problems involving image, speech, and medical data. The chapters convey current state-of-the-art uses of data structures in computer graphics displays and pattern recognition algorithms. Many chapters conclude with exercises that will be useful to students and to instructors who wish to use this book as a supplementary text. Other chapters cover current research topics, including language understanding and syntactic pattern recognition. Such material is not suitable for exercise problems, but in keeping with many of the other chapters, this research literature provides topics for further research.

Finally, a word of thanks to all of the contributors for their care in preparing their manuscripts for this volume, to R. Burns whose organizational skills are reflected here, and to J. Badal and D. Trammel for their help with the typing. The support of the Air Force Office of Scientific Research is gratefully acknowledged.

I

FUNDAMENTAL METHODOLOGY

Data Structure Design

FRANK W. TOMPA

Department of Computer Science
University of Waterloo
Waterloo, Ontario, Canada

1. LEVELS OF DATA REFINEMENT

Many data structures designers realize that data should be specified at two levels: the abstract, user-oriented information structure and the concrete, machine-oriented storage structure. Judging from the experience of algorithm designers, however, data structures should instead be viewed at many levels.

The design methodology suggested here is based on five views of data:

- data reality: the data as it actually exists (including all aspects which are typically ignored except in philosophical treatises)

- data abstraction: a model of the real world which incorporates only those properties thought to be relevant to the application(s) at hand

- information structure: a refinement of the abstraction in which only some of the relevant data relationships are made explicit, the others derivable indirectly (usually through some computations involving relational composition)

- storage structure: a model of the information structure, often expressed in terms of diagrams which represent cells, linked and contiguous lists, and levels of storage media

•machine encoding: a final computer representation,
including .pecifications for encoding primitive
data objects (e.g., the representations for
numbers and characters, the use of absolute as
opposed to relative addresses, and the use of
data packing).

The design of a data structure should proceed through successive
levels, binding only those aspects which are necessary to specify each level. Within a level, the process of stepwise refinement should be adapted from algorithm design methodology to provide as smooth a transition as possible to the more detailed
data level [10, 17, 38].

These five views of data correspond exactly to the levels
of development in the corresponding program which describes the
data operations to be performed. The first step defines the
application's goal in terms of real objects. Next, the approach
to a solution which achieves that goal is specified in terms of
the data abstraction. At the third step, an algorithm incorporating the approach is designed to operate on the information
structure, after which a program implementing the algorithm is
written to manipulate data in terms of its storage structure.
Finally, at the fifth level, the program is translated into object code which operates on data bound to a particular machine
encoding.

2.   AN EXAMPLE OF STEPWISE DATA STRUCTURE DESIGN

Designing the data structure for a hypothetical genealogical application will serve to illustrate the methodology to be
followed. It will be assumed that a historical foundation wishes
to computerize the Habsburg family tree for a fact retrieval system which is to be implemented on an IBM 360/75.

By the time the data structure is to be designed, the data
reality has already been chosen: in this case, the structure of
all the facts concerning the Habsburg lineage. In many cases,
the primitives available for the machine encoding level have
also been fixed: here, those provided by 360 architecture (e.g.
memory addressing structure, cell size). Thus the design process is actually composed of four major steps which serve as
transitions, or mappings, from one data structure level to the
next.

The first step in the design is to identify the aspects of the real world which are relevant to the application. Some facts concerning the Hapsburgs are clearly of no concern to genealogical studies: for example, that the name is derived from Habichtsburg on the Aar, that Albert III was landgrave of Upper Alsace, or that Emperor Maximillian of Mexico did not get along very well with his brother Emperor Francis Joseph I.* The data designer must therefore consider the data reality and select those properties to record; all other information will be impossible to obtain from the data base. From discussions with the directors of the historical foundation, it may be learned that the only relevant facts are persons' names, dates of birth and death, and blood and marital relationships. This information constitutes the data abstraction.

At the level of the data abstraction, all data is equally accessible. In a manner similar to examining a conventional genealogical chart, information can be obtained about any entry without necessarily starting a search from a particular root (e.g., Guntram the Rich). In addition, it must be as easy to ascertain any relationships as any others; for example, at the data abstraction level, finding all the second cousins of Ferdinand III or the great grandchildren of Maria Theresa is conceptually as natural as finding parents, children, a name, or a date of birth. That is, there is no concept of efficiency yet at this stage of the design.

After the data abstraction is designed, the next step is to decide on an information structure by choosing which of the relevant data relations will be stored explicitly and which will remain accessible only via others. For example, it may be that researchers often require the names of the Habsburg cousins of certain Habsburgs. Done often enough, it would be convenient to store the cousin relationship explicitly; thus, for example, associated with Emperor Rudolph II is the set of nineteen cousins (Figure 1). Storing cousins explicitly, however, results in some redundancy, because sets of cousins often intersect. To avoid such redundancy, cousins from different parents could be kept separately, and thus cousins may be found by accessing the children of a person's uncles and aunts. Instead of a simple retrieval of one set, first the uncles and aunts of Rudolph must be collected, yielding Philip II and Joan on his mother's side and Ferdinand of Tirol, Charles, and 11 aunts on his father's

---

*This and all subsequent material concerning the Habsburgs, is obtained from reference 13.

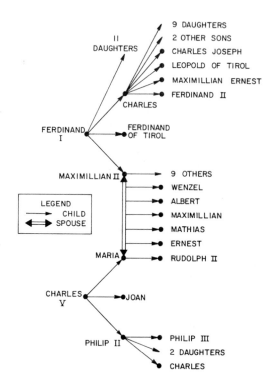

Figure 1:   *Detail From a Habsburg Genealogical Chart*

side; then the union of their children must be found. Thus the
price of less redundancy is more complicated access. By examining the relative frequency of operations to be performed on the
data, the genealogical data designers choose to maintain for
each Habsburg, the name, parents, spouses, children, date of
birth, and date of death:

    set of person Habsburg;

    type person = (string NAME; elders PARENTS;
                    set of offspring FAMILY; life YEARS);

    type elders = (person MOTHER, FATHER);

    type offspring = (person SPOUSE; set of person CHILDREN);

    type life = (date BIRTH, DEATH);

Having chosen this information structure, an algorithm can be written for each data operation required. For example, to find the cousins of Rudolph, the following algorithm is possible:

GRANDPARENTS ← RUDOLPH'S PARENTS' PARENTS

GRANDCHILDREN ← GRANDPARENTS' CHILDREN'S CHILDREN

SIBLINGS ← RUDOLPH'S PARENTS' CHILDREN

COUSINS ← GRANDCHILDREN - SIBLINGS

If many researchers wanted to examine the Habsburgs' life spans, it may be worthwhile to order the Habsburgs by their ages at death; however, given the information structure chosen here, the complete family tree may have to be traversed to answer questions such as how many Habsburgs died before they were thirty. Thus the information structure has a direct effect on the efficiency of operations applied to a data base.

After the explicit relations are chosen and the algorithms for data manipulation are written, the storage structure must be designed. For each occurrence of a complex data type, (such as a tuple, set, sequence, or array) in the information structure, a storage mapping function must be chosen. For example, for each explicit relation it must be decided where pointers should be used in preference to contiguity, whether or not trees should be balanced, and which sets of data objects should be kept together in case of a paging environment. For the application, the set used to represent all the Habsburgs could be stored as a doubly-linked list with no concern for ordering to simplify the code needed to add new members, or it could be stored contiguously, ordered by name to speed up the search for a particular member. To avoid having variable-length fields in the middle of tuples for each person, and thus to simplify access to all fixed-length fields, either the NAME could be stored contiguously in a large fixed-sized field or a fixed-size pointer to an arbitrary-length string containing the NAME could be used. Alternatively, to save space, the variable-length string could be stored in an exact-fitting field as the last entry of each tuple.

Thus the design of the storage structure is heavily dependent on the relative frequencies of operations on each component of information structure (number of retrievals *vs.* insertions and deletions) and on the cost of storage space *vs.* the cost of execution time. Because the genealogical system is to be core-resident on a 360/75, and because the operations tend to cluster around one or two given people (e.g., who are Rudolph's cousins?

was Francis Joseph's father alive when Archduke Francis Ferdinand was assassinated?) the following design is chosen (Figure
2):

- the fields of each tuple will be stored contiguously in the order of the information
  structure, except that each person's name
  will appear last,

- the set of persons representing the whole
  Habsburg family will be linked through the
  PARENTS and CHILDREN fields rather than having
  its own pointers,

- all other sets will be stored indirectly (i.e.,
  a pointer will be stored in the appropriate
  tuple) as a singly-linked list, the families
  ordered by date of marriage and the children
  ordered by date of birth,

- each occurrence of a person within another
  tuple will be represented indirectly.

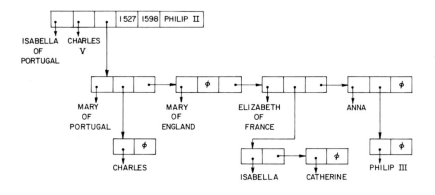

Figure 2: *Detail From the Storage Structure*

The final design step is to map the storage structure onto the machine. Each primitive data object (e.g., integer, real, character, and pointer) must be encoded in terms of bits, bytes, or words. As at the previous step, the choices are usually made in terms of space/time trade-offs. For example, each string can be encoded using data compression to save space or it can be left unpacked to allow efficient input and output; each date can be stored as a four-character string or it can be encoded as binary numbers: the birth as the number of years since the year 1000 and the death as the number of years since the birth (i.e., the age at death).

To save time (at the expense of space) the hypothetical genealogical data base may be stored on the 360/75 as follows (Figure 3):

•strings are headed by a one-byte length field followed by each character stored in EBCDIC,

•pointers are hexadecimal, six-digit absolute memory addresses, stored right-justified in a 32-bit word,

•dates are three-byte EBCDIC characters representing the last three digits of the date.

This completes the design of the data structure. It is important to realize that in actual practice the design will not likely be completed in one pass through the steps outlined here. It may be obvious that the design of one level may give insight into deficiencies in the design of the previous level, thus requiring some backtracking to redesign. For example, if the storage structure were originally designed to place the dates before the pointers to parents and family, it would become obvious during the design of the machine encoding that these pointers will not be word-aligned unless two bytes are left unused after the date fields: thus the storage structure would subsequently be redesigned to resemble Figure 2.

Less obvious is that "one man's storage primitive is another's data reality." For example, strings, which were considered to be primitive objects in this design, may instead be interpreted as an ordered, arbitrarily large collection of characters (i.e., type string = sequence of character). This interpretation requires the design of a storage structure for the sequence and a data encoding for individual characters, thus allowing the designer to decide whether to incorporate text compression.

Figure 3:   *The Machine Encoding for the*
Tuple Representing Philip II

3.   RESEARCH ACTIVITIES

This section examines some aspects of research at each of
the levels of data and at the interfaces between successive
levels. This outline is not a complete review of current activities in data structures, but rather it is intended to provide
additional insight into the interrelationships among the levels.

3.1   Data Reality

Top management must be able to consider all aspects of data
reality. For example, managers in a credit card company *do*
care about the availability of plastics for the cards, the appeal of the design of the cards' faces, and other aspects which
are probably "irrelevant" in the view of computer personnel
dealing with the data. Therefore such information must be included as part of the first view of data. As mentioned in the
previous section, the data reality is usually specified before
the start of data structure design; thus research at this level
falls into non-computer areas, such as business administration,
economics and consumer psychology.

3.2   Transition to Data Abstraction

Translating an application from the reality into an abstraction is the interface at which data managers decide which aspects of data are relevant to the model (possibly by enumerating
the types of queries and updates that may be applied to the
data). It is this step of the design that is usually the most
difficult, for it involves identifying all the aspects of reality which will be relevant to the application: people unfamiliar with a computer program's lack of forgiveness (doing what

is said, not what is meant) cannot specify all details, and people unfamiliar with reality's lack of consistency (changing economics, legalities, technologies) cannot cope with fluid and incomplete specifications. Some work has begun on developing techniques to formalize an application's needs [4], but much is still to be done. Designing methodologies to map data realities into suitable models may be the greatest future contribution from researchers who straddle the fields of computer and management sciences.

3.3 Data Abstraction

Management communicates with computer personnel at the level of the data abstraction. Thus data must be described formally, yet in terms understandable to non-mathematicians. The result is that many data base systems and languages have been designed to operate at this level in terms of a relational model [5, 8]. Such a model presents data as if it were a large table of values, organized as an unordered set of tuples (or records) serving as the table's rows and as an unordered set of (named) domains serving as the columns. This model meets the requirement of the abstraction level that all relationships are equally accessible, and thus there is no "navigation" required to access data.

Other research at this level involves the design of models based on algebra or on graph theory. The latter models represent data items as nodes and data relations as directed edges connecting the appropriate items. Again, to qualify as a model for data abstraction, there cannot be any need for navigating the data base; thus the graphs cannot be rooted, and they must be conceptually equivalent to their transitive closure.

3.4 Transition to Information Structure

Given an abstract specification of a data structure, many relationships can be expressed in terms of other, more basic ones. For example, finding a person's cousins can be accomplished by finding the children of that person's uncles and aunts, by finding the nieces and nephews of that person's parents, or by finding the children of that person's parents' siblings. Thus a data structures designer must determine which of the relationships are to be considered basic and therefore stored explicitly as part of the information structure. The rest will remain accessible only via one or more "access paths" through the stored relationships [1].

The ANSI/SPARC recommendations for data base systems include this transition in a mapping from a conceptual schema
(the enterprise's view -- a composite of users' views) to an
internal schema (the stored data view) [2]. The data base administrator must determine the requirements of all users in order
to decide which of the relationships are the most basic across
the complete application, and to provide algorithms which encode
the rest. The concept of data independence implies that the
users need not be aware of which relationships are stored explicitly and which are not; in fact, the data base administrator
should be able to alter the information structure without
affecting any users' programs.

3.5   Information Structure

Each explicit relationship is encoded by means of a data
type, such as a tuple, sequence, set, tree, or array, for which
certain operations are defined (Figure 4). From these, complete
information structures can be built and associated algorithms
can be expressed in terms of the given primitive operations.

Recently, research at the information structure level has
been concentrated on the specification of data types [21]. Not
only does the format of an instance of each data type need to be
described, but the effect of each of the defined primitive operations must also be specified precisely. There has recently been
much interest in algebraically-based formalisms [16], as well as
in techniques based on graph theory [14].

Another area of study within information structures is the
determination of ordering to be applied to particular data types.
For example, there has been much research into the ordering of
lexicographic search trees, with some results concerning optimal
ordering [18] and others concerning efficiently achievable near-
optimal orderings [36].

3.6   Transition to Storage Structure

For each data type there are many storage structures which
can be used to model the data operations. Consider for example
a sequence as defined in Figure 4. Assuming a pointer to the
start of the sequence, the sequence extent can be represented by
storing the size, by storing a pointer to the last element, or
by incorporating a delimeter after the last element (Figure 5a).

__tuple__

Properties: finite juxtaposition of components, each having a
type and a name which may be used as a selector

Examples: __type__ rational = (__integer__ NUMERATOR; __integer__ DENOMINATOR)
rational PI
__type__ student = (__integer__ ID_NUMBER, AGE; 1..4 YEAR: __logical__ SEX)
student LEE

Operations: initialization: LEE := (75023962,22,2,__true__)

selection: PI(NUMERATOR)

__sequence__

Properties: arbitrarily large, ordered collection of homogenous components

Examples: __type__ queue = __sequence of__ student
queue WAITING_LIST
__type__ string = __sequence of__ character
string TEXT

Operations: initialization: all sequences initialized to __null__ (i.e. size=0)

selection: WAITING_LIST(__first__) WAITING_LIST(__last__)
TEXT(__current__) TEXT(__next__) TEXT(__previous__)
WAITING_LIST(I)

insertion: __insert__ "a" __after__ TEXT(__current__)
__insert__ LEE __before__ WAITING_LIST(__current__)

deletion: __delete__ TEXT(__current__)

__tree__

Properties: root node and a sequence of subtrees, such that all
nodes are of the same type

Examples: __type__ family = __tree of__ person
family JONES
__type__ contents = __tree of__ section
contents   BOOK

Operations: initialization: JONES := LEE

selection: BOOK(2.4.1.2)
__root__ (JONES(__current__))

traversal: __for__ MEMBER ε JONES __do__

insertion: __insert__ CHAPTER3 __after__ BOOK(__current__)
__insert__ LEE __before__ JONES(__current__)

deletion: __delete__ BOOK(__current__)

Figure 4: *Examples of Data Type Descriptions*

a. DENOTING THE EXTENT

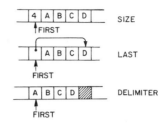

b. DENOTING THE SEQUENTIAL RELATIONSHIP

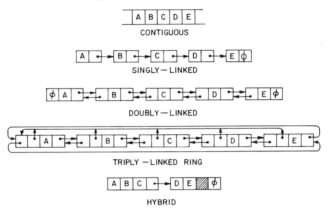

Figure 5:   *Representations for a Sequence*

The sequence itself can be stored contiguously, using one-way, two-way, or multiple pointers (absolute or relative addresses), or a hybrid of contiguity and links (Figure 5b). The alternatives chosen for an application may have dramatic effects on execution time and on storage space efficiency.

Thus, at this interface, the choice of representation includes decisions between contiguity and links, between one-way and multiply-linked lists, and between direct access and scatter storage techniques. Some research has been conducted into choosing an optimal representation from within a limited class of storage structures [30]. To allow automated selection from among more diversified representations, an alternative methodology has been developed for choosing the best storage structure available from a library of representations encompassing many classes of structures [15].

3.7   Storage Structure

Individual storage structures have been studied for many years. Before the mid-sixties numerous novel linking methods were developed in new programming languages. For example, LISP used pairs of contiguous cells for CAR and CDR [23], SLIP introduced two-way lists [37] and CORAL was designed around linked lists in which each element contains a pointer to the next element and a pointer that either references the previous element or the first (i.e., head) element [31].

More recently, quantitative studies have been conducted to determine the performance characteristics for sets of related storage methods. For example, many scatter storage techniques had been proposed in the sixties, each claiming to be efficient for a class of applications; several of these were finally compared on various sets of data to help designers choose among them [22]. Comparison studies have also been conducted on representations for other data types, such as lexicographic search trees [28].

3.8   Transition to Machine Encoding

Binding a storage structure to a machine is the last interface in the design of a data representation. Research at this transition includes the study of alternatives for encoding indivisible units of data. For many applications, much of the encoding is predetermined by the choice of implementation language, operating system, and machine configuration. For example, few applications designers can actually choose between twos complement and signed magnitude representations for integers; between hexadecimal, octal, and binary floating point representations for reals; or between EBCDIC and ASCII representations for characters.

There are two aspects of this transition over which many designers do have control. The first is the option of data compression techniques, including Huffman encoding, blank suppression, differencing, and decimal-to-binary encoding [19]. The advantages of data compression arise from storage savings, increased security, and sometimes run-time savings (when the space requirements are so much reduced that data can reside on a faster storage medium). The other aspect receiving much research attention is the study of portable software (i.e., machine independence), where the same storage structure is mapped onto a variety of machines [35]. The primary advantages here are the ability to exchange data between installations and the ability to upgrade a given installation's machine configuration without extensive software recoding.

3.9 Machine Encoding

Finally, the machine encoding is the level at which all implementations must eventually reside. Research at this level is typically hardware-oriented, though more recently many researchers have become involved with microprogramming. Two areas which will likely have significant effects on data structure design are the study of new memory technologies (e.g., bubble memories, holographic stores) [26] and research into associative memory techniques [29].

4. OTHER DESCRIPTIONS OF DATA LEVELS

The design methodology proposed here is not new, but instead a fresh look at methodologies suggested for several years. It is worthwhile to examine some previous proposals which are related to this framework.

The separation of the storage structure from the machine encoding was first incorporated into the COBOL language. For example, the choice of packed decimal or binary representation for numeric data is specified physically apart from the operations performed on that data. By providing distinct data and program divisions, COBOL programmers were forced to separate the details of data encoding from the programs that manipulate the data, thus achieving a degree of representation independence not previously available in other languages.*

In a paper which is now classic, Mealy described data at three levels [25]. He reminded programmers that their view of data was only a theoretical model of real world objects, and therefore necessarily did not include some properties thought to be irrelevant. Furthermore, Mealy pointed out that the data as stored was, in turn, only a machine representation for the theoretical model. He claimed that programmers must be provided

---

*The format statement in FORTRAN does provide some independence, but at the input/output interface only.

with facilities for accessing data from either of the latter
viewpoints to allow representation independence while still providing control over implementation efficiency.

Following along these lines, d'Imperio explained the advantages of separating the design (and the description) of stored
data into the two stages suggested by Mealy [11].

"There are various ways of representing a given
data structure (e.g., a "tree") in storage structures, and the same storage structure may be used
for several different data structures. Particular
data structures, as defined here, are the products
of a particular human interpretation of a problem,
expressed in the preliminary preparation and recording of the data and in the choice and ordering
of processes that take place in a particular program. They are not invariant, inherent, or
necessary parts of the data itself, but are the
result of a certain way of looking at the data and
the problem solution. Since data structures are
the products of human understanding and purpose
in defining a solution to a problem and are often
chosen without the explicit awareness of the problem solver, they tend to be taken for granted,
and attention is directed solely toward the storage structures in which the data will be arranged
and manipulated and which the problem solver must
explicitly define and arrange. Hence, properties
that belong to the interpretation of the data and
the meaning of the data in the problem easily become confused with and unnecessarily tied down to
the particular storage structures that were selected to handle them in a particular programming system." [page 3]

She then reviewed several common structures in terms of those
two levels. This analysis aided her in comparing the facilities
and efficiency of the data structures provided by a chosen set
of programming languages.

A two-level approach to data has led several language designers to provide a syntax and semantics which will aid programmers in separating the design of the theoretical model from
the design of the machine representation. Balzer developed a
system which provided a uniform syntax for manipulating several
data types [3]. For example, the construct PERSON(AGE) could
be used to access a component of a PL/1 structure, access an

element in some array, or call a function which takes one parameter and returns some value. The particular machine representation to be used could be chosen after the program was completely written, and if inadequate it could be redesigned without any programming changes. Separating the two design decisions by this technique has since become known as uniform referents [32].

An extension and formalization of these ideas has recently received much attention under the name of abstract data types. One major approach was incorporated in SIMULA 67 which includes a construct named a "class," through which the properties of a user-defined data type and valid operations on that type are defined separately from its representation [7]. Using a similar approach, a language's translator can enforce this separation by allowing access to a data type's representation inside the class which encodes it and disallowing such access elsewhere [20, 27]. The data encoding can thus be altered without affecting the rest of the program. In addition, the separation permits proofs of correctness to be established in two stages: the uses of the abstract data type can first be shown to model reality, and the representation can then be shown to be a faithful implementation of that data type. Through type-checking, a language's translator can ensure that only valid instances of a data type are submitted for processing under that type's operations.

While some researchers explored the separation of the theoretical model from the machine representation, others realized that it is worthwhile to view data structures as consisting of more than two levels. McCuskey described a model containing four data views: the real world (problem level), the theoretical model (problem interpretation), the information structure (logical organization), and the machine representation (physical organization) [24]. McCuskey thus separated Mealy's theoretical model level into two stages to distinguish between the specification of the relevant relations (to be made at the level of the problem interpretation by using a set-theoretic framework) and the specification of the explicit relations (to be made at the level of the logical organization). Earley furthered the ideas of McCuskey's model by developing unified language constructs to encompass the three levels dealing with stored data [12].

A data model developed more recently is the Data Independent Accessing Model (DIAM) [33]. DIAM has four levels of data specification: the entity set model for describing the data abstraction, the string model for describing the access structure, the encoding model for mapping access structures into an address space, and the physical device model for binding the address space to a machine. Thus, Mealy's machine representation has also been separated into two stages: the linking method (sometimes called the "storage mapping function") is to be specified at the former and the actual data layout at the latter.*

Figure 6 compares the several related proposals. From this summary, it should be apparent that the five views of data suggested here are not without a history, and that further motivation for each level can be found elsewhere.

	data reality	data abstraction	information structure	storage structure	machine encoding
COBOL	-	-	-	program division	data division
Mealy	real world	theoretical model		machine representation	
d'Imperio	-	data structure		storage structure	
McCuskey	problem	problem interpretation	logical organization	physical organization	
Earley	-	relation	access path	machine	
Senko,et al	-	entity set	string	encoding	physical device

Figure 6: *Comparison of Data Level Models*

---

*McCuskey also recognized this division, which he named the relative *vs.* absolute organization and incorporated into his model as sublevels of the physical organization.

5. A SECOND EXAMPLE OF DATA DESCRIPTION BY LEVELS

To appreciate the role of each view of data structures, it is worthwhile to examine an application taken from actual practice. This section therefore contains the description of a system for natural language understanding which has recently been developed [6]. As an example, Cohen described the following dialogue:

Sentence: "The Rag Doll stayed in the holly bush."

Question:	Where is the Rag Doll?
Answer:	In the holly bush.
Question:	Who is in the holly bush?
Answer:	The Rag Doll.
Question:	Which doll is in the plant?
Answer:	The Rag Doll.

Since it would be tedious, and likely confusing, to include all details of the design process or even of the final data design many aspects are omitted or simplified.

For this application, the data reality was natural language -in particular, written English. The data therefore included at least grammar (part of speech, tense, mood, voice), meaning (denotation, connotation), etymology (derivation, form), style, punctuation, and typesetting (type font, line width, spacing). Although it may not be apparent that all these could affect understanding, writers, publishers, and reading teachers might choose a different subset of these data properties as influencing a reader's comprehension.

Since the system was intended to be used to answer questions input from some computer terminal, the relevant relations were derived from some aspects of English syntax and semantics only. In particular, the syntax could be represented by a model in which a sentence consists of a verb together with a set of noun phrases assigned to roles determined by the verb's "case frame." The semantics were modeled by a "structural dictionary" which used a hierarchy of concepts (e.g., "pen $\subset$ writing implement $\subset$ tool $\subset$ artifact"), some definitional information encoded using case grammar (e.g., "pens use ink"), and links to specific instances occurring in some text (e.g., "John holds the pen and the paper"). Cohen chose to represent this data abstraction by a labeled, directed graph in which the edges served either to identify a node or to link a verb to its noun phrases, a concept to its superset, or an instance to its dictionary entry (Figure 7).

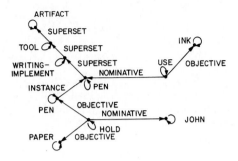

Figure 7:   *A Graph Representing the Data Abstraction for
            the Concepts "John holds the pen and the paper,
                           Pens use ink,
                           Pens ⊂ writing implements ⊂ tools
                              ⊂ artifacts"*

At the level of the information structure, only some relationships from the graph can be made explicit. It was decided
that connectivity, reachability, and planarity, for example,
were not used sufficiently often to justify their explicit inclusion. Furthermore, it was decided that the graph would be
stored uniformly, that is, that all nodes and edges would be
treated equally, whether used in the dictionary or in the particular dialogue. Because graph traversal was originally expected to be performed in the direction of the edges more often
than in reverse, edges originating at a node would be represented explicitly (those sharing a common label being grouped
together), but those terminating at that node would only be
accessible implicitly through a set of predecessor nodes (i.e.,
nodes from which there originates at least one edge terminating
at the particular node in question). The following declarations
could thus be used for the information structure (Figure 8):

type graph = set of node;

type node = (set of node PREDECESSORS;
            set of edge_class OUT_EDGES);

type edge_class = (string LABEL; set of node SUCCESSORS);

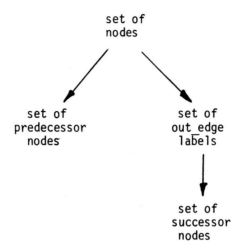

Figure 8: *Information Structure*

At the next level, the storage structure must be chosen to represent each of the data types comprising the information structure: in this example, the two tuples (node and edge_class), the four sets (graph, PREDECESSORS, OUT_EDGES, and SUCCESSORS), and the string (LABEL). Because pattern matching was to be applied extensively to the strings, it was decided to code the application's programs in Spitbol [9]; thus a string would be represented by a header pointing to a contiguous block of characters and a tuple would be represented contiguously (using "programmer-defined data types"). This left the decision for the sets, which could be represented contiguously (using "arrays"), hashed (using "tables"), or linked (using pointers in "programmer-defined data types"). Because sets were expected to be small and insertions and deletions frequent, headed, singly-linked rings were chosen (Figure 9).

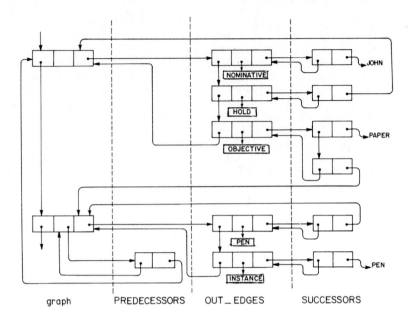

Figure 9: *Detail From The Storage Structure*

Finally, the machine encoding binds the data structure to a machine. Since the application was written in **Spitbol,** and therefore core-resident on an IBM System/370, there was little actual choice at this level: pointers were encoded as full-word, absolute memory addresses and characters were encoded in 8-bit EBCDIC.

6. CONCLUSIONS

The design of a data structure is far too important to leave to chance or to pursue haphazardly. For almost all appli-cations a poorly designed data structure can result in the application's failure: the structure may be too inflexible to allow some data manipulations, the manipulations may be overly costly in run time or in storage space, the data structure may not be transferable to an updated hardware system, or, in the worst case, the manipulation routines may never function cor-rectly because of obscurity and unnecessary complexity in the data structure.

The design methodology presented here attempts to minimize these problems. Foremost, data structure design and description by levels provide a degree of clarity not usually found in traditional methods of documentation. It is far easier to design a complex structure in a top-down manner, where the temporarily irrelevant details of lower levels do not obscure the logic for any design step. A stepwise design also induces a clear description in which each level is comprehensible without preknowledge of the whole design in all its detail. This clarity results in a data structure which is more likely to be a correct model of the application's reality and which furthermore lends itself to rigorous correctness proofs.

Each of the four interfaces contributes to a more flexible data structure. Starting closest to the machine, if the transition from a storage structure to a machine encoding is made explicit, designers will be more easily able to transfer an application from one machine environment to another. Because the encoding of each data primitive (e.g., integer, pointer) is separated from its use, the data structure should not have to be redesigned merely to transform from twos-complement to signed-magnitude or from absolute memory addresses to page-and-offset addresses. As an example, there should be little or no change to the storage structure in Figure 9 to move the natural language understanding system from an IBM 360 to a Honeywell 6050.

At the next transition, the separation of the storage structure from the information structure allows a redesign of any data type's representation without the fear of altering the data type's role or usage within the application. This freedom is often beneficial for optimizing a data type's representation, for example, by choosing to use doubly-linked rings instead of contiguity or hash tables instead of binary search trees. In Figure 9, recoding the representations for sets (to keep the elements sorted and to include in the head element a dummy field having a value lexically greater than any member's value) results in a run time improvement of 14% which is realized as an actual cost reduction of 4% (due to increased space for the dummy fields) [34].

The separation of the information structure from the data abstraction allows data access paths to be redesigned without reconsidering the relevancy of the relationships which they represent. Thus the information structure can easily be altered to optimize the choice of data paths based on the relative frequencies of their accesses. For example, if the edges of the graph in Figure 7 are to be followed in the reverse as often as in the forward direction (e.g., to be required to find the

starting node for an edge labeled "nominative" ending at the
node with edge "John" as often as to find the target node for
an edge labeled "nominative" starting at the node with edge
"hold") and if it is found that there is usually only one suc-
cessor node per label, the information structure can be redesigned as follows (Figure 10):

<u>type</u> graph = <u>set of</u> node;

<u>type</u> node = (<u>set of</u> edge IN_EDGES, OUT_EDGES);

<u>type</u> edge = (<u>string</u> LABEL; node ADJACENCY) ;

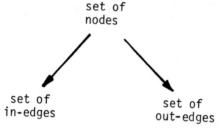

Figure 10:   *Revised Information Structure*

Since such an optimization corresponds to improving the algorithms involved, it is usually far more productive than optimizing at the **storage** structure level (which corresponds to
improving the programs). In particular, whereas the previous
redesign only had a 4% cost reduction, the redesign suggested
here would result in a 16% improvement in efficiency for the
application [34].

Finally at the transition furthest from the machine, the
separation of the data abstraction from the reality promotes
flexibility by documenting which relationships were considered
to be irrelevant. Thus, in reconsidering the application as a
whole, designers are not misled into believing their system is
isomorphic to reality. Instead they realize that theirs is
only a model, and therefore they can alter their design decisions.

ACKNOWLEDGEMENTS

Thanks are due to Richard Peebles, Sylvia Osborn and Bruce Jolliffe for their help in formulating these ideas and to Phil Cohen for his donation of the natural language understanding system. Acknowledgement is also given to the University of Waterloo for its financial support.

PROBLEMS

(Research problems are marked by an asterisk)

1. In section 2, it is claimed that "one man's storage primitive is another's data reality." For each of the five data levels, give an example of a situation in which one could consider an integer to be an object at that level.

2. Design an information structure which corresponds to the following data abstraction for a student record file:

   students may be registered for one to five courses

   courses may have arbitrarily many students enrolled

   each student has an identification number, name, and address

   each course belongs to a faculty, has an identifying number within the faculty, and meets two or three per week

   Assume that the following queries are equally likely:

   Who is taking a course in faculty X?

   List the courses taken by the student having identification number N, ordered by faculty and identifying number.

   Who is enrolled from out of state?

   (Be sure the data description is independent of storage structure.)

3. Describe several alternative storage structures for representing a tree as defined in Figure 4.

4. Describe some alternative information structures which may be represented by a singly-linked list.

5. Describe all five levels of a data structure which could be used to construct a concordance (i.e., a keyword-in-context index) for some text.

6. Design and defend a storage structure for representing sparse matrices for which transposes are required 40% of the time, pairs of matrices are added together 25% of the time, the largest elements on the major diagonals are required 20% of the time, and the percentages of non-zero entries are required 15% of the time.

7*. Devise an algorithmic approach to choosing a "good" information structure for a given data abstraction.

8*. Design and implement a programming language in which data declarations are made at the information structure level only (e.g., in the style of Figure 4).

9*. Examine the computer science literature for other descriptions of stepwise data design, and reconcile any differences.

10*. Use the design methodology suggested here for an application which arises naturally in your research or business.

Some of the material contained here originally appeared in "A Scenario for Data Structure Design," from the 1975 Proceedings of the Conference on Computer Graphics, Pattern Recognition and Data Structure (75 CH 0981-1C). Copyright 1975 by The Institute of Electrical and Electronics Engineers, Inc.

REFERENCES

1. Astrahan, M. M. and Ghosh, S. P. "A Search Path Selection Algorithm for the Data Independent Accessing Model (DIAM)," *ACM SIGMOD Workshop on Data Description, Access, and Control,* 1974, pp. 367-388.

2. Bachman, C. W. "Summary of Current Work: ANSI/X3/SPARC/ STUDY GROUP - Database Systems," *FDT* 6, 3 (1974), pp. 16-39.

3. Balzer, R. M. "Dataless Programming," *Proc. AFIPS 31* (FJCC, 1967), pp. 535-544.

4. Boehm, B. H. "Some Steps Toward Formal and Automated Aids to Software Requirements Analysis and Design," *Proc. IFIP* (1974), pp. 192-197.

5. Codd, E. F. "A Relational Model for Large Shared Data Banks," *Comm. ACM* 13, 6 (June 1970), pp. 377-387.

6. Cohen, P. R. "An Integration of Two Language Understanding Methodologies," *Proc. ACM National Conference* (Nov. 1974), pp. 297-305.

7. Dahl, O.-J., Nygaard, K., and Myhrhaug, B. "The SIMULA 67 Common Base Language," Norwegian Computing Centre, Forskningsveien 1B, Oslo, 1968.

8. Date, C. J. *An Introduction to Database Systems,* Addison-Wesley, Reading, Mass., 1975, pp. 61-131.

9. Dewar, R. B. K. and Belcher, K. E. "SPITBOL--Speedy Implementation of SNOBOL-4, Version 2.1," Illinois Inst. of Tech., 1971.

10. Dijkstra, E. W. "Notes on Structured Programming," in *Structured Programming* (Dahl, Dijkstra, and Hoare, eds.), Academic Press, New York, 1972, pp. 1-82.

11. d'Imperio, M. E. "Data Structures and Their Representation in Storage," *Annual Review in Auto. Prog. 5,* Pergamon Press, Oxford, 1969, pp. 1-75.

12. Earley, J. "Towards an Understanding of Data Structures," *Comm. ACM* 14, 10 (October 1971), pp. 617-627.

13. *The New Encyclopaedia Britannica*, Macropaedia, 8 (1975), pp. 530-536.

14. Gotlieb, C. C. and Furtado, A. L. "Data Schemata Based on Directed Graphs," Department of Computer Science, University of Toronto, Tech. Report 70, October 1974.

15. Gotlieb, C. C. and Tompa, F. W. "Choosing a Storage Schema," *Acta Informatica* 3 (1974), pp. 297-319.

16. Guttag, J. V. "The Specification and Application to Programming of Abstract Data Types," Computer Systems Research Group, University of Toronto, Tech. Report CSRG-59, September 1975.

17. Honig, W. L. "Bringing Data Base Technology to the Programmer," *FDT* 6, 3 (1974), pp. 2-15.

18. Knuth, D. E. "Optimum Binary Search Trees," *Acta Informatica* 1 (1971), pp. 14-25, 270.

19. Lesk, M. E. "Compressed Text Storage," Bell Labs., Tech. Report 3, Nov. 1970.

20. Liskov, B. and Zilles, S. "Programming with Abstract Data Types," *Proc. of Symposium on Very High Level Languages, SIGPLAN Notices* 9, 4 (April 1974), pp. 50-59.

21. Liskov, B. and Zilles, S. "Specification Techniques for Data Abstractions," *IEEE Trans. on Software Engineering* 1, 1 (March 1975), pp. 7-19.

22. Lum, V. Y., Yen, P. S. T., and Dodd, M. "Key-to-Address Transform Techniques: A Fundamental Performance Study of Large Existing Formatted Files," *Comm. ACM* 14, 4 (April 1971), pp. 228-239.

23. McCarthy, J. "Recursive Functions of Symbolic Expressions and Their Computation by Machine - Part 1," *Comm. ACM* 3, 4 (April 1960), pp. 184-195.

24. McCuskey, W. A. "On Automatic Design of Data Organization," *Proc. AFIPS 37* (FJCC, 1970), pp. 184-199.

25. Mealy, G. "Another Look at Data," *Proc. AFIPS 31* (FJCC, 1967), pp. 525-534.

26. Miller, S. W. "Storage Technology: Overview and Projection," *Proc. of ACM Pacific 75*, San Francisco, April 1975, pp. 10-14.

27. Morris, J. H., Jr. "Types Are Not Sets," *Conf. Record of ACM Symposium on Principles of Programming Languages*, Boston, October 1973, pp. 120-124.

28. Nievergelt, J. "Binary Search Trees and File Organization," *Comp. Surveys* 6, 3 (September 1974), pp. 195-207.

29. Parhami, B. "Associative Memories and Processors: An Overview and Selected Bibliography," *Proc. IEEE 61*, 6 (June 1973), pp. 722-730.

30. Randall, L. S. "A Relational Model of Data for the Determination of Optimum Computer Storage Structures," Systems Engineering Lab., University of Michigan, Tech. Report 54, RADC-TR-72-25, February 1972.

31. Roberts, L. G. "Graphical Communication and Control Languages," *Second Congress on the Information Systems Sciences*, 1965, pp. 211-217.

32. Ross, D. T. "Uniform Referents: An Essential Property for a Software Engineering Language," *Software Engineering 1*, (Tou, ed.), Academic Press, New York, 1970, pp. 91-101.

33. Senko, M. E., Altman, E. B., Astrahan, M. M., and Fehder, P. L. "Data Structures and Accessing in Data Base Systems," *IBM Sys. J.* 12, 1 (1973), pp. 30-93.

34. Tompa, F. W., "Choosing an Efficient Internal Schema," *Proceedings of the Second International Conference on Very Large Data Bases*, Brussels, September 1976.

35. Waite, W.M., "The Mobile Programming System: STAGE2," *Comm. ACM*, 13, 7(July 1970), pp. 415-421.

36. Walker, W. A. and Gotlieb, C. C., "A Top-Down Algorithm for Constructing Nearly-Optimal Lexicographic Trees," *Graph Theory and Computing*, (R. Read, ed.), Academic Press, New York, 1972, pp. 303-323.

37. Weizenbaum, J., "Symmetric List Processor," *Comm. ACM 6*, 9 (September 1963), pp. 524-536.

38. Wirth, N., *Systematic Programming: An Introduction*, Prentice-Hall, Englewood Cliffs, New Jersey, 1973.

The Concise Structuring of Geometric
Data for Computer Aided Design

CHARLES M. EASTMAN

*Institute of Physical Planning
Carnegie-Mellon University
Pittsburgh, Pa.*

1. INTRODUCTION

A physical system is a collection of parts which occupy space
and whose performance is a function of their spatial composition. Buildings, automobiles, ships and aircraft are usually
considered during design as physical systems while computers
and electronic systems usually are not.

A growing number of computer data bases are under development oriented toward the design of different types of physical
systems: for ships [1, 5]; for buildings [2, 8, 10], and for
automobiles [18]. In each of these cases, the data base is
used in design as the source of information for making a variety
of complex analyses and for automated drafting. Later in some
cases, they are used for construction and operation. For
convenience, I shall call a data base for physical system design a DESIGN INFORMATION SYSTEM (DIS).

The bottom level description of a physical system in a DIS
is a collection of ELEMENTS. Each element consists of a set of
attributes, including shape, cost, structure, function, etc..
The physical systems described in a DIS typically involve a
large number of elements -- from a thousand to several million.
Many have complex shapes and extensive attributes. Millions of
bytes are often required to hold such a description, which
currently encourages use of some form of secondary memory.

The definition of a physical system description of such a
large size is a difficult and time consuming task. A variety
of aids are necessary to expedite it. Most important is the
reliance on machine readable CATALOGS for standard parts. Thus
only custom parts need to be entered manually. In addition,

a variety of other catalog information can be stored and utilized, from the definition of activity areas and manpower requirements for different tasks [1], to programs that automatically detail some portion of the database [8]. From the parts catalog and manually entered data is built up a PROJECT FILE, which is modified by manual manipulation and application programs. In addition, a variety of data entry techniques have been developed to expedite the entry of information regarding custom parts [11,15].

The standard procedure for building up a description in a DIS is to transfer part descriptions from disc or tape files comprising the parts catalog into the project file. Associated with each part by the user is one or more spatial locations and possibly other idiocyncratic information. Custom parts are entered directly, possibly drawn in on a digitizer tablet and their attributes added from the keyboard. Manipulation, analysis or display of a configuration brings collections of parts into core memory where they may be inspected or altered.

The efficient structuring of large databases has been intensively studied since the 1950s. For numeric or character data, a variety of coding and accessing schemes have been developed, such as inverted lists [7], rings [14], sets [6], hierarchies and plexes [17]. The coding schemes and structures for spatial properties are much less well developed.

The most common approach to the development of spatial datastructutes has emphasized efficient structures for particular operations, such as display [12], possibly with hidden line removal [16] or surface shading [13]. Other operations given consideration are the shape composition operations of union, intersection, and complement [3], [4]. While these efforts have emphasized fast algoithms they have ignored the applications context in which most are likely to be used. Not focussed on is the more general question of very large databases of spatial information and their concise structuring for both efficient storage and fast operations.

Parts catalogs will be much larger than the largest database and will be accessed only once for each part. Usually, they will be organized so as to minimize storage. More critical however is the structure of the project file. It will be added to and manipulated continuously throughout the life of a project.

In this paper, I wish to focus on the structuring of spatial information on project files for computer aided design. A good structure will be one that requires both small amounts of stor-

age and is efficiently operated on. Rather than consider the
detail structure of spatial information -- on the existence or
nonexistence of particular pointers or data -- I will focus one
level higher, on the organization of information into records
and the organization of these records. A general methodology
is outlined for evaluating the alternative record organizations.
An example analysis, based on the development of one design
oriented data base system, Building Description System, (BDS)
is included, which indicates the tradeoffs involved.

A general strategy for reducing storage requirements of data
is to identify redundancies within it. Data that is similar and
repeated throughout the data base may be stored once in a common
form and re-combined as demanded by use. That is, we may save
storage by accepting some amount of additional computation to
recombine data each time it is needed. In most cases, the alternatives regarding what information to store and what and
when to compute it is significant and the tradeoffs are resolved
intuitively. More precise forms of analyses, however, are possible. If the alternative collections of redundant information
can be identified, the average redundancy of each set of information known, its storage requirements identified, both prior
and after computing, and the cost of alternative computation sequences determined, then the optimal mix of computation and storing of information may be derived. This strategy is easily
applied to spatial information.

II.   SHAPE DESCRIPTIONS

Any shape may be considered a POLYHEDRON, made up of vertices, edges, and faces. The faces of a polyhedron may be planar
or curved (to date, all databases using a polyhedron shape representation are restricted to planar or simple curve faces).
The complete description of any polyhedron consists of a TOPOLOGY
of the adjacency relations between its constituent parts and a
GEOMETRY specifying the dimensional aspects of the shape. Without both aspects, a shape description is incomplete and some
operations on it are not possible. In most data structures,
these two aspects are not distinguished.

A polyhedron topology is defined by the relations shown in
Figure 1a. A variety of structures have been developed to store
them. Most store only a subset of the relations and compute
the others when needed. The geometric properties are depicted
in Figure 1b. They too are redundant and only subsets are
usually stored from which the others are computed.

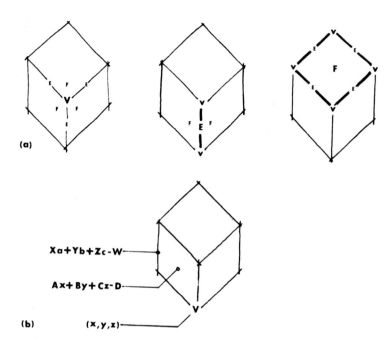

Figure 1:   *The Topological Relations (a) Define All
Adjacencies Between Faces, Edges and Verti-
ces, (b) the Geometrical Relations Specify
Dimensions and Relative Placement.*

A single topology may define the adjacency relations in the
shapes of a large number of parts. In construction, only four
different topologies are needed to represent different types
of structural steel: the wideflange, ell, plate and pipe. All
pipe and tubing is based on a single topology. Most wooden
parts are rectangular and thus also consist of a single topology. Topologies are one repeated set of information that can
be centrally stored for use by a variety of shape descriptions
within a database.

Another form of redundancy is observable within the geometric aspect of a shape description. If a person is asked to
consider a rectangle cuboid three by five by ten, that shape is
unambiguously defined. "Rectangular cuboid" not only specifies
a particular topology (made up of six faces each with four
edges) but also a class of geometries in which all faces join
at right angles. We can consider the concept "rectangular
cuboid" as a MODEL GEOMETRY which defines consistent dimensional
relations within a family of shapes. In a similar way, many

shapes within product brochures are defined with a general
schematic sketch of common dimensions and a table with the variable dimensions for each individual item. In both cases, the
model geometry can be defined by a set of algebraic expressions,
See Figure 2. The expressions define the geometrical aspects
of a shape in terms of a set of critical variables. Different
members from a family of shapes can be easily entered, either
by a user interactively or from a table in the parts catalog.

A commonly used form of redundancy in graphical databases
is the redundancy of whole shapes. The same part or shape may
be used in many different locations. Each need not be defined
separately. Instead, a spatial transformation can be used to
define the location of each instance of a part and to transform
a single shape definition to any location.

Four different types of shape information have been identified. They are the topology, the model geometry, critical
values, and the transformation. These four classes are sufficient to completely define any shape and can be ordered hierarchically. While one topology is likely to be associated with
several geometries, it is not likely (though it is possible)
that one geometry will be associated with several topologies.
Similarly, one model geometry may be associated with several
critical values, but it is not likely that one set of critical
values will be associated with several model geometries. The
same holds true for the transformation; several locations may
be associated with one shape, but not vice versa. Together,
then, these four classes of shape information can be organized
into the hierarchy shown in Figure 2. At each level is a one-
many branching, allowing higher level information to be used
repeatedly to produce a large number of bottom level shape
descriptions.

This hierarchy can be extended to one further level. A
number of topologies can be described according to a family definition. For instance, "a pyramid with a five-side base" is
an unambiguously defined topology, as is "an extrusion with
eight sides". See Figure 3. Both pyramids and extrusions are
families of topologies which take the number of faces on their
base as a defining parameter. The operations to construct a
topology may be organized into a routine capable of defining a
family of them, varied according to the arguments. This addition results in a five level hierarchy that collects together
at higher levels information that is common to a number of
shapes. Instead of storing the higher level information for
each shape, it is stored once and the cost of that storage distributed over all the parts it helps define.

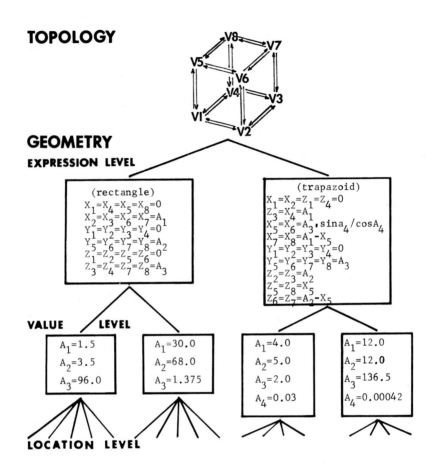

Figure 2: *The Four Level Hierarchy of Spatial Information Which Collects Together Common Data Describing a Set of Elements.*

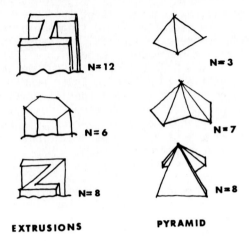

EXTRUSIONS   **PYRAMID**

Figure 3: *Two Classes of Topologies That Can Be Created Through Subroutines.*

III. SHAPE INSTANTIATION

The five level hierarchy has the potential of greatly reducing the storage requirements for shape information within large project files. But this savings comes at a cost; the instantiation of any shape now requires a significant amount of computation. Specifically, the following computations must be executed:

1. The topology routine must receive the topology values and be executed so as to result in a specific topology;

2. the geometry variables must be associated with the model geometry so as to result in a specific shape geometry;

3. the geometric information must be transformed to common coordinates by applying the part transformations;

4. the geometry must be linked to the topology so as to define a complete shape.

Some operations may not require all of the above steps prior to their application. Perspective and orthographic transformations for display do not require step (3) because they can be executed with the part at the origin, albeit in a different placement than initially. A display transformation can be multiplied with the spatial transform so as to result in a single transform being applied to the shape information. The relocating of parts without displaying them also may be done without accessing or linking the topology record. But these are the exceptions. For most operations these four compurations must be applied prior to their application.

Throughout the life of a project file, part information passes through four different stages, corresponding to the different media and representations used. The first stage is when the part information is in a catalog or otherwise initially defined. The second stage is when it resides on the project file but is not in use. The third stage is when the information is residing in core memory so as to be used, possibly by several different shapes. The last stage is when the shape information is prepared so as to accurately depict the shape of a specific part.

These four stages are linked by three state transitions: (a) the transfer from catalog to project file, (b) the transfer from project file to core memory, and (c) any computation just prior to operation. The above four computations required to instantiate a shape are most conveniently made during these transitions. Notice that if compacted information is expanded through computation when it is first entered into the project file, the effect of the compacting is ignored and the result is that the data is stored in its expanded format.

The cost of each of the four computations varies significantly depending upon when they are undertaken. Computations done when the part information is first retrieved from the catalog need only be done once; the result of that computation is stored for later use. If the same computation is done when the part is loaded into core memory from the project file, it will have to be repeated for that part each time the record is loaded. In that at least some of both the topological and geometric information can be used by several parts, it may be desirable to use one copy of that information in core for the definition of several different shapes. Computations may be delayed even later and correspondingly, the number of times that computation will have to be made for a particular part will increase. The state at which these computations are made determines what must be stored both before and after them.

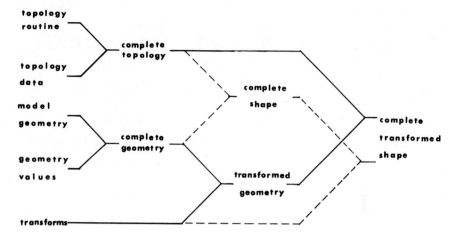

Figure 4:   *The Precedence Ordering and Alternative Instantiation Sequences Possible With the Five Level Hierarchy.*

The four computation steps are partially ordered. The sequence of necessary computations is shown in Figure 4. Steps (1) and (2) must be done before (4); (2) must be done before (3). Thus the five possible computation sequences are (1, 2, 3, 4), (2, 1, 3, 4), (1, 2, 4, 3), (2, 1, 4, 3) and (2, 3, 1, 4). The input to any of the computation steps is some data stored on one or more records. The output is also a record. Thus for each of the computations, specific input and output records can be defined. If two of the computational steps are back-to-back the record defined between them is used only temporarily and can be ignored in evaluating overall storage requirements.

IV. A QUANTITATIVE FORMULATION

The compute versus store question is essentially an optimization problem seeking the best combination of storage and compute costs. The range of alternatives for the organization of shape information is not large and can be easily enumerated. Specifically, the range of alternatives consists of alternative assignments of the four computation steps to the three state changes, limited to the three instantiation sequences defined above. The alternatives are defined in Figure 5.

ALTERNATIVE COMPUTATION METHOD	ONE	TWO	THREE	STORAGE REQUIREMENTS
1			1,2,3,4	$S_1+S_2+S_4+S_5+S_7$
2		1	2,3,4	$S_1+S_2+S_4+S_5+S_7$
3	1		2,3,4	$S_3+S_4+S_5+S_7$
4		2	1,3,4	$S_1+S_2+S_4+S_5+S_7$
5	2		1,3,4	$S_1+S_2+\quad S_6+S_7$
6		1,2	3,4	$S_1+S_2+S_4+S_5+S_7$
7	1,2		3,4	$S_3+\quad S_6+S_7$
8		2,3	1,4	$S_1+S_2+S_4+S_5+S_7$
9	2,3		1,4	$S_1+S_2+\quad S_8$
10	1	2	3,4	$S_3+S_4+S_5+S_7$
11	2	1	3,4	$S_1+S_2+\quad S_6+S_7$
12	2	3	1,4	$S_1+S_2+\quad S_6+S_7$
13		1,2,3	4	$S_1+S_2+S_4+S_5+S_7$
14	1	2,3	4	$S_3+S_4+S_5+S_7$
15	1	2,4	3	$S_3+S_4+S_5+S_7$
16	2	1,3	4	$S_1+S_2+\quad S_6+S_7$
17	2	1,4	3	$S_1+S_2+\quad S_6+S_7$
18	1,2	3	4	$S_3+\quad S_6+S_7$
19	1,2	4	3	$S_3+\quad S_6+S_7$
20	2,3	1	4	$S_1+S_2+\quad S_8$
21	1,2,3	4		$S_3+\quad S_8$
22	1,2,4	3		$S_3+\quad S_6+S_9$
23		1,2,3,4		$S_1+S_2+S_4+S_5+S_7$
24	1	2,3,4		$S_3+S_4+S_5+S_7$
25	2	1,3,4		$S_1+S_2+\quad S_6+S_7$
26	1,2	3,4		$S_3+\quad S_6+S_7$
27	2,3	1,4		$S_1+S_2+\quad S_8$
28	1,2,3	4		$S_3+\quad S_8$
29	1,2,4	3		$S_3+\quad S_6+S_9$
30	1,2,3,4			S_9

Figure 5: *The thirty alternative computation methods possible for the five level shape hierarchy outlined in Section II. Storage requirements identify those records which are used by each method.*

Figure 5 represents the 30 alternative computation methods possible for the five level shape hierarchy outlined in Section II. Storage requirements identify those records which are used by each method.

Thirty alternative methods exist for instantiating the shape information. Notice that all sequences of computations made within a single state change are equivalent; each involves the same storage and computations. Alternative 1 keeps all information about a shape in the form in which it is received from parts catalog until it is about to be operated on. This alternative seems to minimize storage. Alternative 3 computes the topological information when the part is first defined in the project file, while putting off all other computations until the last moment. Alternative 6 computes the topology and geometry information when a part is accessed from the project file into core. In this case, the possibility of using one core record for several different part descriptions is facilitated. Alternative 21 makes all computations when the part is first defined, except for the linking of topology and geometry, which is done just prior to operation.

Corresponding to each of the four computations is a cost in terms of time, C_i, where i = 1,2,3,4. The cost can be approximated as:

$$C_i = \sum_k (d_{ik} \cdot td_k) + c_i$$

where d_{ik} = the number of accesses to storage media k required to retrieve all records for input to computation i plus the number of accesses for storing the results.

td_k = the average record access time for media k,

c_i = cpu time for computation i and the time required to read and write input and output records.

Many of the computations, especially if done early, generate information used in a number of part descriptions later and the cost of the computation can be distributed over this number. The number of parts effected by a computation depends upon the use of the system, specifically upon the average number of operations on a part and the size of core memory, which determines the likelihood that information in core will be used more than once. The number of times information is likely to be used in any state is denoted p_j, where j = 1, 2, 3. The quotient C_i/p_j defines the average computation time required for each step in instantiating a single part.

The assignment of a computation to a state change can be defined by a boolean matrix $x_{ij\alpha}$. That is, $x_{ij\alpha}$ depicts method α of computation as defined in one of the rows of Figure 5. Putting these functions together, we are interested in T, the average cost of computation to instantiate a part in the database by method α , where:

$$T_\alpha = \sum_{j=1}^{3} \sum_{i=1}^{4} (C_i/p_j) \cdot x_{ij\alpha}$$

T_α does not depict the efficiency of alternative algorithms for manipulating the database, of course. Rather it denotes the fixed overhead cost involved in setting up the shape information for a part so that it may be operated on later.

Associated with any computation sequence is a storage requirement. In general, we can expect that the most efficient method for instantiating shapes time-wise will be the most expensive space-wise. But some of the sequences offer significant marginal advantages, as we shall see. The storing of a record is only considered if it is part of the project file; core records and those on the parts catalog will be ignored. Also, operations concatonated within a state change require only temporary storage, which need not be considered.

Each of the initial and intermediate records has a size s_n, n = 1-9 and that size can be distributed over the number of parts they describe, in the same manner as we treated computation time. In this case, the efficiency of storing information is not based on p_j, a measure of use, but rather the number of parts used by information at different levels in the hierarchy. We denote the average number of records attached to one record above it in the hierarchy as l_m, where m = 1,2,3,4. The the effective storage cost of each record type is:

RECORD	NOTATION	EFFECTIVE STORAGE COST
topology routine	s_1	$S_1 = s_1/l_1 \cdot l_2 \cdot l_3 \cdot l_4 \cdot l_5$
topology values	s_2	$S_2 = s_2/l_1 \cdot l_2 \cdot l_3 \cdot l_4$
complete topology	s_3	$S_3 = s_3/l_1 \; l_2 \; l_3 \; l_4$
geometry values	s_4	$S_4 = s_4/l_1 \cdot l_2$
model geometry	s_5	$S_5 = s_5/l_1 \cdot l_2 \cdot l_3$
complete geometry	s_6	$S_6 = s_6/l_1 \cdot l_2$
transform	s_7	$S_7 = s_7/l_1$
transformed geometry	s_8	$S_8 = s_8/l_1$
complete shape	s_9	$S_9 = s_9/l_1$

The record sizes s_n should include the directory entries associated with the record type to access them. The storage requirements for each of the computation methods, defined in terms of the above size variables, are also shown in Figure 5.

The above analysis provides the information needed to determine the space and time requirements for each of the 30 computation methods allowed by the redundancies identified in Section II. Other redundancies may also exist, especially within the shapes encountered in specialized classes of problems. The optimal storage and computation method for any set of redundancies will depend upon the size of the records used to store the information, the characteristics of the typical data encoded and how it will be used. Thus no general decision rules can be provided. In the following section, however, a

detailed example is presented, which indicates the magnitude of
the savings that can be gained from this type of analysis and
some of the trade-offs involved.

V. THE STRUCTURING OF BDS

Building Description System (BDS) is a prototype DIS for the
building industry under development at Carnegie-Mellon University. It is conceived as an integrated database for automated
drafting, data preparation for engineering analysis programs and
as a medium for recording and facilitating intuitive evaluation
of design and construction decisions [8, 9]. Its purpose is to
replace paper and drafting tools as the media for design.

Graphics plays a special role in BDS. It is used not only
as a means for producing finished architectural and engineering
drawings, but also as an important database interrogation format
that is mandatory if BDS is to be used by professionals. Perspective and orthographic displays are used to facilitate examination of the database organization, as a quick means for intuitive evaluation and for identifying problem areas during design. Also considered important is the capability to graphically
represent spaces, activity areas, and other abstract spatial
configurations.

Early analysis of some typical buildings of the types for
which BDS may be used indicated that they consisted of a large
number of parts. Medium sized buildings could easily include
500,000 orderable items. Building parts vary greatly in their
spatial complexity. Many are simply cuboids, such as doors and
bricks. Others, such as metal window frames and some mechanical
equipment, however, involve hundreds of vertices and faces.

The data flow rate for convenient graphical manipulation of
a DIS is such as to preclude anything but local computation for
at least some operations and local residency of the database.
A minicomputer configuration seemed to be the only alternative
satisfying these criteria economically so as to allow transfer
of the ideas in BDS to practice in the near future. A minicomputer configuration, however, implies small word size and limited real arithmetic capabilities.

Allocation of records to secondary memory is usually done by
files or sectors. The sector size on our equipment is 512 bytes.
Thus where large records are anticipated, they will be allocated
in 512 byte blocks. We chose a variable length allocation
scheme, so as to facilitate dynamic definition and extension of
records.

The accessing of records is through a directory, which is itself accessed through a hash code. Almost all record accesses thus require two disc reads, one for the directory to identify the location of the record and the second for the record itself.

Careful analyses were made of the data structures and computations needed for storing and manipulating the shapes of building components. These are described below.

Records for topology routines will store executable code that will most likely call other routines. We estimate that 90% of all topology routines can reside within a disc sector and the rest will require two. Only a few parameters will be needed to define a topology; more space will be consumed by its directory and name. Each set of parameters is estimated to need a total of 64 bytes. Only a few sets of parameters will be associated with any particular routine. If topologies and the values associated with it are combined on a single record, some compacting is possible, with 85% on one sector and the rest on two.

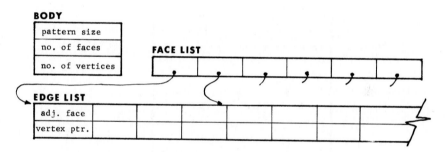

Figure 6:   *The Compacted Topology Data Structure Used in BDS.*

The initial data structure for storing complete topologies in BDS is shown in Figure 6. Notice that it makes reference to geometric information only at the vertices. All other geometric information has been suppressed. By associating a base address with a particular geometry, the vertices in the topology are easily associated with different sets of geometry coordinates. We expect 90% of all topologies to fit within one sector and all others to fit within two. (A topology of about forty vertices can fit within one sector.) This record stores only the minimal relations needed to define a topology. An expanded structure is computed from it temporarily when required by complex operations [8].

In computing a complete topology from its defining parameters, at least three directory and record accesses will be required, with two more to store the results. If the topology routines and the topology parameters are stored on a single record, only four accesses are needed total. Computation time to create a complete topology will probably average about 20 milliseconds.

The routine depicting the model geometry consists of a set of algebraic expressions. About 70% of the records holding these routines are expected to fit within one sector and the rest in two. The critical values input to the model geometry will be stored in tabular form in a record grouping all value sets for a particular model geometry. For estimation purposes, we expect each set of values to occupy an average of 64 bytes. The model geometry and critical values can also be collected on a single record. We estimate for each model geometry there will be about ten sets of values. About 30% of the combined records will fit in 512 bytes, 50% in two sectors and the rest in three.

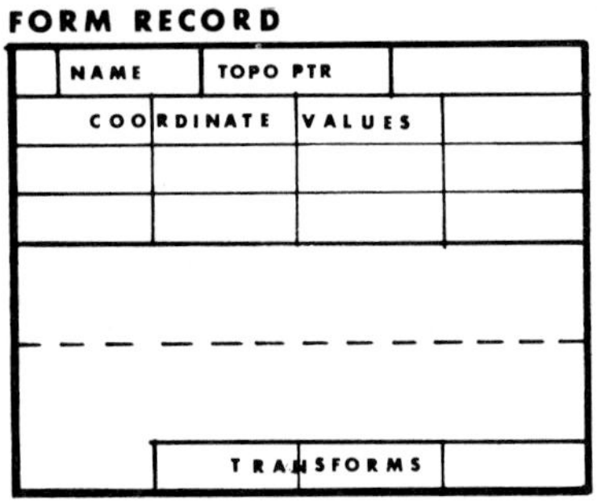

FORM RECORD

NAME	TOPO PTR	
COORDINATE	VALUES	
— — — — — — — — —
	TRANSFORMS	

Figure 7: *Record Format for Storing a Complete Geometry and Its Transforms.*

Computation times for deriving a geometry from a model and a set of values will involve four disc accesses, plus about 20 milliseconds computation, due to the real arithmetic involved. About 75% of the geometry records will fit in a single sector, the rest in two.

In BDS, the record holding the complete geometry is called a FORM Record. Its format is shown in Figure 7. The transformations are of fixed length, 32 bytes and located at the far end of the record. It is expected that 30% of the Form records will be one sector long, 40% two sectors long, and 30% three sectors.

Record Name	Size Distribution and Mean	Effective Space	Symbol
topology routine	$(.9 \times 512) + (.1 \times 1024)$ $=563.2$	$563.2/4500 =$ $.125$	S_1
topology data	64 (fixed length)	$48/3000 = .016$	S_2
combined topology routine & data	$(.85 \times 512) + (.15 \times 1024) = 589$	$589/4500 = .13$	$S_1 + S_2$
complete topology	$(.90 \times 512) + (.1 \times 1024)$ $= 563.2$	$563.2/3000 = .19$	S_3
model geometry	$(.7 \times 512) + (.3 \times 1024)$ $= 665.6$	$665.6/300 = 2.19$	S_4
geometry values	64 (fixed length)	$64/30 = 2.13$	S_5
combined model, geometry and values	$(.3 \times 512) + (.5 \times 1024)$ $+ (.2 \times 1536) = 973$	$973/300 = 3.24$	$S_4 + S_5$
complete geometry	$(.75 \times 512) + (.25 \times 1024) = 640$	$640/30 = 21.3$	S_6
transformations	32 (fixed length)	32	S_7
combined geometry & transformations	$(.3 \times 512) + (.4 \times 1024)$ $+ (.3 \times 1536) = 1024$	$1024/30 = 34.13$	$S_6 + S_7$
transformed geometry	$(.75 \times 512) + (.25 \times 1024)$ $= 640$	640	S_8
combined geometry & topology	$(.3 \times 512) + (.5 \times 1024) +$ $(.2 \times 1536) = 973$	973	S_9
combined shape	$(.1 \times 512) + (.4 \times 1024) +$ $(.3 \times 1536) + (.2 \times 2048)$ $= 1741$	$1741/30 =$ 58.0	$S_7 + S_9$

Figure 8: *The size distribution of each potentially useful record type in BDS and their Effective space, as denoted by* $S_i / \sum_{1m}$. *All units are in bytes.*

The transformation of coordinates to common "world" coordinates can be done in place and will require the same storage requirements as the coordinates without transforms. The transforms and coordinates can be on the same record. About ten milliseconds of cpu will be required to make the transformation.

The linking of topology and the transformed geometry is the last operation required to instantiate a shape. The cpu time required is negligible. If a record with the result were stored, it would have a size of about 973 bytes (see Figure 8).

A summary of the space requirements for the alternative record types is shown in Figure 8. It presents the numerical estimates for the values of S_i. These estimates were derived from alternative configurations of BDS-type datastructures. Other record layouts, responding to different applications, could result in quite different sizes.

Figure 9 presents the estimated computation times for deriving the various records. The number of disc accesses are indicated, as they will vary with different organizations of operations.

	INPUT RECORDS AND READS	OUTPUT RECORDS AND READS	COMPUTATION (μs)
C_1	two	two	twenty
C_2	two	two	twenty
C_3	two	two	ten
C_4	two	two	zero

Figure 9: *Computation and access requirements for each of the four steps required to instantiate a shape.*

HARDWARE CONSTANTS:

HIERARCHY USE:

$$l_1 = 1$$

disc access time = 50 ms.

$$l_2 = 30$$

disc read time = 5.6 μS/byte

$$l_3 = 10$$

$$l_4 = 10$$

USE ESTIMATES:

$$l_5 = 1.5$$

times a part is in $state_1 = 100$

$$state_2 = 1.2$$

$$state_3 = 1.0$$

Figure 10: *User and Hardware Data for BDS*

Other parameters defining the expected use of BDS are shown in Figure 10. The average disc access time is 50 milliseconds and the disc read rate is 5.6 microseconds per byte. The average total number of operations on a part, over the lifetime of a project file, is expected to be about one hundred. The times a part is in core and used again is expected to be about sixteen percent of the time. We have assumed that a typical BDS database incorporates about 30 transforms for each geometry, about ten value sets for each model geometry, about ten geometries for each topology, and about 1.5 topology value sets for each topology routine. Good use of the system can result in more compact organizations, while some users may define a separate topology for every part in his project file.

By assigning the numerical values in Figures 8, 9, and 10, to each of the thirty alternative instantiation methods, the whole range of alternative schemes can be evaluated. The results are shown in Figure 11, in plot form. To indicate the nature of the numerical computations, those for Alternatives 7, 16, 18, 22, 29, and 30, are presented below.

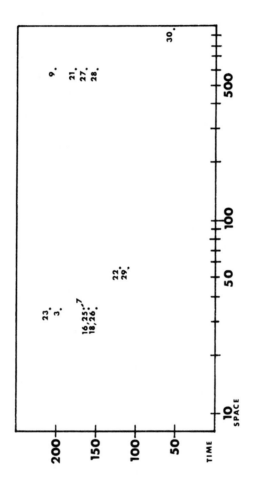

Figure 11: *The Time and Space Requirements for the Best Performing Computation Method, Defined in Figure 5.*

$$T_\alpha = \frac{(\text{\# reads} \times (dt + \text{read rate} \times (\sum \text{record I-0})) + \text{cpu time})}{\text{\# of times a part is in state i}}$$

	disc reads	record I-0	cpu time

ALTERNATIVE 7

state	disc reads	record I-0	cpu time
state1	6	512+589+973+512+563.2+1024	40
state2	0	0	0
state3	3	512+563.2+1024	10

T = 175.3 milliseconds   average space per shape = 34.32 bytes

ALTERNATIVE 16

state	disc reads	record I-0	cpu time
state1	4	512+973+512+1024	20
state2	3	512+589+1024	30
state3	0	0	0

T = 162.3 milliseconds   average space per shape = 34.26 bytes

ALTERNATIVE 18

state	disc reads	record I-0	cpu time
state1	6	512+589+973+512+563.2+1024	40
state2	3	512+563.2+1024	10
state3	0	0	0

T = 146.7 milliseconds   average space per shape = 34.32 bytes

ALTERNATIVE 22

state	disc reads	record I-0	cpu time
state1	5	512+589+973+512+973	25
state2	0	0	0
state3	2	512+1741	10

T = 121.5 milliseconds   average space per shape = 58.02 bytes

ALTERNATIVE 29

state1	5	512+589+973+512+973	25
state2	2	512+1741	10
state3	0	0	0

T = 105.1 milliseconds   average space per shape = 58.02 bytes

ALTERNATIVE 30

state1	6	512+589+973+32+512+973	50
state2	0	0	0
state3	2	512+973	0

T = 52.2 milliseconds   average space per shape = 973.0 bytes

Space requirements vary from 35 bytes per part to almost 1000. At the same time, the computation time to set up the shape descriptions varies from about fifty milliseconds to over five hundred. While the separate storage of topologies and transforms were significantly effective and the topology computation marginally effective, the computation of geometric data offered no space savings. The significant alternatives are 18, 22, 26, 29, and 30. A twenty to one jump in size results from early execution of computation step three. The effect of this step is to derive a unique set of vertex coordinates for an individual part, thus requiring a separate set for each. Alternatives 16 and 18 produce identical results with Alternatives 25 and 26. The reason is that the linking of the topology (step 4) takes negligible time once the records are in core and both alternatives require the same disc accesses.

The methods worth serious consideration are 18, 26, and 29. Both 18 and 26 require 34 bytes of storage and 146 milliseconds for instantiation, while alternative 29 requires only 105 milliseconds for instantiation but 58 bytes of storage. The tradeoff between faster computation versus smaller storage is clear. Alternative 29 assumes that a shape, e.g., geometry and topology, plus all its transforms can be located on a single record and require only one disc access. Either alternative is acceptable for the considerations defined here.

BDS incorporates Alternative 16 as its shape computation method. A thirty to one compaction is gained in the total size of the database. The 34 byte density easily allows 500,000 parts to reside on a discpack storage devise. The cost of this compaction has been to triple the instantiation time, essentially reducing the rate at which parts can be operated on from 21 to 7 per second. (This figure differs from previously published estimates of BDS performance.)

This alternative has been fully implemented and tested within BDS on a PDP-10 and is currently being implemented on a PDP-11. BDS is used for a variety of studies regarding physical system design. It allows effective real-time manipulation of large design databases, of buildings, factories or mechanical systems. Figure 12 presents some display projections derived from a database as it is being manipulated.

Most of the computation methods considered here are I-O bound, limited by disc access and read rates. Significantly faster equipment would alter these times and may change the marginal advantages among them. Some further advantages may be derived that were not considered in this analysis. Overlapping cpu operations with disk I-O can effectively eliminate most cpu computation times from consideration.

This analysis has assumed that hierarchical shape information can be retrieved from the disc directory with only one disc access. This requires that pointers in records, such as from the Form record to the topology that created it, be in terms of disc sector addresses, rather than directory addresses. This calls for a quite specialized memory management and directory scheme. If such a management scheme cannot be devised, then significantly longer computation times will result.

This analysis considers the cost of creating and using a large design database. Definition of the database has emphasized use of a parts catalog. If primary input of shapes is from some other data device, such as a tablet, the creation of shape information may involve costs that would alter the outcomes derived here. The results also are sensitive to the total size of the database. If it is small, then the number of branches from one level in the record hierarchy to another will be fewer, resulting in less efficient storage.

VI. SUMMARY

In this chapter, a methodology has been presented for analyzing alternative schemes for storing spatial information in
very large databases. This methodology may be applicable to
many other types of databases, beside spatial ones. The methodology consisted of identification of all possible forms of
compaction of the final data to be presented, by bringing together information used by many unit records. Later, when an
individual unit record is desired, it must be recomputed from
the various stored information.

The information in any database goes through a variety of
states, where a state is defined by the storage medium and representation of data. These states define the alternative times
in which compacted data can be expanded. Notice that among the
alternatives considered are those which involve not utilizing
one or more possible compactions. By systematic evaluation of
the alternatives an optimal scheme can be derived, resulting in
both practical storage requirements and reasonable computation
times.

ACKNOWLEDGMENTS

Work on BDS is supported by the National Science Foundation.
BDS is the result of many peoples efforts, especially Joseph
Lividini, Adrian Baer, Max Henrion and Gilles Lafue.

STUDY QUESTIONS

1. In your area of design expertise, identify the shape con-
   sistancies or redundancies that could be used to compact
   spatial information in a database.

2. Devise a record directory scheme with the following capabilities:

   a. Allows variable length records;
   b. allows relocatable records, and
   c. allows references to other records to be direct
      addresses, without going through a directory.
      Outline the bookkeeping operations required to
      relocate a record.

3. Assume a greatly different distribution of part shapes, for
    example, each geometry has only ten transforms and each
    model geometry has 20 sets of values. How do the trade-offs
    between storage and computation time vary?

4. The analysis developed here applies to polyhedral shapes.
    What consistancies of data could be used for shapes with
    multi-curved surfaces to reduce their storage requirements?

    (a) Develop a set of records and define their contents
         and size for compactly storing multi-curved shapes.

    (b) Carry out an analysis similar to this one to derive
         the significant alternative data organizations.

REFERENCES

1. Bandurski, A. and D. Jefferson, "Enhancements to the BBTG Model for Computer-Aided Ship Design,"*Proceedings of the Workshop on Databases for Interactive Design,* University of Waterloo, September 15-16, 1975.

2. Barnard, D. F., "Data Structures for Interaction," *Proceedings of the Workshop for Interactive Design,* University of Waterloo, Ontario, September 15-16, 1975.

3. Baumgart, B. G., "Geometric Modeling for Computer Vision," Stanford Artificial Intelligence Memo 249, Computer Science Department, Stanford University, October 1974.

4. Braid, I., "The Synthesis of Solids Bounded by Many Faces," *Communications to the ACM,* 18:4, April 1975, pp. 209-216.

5. Brainin, J., "Use of COMRADE in Engineering Design," *1973 National Computer Conference (NCC),* AFIPS Press, Montvale, New Jersey.

6. Dodd, G. G., et. al., "APL-A Language for Associative Data Handling in PL1," *Proceedings AFIPS 1966 Fall Joint Computer Conference,* Vol. 29, Spartan Books, New York.

7. Dodd, G. G., "Elements of Data Management Systems," *Computing Surveys,* 1:2, June 1969, pp. 117-133.

8. Eastman, C. M. and A. Baer, "Database Features for a Design Information System," *Proceedings of the Workshop on Databases for Interactive Design,* University of Waterloo, Ontario, September 15-16, 1975.

9. Eastman, C. M., "The Use of Computers Instead of Drawings in Building Design," *American Institute of Architects Journal,* March 1975, pp. 46-50.

10. Hoskins, E. M., "Computer Aids in Building," *Computer Aided Design,* J. Vlietstra and R. F. Willinga (eds.), American Elsevier, New York 1973.

11. Lafue, G., "Computer Recognition of Three-Dimensional Objects From Orthographic Views," Institute of Physical Planning Research Report, No. 56, Carnegie-Mellon University, Pittsburgh, Pa.

12. Newman, W. and R. Sproull, *Principles of Interactive Computer Graphics*, McGraw-Hill, New York, 1973.

13. Phong, B. T., "Illumination for Computer Generated Pictures," *Communications of the ACM*, 18:6 (June, 1975), pp. 311-317.

14. Ross, P. T., "The AED Free Store Package," *Communications of the ACM*, 10:8, August 1967, pp. 481-492.

15. Sutherland, I., "Three Dimensional Data Input by Tablet," *Proceedings of the IEEE*, 62:64 (April 1974).

16. Sutherland, I., R. F. Sproull and R. Schumacker, "A Characterization of Ten-Hidden Surface Algorithms," *Computing Surveys*, 6 (March 1974), pp. 1-56.

17. Thomson, B. M., "Plex Data Structure for Integrated Ship Design," *1973 National Computer Conference (NCC)*, AFIPS Press, Montvale, New Jersey.

18. Warn, D. R., "VDAM - A Virtual Data Access Mechanism for Computer Aided Design," *Proceedings of the Workshop on Databases for Interactive Design*, ACM, New York, September 1975.

Data Structures for Pattern Recognition Algorithms

CHARLES T. ZAHN, JR.

Computation Research Group
Stanford Linear Accelerator Center*
Stanford, California 94305

ABSTRACT

This paper will describe experiences gained while programming several pattern recognition algorithms in the languages
ALGOL, FORTRAN, PL/1 and PASCAL. The algorithms discussed are
for boundary encodings of two-dimensional binary pictures,
calculating and exploring the minimum spanning tree for a set
of points, recognizing dotted curves from a set of planar points
and performing a template matching in the presence of severe
noise distortions. The lesson seems to be that pattern recognition algorithms require a range of data structuring capabilities for their implementation, in particular arrays, graphs
and lists. The languages PL/1 and PASCAL have facilities to
accommodate graphs and lists but there are important differences for the programmer. The ease with which the template
matching program was written, debugged and modified during a 3
week period, using PASCAL, suggests that this small but powerful language should not be overlooked by those researchers who
need a quick, reliable, and efficient implementation of a pattern recognition algorithm requiring graphs, lists and arrays.
A number of pattern recognition data-structures are defined
and manipulated by sample PASCAL programs, including the major
parts of the noisy template matching program.

*Work supported by U.S. Energy Research and Development
Administration.

ALGORITHMS

Encoding Digital Pictures

The storage of digital pictures[1] generally requires a rectangular array of picture elements (pixels), each represented by a small integer. The large number of pixels and the small number of bits (1 to 8) per pixel suggest packing the array with one machine word containing several pixels. For efficiency in performing local preprocessing on pixel neighborhoods, it seems natural to unpack several rows of the digital picture and then repack.

Binary digital pictures (see Fig. 1a) consist of connected regions of black or white color which can be represented by a set of polygonal boundary curves. One method[2] for calculating these curves scans the binary picture from top to bottom, extracting curvature points where some boundary curve changes direction. These curvature points are maintained in several linked lists which grow and merge and eventually become cyclic lists corresponding to a completed closed polygon (see Figure 1). There is also a natural insidedness relation among these non-intersecting boundary curves which can best be represented as a directed rooted tree of curves.

A similar method for binary pictures on a triangular grid[3] requires a top-down processing of the strips (corridors) between two adjacent picture rows (see Figure 2). The small pieces of boundary which touch the edges of the corridor are recognized as tops or bottoms according to which edge they touch, and by maintaining a queue of bottom elements, the processing of corridor sequences becomes quite simple: bottoms are added to the queue and tops are linked to the first queue element which is then taken off the queue. This queueing procedure doesn't even need to know where one corridor leaves off and the next begins.

Processing Region Boundaries

It is often appropriate to smooth the polygonal region boundaries by the elimination of wiggly sequences of curvature points caused by quantization noise (see Figure 1). This requirement provides further motivation for representing the curves as linked lists. Not only is the deletion more convenient, but the storage for the deleted points can be re-used for other curves. Computing the convex hull of a closed polygonal curve retains more information if the portion of boundary

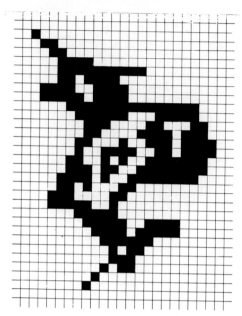

Figure 1:   (a) *Binary Digital Picture on Square Grid*

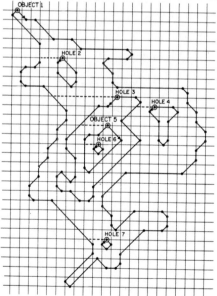

Figure 1:   (b) *Curvaturepoints and Boundary Curves*

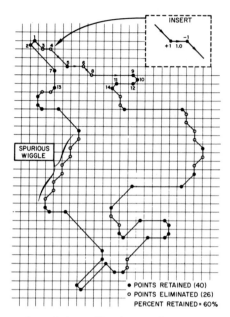

Figure 1:   *(c) Inflexion Points on Outer Curve*

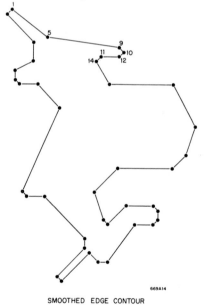

SMOOTHED EDGE CONTOUR

Figure 1: *(d) Smoothed Boundary Curve*

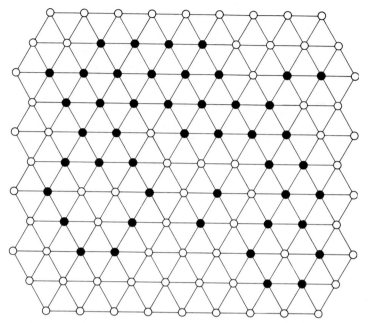

Figure 2: *(a) Binary Picture on Triangular Grid*

Figure 2: *(b) Connectivity Graph of Picture*
            Points and Boundary Graph of Edge Contours

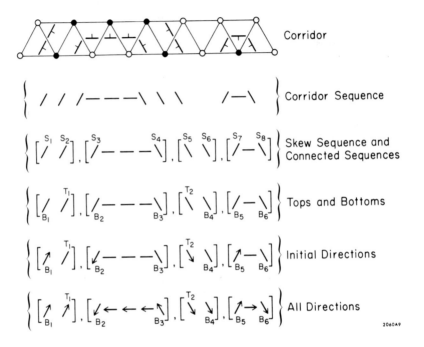

Figure 2(c)   *Analysis of Corridor C_6 Between Rows r_5 and r_6 of (b).*

delineating each concavity is extracted to form a polygonal boundary for the concavity. Once again the flexibility of linked lists is useful.

For the computation of area and local curvature[4] as well as Fourier Descriptors of the boundary shape,[5] it is very convenient to have the boundary represented as a cyclic doubly linked list in close correspondence to the true geometric relationship of the curvature points. The storage for Fourier Descriptors is naturally a static array.

Cluster Analysis

An important problem in pattern recognition is the description of structural properties of a set of points in a multidimensional space. One approach to this problem which applies in a general metric space[6] is to compute the minimal spanning tree (MST) from the complete graph of points with metric distance as edge-weight (see Figure 3). Each point can be represented as an array of coordinate values, and the set as an array of points. An efficient algorithm for constructing the MST begins with a single node (point), and repetitively adds a new node and edge to the growing tree until all points are nodes of the tree. Since the tree grows and the local degree (number of connecting edges) of nodes is not known a priori, it is convenient to associate with each node a list of node-edge adjacencies which refer to actual edges. Each edge has length information and is referred to by two node-edge adjacencies. Two arrays are used to select the next edge to add to the growing tree.

Well-defined clusters can be found by deleting certain "inconsistent" edges of the MST; to determine inconsistency, one must compute simple statistical properties of small sets of edges near the two end-nodes of a given edge. Forming a list of the edges of a subtree can be done by a recursive procedure or using an explicit stack. The connected subtrees which result from deletion of inconsistent edges can be further investigated by calculating the diameter path (longest), considering it as a one-dimensional domain and plotting other functions (e.g., point density estimates) along this coordinate. An especially elegant computation can be constructed to determine, for a given node-edge adjacency, the maximum path length between the given node and all nodes of the subtree defined by the given node-edge adjacency. These "relative-depths" allow almost immediate calculation of "relative-diameters" and the "global" diameter. They are properties of the node-edge adjacencies and would have been

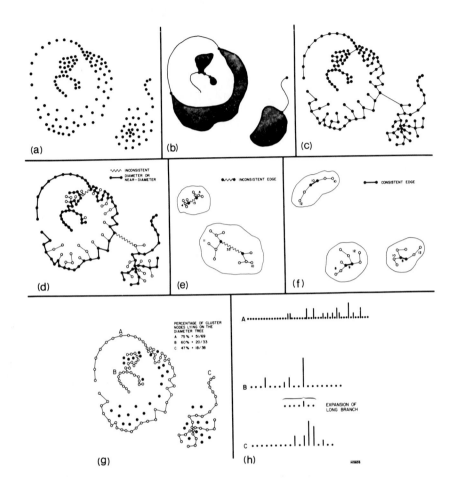

Figure 3: (a) *Planar Point Set*
(b) *Possible Perceptual Gestalt*
(c) *Minimal Spanning Tree*
(d) *Inconsistent Edges and Diameter Paths*
(e) *Closer Look at Inconsistent Edges*
(f) *Consistent Edges*
(g) *Near-Diameter Trees*
(h) *Plotting Tree Depth Along Diameters*

awkward to include in the data-structure if lists of node-adjacencies had not been directly represented. When the diameter path has been found, it may be convenient to represent it as a list or array, depending on the subsequent uses of the path.

Dotted Curve Recognition

As implied by Figure 4, the MST can be useful for the recognition of curves formed by a set of points in the plane. To realistically apply the MST to recognize particle tracks from physics photographs,[7] some shortcuts were necessary. The scanner transforms the photo into a list of points corresponding to the normal top-down left to right TV raster scan of a rectangular area. The sorted order of rows was exploited for its geometric content in the following way: a quasi-minimal spanning forest (Q-MSF) was constructed by restricting the tree to edges connecting a point to other points in a fixed rectangular window around the point. Because of this modification, it became appropriate to maintain a queue of current candidate edges for entry into the tree sorted on edge length (i.e., a priority queue[8]). The crucial aspect of this method is that searching the rectangular window around a new MST node requires looking at only a small horizontal strip of the entire picture -- a small subset of the sorted rows. With these modifications, it became feasible to compute quasi-minimal spanning forests for 1000-2000 points. To economize on storage requirements, the Q-MSF was represented as directed rooted trees with each new edge pointing back into the growing tree. Although this restricts the subsequent tree explorations to follow directed paths, for this type of line-like data the restriction was quite tolerable.

The procedure for curve recognition extracts directed paths from the Q-MSF (possibly after deletion of "hairs": see Figure 4), and applies a variant of the iterative endpoint fit method[9] to recursively decompose the path into approximately linear segments.[7] This requires recursion or an explicit stack. Figure 5 depicts how the method works by breaking path (AB) at C, accepting (AC) as a sufficiently linear segment, breaking (CB) at D, and then accepting (CD) and (DB). The resulting segments are connected into lists which represent curves with slowly varying direction. It is useful to provide links which associate each segment back down to the lower level path of points constituting it.

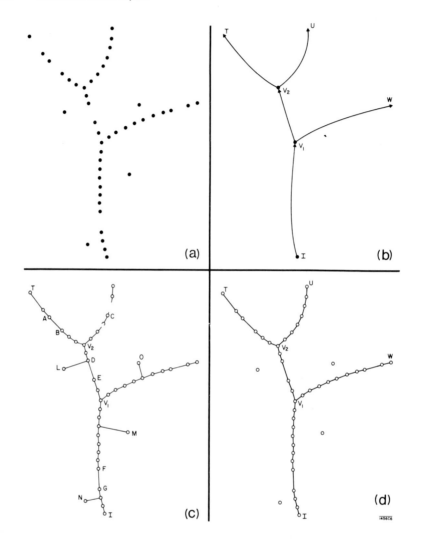

Figure 4: (a) Dotted Particle Tracks (simulated)
           (b) Physical Interpretation as Curves
           (c) Minimal Spanning Tree
           (d) MST with Hairs Deleted

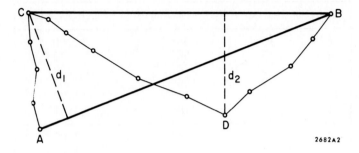

Figure 5:   *Iterative End-Point Fit*

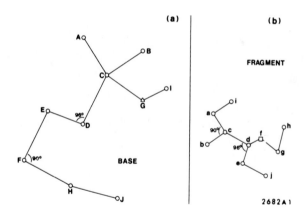

Figure 6:   *(a) & (b) MSTs for Nearly Similar
Planar Point Sets*

Node	Degree	Minimum Angle	Length Ratio
c	3	90°	1.00
d	3	96°	.70
g	2	70°	.89
a	2	90°	1.00
e	2	96°	.70
f	2	118°	1.64
C	4	67°	1.00
F	2	90°	1.00
D	2	96°	.70
E	2	96°	.70
G	2	118°	1.64
H	2	162°	1.07

Figure 6(c): *Node Lists, Minimum Angles and Length Ratios*

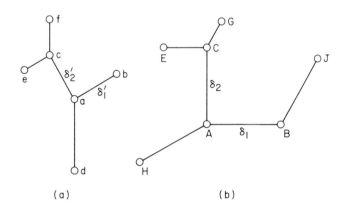

(a)   (b)

Figure 7: *(a) Neighborhood of Test Node in MST for Base Point Set*
(b) Neighborhood of Match Node in MST for Fragment Point Set

Noisy Template Matching

A program has been designed[10] to recognize a partial fragment of an original base point set in the plane even after rotation, uniform scale change, and extremely heavy noise distortions. The method used depends on invariance of local structure of the MST to these forms of distortion. Figure 6 shows the MSTs for two almost matching sets; the local structure invariant to scale changes consists of the angles formed by the sequence of edges about a node, as well as the ratios between lengths of pairs of edges subtending such angles. To adjust to these needs, we calculate a direction for each node-edge adjacency while growing the MST, and keep each node's adjacency list ordered by edge-direction counter-clockwise around the node. When the MST is complete, we calculate angles around each node, storing the information at node-edge adjacencies. The minimum angle at each node is calculated along with the ratio between the lengths of the edges subtending this minimum angle. This information is stored at the node. The nodes of the MST are next arranged into separate lists based on local degree (≤ 6 for a planar MST), and each list is ordered by the value of minimum angle. This structure is computed for both base and fragment point sets so that the matching algorithm will be very efficient (see Fig. 6c). Attempts to find nodes with similar local structure restrict their attention to nodes of nearly the same degree and with compatible minimum angle and length ratio. This focuses the search dramatically.

When there is reasonable evidence of matching local structure between two nodes, then a global least squares fit is performed to obtain a final verification. This requires a 4×4 matrix which defines the linear system to be solved.

A more detailed description of this algorithm and its data-structures in PASCAL will be given in a later section.

DATA-STRUCTURES

The functional requirements of the various algorithms described above dictate the use of a wide range of data structures including arrays, matrices, singly and doubly linked lists, cyclic lists, rooted directed and symmetric trees, simple and priority queues, stacks, and sorted lists. These are fundamental data-structures for general programming,[11] and pattern recognition methods appear to need a rich blending of the entire range for their convenient implementation. We have attempted to describe the algorithms in sufficient detail to indicate that the chosen data-structures were the natural consequence of certain requirements for efficiency or convenience.

Lists, trees, queues, and stacks can be implemented in terms of two more primitive data-types called records and references. A record is a data-structure consisting of several named fields of possibly different types, and a reference is a variable which points to some record. If records containing references to other records can be dynamically created and destroyed during the execution of a program, then one has all the facilities needed to create arbitrary graphs; lists, trees, queues and stacks are special instances of general graphs.

While there are ways to implement lists and trees in some cases using arrays, the lack of dynamic storage allocation can make such solutions awkward. The clarity of programs can also suffer when arrays are used for purposes never intended.

LANGUAGE COMPARISON

FORTRAN and ALGOL-60

From the point-of-view of data-structures, FORTRAN and ALGOL-60 are almost identical since arrays are all that is offered. The curvature points algorithm[2] was implemented in ALGOL-60 (see Appendix A,B in[12]) with arrays named X,Y,EDGEIN, EDGEOUT to represent the curvature points themselves, and arrays named TOP, BOTTOM, NEXTPOINT, NEXTEDGE, LASTPOINT, LASTEDGE, ANGLE, LENGTH to represent the cyclic polygonal curves. The program is reasonably clear but there is some waste of storage, and misuse of the integer pointers cannot be detected by the language compiler as it can be in languages with references declared as bound to one particular record class.

The dotted curve recognition program for particle tracks[7] was implemented in FORTRAN although originally developed and debugged in PL/1. The clarity of the program suffered considerably in the translation while the efficiency was not substantially enhanced. It was probably quite fortunate that the program was correct before being translated to FORTRAN since the array implementation of pointers has the same problem as mentioned above for ALGOL-60.

The MST cluster analysis algorithm has been programmed in FORTRAN[13] making it more accessible, but the FORTRAN version lacks something in clarity, for the usual reasons, even though the author made a valiant attempt.

PL/1

The PL/1 language offers structures (similar to records) and pointers (references), and allows for dynamic storage allocation and deallocation. Unfortunately, pointers are not restricted to refer to a particular class of structure and, as a result, detecting misuses of pointers by traditional debugging can be quite painful. We implemented the minimal spanning tree clustering[6] in PL/1 as well as the earlier versions of the dotted curve recognition.[7] In general, we found PL/1 to be an adequate programming tool for these algorithms if used in a very constrained way, avoiding the more dangerous or mysterious aspects of the language.

ALGOL-W

The language ALGOL-W[14] (implemented extremely well on the IBM/360) is based on ALGOL-60 but includes records separated into disjoint classes, and references which are restricted to refer to a particular class or set of classes. The compiler can, therefore, diagnose most misuses of references and save the programmer many grey hairs. The algorithms we have implemented in PL/1 could have been programmed almost identically in ALGOL-W with a gain in efficiency as well as programmer convenience.

PASCAL

The language PASCAL[15,16,17] is based on ALGOL-60 and ALGOL-W, but implements many of the important data structuring facilities described and motivated by Hoare.[18] It has the records and references (here called pointers) of ALGOL-W but includes programmer defined data types, constants, sets, etc. It enjoys most of the desirable properties of ALGOL-W but was more consciously designed to support modern ideas of hierarchical refinement of data-structures and procedures.

We programmed, debugged, experimented with, and modified the noisy template matching algorithm[10] as well as writing the paper -- all within 3 weeks. The initial computer run was an attempted compilation of approximately 900 lines of PASCAL and the final production run occurred 8 working days later with a 1300 line program! Only two programming errors slipped past the compiler and they caused no severe difficulty. This was, moreover, our first serious effort at programming in PASCAL, although familiarity with ALGOL-W helped.

In PASCAL, the programmer can define the type pixel to be a subrange 0..7 of integer values, and then a packed array [1..500,1..500] of pixel would require only 25,000 32-bit words of storage. The programmer must consciously pack and unpack, but need not be concerned with the machine dependent details of shifting, masking and field extraction.

SKOL

SKOL is a language which is currently under experimental development, and which represents an attempt to implement some of the features of PASCAL, along with structured control as advocated by Knuth,[19] and a form of coroutines adapted from SIMULA[22]; the MORTRAN2 macro-translator[20] is used to translate SKOL programs into equivalent FORTRAN.

The language MORTRAN2 is a structured extension to FORTRAN which can be translated into standard FORTRAN by a very small standard FORTRAN program (800 cards). The translator is driven by a list of macro-rules for text replacement, and SKOL → FORTRAN translation is achieved simply by using a list of macro-rules appropriate to SKOL. The most interesting development to date has been the relative ease with which records and references can be implemented[21] with very good protection against misuse of references.

The macro-based implementation of a structured language allowing records and references by a standard FORTRAN program which translates the given language into standard FORTRAN has large implications. The major advantages of FORTRAN (i.e., frequency of implementation and program libraries) are retained while its considerable deficiency as an intellectual tool for problem solving is not relevant. Other data structures such as stacks and queues are easy to implement in the macro-based fashion, as are other user-defined facilities. In its present state of development, SKOL would be a fairly convenient vehicle for programming the pattern recognition algorithms discussed above.

PASCAL DATA-STRUCTURES

The PASCAL language has data-definition and data-structuring facilities which, in conjunction with records and references, allow the programmer to structure data in a conceptually natural way. The programmer may define a name

(i.e., identifier) to be synonymous with a constant value
(e.g., PI=3.14159). He may define a new type (i.e., range of
values) as a finite set of distinct names which become the
constant values of the new type (e.g., Color=[Red,Yellow,
Green]) or as a subrange of the integers (e.g.,
Age_range=0..150).

We shall present some concrete examples of PASCAL data-
structures in the context of pattern recognition algorithms.

General Digital Pictures

Suppose we wish to represent general digital pictures --
that is, colored (trispectral) as well as black and white. We
begin by defining several constant names which will be used
uniformly in all subsequent data-definitions, data-declarations
and commands.

constant Pix_size = 100; Black=63; White=0;

Next, we define four new types - Color, Pixel, Pix_type and
Pix_range

```
type    Color    = [Red,Yellow,Green];
        Pixel    = White .. Black;
        Pix_type = [Colored,Black_white];
        Pix_range = 1 .. Pix_size;
```

and then new structured types called Simple_pix and
Colored_pix

```
type   Simple_pix = packed array[Pix_range,Pix-range]
                          of Pixel;
       Colored_pix = array[Color] of Simple_pix;
```

Now we can define the new type Picture

```
type   Picture =

       record

          Name: Text_string;

          case P_T: Pix_type of

             Colored: (C_P : Colored_pix);

             Black_white: (S_P : Simple_pix)

       end;
```

The case variant construction within a record is peculiar to
PASCAL; in this case, it means that each variable of type
Picture will have a field called P_T of type Pix_type (i.e.,
Colored or Black-white) and subsequent fields will have names

and types depending on the particular value of P_T. We have
thus defined a single data-type which can be used to represent
general digital pictures.

Should we need to handle pictures 150×150 with picture
elements in the range 0=White to 15=Black, then all that is
required is to change the constant definitions for Pix_size
and Black! All other adjustments required throughout the
program are obtained consistently by recompilation of the
program.

Minimal Spanning Trees

The PASCAL data-structures employed to represent a minimal
spanning tree (MST) included the following four new types. The
symbol "@" means "reference to".

```
type
    POINT_TYPE=
        array [1..MAX_DIM] of real;
    NODE_TYPE=
        record
            FIRST_ADJ: @ADJ_TYPE;
            DEGREE:  integer;
            X: POINT_TYPE;
            NEXT: @NODE_TYPE;
        end;
    ADJ_TYPE=
        record
            NEXT: @ADJ_TYPE;
            EDGE: @EDGE_TYPE;
        end;
    EDGE_TYPE=
        record
            END_NODE: array [1..2] OF @NODE_TYPE;
            LENGTH: real;
        end;
```

This introduces a new type named Point_type into the
language. A value of this new type must be a sequence of real
values, each one identified by an integer between 1 and
Max_dim (a constant). If Max_dim has been defined as 3 then
the following triple is a Point_type value:

$$(3.412 , 0 , 5.2E20)$$

with the understanding that 1,2,3 are the respective names of
the real values constituting this Point_type value.

Two new variables U,V can now be introduced by the declaration

      var U,V : Point_type ;

and the notation for referring to its subvalues is the familiar array subscript notation. The following three PASCAL statements will initialize variable U to the value above

      U[1] := 3.412; U[2] := 0; U[3] := 5.2E20;

The statement V := U; will replace the value (all three parts) of V by the current value of U and is equivalent to

      for I := 1 to 3 do V[I] := U[I];

The new type called Node_type also consists of a structured value constructed from other subvalues (as in Point_type) but record differs from array in two significant ways. First, the subvalues may be of different type from one another and second, these constituent subvalues are identified by field names rather than by integer subscripts. The fields of Node_type are X,Degree,Next,First_adj. The last two fields identify values which are references (or pointers) to other values of type Node_type or Adj_type which are created dynamically at run-time. Notice that the subvalue identified by fieldname X is itself of a non-primitive programmer-defined type. A typical value of Node_type might be

      ((3.412, 0, 5.2E20),3,?,?)

If ND has been introduced as a variable of type Node_type by the declaration

      var ND : Node_type;

then the field X of variable ND is identified by the notation ND.X and the second coordinate of X within ND is referred to as ND.X[2].

Dynamic creation of Nodes, Edges and Adjacencies to "grow" graphs at run-time is accomplished by declaring some variables to be references to ("@") values of Node_type, Edge_type or Adj_type as follows:

      var N : @ Node_type; A :@Adj_type; E : @Edge_type;

A special PASCAL command new (RV); will create a new value of the type referred to by the variable RV. A new node is created by

      new (N);

and the value of Node_type so created is identified by the notation N@. The subvalues of N@ are denoted by N@.X,

N@.Degree, N@.X[3], N@.Next etc. The following iteration creates a list (or sequence) of 5 nodes and then initializes the points to zero:

```
var Head,N : @Node_type;

Head := nil;
for I := 1 to 5 do
    begin
        new(N);
        N@.Next := Head;
        Head := N
    end;

N := Head;
while N ≠ nil do
    begin
        for I := 1 to 3 do N@.X[I] := 0 ;
        N := N@.Next
    end;
```

The special value nil serves the role of an undefined reference value which is used to mark the end of lists.

The adjacencies (values of type Adj_type) are employed to link nodes to their adjacent edges in an environment where the graph "grows" and the local degree of nodes is not known in advance. Within each node the First_adj field refers to the first adjacency in a list of adjacencies defined by the field Next within the adjacencies. Field Edge within each adjacency refers to the edge in question and each edge has references back to its end nodes.

Tree of Figure Boundaries

The curvaturepoint method mentioned earlier[2] transforms a binary digital picture (see Fig. 1a) into a tree of polygonal boundary curves (see Fig. 1b). For example, the tree corresponding to Fig. 1b has a top node consisting of the outermost boundary curve around "object 1" and the 4 descendants of this top node are the four "holes" 2,3,4,7. Hole 3 has a descendant "object 5" which itself has a descendant "hole 6". Each curve consists of a cyclic sequence of curvaturepoints, each identified by an incoming and outgoing boundary edge direction as well as the length of the outgoing edge. It amounts to a variable-length Freeman chain-encoding[4] of the curve.

PASCAL data-structures for the boundary tree might be as follows:

```
type Point_type = record X,Y : real end;
     Direction_type = 0..7;
     Angle_type = record In,Out : Direction_type end;
     Cp_type =
         record Bend:Angle_type; Outlength:integer;
                Next,Previous:@Cp_type end;
     Curve_type =
         record Top,Bottom:
                   record Cp:@Cp_type;
                          Pt:Point_type end;
                Inside,Same,Outside,Next:@Curve_type end;

var Outer_curve:@Curve_type;
```

These type definitions introduce "points" in the plane
with coordinates (X,Y); a set of 8 compass "directions" denoted
by integers 0,1,2,...,7 corresponding to the direction in units
of 45° measured counterclockwise from the positive X-axis;
"angles" consisting of pairs of directions; "curvaturepoints"
which are "angles" with an outgoing length and forward and
backward links to other curvaturepoints; "curves" each containing a top and bottom curvaturepoint along with actual coordinates as well as links to the inside and outside curve. The
outer curve of the boundary tree is accessed by the curve-
reference variable named Outer_curve.

The tree is represented by having the Outside curve-
reference point to the unique curve immediately enclosing the
given curve and Inside point to one of the possibly several
immediately enclosed curves. The set of curves having a common
Outside are linked together in a list by the Same field.

Each curve has a cyclic sequence of curvaturepoints which
can be entered at top or bottom. To exemplify the manipulation of the boundary curves we give a program to compute area:

```
{Compute signed area of simple closed polygon}
var P1,P2:@Cp_type;
    Crv:@Curve_type;
    X1,X2,X3,Y1,Y2,Area : real;
    Delta:array[Direction_type] of Point_type;
Area := 0.0;
P1 := Crv@.Top.Cp; X1 := Crv@.Top.Pt.X;Y1 := Crv@.Top.Pt.Y;
repeat
    P2 := P1@.Next;
    Y2 := Y1 + Delta[P1@.Bend.Out].Y*P1@.Outlength;
    X2 := X1 + Delta[P1@.Bend.Out].X*P1@.Outlength;
    X3 := X2 + Delta[P2@.Bend.Out].X*P2@.Outlength;
    Area := Area + .5*Y2*(X3 - X1);
    P1 := P2; X1 := X2; Y1 := Y2;
until P1 = Crv@.Top.Cp;
```

This algorithm uses an interesting variable Delta which is an array of point-vectors indexed by the values of type Direction_type. It is assumed to define "unit" vectors in each of the 8 directions except that the length of diagonals (the odd ones) is $\sqrt{2}$.

The assignments to X2 and Y2 inside the repetition deserve some special comment. P1 refers to a curvaturepoint, P1@.Bend denotes the "angle" of this curvaturepoint and P1@.Bend.Out denotes the outgoing direction of this angle. This direction is used as subscript into array Delta and the appropriate coordinate of the resulting unit vector is multiplied by P1@.Out-length, the integral number of unit vectors representing the length of the outgoing boundary edge at curvaturepoint P1@.

These examples do not involve all the nice data-representation facilities of PASCAL, but we hope to have indicated that this language allows a very pleasant implementation of algorithms which manipulate graphs, lists and arrays.

PASCAL PROGRAM FOR NOISY TEMPLATE MATCHING

Major Data-Structures

The most important data for the noisy template matching[10] program (see earlier discussion for an overview) consists of two minimal spanning trees constructed from the "base" and "fragment" point sets in 2-dimensional space. The data-structure definitions for this basic data are as follows:

```
const
    MAX_DIM=2; NN_MAX=200;

type
    POINT_TYPE=
        array [1..MAX_DIM] of real;
    NODE_PTR=
        @NODE_TYPE;
    ADJ_PTR=
        @ADJ_TYPE;
    EDGE_PTR=
        @EDGE_TYPE;
    NODE_TYPE=
        record
            FIRST_ADJ: ADJ_PTR;
            DEGREE: integer;
            X: POINT_TYPE;
            NEXT: NODE_PTR;
            MIN_ANGLE: real;
            LEN_RATIO: real;
            MIN_ADJ: ADJ_PTR
        end;
    ADJ_TYPE=
        record
            NEXT: ADJ_PTR;
            EDGE: EDGE_PTR;
            DIRECTION: real;
            ANGLE: real
        end;
    EDGE_TYPE=
        record
            END_NODE: array [1..2] of NODE_PTR;
            LENGTH: real
        end;
    N_ARRAY=
        array [1..NN_MAX] of NODE_PTR;

var
    NODES,FRAG_NODES:
        N_ARRAY;
    N_FRAG_PTS,N_ALL_PTS:
        integer;
```

The definitions of Node_type, Adj_type and Edge_type are the same as for a general MST described earlier but "nodes" contain extra fields for minimum angle, length ratio across this angle and a reference to the adjacency representing the first edge of the minimum angle (reading counterclockwise, of course). Each "adjacency" now has an angular direction and the angle formed by this edge and the next. An N_array is an array of upto NN_max node references and two such variables NODES and FRAG_NODES are introduced to define the "base" and "fragment" point sets respectively. The size of these two sets are maintained in variables N_ALL_PTS and N_FRAG_PTS respectiveiy.

The list of edge-adjacencies for each node will be maintained in a counterclockwise order around the node starting at the 0 direction (i.e., 3 o'clock).

Planar Minimal Spanning Tree

The following PASCAL program computes the MST using the above data-structure; it assumes that an array NODES[1..N_POINTS] contains references to the nodes containing the points and that a function EUCLIDIST of two points will give the euclidean distance. The procedure GET_THETA of two nodes will set THETA to the angular direction from first node to second node.

```
procedure
    MST( N_POINTS : integer; var NODES : N_ARRAY );
    (* COMPUTE THE MINIMAL SPANNING TREE FOR THE POINTS X(1..MAX
    DIM) OF NODES REFERENCED BY NODES (1..N_POINTS).  COMPUTE
    THE DIRECTION OF EACH NODE/EDGE ADJACENCY MEASURED AS
    (0..2*PI) AND ARRANGE LIST OF ADJACENCIES AT EACH NODE IN
    COUNTERCLOCKWISE ORDER FROM 0).  PRIM/DIJKSTRA SINGLE FRAG-
    MENT METHOD IS USED.
    *)
var
    NEAR:
        array [1..NN_MAX] of
            record NODE:NODE_PTR; DISTANCE:real; FREE:boolean end;
    NEW_NODE, OLD_NODE: NODE_PTR;
    THIS_ADJ,LAST_ADJ,NEW_ADJ: ADJ_PTR;
    NEW_EDGE: EDGE_PTR;
    MIN_DIST,T,RHO,THETA: real;
    K,J: integer;

begin (* MST BODY *)
    with NODES[1]@ do
        begin DEGREE := 0; FIRST_ADJ := nil end;
    with NEAR[1] do
        begin NODE := nil; FREE := false end;
    for K := 2 to N_POINTS do
        with NEAR[K] do
            begin
                NODE := NODES[1];
                DISTANCE := EUCLIDIST(NODES[1]@.X,NODES[K]@.X);
                FREE := true
            end;
    for J := 1 to N_POINTS-1 do
        begin
            CLOSEST;
            GET_THETA(OLD_NODE,NEW_NODE);
            new(NEW_EDGE);
            with NEW_NODE@ do
                begin
                    new(FIRST_ADJ); DEGREE := 1;
                    with FIRST_ADJ@ do
                        begin
                            EDGE := NEW_EDGE;
                            NEXT := nil;
                            if THETA >= PI then
                                DIRECTION := THETA-PI
                            else
                                DIRECTION := THETA+PI
                        end
                end;
```

```
with OLD_NODE@ do
    begin
        DEGREE := DEGREE+1;
        LAST_ADJ := FIRST_ADJ;
        while THIS_ADJ ≠ nil do
            begin
                if THIS_ADJ@.DIRECTION <= THETA then
                    begin
                        LAST_ADJ := THIS_ADJ;
                        THIS_ADJ := LAST_ADJ@.NEXT
                    end
                else
                    THIS_ADJ := nil
            END;
        new(NEW_ADJ);
        with NEW_ADJ@ do
            begin EDGE := NEW_EDGE; DIRECTION := THETA end;
        if LAST_ADJ = nil then
            FIRST_ADJ := NEW_ADJ
        else
            LAST_ADJ@.NEXT := NEW_ADJ;
        NEW_ADJ@.NEXT := THIS_ADJ
    end;
with NEW_EDGE@ do
    begin
        END_NODE[1] := NEW_NODE;
        END_NODE[2] := OLD_NODE;
        LENGTH := MIN_DIST;
    end;
for K := 1 to N_POINTS do
    with NEAR[K] do
        if FREE then
            begin
                T := EUCLIDIST(NEW_NODE@.X,NODES[K]@.X);
                if T < DISTANCE then
                    begin
                        DISTANCE := T;
                        NODE := NEW_NODE
                    end
            end
    end
end
end (* PROCEDURE MST *) ;
```

The major auxiliary data-structure required to build the MST using Prim's single fragment approach is a variable NEAR consisting of an array of records (one per node), each record indicating if the node is FREE (i.e., outside the fragment) and if so which NODE of the fragment is closest to it and at what DISTANCE.

The program begins by making the first node of the input array NODES become the initial fragment* and by making all other nodes "free" with this sole fragment node the closest for all of them. The first statement of MST uses the PASCAL with statement which allows the programmer to abbreviate the usual notation for fields within a record. It is exactly equivalent to the two statements
```
NODES[1]@.DEGREE := 0;
NODES[1]@.FIRST_ADJ := nil;
```

Similarly the second with statement records that the first node is not FREE and that it has no nearest node in the fragment. The statement is equivalent to
```
NEAR[1].NODE := nil;
NEAR[1].FREE := false;
```
The next statement of the program can be considered as a refinement of the command
```
for K := 2 to N_POINTS do
      Initialize_NEAR[K]
```
and the phrase "with NEAR[K] do" focuses attention on the three fields of that specific record called NEAR[K] in a fashion that is a clear reflection of what is being accomplished. In particular, notice the strong parallel between the hierarchical dynamic nesting of this for statement and the hierarchical static nesting of the declaration of variable NEAR.

The remainder of the MST program is an elaboration of the following rough sketch:

---

* this use of the word fragment is not related to the meaning as used for template matching.

```
for J := 1 to N_POINTS-1 do
    Find_closest_free_node
    Compute_theta_for_this_edge
    Create_new_edge
    Initialize_new_node
    Update_old_node
    Initialize_new_edge
    for K := 1 to N_POINTS do
        Update_NEAR[K]_if_FREE
```

The command "Initialize_new_node" becomes:

```
with NEW_NODE@ do
    DEGREE := 1
    Create_new_adjacency_for_FIRST_ADJ
    Initialize_FIRST_ADJ_list
```

and the command "Initialize_FIRST_ADJ_list" becomes:

```
with FIRST_ADJ@ do
    EDGE := NEW_EDGE
    NEXT := nil
    DIRECTION := Rotate_theta_by_180°
```

Because of the nesting of with statements the assignment NEXT := nil in this context actually means

```
NEW_NODE@.FIRST_ADJ@.NEXT := nil
```

The purpose of performing the above exercise was to indicate how the top-down stepwise-refinement of complex programs involving complex data-structures can be gracefully accomplished in PASCAL. The reader is encouraged to read the remainder of the MST program to test his understanding of these data-structure manipulations.

The procedure CLOSEST which follows is also instructive

```
procedure
    CLOSEST;
    (*COMPUTE FREE NODE CLOSEST TO CURRENT FRAGMENT OF GROWING
     MST. *)

    var K,KMIN: integer;
    begin (* CLOSEST BODY *)
        MIN_DIST := BIG_REAL; KMIN := 0;
        for K := 1 to N_POINTS do
            with NEAR[K] do
                if FREE then
                    if DISTANCE < MIN_DIST then
                        begin MIN_DIST := DISTANCE; KMIN := K end;
        if KMIN ≠ 0 then
            begin
                NEAR[KMIN].FREE := false;
                NEW_NODE := NODES[KMIN];
                OLD_NODE := NEAR[KMIN].NODE
            end
        else (* NO FREE NODES FOUND *)
            NEW_NODE := nil
    end (* PROCEDURE CLOSEST *) ;
```

The repetition in this procedure might be expressed in English as "Go through the node-array NEAR changing MIN_DIST to the NEAR DISTANCE if the node is still FREE and the NEAR DISTANCE is smaller than the current value of MIN_DIST". The text of the PASCAL version is reasonably close to this while being more precise.

Although not central to the process of template matching, the following program to print an entire MST was very useful in program development. It assumes that the nodes are arranged into 6 lists based on degree and the type FN_ARRAY is defined by

```
    type FN_ARRAY = array[1..6] of NODE_PTR;
```

This program has with statements nested four deep! It traverses every structural link (i.e., reference) in the MST data-structure. It has been written using indentation instead of the delimiters begin ... end to indicate groups of statements and a for statement which traverses linked lists has been used for added clarity. The latter would be a very nice addition to the PASCAL language.

```
procedure FULL_PRINT ( FIRST_NODE : FN_ARRAY );
    var I,J,K : integer ; ND : NODE_PTR; A: ADJ_PTR;
    for K := 1 to 6 do
        writeln; writeln('0'); writeln(' DEGREE ',K:I);
        for ND:= FIRST_NODE[K] by NEXT do
            with ND@ do
                write ('0',' DEG ',DEGREE:2,' COORDS ');
                for I := 1 to MAX_DIM do
                    write (' ',X[I]:10);
                writeln;
                for A := FIRST_ADJ by NEXT do
                    with A@ do
                        write (' DIR ',DIRECTION:10,' ANG ',ANGLE:10);
                        with EDGE@ do
                            write (' LEN ',LENGTH:10,' ENDS ');
                            for J := 1 to 2 do
                                with END_NODE[J]@ do
                                    for I := 1 to MAX_DIM do
                                        write (' ',X[I]:10)
        writeln;
```

Notice that the innermost nested write statement is equivalent to

        write(' ',ND@.A@.EDGE@.END_NODE[J]@.X[I]:10)

which asks to print the I-th coordinate of the J-th end node of the edge associated with adjacency A of node ND.

Fragment Matching

After MST, GET_ANGLES and NODE_LISTS have been performed on the nodes of both "base" and "fragment" then the fragment matching can begin in earnest. The procedures GET_ANGLES and NODE_LISTS compute the angles between consecutive (counter-clockwise) edge-adjacencies at each node, the minimum angle and associated length ratio for each node and arrange the nodes in separate lists based on degree, these lists being sorted according to increasing minimum angle. The variables FIRST_NODE and FST_FRG_ND (read "first fragment node") are the first node arrays for the base and fragment respectively.

The following procedure FRAG_MATCH is written in pseudo-PASCAL using indentation and the extension of the for statement to linked lists. It also employs the new "situation case" control statement[19,23,24] to handle the double-outcome Match or No_match of the attempt to find the fragment hidden somewhere in the base. The definition of the array INC[1..3] as a constant (0, 1, -1) is not allowed in PASCAL but is precisely what the program requires.

The procedures LOCAL_FIT and GLOBAL_FIT perform the most complex part of the fragment matching and will be described later. MND and TND are abbreviations for "match node degree" and "test node degree." On the presumption that the fragment has fewer points than the base this program tries each fragment node as a Match-node and looks for Test-nodes among the base nodes which might correspond. The search is restricted to Test_nodes whose degree differs from that of the Match_node by at most one.

EPS_ANGLE and EPS_RATIO are tolerances defined as constants at the beginning of the program.

```
var FIRST_NODE,FST_FRG_ND : FN_ARRAY
procedure FRAG_MATCH
const INC[1..3] = (0,1,-1)
until Match or No_match do
    for MND := 6 downto 2 do
        for MATCH_NODE := FST_FRG_ND[MND] by NEXT do
            with MATCH_NODE@ do
                M_A := MIN_ANGLE ;L_R := LEN_RATIO
            for TRIAL := 1 to 3 do
                TND := MND + INC[TRIAL]
                if TND in [2..6] then
                    for TEST_NODE := FIRST_NODE[TND] by NEXT do
                        with TEST_NODE@ do
                            if (abs(MIN_ANGLE-M_A) < EPS_ANGLE
                              and (abs(1-LEN_RATIO/L_R) < EPS_RATIO
                            then
                                SMPL_MATCH := true
                            else
                                SMPL_MATCH := false
                        if SMPL_MATCH then
                            if LOCAL_FIT then
                                if GLOBAL_FIT then
                                    Match
No_match
then case
    Match : nop
    No_match: writeln ; writeln (' NO MATCH')
```

Local Fitting

When a Match_node and Test_node have been found with nearly equal minimum angle and length ratio, a search is made in the neighborhoods of these two nodes for additional nodes and edges whose relative positions are compatible with a similarity transformation between base and fragment.

For example, suppose that Match_node A in figure 7b and Test_node a in figure 7a have been found to match up at angles BAC and bac respectively. An approximate scale-factor S_F is computed by the formula

$$S\_F := \left(\delta_1 * \delta_1' + \delta_2 * \delta_2' \right) \bigg/ \left(\delta_1^2 + \delta_2^2 \right)$$

where the δ_k and δ_k' are as shown in figure 7. This scale-factor is used to test all edge correspondences whose directions are consistent relative to the original minimum angle correspondence.

The search for extra node correspondences begins by scanning through the adjacency lists for nodes A and a cyclically starting respectively at edges AB and ab. The two edge-adjacency lists are scanned synchronously and the angular change since the starting edge-direction is continuously inspected for potential matches between base and fragment. These angular changes are kept in variables DTHETA_M and DTHETA_T. When the edges corresponding to nearly equal DTHETA_M and DTHETA_T also have lengths differing by the ratio S_F then the respective end-nodes at the other ends of these matching edges are investigated in a similar way.

In the case depicted in Figure 7 nodes B and b will correspond since both DTHETA_M and DTHETA_T are zero initially and $\delta_k'/\delta_1 \approx S\_F$. The local neighborhoods of B and b will reveal no further structural similarities because node b has degree 1. Next the nodes C and c will correspond at DTHETA_M and DTHETA_T, both approximately 90°. The scan around nodes C and c begins with respective edges CA and ca linking back to the Match_node (A) and Test_node (a). Edges CG and cf will have nearly equal angular changes (variables DTHETA_M2 and DTHETA_T2) but will fail the length ratio test. Finally, edges EC and ec will have angular change 270° and compatible length ratio. No further nodes or edges will be found to correspond.

The local fit is successful because 4 nodes (A,B,C,E) and (a, b, c, e) correspond in a fashion compatible with a similarity transformation. These "points" are stored in the arrays FRAG and BASE at positions 1..N_LOC_MTCH for use by the global fitting program. The variables FRAG and BASE are declared to be of type PT_ARRAY defined by

type PT_ARRAY = array [1..NN_MAX] of POINT_TYPE;

The following PASCAL program implements the local fitting as described. The tests of DTHETA_? against 1.8*PI are valid because all local angles in a planar MST are at least 60°.

```
function
    LOCAL_FIT:boolean;
    var
        F_M,F_T,A_M,A_T,F_M2,F_T2,A_M2,A_T2: ADJ_PTR;
        IN_EDGE_M,IN_EDGE_T: EDGE_PTR;
        DTHETA_M,DTHETA_T,S_F,D1,D2,D1_P,D2_P,LEN_M23,LEN_T23,
            DTHETA_M2,DTHETA_T2: real;
        N_M,N_T,F_ND,B_ND: NODE_PTR;
        K: integer;
    begin (*LOCAL_FIT BODY *)
        with MATCH_NODE@ do
            begin F_M := FIRST_ADJ; A_M := MIN_ADJ end;
        with TEST_NODE@ do
            begin F_T := FIRST_ADJ; A_T := MIN_ADJ end;
        DTHETA_M := 0; DTHETA_T := 0;
        D1 := A_M@.EDGE@.LENGTH; D2 := MATCH_NODE@.LEN_RATIO*D1;
        D1_P := A_T@.EDGE@.LENGTH; D2_P := TEST_NODE@.LEN_RATIO*D1_P;
        S_F := (D1*D1_P+D2*D2_P)/(sqr(D1)+sqr(D2));
        N_LOC_MTCH := 1;
        FRAG[N_LOC_MTCH] := MATCH_NODE@.X;
        BASE[N_LOC_MTCH] := TEST_NODE@.X;
        repeat
            if abs(DTHETA_M-DTHETA_T) < EPS_ANGLE then
            if abs(1-(A_M@.EDGE@.LENGTH*S_F)/A_T@.EDGE@.LENGTH)<EPS_RATIO then
                begin
                    N_M := OTHER_NODE(MATCH_NODE,A_M);
                    N_T := OTHER_NODE(TEST_NODE,A_T);
                    N_LOC_MTCH := N_LOC_MTCH+1;
                    FRAG[N_LOC_MTCH] := N_M@.X;
                    BASE[N_LOC_MTCH] := N_T@.X;
                    if (N_M@.DEGREE>=2) and (N_T@.DEGREE>=2) then
                        begin
                            IN_EDGE_M := A_M@.EDGE;
                            with N_M@ do
                                begin
                                    F_M2 := FIRST_ADJ;
                                    A_M2 := FIRST_ADJ;
                                    while A_M2@.EDGE ≠ IN_EDGE_M do
                                        A_M2 := A_M2@.NEXT
                                end;
                            IN_EDGE_T := A_T@.EDGE;
                            with N_T@ do
                                begin
                                    F_T2 := FIRST_ADJ;
                                    A_T2 := FIRST_ADJ;
                                    while A_T2@.EDGE ≠ IN_EDGE_T do
                                        A_T2 := A_T2@.NEXT
                                end;
```

```
                    DTHETA_M2 := 0;   DTHETA_T2 := 0;
                    repeat
                        if DTHETA_M2 <= DTHETA_T2 then
                            begin
                                DTHETA_M2 := DTHETA_M2+A_M2@.ANGLE;
                                if A_M2@.NEXT = nil then
                                    A_M2 := F_M2
                                else
                                    A_M2 := A_M2@.NEXT
                            end
                        else
                            begin
                                DTHETA_T2 := DTHETA_T2+A_T2@.ANGLE;
                                if A_T2@.NEXT = nil then
                                    A_T2 := F_T2
                                else
                                    A_T2 := A_T2@.NEXT
                            end;

                        if abs(DTHETA_M2-DTHETA_T2) < EPS_ANGLE then
                            begin
                                LEN_M23 := A_M2@.EDGE@.LENGTH;
                                LEN_T23 := A_T2@.EDGE@.LENGTH;
                                if abs((LEN_M23*S_F)/LEN_T23-1)<EPS_RATIO then
                                    begin
                                        N_LOC_MTCH := N_LOC_MTCH+1;
                                        F_ND := OTHER_NODE(N_M,A_M2);
                                        FRAG[N_LOC_MTCH] := F_ND@.X;
                                        B_ND := OTHER_NODE(N_T,A_T2);
                                        BASE[N_LOC_MTCH] := B_ND@.X;
                                    end
                            end
                    until (DTHETA_M2>1.8*PI) or (DTHETA_T2>1.8*PI);
                end
            end;
        if DTHETA_M <= DTHETA_T then
            begin
                DTHETA_M := DTHETA_M+A_M@.ANGLE;
                if A_M@.NEXT = nil then
                    A_M := F_M
                else
                    A_M := A_M@.NEXT
            end
        else
            begin
                DTHETA_T := DTHETA_T+A_T@.ANGLE;
                if A_T@.NEXT = nil then
                    A_T := F_T
                else
                    A_T := A_T@.NEXT
            end
    until (N_LOC_MTCH>10) or (DTHETA_M>1.8*PI) or (DTHETA_T>1.8*PI);
    LOCAL_FIT := (N_LOC_MTCH > 3)
end (* FUNCTION LOCAL_FIT *) ;
```

Global Fitting

If the local fitting has been successful then N_LOC_MTCH points of the fragment and base have been paired and stored in the point arrays FRAG and BASE; furthermore, N_LOC_MTCH $\geq$ 4. Next, the procedure GLOBAL_FIT determines the "best" similarity transformation mapping the base nodes matched by LOCAL_FIT into their corresponding fragment nodes. Then this transformation is applied to all base nodes and a count is made of how many fragment nodes are within a given tolerance of some transformed base node. If a large enough percentage of all fragment nodes are thus counted then the global fit is considered successful.

The "best" similarity transformation in the sense of least squares mapping n points (x_k, y_k) into corresponding points (u_k, v_k), $1 \leq k \leq n$, is defined by the formulas

$$u = ax + by + c$$
$$v = ay - bx + d$$

where the 4 coefficients (a,b,c,d) are such as to minimize

$$\sum_{k=1}^{n} \left(u_k - (ax_k + by_k + c)\right)^2 + \left(v_k - (ay_k - bx_k + d)\right)^2$$

This leads to the linear system:

$$
\begin{bmatrix}
\sum(x_k^2 + y_k^2) & 0 & \sum x_k & \sum y_k \\
0 & \sum(x_k^2 + y_k^2) & \sum y_k & -\sum x_k \\
\sum x_k & \sum y_k & n & 0 \\
\sum y_k & -\sum x_k & 0 & n
\end{bmatrix}
\cdot
\begin{bmatrix}
a \\ b \\ c \\ d
\end{bmatrix}
=
\begin{bmatrix}
\sum(u_k x_k + v_k y_k) \\
-\sum(v_k x_k - u_k y_k) \\
\sum u_k \\
\sum v_k
\end{bmatrix}
$$

The coefficients COEFF [1..4] $\equiv$ (a,b,c,d) are determined by procedure SIMILAR using Moler's DECOMP and SOLVE[25] in PASCAL versions. The details of SIMILAR will not be given here but the following data-structures were appropriate:

```
const NMAT = 4;
type  VECTOR = array [1..NMAT] of real;
      MATRIX = array [1..NMAT,1..NMAT] of real;
```

The GLOBAL_FIT procedure follows:

```
function
    GLOBAL_FIT:boolean;
    var
        I,T,M,N_GLB_MTCH,MIN_T: integer;
        MIN_DIST,DIST_M_T,SCALE,RMS_FIT: real;
        COEFF: VECTOR;

    begin (* GLOBAL_FIT BODY *)
        SIMILAR(N_LOC_MTCH,BASE,FRAG,COEFF,RMS_FIT);
        WRITELN(' SIMILAR ',RMS_FIT,COEFF[1],COEFF[2],COEFF[3],COEFF[4]);
        SCALE := sqrt(sqr(COEFF[1])+sqr(COEFF[2]));
        for I := 1 to N_FRAG_PTS do
            FRAG[I] := FRAG_NODES[I]@.X;
        for I := 1 to N_ALL_PTS do
            with NODES[I]@ do
                begin
                    BASE[I][1] := COEFF[1]*X[1]+COEFF[2]*X[2]+COEFF[3];
                    BASE[I][2] := COEFF[1]*X[2]-COEFF[2]*X[1]+COEFF[4]
                end;
        N_GLB_MTCH := 0;
        for M := 1 to N_FRAG_PTS do
            begin
                MIN_DIST := BIG_REAL;  MIN_T := 0;
                for T := 1 to N_ALL_PTS do
                    begin
                        DIST_M_T := EUCLIDIST(FRAG[M],BASE[T]);
                        if DIST_M_T < MIN_DIST then
                            begin
                                MIN_DIST := DIST_M_T;
                                MIN_T := T
                            end
                    end;
                if (MIN_DIST<EPS_DIST*SCALE) then
                    N_GLB_MTCH := N_GLB_MTCH+1
            end;
        GLOBAL_FIT :=
            ((N_GLB_MTCH/N_FRAG_PTS) > PCT_LIMIT)
    end (* FUNCTION GLOBAL_FIT *) ;
```

We draw the reader's attention especially to the expressions BASE[I][1] and BASE [I][2] which may look strange at first since few languages allow arrays of arrays. These expressions are, however, perfectly natural consequences of our type definitions and variable declarations

```
const MAX_DIM = 2; NN_MAX = 200;
type  POINT_TYPE = array [1..MAX_DIM] of real;
      PT_ARRAY = array [1..NN_MAX] of POINT_TYPE;
var   FRAG, BASE : PT_ARRAY;
```

According to these definitions BASE is of type PT_ARRAY, BASE[I] is of type POINT_TYPE and BASE[I][1] is of type real, being the value of the first coordinate of the I-th point in BASE.

By comparison a variable A of type MATRIX is doubly indexed and is referenced by expressions like A[I,J]. However, MATRIX might have been defined as

```
type MATRIX = array [1..NMAT] of VECTOR;
```
in which case the row-vectors of a matrix could be handled as unit concepts.

Publication Credits

The following figures appeared in previous publications:

Figures 3 and 4: IEEE Transactions on Computers, Vol. C-20, No. 1, Jan., 1971, pp. 73-74.

Figure 5: International Computing Symposium 1973, A. Gunther, et. al. (eds.), North-Holland Publishing Company, 1974, p. 384.

Figure 6: IFIP Congress 74, North-Holland Publishing Company, 1974, p. 699.

An outgrowth of "Data Structures for Pattern Recognition Algorithms: A Case Study," which appeared in the 1975 Proceedings of the Conference on Computer Graphics, Pattern Recognition and Data Structure (75 CH 0981-1C). Copyright 1975 by The Institute of Electrical and Electronics Engineers, Inc.

EXERCISES

1. Design data-structures in PASCAL to represent the
    "triangular picture graph" of figure 2a and the boundary
    curves formed by "contour segments" shown in figure 2b.
    Design a PASCAL algorithm to compute the boundary from
    the triangular picture graph using a simple queue of con-
    tour segments from corridors.

2. Design appropriate data-structures and algorithms to
    compute the convex hull of a simple closed planar polygon
    retaining the "concavities" as a list of closed polygons.

3. Write a program to find "inconsistent" edges in an MST
    (see reference 6). Use an explicit stack rather than a
    recursive procedure.

4. Translate the MST algorithm and data-structures into
    FORTRAN, retaining the flavor of the PASCAL implementa-
    tion as much as possible.

5. Given a sequence of planar points in a one-way linked list,
    write an algorithm to implement the iterative-endpoint-fit
    and represent the derived line segments. You may use a
    recursive procedure in PASCAL.

6. Devise a PASCAL data-structure which represents a binary
    digital picture on a square grid by "slice scans" in both
    horizontal and vertical directions. In a slice scan each
    row (or column) is given as a possibly empty list of
    contiguous runs of black points. For example, the ninth
    row in figure 1a is represented by {(4,7),(10,13)} and
    column 10 by {(7,14), (23,25), (30,30)} while columns 1
    and 2 are empty. Write programs to convert from doubly-
    indexed array format to double slice-scan and vice-versa.

7. Some awkwardness was encountered in the procedure LOCAL_FIT
    used in template matching because the edge-adjacency list
    was not really cyclic whereas the scans around the
    Match_node and Test_node were cyclic starting at the
    minimum angle. Suggest data-structure and program mod-
    ifications in MST and LOCAL_FIT to alleviate this problem.

8. Design a data-structure to represent arbitrary simple
    closed polygons like figure 1d and an algorithm to com-
    pute sequences of bends of the same type (convex vs. con-
    cave). Keep these bend groups in a cyclic list analogous

to the underlying curve. For example, in figure 1d bend
5 is a group of "concave" type and bends 9, 10, 12 form
a "convex" group.

9.   Given a set of points in a general metric space design an
     algorithm to construct a graph in which each point is
     connected to each of the k points nearest to it in the
     point set (the data-structure for MSTs is adequate for
     general graphs). Using these "k-nearest" neighborhoods
     to define a similarity measure based on shared near
     neighbors (proposed by Jarvis and Patrick[26]), construct
     the maximal spanning forest in the resulting graph and
     investigate the use of this data-structure for cluster
     analysis of the original set of points. This maximal
     spanning forest is equivalent to a minimal spanning forest
     in the graph of reciprocals of the similarities.

10. Design a PASCAL data-structure to represent general trees
     without any adjacency records but with 2 extra edge-
     references in each edge and a "first edge" reference
     replacing the old "first adjacency" reference. Hint:
     this will work for any bipartite graph (i.e., having no
     odd length circuits). Modify the MST algorithm to
     reflect the altered data-structure. What restrictions on
     dynamic growth of such trees is imposed by this data-
     structure?

REFERENCES

1.   A. Rosenfeld, Picture Processing by Computer, Academic
     Press, 1969, (see also Computing Surveys, Sept. 1969).

2.   C. T. Zahn, "A Formal Description for Two-dimensional
     Patterns," Proc. INtl. J. Conf. on A. I., Washington,
     D. C., May 1969, available as SLAC-PUB-538 from Stanford
     Linear Accelerator Center, Stanford, California 94305.

3.   C. T. Zahn, "Region Boundaries on a Triangular Grid,"
     Proc. 2nd Intl. J. Conf. on Pattern Recognition,
     Copenhagen, Denmark, August 1974, available as
     SLAC-PUB-1437.

4.   H. Freeman, "Techniques for the digital computer analysis
     of chain-encoded arbitrary plane curves," Proc. Natl.
     Electronics Conf., 1961, pp. 421-432.

5.   C. T. Zahn and R. Z. Roskies, "Fourier Descriptors for
     Plane Closed Curves," IEEE Trans. Computers, Vol. C-21,
     No. 3, March 1972, pp. 269-281.

6.   C. T. Zahn, "Graph-theoretical methods for detecting and
     describing Gestalt clusters," IEEE Trans. Computers,
     Vol. C-20, No. 1, Jan. 1971, pp. 68-86.

7.   C. T. Zahn, "Using the Minimum Spanning Tree to Recognize
     Dotted and Dashed Curves," Proc. of an Intl. Computing
     Symp. (1973), A Gunther et al.,(Editors), North-Holland
     Publ. Co., 1974.

8.   D. E. Knuth, "The Art of Computer Programming: Sorting
     and Searching," Vol. 3, Addison-Wesley, 1973.

9.   R. O. Duda and P. E. Hart, Pattern Recognition and Scene
     Analysis, John Wiley, New York, 1973.

10. C. T. Zahn, "An Algorithm for Noisy Template Matching,"
     Proc. IFIP Congress 1974, pp. 698-701.

11. D. E. Knuth, "The Art of Computer Programming: Funda-
     mental Algorithms," Vol. 1, Addison Wesley, 1968.

12. C. T. Zahn, "Two-dimensional pattern description and
     recognition via curvaturepoints," SLAC Report No. 70,
     Dec. 1966.

13. R. L. Page, "A Minimal Spanning Tree Clustering Method [Z]," Algorithm 479, CACM, June 1974.

14. N. Wirth and C. A. R. Hoare, "A Contribution to the development of ALGOL," CACM, June 1966, pp. 413-431.

15. N. Wirth, "The programming language PASCAL," Acta Informatica, Vol. 1, pp. 35-63.

16. K. Jensen and N. Wirth, "PASCAL-User Manual and Report," Springer-Verlag Lecture Notes in Computer Science, Vol. 18, 1974.

17. C. A. R. Hoare and N. Wirth, "An axiomatic definition of the programming language PASCAL," Acta Informatica, Vol. 3, pp. 335-355.

18. C. A. R. Hoare, "Notes on Data Structuring" in Structured Programming by O. J. Dahl, E. W. Dijkstra and C. A. R. Hoare, Academic Press, 1972.

19. D. E. Knuth, "Structured programming with go to statements," ACM Computing Surveys, Dec. 1974, pp. 261-301.

20. A. J. Cook and L. J. Shustek, "MORTRAN2, a macrobased structured FORTRAN extension," presented at 10th IEEE Computer Society Intl. Conf. (COMP-CON'75), available as SLAC-PUB-1527, Jan. 1975.

21. L. J. Shustek and C. T. Zahn, "Records and references in MORTRAN2," presented at ACM SIGNUM Workshop on FORTRAN preprocessors for Numeric Software, Jet Propulsion Lab, Pasadena, Calif., Nov. 1974.

22. O.-J. Dahl, "Hierarchical Program Structures," in Structured Programming (see 18).

23. C. T. Zahn, "A Control Statement for Natural Top-down Structured Programming" in Programming Symposium: Proceedings, Collogue sur la Programmation, ed. B. Robinet, Berlin, Springer-Verlag, 1974, pp. 170-180.

24. D. E. Knuth and C. T. Zahn, "Ill-chosen Use of Event," letter in ACM Forum section of CACM, Vol. 18, No. 6 June 1975), p. 360.

25. C. B. Moler, "Algorithm 423: Linear Equation Solver,"
     CACM, Vol. 15, No. 4 (April 1972), p. 274.

26. R. A. Jarvis and E. A. Patrick, "Clustering Using a
     Similarity Measure Based on Shared Near Neighbors,"
     IEEE Trans. on Computers, Nov. 1973, pp. 1025-1034.

Organizing Data in Computer
Graphics Applications

ROBIN WILLIAMS

IBM Research
San Jose, California

INTRODUCTION TO THE CHAPTER

Everyone who writes a non-trivial computer program has data
organization problems. The efficient structuring of data is
critical to both storage needs and execution speed. This is
especially true in interactive computer graphics because one
usually deals with large volumes of data at high speeds. There
are also the additional problems of mapping 2 or 3 dimensional
data into a one dimensional memory, formatting data for display,
and sometimes, depending upon the hardware, creating and manag-
ing display files. The need to interact with the data, and to
edit and analyze the data via images are further complications,
particularly when rapid response to interactions are required.
The following three papers in this chapter of the book give some
idea of how these problems are solved in various systems and then
describe an approach to storing graphical data in a self-describing mechanism in a relational data-base.

The first paper gives an overall survey of data structures
used in data-bases generally and in computer graphics systems in
particular. Although this paper is now five years old and hence
some examples are dated, there has been little change in the
basic methods of structuring data and the paper does give an
overall review and includes over 100 references. There have been
some important developments in data-bases and data management
systems recently and much research is being done to investigate
the general problems of large data bases. Specifically data
independence (from application programs), data security, inte-
grity, privacy, sharing of central data-banks and on-line query

languages are all being intensively investigated. A currently
active project at IBM Research in San Jose is investigating the
use of a relational data-base for storing self-describing graphical data. The ideas and concepts are explained in papers
2 and 3. Paper 3 contains the descriptors actually being used,
but paper 2 provides some additional motivation and a geographic
data-base example based on tabular structures.

Some of the material contained here also appeared in "A Picture-Building System,"from the 1975 Proceedings of the Conference on Computer Graphics, Pattern Recognition and Data Structure (75 CH 0981-1C). Copyright 1975 by The Institute of
Electrical and Electronics Engineers, Inc.

A Survey of Data Structures for
Computer Graphics Systems*

ROBIN WILLIAMS

ABSTRACT

This is a survey of data structures and their use in computer graphics systems. First, the reasons for using data structures are given. Then the sequential, random, and list organizations are discussed, and it is shown how they may be used to
build complex data structures. Representative samples of languages specifically designed for creating and manipulating data
structures are described next. Finally some typical computer
graphics systems and their data structures are described. It
is also pointed out that much work remains to be done to develop a satisfactory theoretical foundation for designing data
structures.

1. INTRODUCTION TO THE DATA STRUCTURE PROBLEM IN COMPUTER
   GRAPHICS

Many papers describing data structures and languages for
creating data structures have appeared during the last ten years.
Also, in most of the papers on computer graphics systems, a
description of the data organization is given. It is the purpose of this paper to describe and compare several different
organizations and their use in computer graphics.

---

*Reprinted by permission of ACM; originally in ACM Computing
Surveys, Vol. 3, No.1, March 1971.

This work was partially supported by the Information Sciences
Directorate, Air Force Office of Scientific Research, under
grant AF-AFOSR-68-1367.

First the term "data structure" is explained, and then requirements of data structures for computer graphics are outlined.
Several common, representative types of data structures are described. Also, languages and techniques for constructing and
manipulating data structures are briefly discussed. Finally,
some actual computer graphics systems and their data structures
are described.

Data consists of numerical values, names, codes, and symbols.
Each of these things, considered separately, is called a *data
element*. Data elements are stored in computer memories in an
organized manner to preserve the relationships and logical associations that exist between them and also to provide access from
one data element to another. This organization of data is
called a *data structure*. Take an example - in an electronic
circuit it is not only the component values that are important,
but also the manner in which the components are interconnected.
These component connections must be preserved in a data structure.

A *computer graphics* system is a computer system with a graphical display facility. The display may be used simply as an
output device to display information; but a much more interesting use of the display is to use it as a coupling between the
computer and a human operator. In this case, if the computer is
appropriately programmed, the display can be used for both input
and output of data during program execution and the system is
said to be *interactive*.

The purpose of interactive systems, graphical or otherwise,
is to make efficient use of both man and machine, allowing the
designer to interact with the computer while his program is
running in order to influence the course of his computations.
For example, in electronic circuit design, a human decision is
needed to make a design change, but the computer can perform
circuit analysis much more quickly and accurately than a designer can. Working together, the designer and the computer can
be more effective than either one alone.

If a computer has an interactive graphical display, the designer can communicate with the computer by means of line drawings. The data for creating a line drawing is stored in the
computer. In some cases it may suffice to use a simple list
of the x,y-coordinates of the endpoints of the straight lines
which make up the drawing. On the other hand, there are many
situations for which complex data structures are needed. It
all depends upon the application.

A small point of confusion arises here. The term data structure is often reserved for complex data organizations, but not always. The list of x,y-coordinates of line endpoints mentioned above is an example of a simple data structure. When a drawing is created from this list, the points are accessed sequentially; lines are drawn, or moves are made without drawing lines, from point to point, in order, starting at the first x,y-coordinate position. Any nonsequential order of processing the points would result in a different drawing being displayed. Therefore, the data is structured, and the list is a simple data structure.

Depending upon the application requirements, varying degrees of sophistication and complexity are employed in data structures, resulting in systems with different degrees of interactive capabilities. An interactive graphics system which is to be used for computer aided design has to satisfy certain special requirements. A designer using the system may reference, at any moment, any part of one of the drawings which he has created. For example, he can request that a particular drawing be displayed, and then subsequently indicate, with a lightpen, a line or element of that drawing. When the pen sees the light from the display, an interruption of the normal computer processing occurs, and the program can determine which line is being drawn and consequently to which line the designer is referring. The data structure should be designed to be flexible enough to find out how the line or part fits into the rest of the structure before any actions (erase, for example) can be performed. This should be determined quickly to provide a rapid response to the user; otherwise he becomes impatient and loses interest. Therefore, the data should be structured to allow necessary searching and accessing of related data to be performed efficiently. Also, during a design process, actions like adding or deleting of data and moving or rescaling of picture parts may be required. Such actions may cause considerable changes in a data structure, and the structure should be flexible enough to allow updating to be performed quickly, also. Again it is pointed out that these additional structure and flexibility requirements are problem dependent. In many cases, the requirements are easily satisfied with simple structures, but for complex computer-aided design problems, rather complicated data structures are required. To design a data structure which is satisfactory in memory requirements and processing speeds for a particular situation, according to the above requirements, is the data structure problem in computer graphics.

2. TYPES OF DATA STRUCTURES

In this section the different types of data structures are discussed from the point of view of their suitability for computer graphics. Because Dodd [32] has already described the various forms of data organization in a general way of data management, this section is brief. The reader who wants to know more about particular organizations is referred to the above paper. For consistency, the terms and presentation used by Dodd are followed wherever possible.

Basic Sequential, Random, and List Structures

First, some definitions: a *record* is a collection of data elements; a *data element* is a numerical value, a name, or an *attribute*. The elements of a record are stored in contiguous memory locations. A set of contiguous memory locations is called a *block*. Elements are also called *items*, and attributes are also called *descriptors* or *keys*.

Dodd [32] has pointed out that all data organizations (structures) can be built up from three basic organizations: *sequential, random*, and *list*. Present day computer memories are one-dimensional in access, the memory locations are numbered serially, and computer logic is designed to fetch data or instructions from memory sequentially unless programmed to do otherwise. Therefore, the simplest data organization is the sequential organization because the mechanism for accessing the data is already built into the computer hardware. In this organization, records are stored sequentially and are ordered according to a common attribute. Records can be retrieved quickly, but inserting a new record or deleting an old record is a difficult and slow process because the whole file of records must be updated each time a change occurs. For this reason, the sequential organization by itself is not suitable for computer graphics.

This leaves the random and list organizations. Both of these organizations are used in computer graphics to form complex data structures. In the *random organization* an arbitrary address is associated with a record or an item, which is then stored at that address. The data can subsequently be retrieved from the same address. The address may be assigned by the programmer and specified each time a reference is made to the data. Obviously, this method is not practical for data bases. A second method is to create a table of data names and associated addresses. The table is then used for each data reference as

shown in Figure 1(a); this is probably the most common method
used in random organizations. The table is called a *symbol
table* or a *dictionary*.

For very large data structures, the table becomes very
large, and it takes a long time to search it to find an item
address. Ordering the table sequentially is not a suitable solution for computer graphics because updating then takes a long
time. A possible solution is to order the table in a different way. For example, if the addresses of the previous item
and the following item are stored with each table entry, then
a given item may be found by following a chain of addresses to
that item. This speeds up table searching. Updating may also
be performed quickly because new entries may be physically
located at the end of the table and addresses altered to include
them in the correct order in the table, and unwanted entries
may be deleted by altering addresses to bypass those entries.
Although methods of ordering tables in this way are more flexible and result in shorter searching and updating times, more
storage space is required than for a sequentially ordered table.

A third random method is to use the record name itself,
treat it as a number, and perform a standard calculation on it,
using the result of the calculation as the address for the
data. An example is shown in Figure 1(b). Suppose the name
LINE3 is stored character-by-character in the computer, and
suppose the digits 0, 1,...,9 are represented by character values 0, 1, ..., 9 and the letters A,B, ..., Z by values 10, 11,
35, respectively. Then the character values for LINE3 would be
21, 18, 23, 14, 03. Assume the calculation to be performed is
to add the character values: this gives 79; and to combine this
result with the third character value shifted two places to the
left: thus 23.. + 79 = 2379. Then 2379 is used as the address
for LINE3.

This method of storage assignment is often called *hash coding*, and the calculation is *hashing*. It may happen that two
or more names hash to the same address. This is called a
collision or *conflict*, and many methods have been devised to
solve this problem. One solution is to connect together on a
list, as described below, all the names and corresponding data
that hash to the same address. When a reference to these elements is made, it is necessary, first to perform a hashing operation and, secondly, to search a list to find and identify
the correct data element.

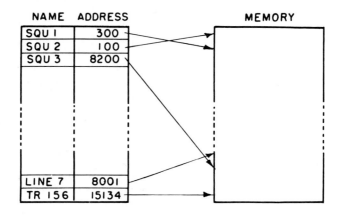

(a)

TABLE METHOD FOR RANDOM DATA ORGANIZATION

NAME		L	I	N	E	3
COMPUTER REPRESENTATION	21	18	23	14	03	

HASHING
CALCULATION
{
FORM SUM   79
FORM ADDRESS (THIRD
CHARACTER AND SUM)   2379

(b)

HASH CODING METHOD FOR RANDOM
DATA ORGANIZATION

Fig. 1
Random Organization of Data

There are many hash coding methods and several ways of dealing with conflicts [68]. Some complex data structures use hash
coding techniques together with list structures [3, 38, 102],
and a language called LEAP, which uses hash coding extensively,
has been used in several graphical applications [38]. LEAP is
described later in Section 3. If computers were built with
associative memories, then random data organizations would be
used much more widely.

A *list* organization is an organization in which records are
chained together by pointers, as shown in Figure 2. A *pointer*
is a means of linking one piece of data to another and, in the
simplest case, is a word which contains an address. Thus one
list may logically connect data elements which are physically
scattered arbitrarily throughout the memory. A block of data
words may also be on many lists and have many pointer chains
running through it. If the last element in a list has a pointer
to the first element in the list, then it is called a *ring*.
Often there is a chain of pointers around the ring in the reverse sense also. Usually one element is designated the *head
element* of the ring, and sometimes pointers from the other ring
elements to this head element can be useful. A ring with all
these pointers, called a full pointer ring, is shown in Figure
2.

It is very easy to update a list or ring structure. For
insertion of a new element, all that is required is to create
the new element at any convenient place in memory and rearrange
the pointers to include the new element in the list or ring.
For deletion, the pointers to the element to be removed are
made to point to the next element beyond the one to be removed,
and then the unwanted element is deleted. For full pointer
chains both forward and backward pointer chains must be altered appropriately.

A more general list structure, called a multilist structure,
is one in which the data elements may belong to several lists.
For example, if a drawing is made up of rectangles and circles,
a list of all rectangles and another list of all rectangles
and circles which have an area greater than some value A may
have several common elements; namely, all those rectangles with
an area greater than A. Therefore some elements may be in more
than one list. It is still quite easy to update such structures. To delete an element, for instance, all lists containing this element must be properly rearranged; a simple example
is shown in Figure 3. In such a situation, however, it is
necessary to search the whole list structure to determine to
which lists an element belongs prior to deleting the element-

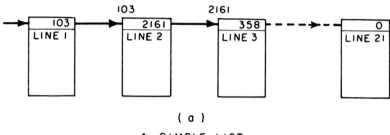

(a)

A SIMPLE LIST

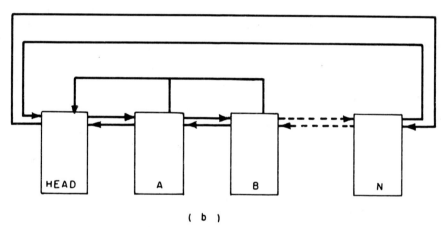

(b)

A FULL POINTER RING STRUCTURE

Fig. 2
Basic List Structures

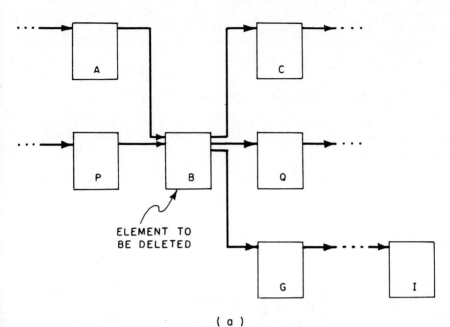

(a)

ORIGINAL LIST STRUCTURE BEFORE DELETION

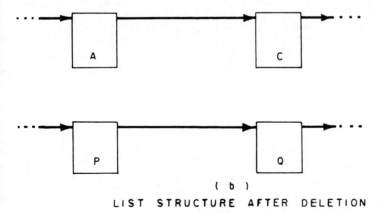

(b)

LIST STRUCTURE AFTER DELETION

Fig. 3
Deletion in a Simple List Structure

a long process for a large structure. If the structure uses
rings, then this problem is avoided because the element has
pointers to the rings in which it exists and only these rings
need be searched and updated. Naturally there is a price to be
paid; more storage is required for ring structures than for list
structures.

Building Complex Structures from Basic Structures

More complex data structures can be created from the basic
forms. Two such structures are tree and hierarchical structures; both are used in graphics systems and applications.

A *tree* structure is defined in graph theory as a structure
which has no closed circuits (rings, in our terminology). This
is equivalent to an organization of blocks and pointers as
shown in Figure 4. A block, as defined in Section 2, is a set
of contiguous memory locations. An identification block is
put at the top of the tree; it has pointers to the second level
blocks, which in turn have pointers to the third level blocks,
and so on. More generally a block at any level may point to a
block further down the tree or even to a block at its own level,
but not to a block higher up the tree.

This level structure provides a basic subroutining capability. In computer graphics if a display structure exists already and it is desired to use it again with different conditions, then a new identification block with parameters is created and a pointer is directed to the existing structure. When
this new node is referred to (processed), the existing structure is used with the parameters specified in the new block.
A simple example is illustrated in Figure 5. A filter stage is
first defined. The filter stage structure is then used four
times, in four different positions, to create the complete
filter. This is more efficient in storage than defining a filter stage four times. In turn, the filter structure may now
be used several times in a more complex circuit. Moreover,
two structures may be combined to form a new structure which
may then be used subsequently as a substructure. The two original structures can still be used separately, also. By building new levels in this way, complex tree structures can be
created.

A *hierarchical* structure is a similar structure with levels
of hierarchy, but it is constructed with rings [32], see Figure
6. From one (initial) ring, there may be branches off from
any element to logically related elements. These related

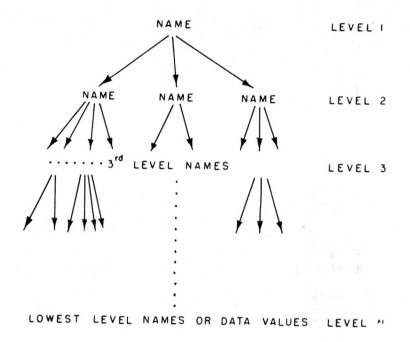

Fig. 4
A Tree Structure

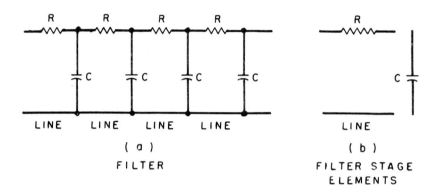

(a)
FILTER

(b)
FILTER STAGE
ELEMENTS

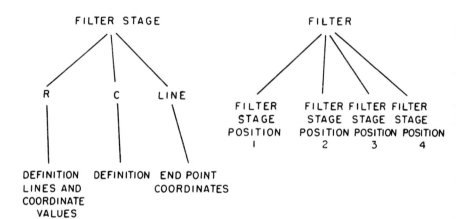

(c)
TREE STRUCTURE

Fig. 5
An Example of a Tree Structure Applied
to an Electronic Circuit

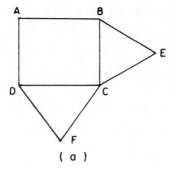

(a)

A LINE DRAWING DESIGN

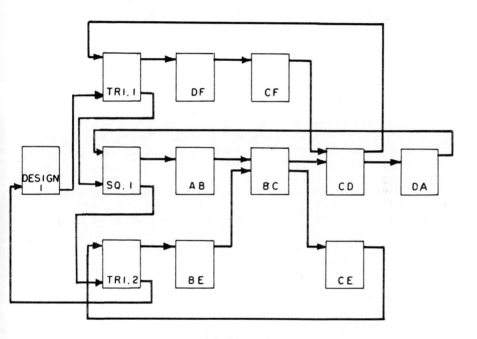

(b)

A POSSIBLE STRUCTURE FOR THE DESIGN IN (a)
(BACKWARD POINTERS AND REVERSE POINTERS
ARE OMITTED FOR CLARITY)

Fig. 6
An Example of an Hierarchical Structure

elements are also arranged in a ring structure, and branches
from these elements to other related elements can occur. These
other elements are also arranged in a ring structure, etc. This
structure allows access from any data item to any other data
item via the rings. It is easy to update the structure since
nothing has to be moved in storage; only pointers have to be
changed. However, the processing can become quite involved in
a deletion operation, especially in making sure that all pointer
chains are properly reconnected. Nevertheless, in hierarchical
structures this operation is considerably easier than in one-
way list structures since pointers go both ways around the rings
horizontally and both ways up and down the hierarchy levels
vertically. The cost for this more versatile organization is
the extra overhead in storage caused by all the pointer chains.
All list organizations have this disadvantage; but ring structures, having the most complex pointer arrangements, suffer
most of all. Another example of an hierarchical structure is
given by Dodd [32].

Theoretical Aspects of Data Structures

Data structures may be represented by *directed graph structures*. Blocks of data (records) are represented in the graph
by *nodes*, and pointers are represented by *directed arcs* between the nodes. A list is then a chain of nodes and arcs. A
ring is a closed chain of nodes and arcs called a *circuit*. A
tree structure corresponds to a directed graph which has no
circuits and which can, therefore, be redrawn to exhibit the
levels in the tree. An hierarchical organization corresponds
to a general directed graph which does contain circuits. As a
result each structure may be classified as a subclass or special
case of the next more general structure.

Also, any operation that can be performed on a directed
graph can be performed on the corresponding data structure.
Apart from the rather obvious correspondence between directed
graphs and data structures, for design purposes, disappoint-
ingly little has been reported in the literature as having resulted from this way of viewing data structures.

Mealy [65] and Chapin [14] have studied data and data processing from a theoretical point of view. They have constructed similar models in which data processing is considered to be
a mapping from one state to another. However, their work does
not appear to have immediate practical use.

Childs [17, 18] has described a set-theoretic data structure (STDS) which has been partially implemented. In this scheme, data is partitioned into mutually disjoint sets called generator sets. Composite sets are then formed from the union of generator sets. Data is stored only once, and there are no explicit pointers between sets of data or between data items. Therefore, data sets can be moved about in memory independently of each other. Set operations are used to retrieve data, and all logical (set theory) questions about the data can be answered. If the data is a personnel file with ten standard facts about each person stored in the structure, then the questions that can be answered are those like "How many people are there satisfying facts 3 and 4 but not 7?" This structure is good for data that can be arranged naturally in set form. However, this is not the case in interactive graphics work. A good feature about this work is that it is based on a mathematical theory.

Hash coding methods have been used for storing data. Feldman and Rovner [36-38, 87, 88] have used this method for storing relationships between data. Their work is discussed in Section 3. There is some theory to hash coding. The randomness of different hashing methods has been studied. Also, comparisons of average retrieval times and average lengths of conflict lists have been made between different hash coding methods. For example, the average retrieval time and the average lengths of conflict lists have been evaluated as a function of the load factor. The load factor is the percentage of memory area allocated for hashing that is actually filled. Although these analyses are useful, more general theory would be needed to design an optimum data structure for a particular application.

One of the biggest problems that arises in interactive systems, especially graphics, is to minimize page swapping between core and secondary memory. To store the display file and the associated data for a non-trivial picture may require several thousand words of storage; to store many pictures, data items, names, and pointers would require many times the available core storage. Therefore, the data structure must be segmented into pages. For general data structures there is no theory on how to do this optimally to minimize page swapping between core and secondary memory. There are several overlay schemes, and there are many ways of operating paging systems for programs in time-sharing situations; but the problem here is different. On large computers, existing system paging and virtual memory methods can be used, but this is not as efficient as when the paging mechanism is especially designed to suit the application data structure. Bobrow and Murphy [10] have implemented a two-level storage system for LISP, and they report good results. Also,

Van Dam and Evans [105], and Rovner and Feldman [38, 87, 88] have implemented paging schemes especially for data structures; these last two schemes are described in Section 3.

One may conclude from this section that, although simple data organizations can be designed quite easily on a basis of searching and updating times, complex data structures cannot. This is because flexible, versatile data structures are tediously intricate and may grow unpredictably in any direction. Also, data structures are dependent upon machine characteristics and, more importantly, on the applications for which they are to be used. For these reasons, many languages have been created to provide programmers with a means to build their own data structures and make their own designs. The programmer of course is still left with the problem of designing a complex data structure, and there is virtually no theory to help him do this.

3. LANGUAGES FOR CREATING AND MANIPULATING DATA STRUCTURES

Languages specially designed for creating and processing list structures have been around for ten years or more: examples are LISP, SNOBOL, IPL and COMIT, to name a few. Ring structures were first used in the SKETCHPAD program [100] developed by I. E. Sutherland at Massachusetts Institute of Technology. Since then, languages for creating and manipulating ring structures have been developed. CORAL [101] was the first of these. More recently other languages with greater flexibility and more complex data structuring capability have appeared.

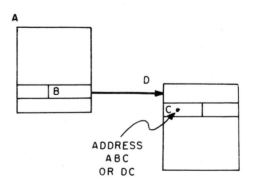

Fig. 7
Addressing in DSPL Structure

Representative samples of the various kinds of languages, together with their characteristics and purposes, are presented
in this section.

Low Level Languages

Some languages allow the user to program very efficiently,
but the user has to program closer to machine language to get
this benefit. Programs written in these languages run much
faster, even one or two orders of magnitude faster, than the
same programs written in higher level list processing languages.
Examples of low level languages are L6 [55] (K. Knowlton, Bell
Telephone Laboratories) and DSPL [105] (D. Evans, University of
Pennsylvania, and A. Van Dam, Brown University) and to some
extent ASP [59] (C. A. Lang and J. C. Gray, Cambridge University,
England).

L6 and DSPL data structures are built up from blocks,
fields, and pointers, A *block* is a sequential number of machine
words, a *field* is a sequential number of bits in a word, and a
pointer is a word address. In DSPL (L6 is similar) a user
can create and name blocks and fields (called baseblocks and
basefields in this language) and can interconnect them with
pointers to form structures. Addresses are formed by concatenating the names of blocks and fields. With reference to
Figure 7, one can use ABC as an address to start in block A,
find a pointer in field B to another block, and then retrieve
the contents of field C in that block. If the block containing
field C is labeled D, then address DC also retrieves the contents of field C. Concatenating pointers in this way is often
called pointer chasing or field sequencing. A powerful feature
of this language is the facility to create templates (blocks
or fields) at any place. The template may be located with respect to an existing block or field. An example is shown in
Figure 8. In this example a mask is formed for bits 0-15 in
word 3 of every block, and block A is specified as a template
with respect to (base) blocks BIG and SMALL.

Operations must also be included in low level languages to
make them useful. These include shifting operations, logical
operations, fixed point arithmetic, storing of pointers, etc.
There must also be a few simple control commands like DO, IF...
THEN, GO TO, IF ALL, and others for input and output.

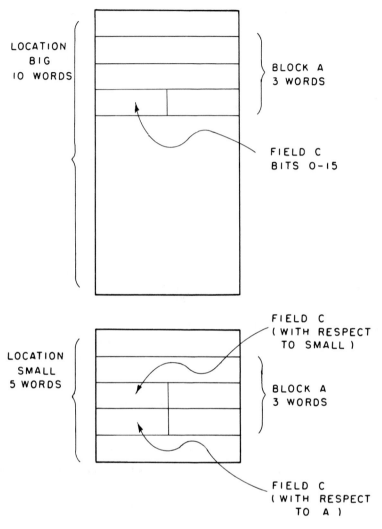

Fig. 8
DSPL Structure With a Template Mask

DSPL also includes a paging facility. Pages have an identification key and a control header that specifies how a page is
structured. There are four other sections to a page: a table
of references to items on other pages: a table of references to
local pages associated with this page: a description of the page
when it is made permanent; and a data section. Local pages are
pages that are associated with a (main) page and which contain
information that is necessary for defining an information structure. A page is temporary while data in it is being created or
altered and may be made permanent when the user indicates that
it is completely defined. The user has access only to the data
section of a temporary page; the other sections are maintained
by the system. When a page is made permanent, it can only be
read and cannot be altered.

A frequency-of-use and recentness-of-use statistic is used
to determine which pages to keep in core or which to write out
on disk when more space is required by other pages coming into
core. When a page is brought into core, a look-ahead mechanism
is used to bring in other pages that may be needed also. This
is done by looking through the reference tables of the page just
brought in to find what other pages may be required; and if there
is room in core for them, they are brought in while the first
page is being processed.

DSPL is one of the few languages for data structures which
has a paging system that is explicitly set up for list-type
data structures. Other languages that use secondary memory
usually use an existing system paging mechanism and would,
therefore, be less efficient.

Low level languages in general can be used to build any
kind of list structure, even hierarchical ring structures, and
are very efficient; however, the user has to concern himself
with all the structuring details.

ASP [59], which stands for *Associated Structure Package*,
is low level language that uses MACRO calls for creating ring
(hierarchical) structures. The language is not at such a low
level as L6 or DSPL, but nevertheless, the programmer creates
and manipulates structures and data items explicitly and controls the form of the structure. The system has been created
for the Titan (Atlas 2) computer, and ASP statements may be
compiled together with programs written in other languages
for this computer. Thus it is possible to build a model in
ASP and to perform analysis on the data with programs written
in other languages - a very desirable feature.

Associations between data elements may also be expressed in ASP. This is done by creating an associative ring and connecting together rings from all associated items on this associative ring. The association is then expressed in the header, called a *ringstart* in ASP, of the associative ring. A data element can have many associations. Using this technique, data relations can be represented in ASP in a similar manner to those which can be represented in LEAP [38, 88] (see Section 3). Figure 9 shows a typical ASP structure; it also shows a clearer way of drawing ring structures.

Higher Level Languages

The reason for developing higher level languages is to free the user from the details concerning the computer and to allow him to concentrate on his problem. The result is that usually a problem may be solved more quickly by using a higher level language, but it is less efficient because it generates more machine code, which uses more storage space and takes longer to run.

PL/1 has the facility to create pointers, and therefore list, ring, and tree structures can be constructed with this language. Dodd has added six statements to PL/1 and formed APL [31] (Associative Programming Language), which is particularly conventient to users who wish to express data associations. The basic elements are called *entities*, which in turn are described by *attributes*. Related entities can be grouped into sets and may be referenced through another entity which owns the set, or they may be referenced independently. An entity is a contiguous block of memory locations and contains the following:

(a) References (pointers) to subsets belonging to the entity.

(b) References to sets to which the entity belongs (called an associative set of reference links).

(c) Data attributes.

Sets are arranged in the form of rings. Figure 10 shows a typical example where D and E belong to B, while E is a member of subset C, which itself is in set A.

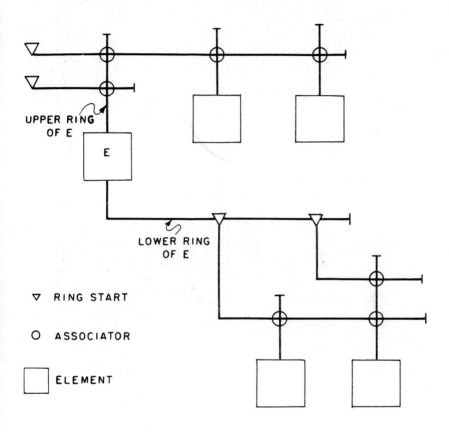

Fig. 9
A Typical Structure in ASP

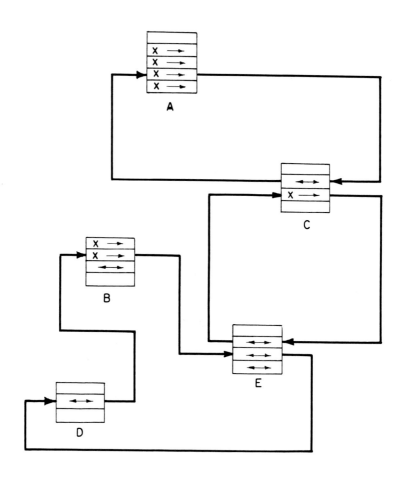

Fig. 10
Multiple Sets of Entities in APL

APL has many special programmer tools, declarations, statements, and control specifications for creating and manipulating data. These are all specified in a higher level language form and the APL structure can be referenced from PL/1 programs, which makes things easier for the user. Therefore, it is not necessary for the programmer to be aware of details such as ring structuring when using the language, and this is a good feature. Also all normal PL/1 language facilities are available to the user.

A language called LEAP, developed for expressing data relations in associative structures, has been developed by Feldman and Rovner [38, 88]. LEAP is an extension of Algol and includes statements for creating and accessing data by a hash coding technique. Data associations are of the form:

"Attribute of Object is Value"
or
$$A(0) = V.$$

An example is: father (jack) = jim - where father, jack, and jim are called *items*. This data is created and stored by a high level statement:

Make father • jack = jim

and jack may be put into a set SONS by

PUT jack in sons.

Data is stored in an A page, an O page, and a V page. Items are treated as integers, and data for an A page, for example, is created by hashing together the A and O values of the triple $A(0) = V$. The system is symmetrical, and each triple is stored on a page of each type. All occurrences of a particular item on an A page are connected together on a ring in the A page; similar rings exist in the O and V pages. Several kinds of requests can be made of the system. If the A, O, and V names are all given, the system checks to see if the triple is in the store. If any two items are given, they are hashed together by the same mechanism that is used to store triples and all the third values that satisfy the triple are returned. Thus, if A and O are given, a position on the corresponding A page is found from hashing A and O. At this position two lists begin. One is a conflict list for all A,O pairs that hash to this address, and the other is a multiple-hit list for all values V that form triples with this particular A and O pair. All values of V for multiple hits and for the appropriate A,O pair in the case of a conflict are returned. Similarly, if any one item in an A,O, or V position of a triple is specified, then all triples in which this item is used in that position are found, using the rings described above, and are returned.

This system allows arbitrary data associations of the form A(O) = V to be created and stored. Storage and retrieval of data are fast and do not require extensive pointer chasing, except to resolve conflicts and to return multiple hits results. Because of the paging structure, extensive page swapping is also avoided. Twice as much storage [38] is required to store data in A, O, and V pages, but it is in secondary memory where the extra storage is needed.

LEAP has been used in several interactive graphical applications. The language is useful in particular applications only if data associations are already in the form A(O) = V or can be expressed in that form. Other developments in associative processing include TRAMP [3], which is an interpretive associative processor, and Symond's associative data structure, which is an extension of PL/1 and which is based directly on Feldman and Rovner's idea of expressing data associations in the form A(O) = V.

4. COMPUTER GRAPHICS SYSTEMS AND THEIR DATA STRUCTURES

It is the intention in this section to show, first, how data structures are actually used in computer graphics and, secondly, to describe some representative graphics systems and their data structures. The first objective can best be achieved by discussing a specific system - the Adage AGT 30, which is currently one of the most advanced computer graphics terminals.

Data Structure and Display Operation of Adage Graphics Terminal

The *Adage Graphics Terminal* (AGT) consists of a medium scale computer, a displayed processor, and a graphical display. Typically the computer has 16K of core memory and a disk secondary memory. The general arrangement of a medium scale computer, a display processor, and a display is typical of many computer graphics systems. Other examples are: IBM 1130/2250, Digital Equipment Corporation PDP9/339, and Control Data Corporation 3200 Digigraphics system. The Adage display has hardware circuits for scaling, translating, and rotating images, a unique Adage feature which in other systems has to be implemented by software. If the computer plus display is used as a terminal to a larger time-shared computer, the terminal can do most of its own local processing. These systems place less demand on a large computer than would a very simple display with limited local processing capabilities.

To display a picture in any graphics system, the designer must create *a display file* in some form or other. This file contains the information on how the picture is to be drawn. From the file, x,y-coordinates are extracted and passed to a vector generator which actually draws the lines in the picture once. However, the CRT has a very short persistence screen and the picture dies away quickly. The picture must be displayed at a rate of 30 frames/second or more so that it does not appear to flicker. Therefore, the display file must be scanned at this rate. This is a requirement for all graphics systems that use a standard cathode-ray tube display.

An Adage *display file* consists of many *images* and *image transformations*. An *image* is a sequential list, often called a *display list*, of graphical commands and arguments or argument addresses; an example of a command is DRAW, with arguments X,Y, Z, which causes a line to be drawn on the display screen from the current beam position to position X,Y,Z. In most other systems it is necessary to calculate a display *list* of move and draw commands for the complete picture frame and put this into a special buffer memory which drives the display. To make changes to a picture, coordinate values in the display list have to be recalculated. In the Adage system the display file is in the main core memory, and a program is used to interpret the commands and control the display. The commands are element-generating or transform-specifying or control commands. Element-generating commands are used to construct the line drawings. Transform-specifying commands allow these line drawings to be scaled, moved, or rotated as a whole. Control commands are used to transfer control to other subprograms, for example, to calculate a new scale or position for an image, to compute new arguments for an element-generating command, to sample a function switch, and to communicate with a central computer.

Images may be treated as subimages of a main image. Each subimage may have its own transformations each time it is used in the main image, and control commands may be used at any point. This gives the programmer the flexibility to create highly-structured images.

Figure 11 shows a typical simple structure. First an analog voltage from a joystick potentiometer is sampled, and transformations proportional to this voltage value are computed

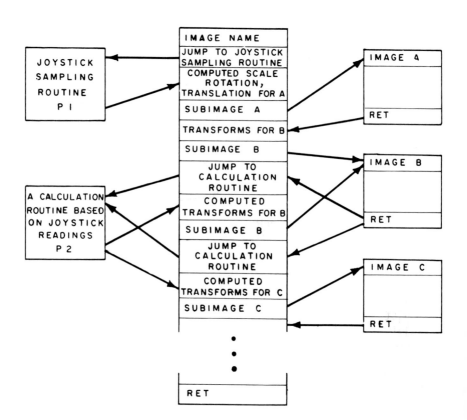

Fig. 11
An Adage Data Structure

for image A. Image A is then displayed. Transforms for an
image B are processed and image B is displayed. Then a calculation is made based upon the joystick reading and image B is
displayed again, but this time with a second set of transformations. Transformations for image C are calculated and image C
is displayed. The process then repeats all over again. The
displayed picture changes as the operator moves the joystick,
and therefore, if the operator moves the joystick continuously,
a simple picture with motion is seen.

A display file usually does not occupy sequential words in
the core memory. It is a list structure, and the references to
subimages are by means of pointers. Many levels of picture
hierarchy may be built up because images may be nested to any
depth. This data structure can be represented by a directed
graph that represents both the structure of images A, B, and C
in terms of lines and points and the instances or uses of these
images in the displayed picture.

The structure described above is only the drawing and
display structure which would be a part of a larger modeling
data structure in a useful application if analysis or some
other computation was required. Display information is, after
all, just one attribute of the data. In a model structure,
blocks would contain both an image definition and other data.
These blocks may be represented by nodes in a directed graph.
Branches in the graph would point to a node and represent a
block of relative transformation data for the image defined at
the node. The display program would reference only the relevant
display commands and transformations while analysis programs
would reference the other data.

Bell Telephone Laboratories GRAPHIC 2 System

A common computer graphics arrangement is to use a small
computer with a display as a terminal connected to a large
time-shared computer.

GRAPHIC 2, developed at Bell Telephone Laboratories [20],
is a typical example of this arrangement. The terminal consists
of a PDP-9 computer and a DEC 340 display. The terminal is
connected to a GE 635 time-shared central computer via a data-
phone communications link. The GE 635 stores the master data
structure for the system, and the PDP-9 stores a copy of it for
the local display generation, control of lightpen interrupt,
etc. When the system was first designed, the PDP-9 had no
large secondary memory. The intention was for the PDP-9 computer

to do local processing and periodically to send information to
the main computer to update the master data structure. It
turned out that two graphics terminals fully occupied the GE
computer and also that the response time at the terminal was
too long. This was because the terminal was constantly communicating with the central computer and the data-phone link
between them was too slow. Now a local disk or drum storage
facility has been added to the PDP-9, and the terminal response
time has improved. The terminal can also be used in a stand-
alone mode (cf. Adage terminal).

The data structure used is based upon a directed graph,
consisting of node blocks, branch blocks, and leaf blocks.
Nodes are connected to nodes or leaves by branches. Display
image information is stored in leaf blocks and transformation
information in branch blocks. Node and branch blocks are used
to store structural information about the overall picture.
Nodes may point to many branch blocks and may be thought of as
graphical subroutines (subimages) which, when called, draw their
image on the screen at the position where the beam happens to
be at the time they are called. A typical GRAPHIC 2 data
structure is shown in Figure 12.

Data, associated with picture elements, is stored in data
blocks. Data blocks are connected to a corresponding leaf block
in a ring structure. Thus a leaf may represent a symbol for
a circuit element, and a ring of data blocks associated with the
leaf could then store the component type, characteristics, and
value. An example for a simple electronic circuit is shown in
Figure 13. This data structure is good for on-line circuit
design work but not so good for other graphical applications,
particularly when frequent searching and updating are required.
Searching this data structure is a slow process because it is
necessary to search the structure to find all instances of a
particular type of item unless additional pointers and rings
are created by the user. Hierarchical ring structures could be
used to speed up searching and updating, but a hierarchical
structure would require more storage space.

General Motors Graphics System

A group at General Motors has been very active in the
computer graphics area; see Jacks [49], and Joyce and Cianciolo
[53]. Some of the ideas that have evolved in their work are
reviewed below. In their system the present large computer is
an IBM 360/67, used in a time-shared mode, and there is a rege-
neration buffer (IBM 2840-II) and a moderate amount of display

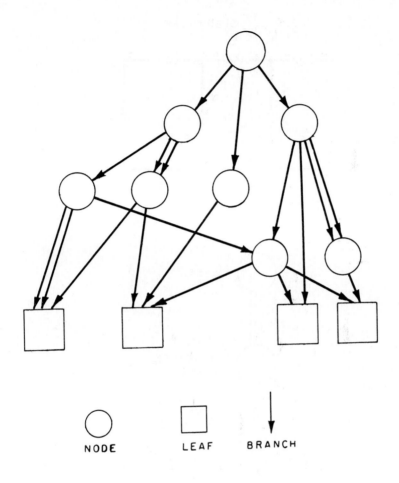

NODE   LEAF   BRANCH

Fig. 12
Typical Graphic Data Structure

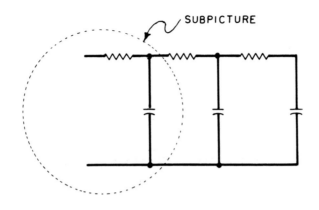

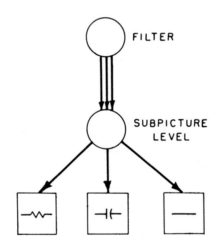

Fig. 13
An Example of the Graphic 2 Data Structure

controller logic for the IBM 2250-III display console. One
feature of this system is that users can write programs in the
PL/1 language.

The most effective computer graphics system is one that
is quickly responsive to the user in a direct manner; such a
graphics system is called a *reactive display system* at General
Motors. Two key points of their reactive display which affect
the internal data structure are *dynamic intensification* and
selective disabling. Dynamic intensification refers to the capability of immediately intensifying the part of the picture
pointed at by a lightpen. If the pen is moved across the screen,
then different parts of the picture will become brightened up
as the pen passes over them. This greatly helps the user to
identify picture parts with the lightpen. To be able to do this
rapidly with as little computation as possible, it is desirable
to have a data structure that stores graphical topology which
can be accessed more rapidly than the rest of the input information. Selective disabling allows the user to select certain
classes or sets of items from the whole picture. For example
if the user wishes to call in a line smoothing subroutine, he
will want to indicate which line to smooth. Then it is desirable in a complex picture that only lines become available for
selection (rejecting all circles, sharp curves, angles, etc.).
Therefore, the display must be organized into sets of items to
satisfy this requirement.

Also, the reactivity of the display is improved by providing easy mechanisms to do various things like changing the
scale, position or orientation of a picture part, changing the
direction of view, and labeling items on the screen.

To cope with these things, the data structure shown in
Figure 14 is used. The display is made up of entities which
are smaller display parts which the user may wish to reference
uniquely. The display data of an entity (lines, points, characters, etc.) may be scattered anywhere on the screen. Each
entity has attributes such as the level of beam intensity and
selectivity or nonselectivity as described above. Each entity
also belongs to a set or to many sets. Thus the relationship
to other entities is established by its belonging to certain
sets in common with other entities. The entities belong to data
elements which in turn have names. Both the entities and the
displayed data elements are arranged in the form of bidirectional
rings. A display buffer, arranged in a unidirectional ring
form by GO TO statements, controls the display, and this buffer
has a two-way linkage to each corresponding entity.

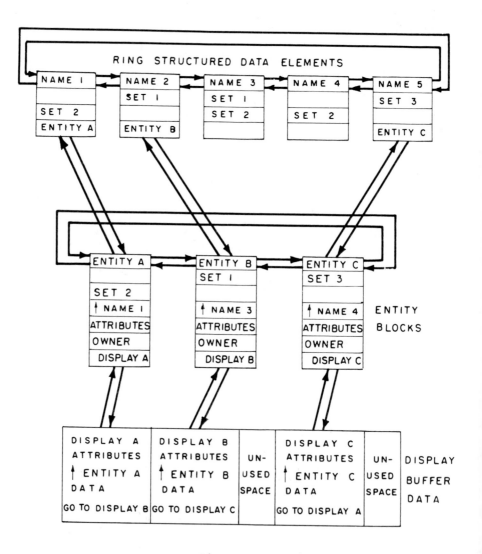

Fig. 14
Data Structure Used in the General Motors
Reactive Display System

As variable-length blocks are brought in and out of the display buffer by changes made to the displayed picture, so there will arise free, unused areas in the buffer. These are connected together in a ring structure called a *free space* ring. Thus free space can be quickly located when additional entities are created. Although at first it seems that the separate ring which describes display entities is unnecessary because the same information is contained in the data element ring, it has been found to speed up the display system considerably. The display entities ring directs the computer to the required data directly; this saves considerable time because otherwise great amounts of CPU processing and long access times to peripheral storage devices are needed to retrieve the display information from the more complicated data elements. This is a major consideration in a graphics system where quick response time is important. The need for fast response to user actions is the argument in favor of having a small satellite computer to serve the display only. The larger computer is then reserved for more complex calculations but is otherwise freed for other work.

Univac Graphics System

A graphics system employing Univac 1557 Display Controllers, 1558 Display Consoles, and remotely accessing a Univac 1108 computer was developed by Adams Associates for Univac (a Division of the Sperry Rand Corporation) [26]. It is a large, comprehensive, and powerful system. An interpretive language processor in the terminal (satellite computer) provides fast responses to user actions and updates a local data structure. Whenever the report block, a core buffer, fills up, data is sent from the terminal to the central computer and a master data structure is updated. Application programs operate on the data structure in the central computer. This approach is seen to be similar to that of GRAPHIC 2; however, the data structures used are different.

There are two principal types of data structure: one is for definition and organization of graphical structures and exists in both the central and terminal computers; the other, derived from the first, is for image display and logical attention handling and exists only in the terminal. The data structure in the central computer is called an *Entity Table;* it acts as a repository for all the data in the system. A hash coded *directory* is used to provide fast access to major structural entities in the table, and an *external directory* is used to correlate user names with internal code names for the data in the Entity Table.

The Entity Table consists of *groups* which are composed of *items* and *uses* of other groups. A group is an organization without absolute positioning and cannot be displayed directly. An item consists of points, lines, and text arranged in a ring, called a component ring, and represents actual display data. It is defined once within a group, but a group may be used many times in different situations, and with different relative trans-formations, within another group. This organization provides a basic subroutining capability. A *master group* is defined with fixed drawing coordinates, and by linking a group use to the master group, the position of a group use may be determined for display purposes.

Each group starts a ring of other group uses and items, and all uses of a group are connected together on a ring. A sample structure is shown in Figure 15. This hierarchical organization "seems to arise naturally" [26] and also provides the subroutin-ing capability.

Attributes may be associated with entries in the Entity Table; they are used to specify whether substructures should be composed of dashed lines, should be intensified or scissored, etc., and in many cases they are just flags. These flags are useful when, for example, data is searched or processed prior to transmission over the communications line because, when a flag is set to indicate that a certain substructure has already been transmitted over the line and another instance of it arises, it is not necessary to send it again. Only the name and the re-ference data need be sent, considerably reducing the amount of data to be transmitted.

In the satellite computer there is a structure of groups, group uses, and items similar to that in the central computer. Also, there is a display file which is used to form an actual picture. It is made up of item blocks which are derived from uses of groups containing items. These item blocks are then connected together in a display list by pointers, the ordering of the blocks being determined from the original hierarchical organization. The display list is, therefore, similar to that in the Adage terminal.

Also in the terminal, there is an interpretive language system called the *Logic Tables*, which reacts to user actions. The tables do more than provide user responses: they allow the data structure to be created or modified, and they also control the transmission of the report blocks to the central computer.

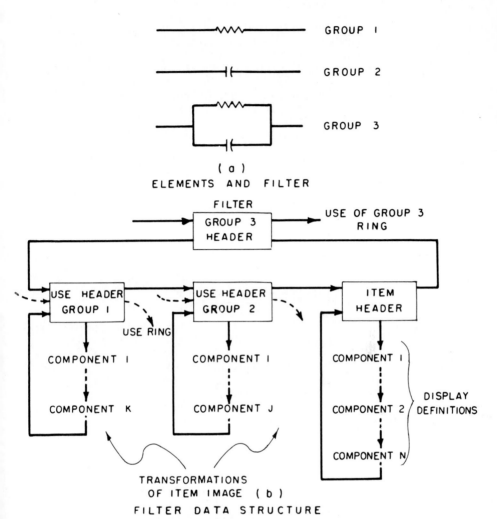

(a)
ELEMENTS AND FILTER

TRANSFORMATIONS
OF ITEM IMAGE (b)
FILTER DATA STRUCTURE
Fig. 15
An Example of the Central Computer
Data Structure in the Univac System

Other Graphics Systems and Developments

Many other computer graphics systems have been developed.
The systems configurations and the data structures employed
are similar to those described above. Control Data Corporation
[39, 77] employing a CDC 3200 computer has developed a system
called the Digigraphics System, which is intended primarily for
industrial use. The data structure is composed of rings connected together in a tree structure. IBM [48] has several
computer graphics systems: its 2250 display may be connected to
a medium scale 1130 computer or to a larger 360 computer. Software provides interactive line drawing capabilities. General
Electric [62, 69] is working on automated design; a hierarchical
data structure is used. Computer aided design, as well as other
significant graphics work, is also being carried on at many
universities including Massachusetts Institute of Technology
[33, 83], Brown University [105], University of Maryland, New
York University, Stanford University, University of California
[87], University of Utah, and in England, Cambridge University
[59] and Brunel University.

5. SUMMARY AND CONCLUSIONS

This paper has explained the reasons for using complex data
structures and has given brief descriptions of the various types
of data organization with which complex structures can be built.
Representative samples of languages for creating and modifying
data structures were described. It was then pointed out that
there is very little theory to help the graphics systems designer and that, as a result, systems are designed on an ad hoc
basis with varying justifications for choosing particular organizations. Finally, some typical computer graphics systems and
their data structures were described.

The data structure used most generally in large graphics
systems is the hierarchical ring structure because it offers
the greatest flexibility. Flexibility, however, also poses the
biggest problems. The more flexible a structure is, the more
difficult it is to implement. Also, the more flexible a structure is, the more pointers it uses, and therefore, the more
core memory space it requires.

In many cases, therefore, a data structure is a compromise
between what is desirable and what can be achieved with the
available resources. In the smaller graphics systems and graphics terminals, computer memory is a limiting factor and forces
the user to use simpler data structures than he might otherwise

prefer. In many cases, the user is supplied with a data
structuring language so that he can design the structure to suit
his own application. This seems to be the best thing to do
since it is generally agreed that there is no optimum data structure that covers all classes of applications.

A previous survey of this subject is by Gray [43]. Some
other related surveys which deal more generally with computer
graphics (including hardware) are by Ninke [73], Van Dam [108],
and Parker [75, 77].

ACKNOWLEDGEMENTS

I am happy to acknowledge the encouragement and guidance
I have received from Professor H. Freeman during the period of
my doctoral research work at New York University. This survey
originated from my research. I would like to thank P. Woon for
his constructive comments on this paper.

6. BIBLIOGRAPHY

Reference Groupings by Main Subject Content

In this grouping only the more significant papers are included, and of these, the ones in italic are considered to be
the most important or novel. This particular grouping has been
determined by the author and might be done a little differently
by others; however, for readers who want to read further it
should provide some direction through the vast amount of available literature.

Computer graphics
    Surveys 51, *73*, 74, *75*, *78*, *107*
    System description (hardware) *20*, *26*, 74, 77
    System description (software) 9, 26, 52, *53*, 77
    Data structure descriptions *20*, *26*, *43*, 53, *100*

Languages
    Data structure languages *43* (survey), 1, 27, *31*, 45, 51, *55*,
        59, 61, *88*, *102*, 105, 109, 112
    Graphical languages 21, *45*, *57*, 58, 69, 89, 101
    Structure (theory) of languages *54*, *67*, *83*, 84, 85, 86, 103
    Associative techniques *31*, 36, 37, *38*, 68, *88*, 92, 97, *102*

Data structure per se
    Survey *32*, *43*
    Theory 14, 17, *18*, *22*, *65*, 68

Picture processing
    Language theory methods 34, *67* (survey), *70*, 71, 91, 94

Application examples
    Electronic circuit design *28*, *29*, *33*, 98
    Computer aided design 15, *83*, 85

Other bibliographies
    The Newsletter of SICGRAPH (Special Interest Committee for
        Graphics sponsored by the Association for Computing Machi-
        nery). Available from ACM Headquarters. Now SIGGRAPH
    fdt, Vol. 1, No. 1 (Aug. 1969). Publication of SICFIDET (Spe-
        cial Interest Committee on File Description and Translation
        sponsored by the Association for Computing Machinery). Con-
        tains papers and information on data description and data
        language. Available from ACM Headquarters. Now SIGMOD.

Document DDC #N68-17113, produced by Lockheed Aircraft.

And at the end of most papers listed in this bibliography, especially [51, 78, 107].

1. Abrahams, P. W., et al. "The LISP Programming Language and System," *Proc. AFIPS 1966 FJCC*, Vol. 29, Spartan Books, New York, pp. 661-676.

2. Allen, T. R. and Foote, J. E. "Input/Output Software Capability for a Man-Machine Communication and Image Processing System," *Proc. AFIPS 1964 FJCC*, Vol. 26, Pt. 1, Spartan Books, New York, pp. 387-396.

3. Ash, W. L. and E. H. Sibley, "TRAMP - An Interpretive Associative Processor with Deductive Capabilities," *Proc. ACM 23rd Nat. Conf.*, 1968, Brandon Systems Press, Princeton, New Jersey, pp. 143-156.

4. Ball, N. A., et. al., "A Shared Memory Computer Display System," *IEEE Trans. Electron. Comput.*, 15, 5 (Oct. 1966), pp. 750-756.

5. Balzer, R. M., "Dataless Programming," *Proc. AFIPS 1967 FJCC*, Vol. 31, AFIPS Press, Montvale, New Jersey, pp. 535-544.

6. Barlett, W. S., et. al, "SIGHT - A Satellite Interactive Graphic Terminal, *Proc. ACM 23rd Nat. Conf.*, 1968, Brandon Systems Press, Princeton, New Jersey, pp. 499-510.

7. Baskin, H. B. and S.P. Morse, "A Multilevel Modelling Structure for Interactive Graphic Design," *IBM Syst. J.*, 7, 3 and 4 (1968), pp. 218-228.

8. Bennett, E., E. C. Haines, and J. K. Summers, "AESOP: A Prototype for On-line User Control of Organizational Data Storage, Retrieval, and Processing, *Proc. AFIPS 1965 FJCC*, Vol. 27, Pt. 1, Spartan Books, New York, pp. 435-455.

9. Berman, M. L., J. W. Machanik, and S. Shellans, "Project Merlin," *Proc. Comput. Graphics 70 Conf.*, Brunel U., Uxbridge, Middlesex, England.

10. Bobrow, D. G. and D. L. Murphy, "Structure of a LISP System Using Two-Level Storage," *Comm. ACM*, 10, 3 (Mar. 1967), pp. 155-159.

11. Bowman, S. and R. A. Lickhalter, "Graphical Data Management in a Time-Shared Environment," *Proc. AFIPS 1968 SJCC*, Vol. 32, AFIPS Press, Montvale, New Jersey, pp. 353-362.

12. Brewer, S., "Data Base or Data Maze," *Proc. ACM 23rd Nat. Conf., 1968*, Brandon Systems Press, Princeton, New Jersey, pp. 623-630.

13. Cameron, S. H., D. Ewing, and M. Liveright, "DIALOG: A Conversational Programming System with a Graphical Orientation," *Comm. ACM*, 10, 6 (June 1967), pp. 349-357.

14. Chapin, N., "A Deeper Look at Data," *Proc. ACM 23rd Nat. Conf., 1968*, Brandon Systems Press, Princeton, New Jersey, pp. 631-638.

15. Chasen, S. H., "The Introduction of Man-Computer Graphics Into the Aerospace Industry," *Proc. AFIPS 1965 FJCC*, Vol. 27, Pt. 1, Spartan Books, New York, pp. 883-892.

16. Chen, F. C. and R. L. Dougherty, "A System for Implementing Interactive Applications, *IBM Syst. J. 7*, 3 and 4 (1968), pp. 257-270.

17. Childs, D. L., "Feasibility of a Set-Theoretic Data Structure," *Proc. IFIP Cong. 1968*, Vol. 1, North-Holland Pub. Co., Amsterdam, pp. 420-430.

18. Childs, D. L., "Description of a Set-Theoretic Data Structure," *Proc. AFIPS 1968 FJCC*, Vol. 33, Pt. 1, AFIPS Press, Montvale, New Jersey, pp. 557-564.

19. Christensen, Carlos, An Example of the Manipulation of Directed Graphs in the AMBIT/G Programming Language, Mass. Comput. Assoc., Div. of Appl. Data Res. Inc., Wakefield, Mass., Nov. 1967.

20. Christensen, C. and E. N. Pinson, "Multifunction Graphics for a Large Computer System, *Proc. AFIPS 1967 FJCC*, Vol. 31, AFIPS Press, Montvale, New Jersey, pp. 697-711.

21. Christensen, C. M., Fischer, D. A. Henderson, Jr. and M. Wolfberg, Third Semiannual Tech. Rep. for Project " "Research in Machine-Independent Software Programming," Mass. Comput. Assoc., Div. of Appl. Data Res. Inc., Wakefield, Mass, March 1970.

22. Codd, E. F., "A Relational Model for Large Shared Data
     Banks," *Comm. ACM 13*, 7 (July 1970), pp. 377-387.

23. Coffman, E. G. and J. Eve, "File Structures Using Hashing
     Functions," *Comm. ACM 13*, 7 (July 1970), pp. 427-432.

24. Cole, M. P., P. H. Dorn, and C. R. Lewis, "Operational
     Software in a Disc Oriented System," *Proc. AFIPS 1964 FJCC*,
     Vol. 26, Part 1, Spartan Books, New York, pp. 351-362.

25. Coons, S. A., "An Outline of the Requirements for a Com-
     puter Aided Design System," *Proc. AFIPS 1963 SJCC*, Vol.
     23, Spartan Books, New York, pp. 299-304.

26. Cotton, I. and F. S. Greatorex, Jr., "Data Structures and
     Techniques for Remote Computer Graphics," *Proc. AFIPS
     1968 FJCC*, Vol. 33, Pt. 1, AFIPS Press, Montvale, New
     Jersey, pp. 533-544.

27. Crespi-Reghizzi, S. and R. Morpurgo, "A Language for
     Treating Graphs," *Comm. ACM 13*, 5(May 1970), pp. 319-323.

28. Dertouzos, M. L., "An Introduction to On-Line Circuit
     Design," *Proc. IEEE 55*, 11 (Nov. 1967), pp. 1961-1971

29. Dertouzos, M. L., and C. W. Therrien, CIRCAL, on-line
     analysis of electronic networks. Tech. Rep. ESL-R-248,
     Oct. 1966, MIT, Cambridge, Mass. Also, *Proc. IEEE 55* (May
     1967), pp. 637-654.

30. D'Imperio, M, "Data Structures and Their Representation
     in Storage," In *Annual Review in Automatic Programming*,
     Vol. 5, Pergamon Press, New York, 1968.

31. Dodd, G. G, "APL- A Language for Associative Data
     Handling in PL/I," *Proc. AFIPS 1966 FJCC*, Vol. 29,
     Spartan Books, New York, pp 677-684.

32. Dodd, G. G, "Elements of Data Management Systems,*Comput.
     Surv. 1,2* (June 1969) pp. 115-135.

33. Evans, D. D., and J. Katzenelson, "Data Structure and
     Man Machine Communication for Network Problems," *Proc.
     IEEE 55,*7 (July 1967), pp. 1135-1144.

34. Evans, T. G, "A Grammar Controlled Pattern Analyzer,"
     Proc. IFIP Cong. 1968, Vol. 2, North-Holland Pub. Co.,
     Amsterdam, pp. 1592-1598.

35. Feingold, S. L., "PLANIT - A Flexible Language Designed for Computer-Human Interaction," *Proc. AFIPS 1967 FJCC*, Vol. 31, AFIPS Press, Montvale, New Jersey, pp. 545-552.

36. Feldman, J. A., Aspects of Associative Processing, TN 1965-13, Lincoln Lab., MIT, Lexington, Mass., 1965.

37. Feldman, J. A. and P. D. Rovner, An Associative Processing System for Conventional Digital Computers, TN 1967-19, Lincoln Lab., MIT, Lexington, Mass., 1967.

38. Feldman, J. A. and P. D. Rovner, "An Algol-based Associative Language," *Comm. ACM 12*, 8, (Aug. 1969), pp. 439-449.

39. Fitzgerald, E. L., "Introduction to Computer Graphics," *Proc. IEEE*, Reg. III Con., Atlanta, Ga., 1966.

40. Fox, L. (ed), *Advances in Programming and Non-Numerical Computation*, Pergamon Press, New York, 1966.

41. Frank, A. J., "B-LINE, Bell Line Drawing Language," *Proc. AFIPS 1968 FJCC*, Vol. 33, Pt. 1, AFIPS Press, Montvale, New Jersey, pp. 179-191.

42. Gorn, S., "Handling the Growth by Definition of Mechanical Languages," *Proc. AFIPS 1967 SJCC*, Vol. 30, AFIPS Press, Montvale, New Jersey, pp. 213-224.

43. Gray, J. C., "Compound Data Structure for Computer Aided Design - A Survey," *Proc. ACM 22nd Nat. Conf., 1967*, MDI Publications, Wayne, Pa., pp. 355-365.

44. Hargreaves, B., J. D. Joyce, G. C. Cole, et. al., "Image Processing Hardware for a Man-Machine Graphical Communication System," *Proc. AFIPS 1964 FJCC*, Vol. 26 Spartan Books, New York, pp. 363-386.

45. Henderson, D. A., Jr., A Description and Definition of Simple AMBIT/G, A Graphical Programming Language, Mass. Comput. Assoc., Div. of Appl. Data Res., Inc., Wakefield, Mass., Apr. 1969.

46. Hsiao, D., and F. Harry, "A Formal System for Information Retrieval From Files," *Comm. ACM 13*, 2(Feb. 1970), pp. 67-73.

47. Hurwitz, A., and J. P. Citron, "GRAF: Graphic Additions to FORTRAN, *Proc. AFIPS 1967 SJCC*, Vol. 30, AFIPS Press, Montvale, New Jersey, pp. 553-557.

48. *IBM Systems Journal, Vol. 7,* Nos. 3 and 4, 1968. The whole issue was devoted to computer graphics.

49. Jacks, E. L., A Laboratory for the Study of Graphical Man-Machine Communication, *Proc. AFIPS 1964, FJCC,* Vol. 26, Spartan Books, New York, pp. 343-350.

50. Jensen, P. A., A Graph Decomposition Technique for Structuring Data, AD-658-756, Clearing House, Springfield, Va., 22151, Sept. 1967.

51. Johnson, C. I., "Principles of Interactive Systems," *IBM Syst. J. 7,* 3 and 4 (1968), pp. 147-173.

52. Johnson, T. E., "SKETCHPAD III: A Computer Program for Drawing in Three Dimensions," *Proc. AFIPS 1963 SJCC,* Vol. 23, Spartan Books, New York, pp. 347-353.

53. Joyce, J. D. and M. J. Cianciolo, "Reactive Displays: Improving Man-machine Graphical Communication," *Proc. AFIPS 1967 FJCC,* Vol. 31, AFIPS Press, Montvale, New Jersey, pp. 713-721.

54. Kirsch, R. A., "Computer Interpretation of English Text and Picture Patterns," *Trans. IEEE Electron. Comput. 13,* 4 (Aug. 1964), pp. 363-376.

55. Knowlton, K. C., "A Programmer's Description of L6," *Comm. ACM 9,* 8 (Aug. 1966), pp. 616-625.

56. Krull, F. N. and J. E. Foote, "A Line Scanning System Controlled from an On-Line Console," *Proc. AFIPS 1964 FJCC,* Vol. 26, Spartan Books, New York, pp. 397-410.

57. Kulsrud, H. E., "A General Purpose Graphic Language," *Comm. ACM 11,* 4 (Apr. 1968), pp. 247-254.

58. Lang, C. A., R. B. Polansky and D. T. Ross, Some Experiments with an Algorithmic Graphical Language, ESL-TM-220, Electron. Syst. Lab., MIT Tech. Memo., Aug. 1965.

59. Lang, C. A. and J. C. Gray, "ASP - A Ring Implemented Associative Structure Package," *Comm. ACM 11,* 8 (Aug. 1968), pp. 550-555.

60. Laurance, N, "A Compiler Language for Data Structures," *Proc. ACM 23rd Nat. Conf.,* 1968, Brandon Systems Press, Princeton, New Jersey, pp. 387-394.

61. Lawson, H. W., Jr., "PL/I List Processing," *Comm. ACM 10*, 6(June 1967), pp. 358-367.

62. Ling, M. T. S., "General Electric Reactive Display System," *Proc. IEEE*, Reg. III Conven.,Atlanta, Ga., 1966.

63. Madnik, S. E., "String Processing Techniques," *Comm. ACM 10*, 7(July 1967), pp. 420-424.

64. McGee, W., "File Structures for Generalized Data Management," *Proc. IFIP Cong.*, 1968, Vol. 2, North-Holland Pub. Co., Amsterdam, pp. 1233-1239.

65. Mealy, G. H., "Another Look at Data," *Proc. AFIPS 1967 FJCC*, Vol. 31, AFIPS Press, Montvale, New Jersey, pp. 525-534.

66. Mezei, L. "Sparta, A Procedure Oriented Programming Language for the Manipulation of Arbitrary Line Drawings," *Proc. IFIP Cong.*,1968, Vol. 1, North-Holland Pub. Co., Amsterdam, pp. 597-604.

66. Miller, W. F., and A. C. Shaw, "Linguistic Methods in Picture Processing-A Survey," *Proc. AFIPS 1968 FJCC*, Vol. 33, Pt. 1, AFIPS Press Montvale, New Jersey, pp. 279-290.

68. Morris, R., "Scatter Storage Techniques," *Comm. ACM 11*, 1(Jan. 1968), pp. 38-44.

69. Morrison, R. A., "Graphic Language Translation With a Language Independent Processor," *Proc. AFIPS 1967 FJCC*, Vol. 31, AFIPS Press, Montvale, New Jersey, pp. 723-731.

70. Narasimhan, R., "Syntax Directed Interpretation of Classes of Pictures," *Comm. ACM 9*, 3(Mar. 1966), pp. 166-173.

71. Narasimhan, R., Labeling Schemata and Syntatic Descriptions of Pictures, Information and Control 7 (Sept. 1964), pp. 151-179.

72. Newman, W. M., "A System for Interactive Graphical Programming," *Proc. AFIPS 1168 SJCC*, Vol. 32, AFIPS Press, Montvale, New Jersey, pp. 47-54.

73. Ninke, W. H., Man Computer Graphical Communication, In System Analysis by Digital Computer, Franklin F. Kuo and J. F. Kaiser (Eds.), Wiley, New York, 1966, Ch. 12.

74. Ninke, W. H., "Graphic I-A Remote Graphical Display Console," *Proc. AFIPS 1965 FJCC*, Vol. 27, Spartan Books, New York, pp. 839-846.

75. Parker, D. B., Solving Design Problems in Graphical Dialogue, Computer Group News IEEE 1,2 (Sept. 1966), pp. 1-12

76. Parker, D. B., Graphical Communication in an On-Line System, in *On-Line Computing Systems*, E. Burgess(Ed.), Amer. Data Process., Inc., Detroit, Mich., 1965.

77. Parker, D. B., Solving Design Problems in Graphical Dialogue, in *On-Line Computing Systems*, W. J. Karplus (Ed.), McGraw-Hill, New York, 1967, pp. 179-219.

78. Prince, M. D. "Man Computer Graphics for Computer-Aided Design," *Proc. IEEE 54*, 12 (Dec. 1966), pp. 1698-1708.

79. Prywes, N. S., "Man Computer Problem Solving With Multilist," *Proc. IEEE 54*, 12(Dec. 1966), pp. 1788-1801.

80. Roberts, L. G., "A Graphical Service System With Variable Syntax," *Comm. ACM 9*, 3(Mar. 1966), pp. 173-176.

81. Roberts, L. G., Graphical Communication and Control Languages, In Second Congress on the Information System Sciences, Spartan Books, New York, 1965.

82. Ross, D. T., "The AED Free Storage Package," *Comm. ACM 10*, 8(Aug. 1967), pp. 481-492.

83. Ross, D. T., The AED approach to Generalized Computer Aided Design, ESL-R-305, Electronic Syst. Lab., MIT, Cambridge, Mass., 1967.

84. Ross, D. T., AED JR. An Experimental Language Processor, ESL-TM-211, Electronics Syst. Lab., MIT, Cambridge, Mass., 1964.

85. Ross, D. T., and J. E. Rodriguez, "Theoretical Foundations for the Computer-Aided Design System," *Proc. AFIPS 1963 SJCC*, Vol. 23, Spartan Books, New York, pp. 305-322. Complete Report: EST-TM-170, Electronic Syst. Lab., MIT, Cambridge, Mass., 1963.

86. Ross, D. T., An Algorithmic Theory of Language, ESL-TM-156, Electronic Syst. Lab., MIT, Cambridge, Mass., 1962.

87. Rovner, P. D., Investigation into paging a Software
     Simulated Associative Memory System, Doc. No. 40 10 90,
     U. of California, Berkeley, Cal., 1966.

88. Rovner, P. D., and J. A. Feldman, "The LEAP Language and
     Data Structure," *Proc. IFIP Cong. 1968*, Vol. 1, North-
     Holland Pub. Co., Amsterdam, pp. 579-585.

89. Rovner, P. D., and D. A. Henderson, Jr., On the Imple-
     mentation of AMBIT/G: A Graphical Programming Language,
     Preprint, Lincoln Lab., Lexington, Mass., Feb. 1969.

90. Rully, A. D., "Subrouting Package for FORTRAN," *IBM SYST.
     J. 7*, 3 and 4 (1968), pp. 248-256.

91. Rutovitz, D., Data Structures for Operations on Digital
     Images, In *Pictorial Pattern Recognition*, G. C. Cheng,
     et al. (Eds.), MDI Publications Wayne, Pa., 1968,
     pp. 105-133.

92. Savitt, D. A., H. H. Love, Jr., and R. E. Troop, "ASP: A
     New Concept in Labguage and Machine Organization," *Proc.
     AFIPS 1967 SJCC*, Vol. 30, AFIPS Press, Montvale, New Jersey,
     pp. 87-102.

93. Schoor, H., and W. M. Waite, "An Efficient Machine Inde-
     pendent Procedure for Garbage Collection in Various List
     Structures," *Comm. ACM 10*, 8(Aug. 1967), pp. 501-506.

94. Shaw, A. C., The Formal Description and Parsing of Pictures,
     Tech. Rep. No. C594, Ph.D. Th., Stanford U., Stanford,
     Ca., Apr. 1968.

95. Shepherd, B. J., Hardware Manipulation of Three-Dimensional
     Graphics, Contact author, IBM, Advanced Syst. Develop.
     Div., Los Gatos, Ca.

96. Shepherd, B. J., A. S. McAllister, and P. Falk, "Micro-
     coded Multiprogramming Display Control Unit," *Proc.
     Computer Graphics '70 Conf.*, Brunel U., Uxbridge, Middle-
     sex, England, Apr. 1970.

97. Sibley, E. H., D. G. Gordon, and R. W. Taylor, "Graphical
     Systems Communications: An Associative Memory Approach,"
     Proc. AFIPS 1968 FJCC, Vol. 33, Pt. 1, AFIPS Press,
     Montvale, New Jersey, pp. 545-555.

98. So, H. C., "OLCA-An On-Line Circuit Analysis System," *Proc. IEEE 55*, 11 (Nov. 1967), pp. 1954-1961.

99. Stotz, R., "Man-Machine Console Facilities for Computer Aided Design," *Proc. AFIPS 1963 SJCC*, Vol. 23, Spartan Boods, New York, pp. 323-328.

100. Sutherland, I. E., "SKETCHPAD: A Man Machine Graphical Communication System," *Proc. AFIPS 1963 SJCC*, Vol. 23 Spartan Books, New York, pp. 329-346. A more complete description is contained in: Tch. Rep. No. 296, Lincoln Lab., MIT, Lexington, Mass. Jan. 1963.

101. Sutherland, W. R., On-Line Graphical Specification of Computer Procedures, Tch. Rep. 405, Lincoln Lab., MIT, Lexington, Mass., May 1966.

102. Symonds, A. J., "Auxiliary Storage Associative Data Structure for PL/I," *IBM Syst. J. 7*, 3 and 4 (   ), pp. 229-245.

103. Tabory, R., Survey and Evaluation of AED Systems at MIT, Tech. Rep. TR 00.1383, IBM Syst. Delevop. Div., Poughkeepsie Lab., Poughkeepsie, New York, Feb. 1966.

104. Uber, G. T., P. E. Williams, and L. H. Bradner, "The Organization and Formatting of Heirarchical Displays for On-Line Input of Data," *Proc. AFIPS 1968 FJCC*, Vol. 33, Pt. 1, AFIPS Press, Montvale, New Jersey, pp. 219-226.

105. Van Dam, A., and D. Evans, "Data Structure Programming System," *Proc. IFIP Cong., 1968,* Vol. 1, North-Holland Pub. Co., Amsterdam, pp. 557-564.

106. Van Dam, A., and D. Evans., "A Compact Data Structure for Storing, Retrieving and Manipulating Line Drawings," *Proc. AFIPS 1967 SJCC*, Vol. 30, AFIPS Press, Montvale, New Jersey, pp. 601-610.

107. Van Dam, A., Computer Driven Displays and Their Use in Man Machine Interaction, In *Advances in Computers,* Vol. 7, F. L. Alt and M. Rubinoff (Eds.), Acakemic Press, New York, ;966, pp. 239-290.

108. Wegner, P. *Programming Languages, Information Structures and Machine Organization,* McGraw-Hill, New York, 1968.

109.   Weston, P. E., Cylinders: A Relational Data Structure,
        Tech. Rep. No. 18, Biological Comput. Lab., U. of Ill.,
        Urbana, Ill., Feb. 1970.

110.   Wexelblat, R. L., and H. A. Freedman, "The MULTILANG On-
        Line Programming System," *Proc. AFIPS 1967 SJCC*, Vol. 30,
        AFIPS Press, Montvale, New Jersey, pp. 559-569.

111.   Williams, R., "On the Application of Graph Theory to
        Computer Data Structures," *Proc. Computer Graphics '70
        Conf.*, Brunel U., Uxbridge, Middlesex, England, Apr. 1970.

112.   Wolfberg, M. S., An Interactive Graph Theory System,
        Ph.D. Th., Moore School Rep. No. 69-25, U. of Pennsylvania,
        June 1969.

113.   Wolfberg, M. S., "An Interactive Graph Theory System,"
        Proc. Computer Graphics 70 Conf., Brunel U., Uxbridge,
        Middlesex, England, Apr. 1970.

On the Application of Relational Data Structures
in Computer Graphics*

ROBIN WILLIAMS

ABSTRACT

Computer graphics provides a user-oriented communication
link to a computer and relational data bases provide a convenient way for users to view large data organizations. Potentially the combination of graphics and relational data bases is
very promising. This paper describes how relational data bases
can be used in graphics applications and how user functions can
be constructed in terms of operations on relations. For application development, it is shown that the use of relational data
bases simplifies the handling of data but with some loss of machine efficiency. Example structures are presented.

1. INTRODUCTION

There is no doubt that the impact of interactive computer
graphics on the computing scene is considerably less than was
predicted a few years ago. One can blame the hardware and say
that it is too expensive, or too simple, or both, but there is
another more serious problem. Systems support for computer graphics is quite inadequate. Software is usually device dependent
and only provides very low-level programming interfaces. Consequently, for all but the simplest applications, each user must
develop his own graphics support. He must first choose a representation for his basic graphic elements or building blocks,
which must be constructed from the available primitives and then
he must design methods to group elements together logically so
that they can be operated on as single entities. He must also
create mechanisms to represent relationships between elements or

*Reprinted by permission of North Holland Publishing Company;
 originally in Information Processing, 1974, IFIP Congress,
 Stockholm, Sweden.

groups of elements and to associate non-graphical data with
elements. Whenever operations are performed at a graphical console, it is necessary to identify which entities are affected
and hence which other relationships and associated data are
affected by the operation. Usually a means for handling atten-
tions to service tablet, light pen and function switch operations
must also be included in the application support.

If an application spans two computer systems, a graphics
satellite and a large time-shared machine, then there are a
number of additional problems, including communications protocol
and the controlling of two sets of programs and data. These
problems are more than enough to put off those who are not already systems programmers. This is very unfortunate because it
was hoped that the display interface would simplify the use of
computers and enhance the development of new application programs.
It is clear that both the end-user and the applications developer
would benefit greatly from better high-level graphics support
than that which is provided today.

2.   INHERENT PROBLEMS IN COMPUTER GRAPHICS

Standing back from the myriad of details and observing the
larger picture one can see the inherent difficulties of interactive graphics. First there is a representation problem.
Graphical data, diagrams, drawings, maps etc. are two-dimensional
but computer storage is one-dimensional. Consequently, there
is a mismatch and the two-dimensional data must be mapped into
a one-dimensional store. Furthermore there are many implicit
relationships in a two-dimensional plane that must be preserved
in a computer representation. The problem becomes worse when it
is necessary to represent three-dimensional objects in a one-
dimensional store and to display two-dimensional views of the
objects.

Secondly, there is a computation problem. Computation
proceeds serially in one dimension and so there is a problem
of converting essentially two-dimensional operations into sequences of processing steps. Both problems are magnified by the
high-speed presentation of data on a display screen.

Thirdly, problem solving and computer aided design with
graphics is an environment where highly complex interactions
take place. Thus the user's data structures are constantly
changing. This is a problem because it is very difficult to
manage dynamic data structures.

Finally, we have data presentation problems. In most applications users want to work at different levels of detail and they also want to vary the scope of the data presentation at each level. When working with urban maps for example, one wants to view major features such as main roads separately from minor features such as housing developments and secondary roads. Therefore it is important to be able to define data subsets and selectively alter the detail associated with such a subset. Conversely, it must be possible to combine or aggregate data from different sources into a displayable entity. In both cases an ability to explore and peruse the data is very desirable, for example, to follow a major highway that goes off the screen.

All these basic problems are related to the representation of images in the computer. Therefore, the data structures used to store the pictorial information are of prime importance. Most realistic applications use large data bases and the graphical aspects of the data constitute only a fraction of the data attributes. Hence, it is necessary to consider these more global data-base requirements and also the overall environment for graphical applications in order to make sensible choices for data structures. As computing hardware costs continue to decrease one can reasonably expect a large percentage of graphical programs to run on dedicated machines that provide good response times and that are highly interactive. The dedicated machine would only need to communicate with other machines in order to share data. Indeed there could be several dedicated machines communicating with one larger machine for purposes of sharing one large integrated data base. Each dedicated machine would contain its own working set of data, as well as all its own programs, and would access the central data bank only to get new data or to update existing data. There are many applications where one can work on a design, a plan, or a drawing, locally without the need for continuous communication with a central data base. When the design is finished the relevant data can be incorporated into the central data base. It is important therefore to achieve a maximum independence of the data base from application programs so that data base alterations and reorganizations will not affect program operation. It is also necessary to permit users to view different subsets of data according to their own needs and also to allow users to extract and integrate data easily. These considerations affect local data structures because one would prefer to avoid conversion problems and the aided complexity of using two different structures.

To solve some of these problems many different data organizations have been proposed [7]. Recently, however, there has developed a considerable interest in relational data bases primarily for non-graphical applications [1, 2, 5]. Relational data

'e some appealing properties; they allow increased data
ₐₑnce, they permit different logical views of data and
..ₑy provide an easily understood data base organization. Because of these properties the suitability of the relational view
of data for graphical applications has been studied and some
results are given below.

3. RELATIONAL DATA BASES

A relation R on sets S_1, S_2,...S_n, is a set of n-tuples
each of which has n elements, the first from S_1, the second
from S_2,..., and the nth from S_n, (i.e., R is a subset of the
Cartesian product S_1 x S_2...x S_n). The set S_i is called the
i^{th} domain of R. A relation with n domains has degree n and
is called an n-ary relation. Each domain can be given a name;
these names are then attributes of the relation. A relation
can be represented conveniently as an array in which each row
is an n-tuple and each column is a domain, (this representation
is not essential however). The ordering of rows and columns
assuming unique domain names is immaterial. An example is
shown in Figure 1.

PNAME	NPOS	TRANSF.	ELEMENT	V1	V2	COLOR	....
PART1	X_1, Y_1	T1	DEF. 1	10	1000	RED	
PART2	X_2, Y_2	T2	DEF. 3	2	10000	BLUE	
⋮	⋮	⋮	⋮	⋮	⋮	⋮	
PART6	X_6, Y_6	T6	DEF. 1	3	1000	RED	
⋮	⋮	⋮	⋮	⋮	⋮	⋮	

(a) An example relation

SUBASSEMBLY (PNAME, NPOS, TRANSF., ELEMENT, V1, V2, COLOR, ...)

(b) The relation structure or type definition.

Figure 1. An example relation and its structure definition.

The name(s) of the key attribute by which tuples can be uniquely identified is shown underlined. For example PART 1 is positioned at X_1, Y_1 has value 10 for domain V_1, has COLOR value red, etc. The structural definition of a relation can be expressed as shown in Figure 1b.

4. RELATIONAL STRUCTURES IN COMPUTER GRAPHICS

The on-line design process is typical of graphical applications. The basic processes, each of which may include many editing functions, are:

Definition of graphic elements (building blocks.

Creation of instances of graphic elements.

Grouping of elements into larger entities (with constraints).

Association of data with parts or entities.

Addition of other relationships.

Frequently, a tree structure or a hierarchical ring structure is constructed as a result of these design actions. A typical hierarchical structure is shown in Figure 2. The details of this structure will differ with different machine capabilities but essentially to create an image from this structure an interpreter program traces through the structure and produces a display list which maintains a display. (Similar reasoning to that presented in this paper applies to systems in which "graphical subroutines" are called to generate display lists.) The display list may be generated on the fly for every frame or may be stored explicitly. The transformations Tl, T2, etc., are transformation factors (scale, displace, rotate) that apply to an instance of a definition and may be hardware or software implemented.

The same information can also be stored conveniently in a relational form. The definition of a graphic element is simply a relation of x, y values that define each line and its attributes as shown in Figure 3. Because each line is drawn from the current position, to the next, only one end point of each line is stored in each tuple and the tuples in this relation are considered to be ordered. This is different from the more usual relation in which tuples are unordered. However unordered

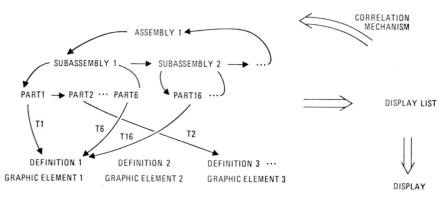

Figure 2. A hierarchical structure for a display system.

Definition 1

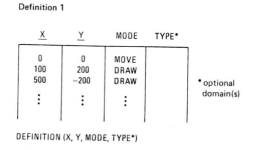

DEFINITION (X, Y, MODE, TYPE*)

Figure 3. Relation for defining graphical elements.

relations could be used if both end points of a line are stored
in a tuple. This costs extra storage space but simplifies some
processing because logically addition or deletion of a line is
then simply a matter of adding or deleting a tuple.

Properties of each line are represented in additional domains of the relation. A line can be specified as visible or
invisible (DRAW, MOVE) and (optionally) it can be solid, dotted
or dashed. It can also be assigned a color and given a gray
scale value.

Relations like those shown in Figures 1 and 3 can be used
instead of the hierarchical structure of Figure 2. Each tuple
in a SUBASSEMBLY relation has a name (PNAME) and if this name is
displayable, its relative position is given in (NPOS). Each
tuple contains a reference to an (ELEMENT) and has transformation parameters (TRANSF) that specify the scale, position and
rotation of the referenced element (whether the transformations
are actually performed by hardware or by software does not
matter for the purposes of this paper.) The entire referenced-
element may be given a COLOR and could be specified to have
solid, dotted or dashed lines, etc. Other non-graphical data,
characteristic values, geometric dimensions, topological connections to other parts and so on, can be included in other domains
of the relation. The tuples and columns are not ordered and the
entries in each particular column are identical in type.

A similar relation could be used to group sub-assemblies
together, and, if necessary, there can be a further grouping
of assemblies and so on.

As shown in Figures 1 and 3, there are many types of graphical data and to display the data it is necessary to know
which domains contain graphical data and what type of data each
domain contains. Then an interpreter can trace through the
relations, given the starting point, and extract and compute
coordinates for display purposes. Here again we are concerned
about logical processing and not the detailed refreshing mechanism, the display could be refreshed from a vector display-
list or a raster of bits or it could be a storage-tube display.

The graphical data can be identified by the interpreter
in different ways. One possibility is to associate a type with
each domain name for the data in that domain and specify the
types of relations and the domains containing graphical data.
However, if the data is part of a larger relational data base
then there will be a catalog that defines the data base contents and there will probably be a data definition language
(DDL) for defining catalog entries. Consequently a graphical

DDL (DDL/G or GDDL) can be defined as an extension of a DDL.
The idea is not limited to any particular data base or data
organization but applies quite generally, for example a DDL/G
could be defined to extend the DDL in the CODASYL DBTG report
[4]. The definition of the graphical information can be represented as shown in Figure 4a. RTYPE indicates the relation type.

RTYPE	DOMAINS	DTYPE
ASSEMBLY	SNAME	RELC
SUBASSEMBLY	PNAME	TEXT
	NPOS	TRPOS
	TRANSF.	TPARAM
	ELEMENT	RELC
	COLOR	DMODE
DEFINITION	X1	RXCOORD
	Y1	RYCOORD
	MODE	VISIBILITY
	TYPE*	DMODE

(a) Display Domains

RELC	Relation call
TEXT	Character string for display
TRPOS	Text relative position
TPARAM	Transformation parameters
DMODE	Display mode
RXCOORD	Relative X coordinate value
RYCOORD	Relative Y coordinate value
VISIBILITY	MOVE or DRAW

(b) Display Types Used in (a)

Figure 4. Definition of graphical data.

For each domain of each relation there is a display type (DTYPE)
which specifies how the interpreter is to process that domain,
for example a relation call means process the specified relation using transformation and type "arguments" from the current
tuple, then restore the original state (transformation etc.)
and return to the next tuple in the current relation. Some
other display types are shown in Figure 4b. Additional display
types would include the third coordinate dimension Z, absolute
as well as relative coordinate values, and descriptors for
images used in image processing.

In practice it would be necessary to store the graphic-
display type information in the catalog but it would also be
desirable to keep the same information locally in a header descriptor with each domain to increase the efficiency of the display interpreter/processor. This does not create a maintenance
problem because this information changes infrequently.

5. GRAPHICAL OPERATIONS USING RELATIONAL STRUCTURES

Working with a relational data base, and a DDL/G, the user sees a conceptually simple, logical interface. He sees no pointers, in contrast to the large number of pointers usually found in hierarchical ring structures. Most user actions involve insertion/deletion of tuples in relations, conditional tests on domain values, extraction of data subsets satisfying given conditions, the formation of new relations from existing data to bring together related data and so on. Graphical editing, model building and analysis of geographical data on maps can all be viewed in this way. Consider the following examples:

(i)   Deletion: To delete an instance of a graphic element, the user first points to the element with a light pen or positions a cursor on it by adjusting an input device. Via a correlation mechanism, the relation and tuple containing the call to the element definition are identified. The user then selects the delete action and the whole tuple can be deleted (thus all data that relates to this instance is deleted automatically).

(ii) Reposition: An element instance is identified as above. The displacement values (or coordinate values in some systems) can then be recomputed.

(iii) Intensification of all elements with a common value in one domain. The element type is selected and the value and its domain name are specified (e.g., SIZE = 12 or VALUE <15, >12). The set of tuples satisfying the condition are found and the corresponding values in a domain BRIGHT are altered for the set of tuples.

For many applications it is important that a working set of data can be extracted from a large integrated data base and used locally and then reintegrated after modification into the central data base. Conceptually it is quite easy for the user to request a working set of data because he can specify the relation and domain names. Similarly, modified domains can be transmitted back and reincorporated into the central data base. These extraction and integration operations are conceptually simpler for the user to specify than corresponding operations with directed graph structures, because of the independence of the relations and the absence of pointers.

Other graphical operations such as windowing, display screen selection and light-pen initiation apply to whole relations or sets of relations and can be treated as global parameters. For example, they can be treated as commands to set modes for the display interpreter; the actual parameter values could be stored in relation headers or even in separate relations.

6. A GEOGRAPHIC DATA SYSTEM EXAMPLE

Consider as a particular example, a geographic-data system, which is a system for displaying geographically distributed data on maps. The inputs to the system shown in Figure 5, are (1) a detailed map, e.g., a street map of a town, Figure 5a, (2) data useful to the application, e.g., data on houses, on schools, on traffic, on police activities, etc., Figure 5b, (3) a zone-map that divides the map into small areas called zones, Figure 5c. A selection mechanism is then used to extract data from the application data and aggregate it into zones and many such extractions of data are created, Figure 5d. Each set of extracted data contains data for each zone such as the number of people in each zone, the average income per zone, the number of traffic accidents per zone, etc. A query language is used to specify logical combinations of conditions on the extracted data and the result is used to "color" the zone map. A simple example of an operation on an extracted data-base relation is to put an asterisk (*) in each zone where the average income is less than $6,000 and the population is greater than 100.

Such a system, with more elaborate graphical features than mentioned above, was implemented at the IBM Research Laboratory (San Jose) and used by policemen to allocate manpower for San Jose so that each police beat had an approximately equal workload [3, 6].

Graphic-data systems in general could employ relational data bases with potentially many advantages. The data base can contain the data for many applications, for all functions of urban government for instance, and because it is logically possible to add new relations or domains at any time the data base can grow in an orderly manner to accommodate new data and new applications. With relational operations a user can conveniently select a subset of the data base and extract domains useful for his application. Data could be selected by specifying input and output relations and selection criteria (probably by graphical means). The same selection or query language could then be used with the extracted data for "coloring" the zone map. Thus the user and the implementer would benefit from the consistency and simplicity of the system.

```
STREETS(STNAME,STTYPE,LOWADDRESS,HIGHADDRESS,XFROM,
        YFROM,XTO,YTO, . . .)
  •
  •
A)  GEOGRAPHIC DATA STRUCTURE


HOUSES (STREET,NUMBER,ROOMS,TAX,. . .)
PERSON (NAME,SOCIAL#,MSTATUS,#CHILD,STREET,NUMBER, . . .)
POLCALL (EVENTTYPE,DATE,TIME,DURATION,STREET, . . .)
  •
  •
B) APPLICATION DATA STRUCTURE


SCHOOLS (NAME,LOCX,LOCY,BOUNDARYNAME)
BOUNDARY1(XPOINT,YPOINT)
ZONE (ZONE#,X,Y)
  •
  •
C) ZONE DATA STRUCTURE


YEAR65 (ZONE#,POPULATION,AVERINCOME)
YEAR66 (ZONE#,POPULATION,AVERINCOME)
  •
  •
CALL1(ZONE#,#CALLS,AVERDURATION)
CALL2(ZONE#,#CALLS,AVERDURATION)
  •
  •
D) EXTRACTED DATA BASE
```

Fig. 5 An example geographic data-base.

7. CONCLUSIONS

A case has been made for the use of relational data bases in computer graphics applications. It is argued that relational data bases have important properties that are as valid for graphical applications as for non-graphical applications and it has been shown that a relational data base system can support graphics applications. Example relational data structures and operations have shown the advantages of using relational data bases. The disadvantages of using relational data bases is that execution efficiency can never be as high as with tailored data structures. Also the implementation of a relational data base system is not necessarily easier than the implementation of other data bases.

However, computer costs, both for memory and processing hardware are still decreasing while application development costs are rising, and it is necessary to give greater attention to the efficiency of the application designer and the end-user and to provide more conveniences for these users. Relational data bases provide conceptually simple views of data and graphical displays provide an easily understood communications link to the computer. Therefore the combination of a computer graphics system using a relational data base offers many potential benefits to users of such systems.

REFERENCES

1. Codd, E. F., "A Relational Model of Data for Large Shared
    Data Banks," *Comm. ACM*, Vol. 13, No. 6, June 1970, pp. 377-
    387.

2. Codd, E. F., "Normalized Data Base Structure: A Brief Tu-
    torial," *Proc. ACM-SIGFIDET Workshop on Data Description,
    Access and Control*, 1971, available from ACM Headquarters,
    New York City.

3. Cristiani, E. J., R. J. Evey, R. E. Goldman, P. E. Mantey,
    "An Interactive System for Aiding Evaluation of Local Govern-
    ment Policies," *IEEE Trans. on Systems, Man & Cybernetics*,
    Vol. SMC-3, No. 2, March 1973, pp. 141-146.

4. Data Base Task Force Group Report to the CODASYL Programming
    Language Committee, April 1971, available from ACM Head-
    quarters, New York City.

5. Lorie, R. A. and A. J. Symonds, "A Relational Access Method
    for Interactive Applications," chapter in *Data Base Systems*,
    Randall Rustin (ed.), (Courant Computer Science Symposium,
    6), Prentice Hall, New York, May 1971.

6. Mantey, P. E., J. L. Bennett, E. D. Carlson, "Information for
    Problem Solving: The Development of an Interactive Geogra-
    phic Information System," *IEEE Int. Conf. on Communication*,
    Vol. II, Seattle, Washington, June 1973.

7. Williams, R., "A Survey of Data Structures for Computer Gra-
    phics Systems," *ACM Computing Surveys*, Vol. 3, No. 1, March
    1971, pp. 1-21. First part of chapter in this book.

Data Structures in Computer Graphics*

ROBIN WILLIAMS
GARY M. GIDDINGS
WARREN D. LITTLE
W. GERALD MOORHEAD
DANIEL L. WELLER

1. INTRODUCTION

A central problem in interactive graphical applications is that of structuring the data. Frequently the graphical data and the non-graphical data are maintained in separate data-bases with different structures. If one attempts to use the graphical medium as a window to the data in the data base and attempts to make changes in the data-base by interactively altering displayed images, then conversions are required between the graphical structures and the primary data files. Some of the ways that have been proposed and used to structure graphical data are discussed in [1].

A project is under way at IBM to evaluate some ideas for storing graphical data together with related non-graphical data in a relational data-base. This approach allows each application to use structures appropriate to the particular application and does not force a particular structure on all applications. Although the data must be organized in a (hierarchical) relational form, any relations can be created to suit the application requirements. The graphical data is self-describing and can be interpreted by an interpreter program that produces calls to a graphic subroutine package to generate displays. It is the use of graphic meanings in a standard data-base environment, separating data from application programs, that makes this approach different from other interpreter approaches (e.g., Sketchpad, [2] and Adage [3]). Thus the data base can be managed separately by a data-base management system and shared by many people without altering the validity of application programs.

*Reprinted by permission of ACM; originally in Proceeding of Workshop on Data Bases for Interactive Design, University of Waterloo, September 1975.

Furthermore, the use of self-descriptive data should allow stan-
dardized program modules to be written to process the data in
such a way that they are usable in diverse applications without
alteration, thus simplifying the job of graphical application
programming. This is in contrast to the common approach in
which each application is programmed independently starting at
a low level. In addition, with our approach all high-level software is device independent, which greatly simplifies application
programming. A brief description of a part of this project
which has been called "A Picture Building System" follows.

2. THE CONCEPT OF PICTURE-BUILDING

Many applications deal with pictorial representations of
objects and data. Line drawings and images are presented to the
user together with menus of commands, and the user interacts with
the graphical presentations to specify actions. The application
program frequently employs a graphic subroutine package to perform the graphical I/O and in many cases this works quite well
with simple arrays of coordinates and text strings. However,
in many applications there is a need to build more complex structures than simple lists of x, y, z coordinates. Imagine for
example, trying to locate a carburetor in an engine from a large
array of coordinate values!

It has been argued in earlier papers [4, 5, 6] that the
important thing to do is to build a model in the computer to
represent the parts, their attributes and their interrelationships so that a whole variety of processing can be performed on
the model. However, many attributes of data are not graphical.
It would be beneficial, therefore, to store graphical data together with non-graphical data in a manner that is consistent
with current or future standard data-bases. A major aim is to
separate data from application programs so that reorganizations
of the data do not affect the validity of application programs
and so that many users (application programs) can share the same
data easily. A general mechanism to achieve this data independence is presented.

The Picture-Building System consists of three parts: (1) a
mechanism for creating structures for graphical and non-graphical
data, (2) a mechanism for interactively loading data into these
structures, and (3) a mechanism for viewing and interactively
manipulating the graphical data via pictures.

3. DATA DEFINITIONS

A relational data-base model was chosen for our work because it employs simple tabular structures that are conceptually
simple to understand and also because there is much research
activity on relational data-bases. In the relational model it
is easier to express data integration and extraction than with
network structures. It is also fairly easy to construct hierarchical structures using relations by allowing a domain to
contain names of other relations. Also, since there is a great
deal of activity on relational data bases for non-graphical data,
it is desired to find out if the same relational structures are
sufficient for graphical data.

The concept of a data definition language for defining relational structures is extended for graphical data by assigning
"meanings" to domain names. For example, a domain of a relation
may contain integers that are to be interpreted graphically as
scale factors: another domain may contain simple byte data that
represents intensities, while another domain may contain reals
representing annual rainfall.

Three domains of a relation SYMBOL1 containing coordinate
data are shown. X, Y, and XYOPERATION are the domain names of
the relation. SYMBOL1 might be considered a "primitive" for an
application that draws pictorial symbols on maps. A "primitive"
is self contained, i.e., it does not refer to other relations.

SYMBOL1	X	Y	XYOPERATION
	0	0	MOVE
	100	200	DRAW
	200	300	DRAW
	.	.	.
	.	.	.
	.	.	.

In this case the order of the tuples (rows) in the table is important and must be preserved. Tuple ordering could be avoided
if desired, by specifying both line end-points, e.g., 0, 0, 100,
200, in each tuple, but that would be inefficient in storage.
In other cases (where drawings overlap) preservation of drawing
order is necessary.

The structure of the relation SYMBOL1 is defined with the
extended data definition language as follows:

DEFINE SYMBOL1

	DOMAIN NAME	GRAPHIC MEANING	DATA TYPE
1.	X ,	X ,	INTEGER
2.	Y ,	Y ,	INTEGER
3.	XYOPERATION,	XYZOPERATION ,	CHARACTER

One or several domains may be defined to be a key as usual; however it is necessary to allow duplicate data in relations containing only coordinate data. Similarly other relation structures can be defined, and other attributes of lines could be specified (e.g., color, line style, intensity, thickness, etc.). Typically in a given application one would define several primitives with which to build more complex drawings or images and then other relations to express groupings and interrelationships between instances of the primitives. For example, the relation MAP-SYMBOLS is shown. This relation positions the primitives SYMBOL1, SYMBOL2 ... in a display when an interpreter is called to display MAP-SYMBOLS (as explained in section 3.1). Non-graphical data is given the meaning datum and is ignored by the interpreter.

MAP-SYMBOLS

GRAPHIC MEANING:	DATUM	X	Y	COLOR	DATUM	RELATION
DOMAIN NAMES:	SYMBOL#	POSX	POSY	COLOR	VALUE	NAME
USER DATA:	1	373	141	RED	10	SYMBOL1
.	2	236	121	GREEN	100	SYMBOL2
.	3	150	207	RED	15	SYMBOL1
.	.	.	.	.	.	.
.	.	.	.	.	.	.
.	.	.	.	.	.	.

So far we have shown how the data definition language is used to define the structures needed for the application. It is also necessary to have a data specification and manipulation mechanism to insert the data into the relational structures and an interpreter to display the images represented by the data in the relations.

4. DATA SPECIFICATION AND MANIPULATION

The basic operations needed are the six operations needed for standard data base operations plus two extra operations: display and correlate. Correlation is the identification of an entity by pointing to its image on the screen, as explained in section 4.2. The following operations are sufficient:

1. Create relation
2. Delete relation
3. Insert tuple (row)
4. Delete tuple
5. Get tuple (Ith, next, or by key)
6. Change domain value in a tuple
7. Display relation
8. Correlation

Other useful operations (e.g., copy relation) can be defined using these basic operations. An application programmer would write procedures to maintain a dialog with the end-user in order to manipulate his data. Typically the application programmer would create menus and corresponding procedures to carry out menu commands. Thus these procedures form the connection between the user and the data-base and would use the basic data-base operators. The end-user however, sees pictures and menus as the interface with which he interacts to perform such operations as move, delete, and copy. Standard procedures could be created or adapted to edit the graphical data. It may be possible to use other standard mechanisms, e.g., a query language function, to simplify the preparation of new applications. An interactive graphical editor is also being developed to help load and manipulate data in relational structures.

4.1 The Interpreter

The operation DISPLAY for a relation or a tuple invokes an interpreter. The interpreter looks up the graphic meaning of the data as specified in the relation domain description and begins processing the first tuple. The interpreter initially assumes a standard, default transform, color, intensity, etc. If the tuple being processed has a call to another relation with some transformation, then the current transform is stacked, a compound transform is computed, and the relation referred to in the current tuple is then processed according to the compound transform. When the interpreter has finished processing the called relation the transform at the top of the transform stack is reinstated. This is similar to other interpreters of graphical structures [2,3]. The difference is that the structures in this case are self-describing relations in a relational data base. The relational approach means that the columns in the tables are homogeneous which makes processing simpler and helps separate data from programs. Also graphic meanings, like SCALE, are given once per entry as in [3]. Furthermore, relations can be created and changed without altering the application programs.

The following graphical meanings have been identified:

RX,RY,RZ   rotation about x,y,z axis
SCALE   scale equally in x,y and z directions
SCLX,SCLY,SCLZ,SCALE   scales in x,y or z directions
SHIFTX, SHIFTY, SHIFTZ   displacement along x,y,z axis
COR   correlatability
COLOR, INTENSITY
STYLE   different line styles and fonts
X,Y,Z   coordinates
XYZOPERATION   specifies operation to be performed
TSTRING   text string of characters
RSTRING   raster bit data
SCREEN   logical screen #
WINDOW and VIEWPORT   bounds in x,y,z dimensions
DATUM   non-graphical data
P1,P2,...Pn   any parameter to be passed to a
                              called RELATION
RELATION   relation name or procedure to be
                              invoked.

An XYZOPERATION can specify drawing a visible or invisible line, drawing an area, positioning text or raster data and some other possibilities to be explained in a subsequent paper. RSTRING, RELATION and parameters P1,...Pn have special meanings in this context. An RSTRING is an array of bits representing an area of any size and is treated as primitive data like lines and coordinates. RSTRINGS can be included in the relational structure, and hence can be invoked, transformed and located anywhere on the screen. An example of this use would be to define symbols to be placed on a map as two-dimensional bit patterns in various locations and colors as a means of displaying data on a map. Thus in the relation MAP-SYMBOLS, SYMBOL1 could be a relation which is an RSTRING rather than a line drawing as actually was shown in relation SYMBOL1 in section 2.

An entry in a domain can be a relation name, thus hierarchical structures (trees) can be built. This is both desirable and necessary in many applications (and has been assumed throughout our work). Such a domain is given the meaning "RELATION".

We have found it convenient to allow procedures as well as tabular data to be used to define graphical entities. We allow a procedure to be callable from a relation (Graphic Meaning RELATION) and executed when needed. The procedure can output graphic commands directly, whenever it is called. For example, a 2.5 inch gear wheel with 27 teeth can be specified by invoking a procedure that computes a gearwheel with teeth and specifying

the parameters 2.5 and 27. Since changing a parameter is easier
than changing an entire table, direct output will be more efficient for this case if the number of teeth on the gear wheel
changes. Even simple arcs can be conveniently defined by a
procedure with parameters. This mechanism allows several gear-
wheels with different numbers of teeth to be created with one
procedure. These ideas are similar to those of T. L. Kunii [7].
More details and examples will be given in a subsequent paper.

4.2 Correlation

Correlation is the identification of a line, entity, or
group of entities in the data-base structure by pointing at its
representation on the screen. The correlation mechanism also
returns the X,Y coordinates of the position pointed to, in user
coordinates. The graphical subroutine package and hardware together must have a correlation mechanism to identify a line or
a text string pointed to by the user via a light-pen, cursor,
etc. In beam-directed display systems with a hardware refresh
buffer a table of starting addresses for each segment can be
kept and when an interrupt occurs the address in the buffer will
identify the item. (Note: If sophisticated hardware that
allows nested subrouting of images is used, then one might have
to return a stack of buffer addresses!) Similarly in a storage
display system, including raster refresh CRT systems, a comparison can be made between a cursor position set by the user and
every line that is drawn on the screen. This is often done by
redrawing the picture and making a comparison for line intersection with the cursor position in a hardware comparison circuit which gives an interrupt when the correct line is found.
Alternatively a table can be constructed with an entry for every
line drawn or text output together with a segment # for the item.
The table is searched to find which item intersects the cursor
position. The mechanism used here is best explained by an example. Relation T is to be displayed. T consists of invoca-
tions, or instances as it is called in graphics, of other (primitive) relations A, B, and C, which contain coordinate data.
The essential structure omitting unnecessary attributes is shown
below:

		RELATION
T	PART # (KEY)	REFERENCE
	a	A
	b	C
	c	B
	d	A

A	X	Y	XYOPERATION
	10	20	Move
	30	40	Draw
	.	.	.
	.	.	.

B, C similar to A.

Then as the interpreter traces through T, calling A, C, B, and A it outputs calls to draw four line-drawings (logical display segments)on the screen and can keep a table of the fully qualified names (to 2 levels) of these line-drawings which are:

Name	Logical Segment
T.a.A	1
T.b.C	2
T.c.B	3
T.d.A	4

Suppose that segment 2 and hence the fully qualified name T.b.C is identified. There is no way to know if the user means to identify an instance of a line in C, C itself, or the entire relation T and the only way to solve this is to request more feedback from the user. First the intensity or color of T.b can be altered to tell the user that the invocation of C has been identified. This is done either by calling the interpreter to display the tuple T.b, or by redisplaying the whole picture and giving the segment T.b.C a different color of intensity. If a local transformed file has been created then only segment T.b.C need be reoutput. Also, commands can be supplied to allow the user to move up or down the structure i.e. view other possibilities from the qualified name until the intended section of the complete image is correctly identified. The important point is that the user can identify different objects, pieces of objects or groups of objects and can perceive this on the screen.

If relation T is referenced by a higher relation then more and longer names are generated during picture interpretation. However the same correlation mechanism applies for any hierarchical structure.

5. ENVIRONMENT OF PICTURE BUILDING SYSTEM

The picture-building system is being programmed to run on

a number of display terminals, including a color display system
called RAINBOW, a color refresh raster display exploiting commercial quality TV monitors, and driven via an IBM System/7.
This intelligent terminal facilitates both the support of color,
and the mixing of analog scanned images (via TV camera) with
computer-generated displays. The RAINBOW terminal appears to
the host computer as a remote terminal (such as an IBM 2741 or
Tektronix 4013). Host computer output is sent to RAINBOW over
voice-grade telephone lines, and the System/7 converts this
output into inputs to the (RAMTEK) display processor, which in
turn drives the refresh memory. Many inputs to our work, the
need for color and images for example, come from the work we
do with application-oriented end users having applications
problems as reported by Carlson et al. [8].

6. CONCLUSIONS

     The concept of the Picture-Building System with data
definition and data manipulation facilities is intended to help
standardize and simplify the programming of interactive graphics
applications. The design includes all forms of graphical data
storage and presentation. This graphical data may be raster data,
vector data, or text. There is a specific emphasis on separating data from programs and on incorporating graphical data
together with non-graphical data in a standard data-base. We
have found some extensions to a basic relational data-base to
be necessary or desirable for storing graphical data. These
are a) row/tuple ordering, b) an extra domain descriptor called
a "graphic meaning", c) duplicate rows (hence non-unique keys),
d) hierarchical structures and e) a procedural capability.

EXERCISES RELATING TO STRUCTURING OF GRAPHICAL DATA

1) Design a display file for a line drawing for any display
   system you know to allow for
   a) selective erasure of any line from the screen
   b) **selective transformation** (movement, rotation) of
   a group of lines (an entity) on the screen.
   NOTE: With storage systems, use a software controlled
   display file that gets reinterpreted or reoutput.

2) What are the problems of a list structure organization in
   main memory?

3) Design a data-definition language for a tree structured or
   network organized data-base to allow for <u>graphical</u> data.
   How would the interpreter work in your case? Note that the
   data (and network) must be self-describing and not just
   a particular example! How are the definitions stored
   and managed?
   NOTE: This leads to "Research issues."

4) Could one write a generalized graphical editor to edit
   data stored in the data-base in problem (3)? The editor
   should be capable of editing data input and stored previously in the data-base and using the descriptors for displaying the data.

5) How can correlation be performed with a raster (CRT) TV
   display system using (a) a light pen, (b) a joystick controlled cursor?

6) How might one store, transform and interact with raster
   data, such as areas, symbols, surfaces etc? How can the
   techniques be added to those for vector and text graphics?

7) Can graphical operations be mapped into queries in a query
   language to cause interactions with graphical data stored
   in a graphical data-base?

8) How does one represent and maintain interrelationships
   among relations in relational data-base? For example,
   how can geometric constraints be handled?

   The authors are interested in corresponding with people
   working in areas represented by "exercises" 6, 7 and 8.

REFERENCES

1. Williams, R., "A Survey of Data Structures for Computer Graphics Systems," *ACM Computing Surveys*, Vol. 3, No. 1, March 1971, pp. 1-21. First part of chapter in this book.

2. Sutherland, I. W., "Sketchpad: A Man-Machine Graphical Communication System," *Proc. SJCC 1963*, Vol. 23, AFIPS 1963, pp. 329-346.

3. Hagan, T. G., Nixon, R. J., and Schaeffer, L. J., "The Adage Graphics Terminal," *Proc. FJCC 1968*, Vol. 33, Pt. 1, AFIPS 1968, pp. 179-191.

4. Sutherland, I. E., "Hardware and Software," Final Report - Special Conference on Computer Graphics as related to Engineering Design, Vol. 2, Contact Sami Al Bana, Columbia University, New York or L. J. Feeser, Rensselaer Polytechnic Institute, Troy, New York or the National Science Foundation, July 1973.

5. Williams, R., "On the Application of Relational Data Structures in Computer Graphics," *Proc. of IFIP Congress 1974*, Stockholm, Sweden, pp. 722-726. Second part of chapter in this book.

6. Williams, R., "A Systematic Method for the Creation of Data Structures in Computer Graphics Applications," Technical Report No. 403-19, New York University, April 1971.

7. Kunii, T. L., Weyl, S., and Tenenbaum, J. M., " A Relational Data Base Schema for Describing Complex Pictures with Color and Texture," *Proc. of the Second Joint Conference on Pattern Recognition*, Lyngby, Copenhagen, Denmark, August 1974.

8. Carlson, E. D., Bennett, J. L., Giddings, G. M. and Mantey, P. E., "The Design and Evaluation of an Interactive Geo-Data Analysis and Display System," IFIP 1974, North-Holland Publishing Company, pp. 1057-1061.

Some Observations on Linguistics
for Scene Analysis

T. KASVAND

Computer Graphics Section
Radio and Electrical Engineering
National Research Council of Canada
Ottawa, Ontario
K1A OR8 CANADA

ABSTRACT

Despite the numerous linguistic and syntactic procedures
proposed for scene analysis, the features in terms of which a
real scene can be modelled have not been defined in a comprehensive manner. In the processing of the image of a real scene a
profusion of features are obtained. A large percentage of these
are extraneous while some critical ones used in the linguistic
description will be missing. To find a predefined combination
of features from such a collection, even on a probabilistic
basis, results in a combinatorial explosion.

Yet, in the literature on psychology of vision, on the
effects of brain damage, on how to draw pictures, etc., there
is a wealth of hints on how "biological systems" appear to solve
the scene analysis problem. To biological systems scene analysis "comes naturally"; one is not even aware that the problem
exists. Some observational results will be compared with computational procedures.

INTRODUCTION

Pattern recognition, scene analysis and numerous activities
of this type can be compared with our own innate abilities.
Frequently the results of such comparisons are devastating to

the computational procedures. This is especially true in pattern recognition if the scene has any complexity at all. The procedures which are successful in very simplified and specific cases cannot be generalized and still remain practical. The linguistic procedures, on which our hopes are pinned, quote equal or even simpler recognition problems as examples of applicability.

The pattern recognition and scene analysis problem is further confused by our own superbly developed ability to abstract the significant descriptors of a scene and to elaborate on them in terms of our stored knowledge and "built-in" instinctive reactions. The well-drawn caricature of a face, for example, is only in remote (mathematical) correspondence with a photograph of the same face. The line drawing is one end result of our analysis of a scene; it is an abstraction. A mechanical procedure, which is based on "perfect" line drawing as a starting point, will experience difficulties with the real scene, and may be in trouble even with a "non-perfect" line drawing where some lines do not connect, some are missing, etc.

Biological systems always start their analysis with the real scene. The line drawing is only a pleasant diversion. This paper is trying to point out that the "biologically derived" solutions to these problems are not entirely unknown. In fact, an enormous amount of observational experimental data is available. There is a wealth of thought-provoking material in the fields of neurology, psychology, electrophysiology, etc. Even though their findings are extremely interesting and appear very pertinent to, for example, the problem of constructing a picture language, the ideas cannot, unfortunately, be captured as yet as simple algorithms. The author claims no special expertise in these fields except for having taken some courses, read numerous articles and books and having attempted to summarize these findings during lectures to students. To quote from Knowing and Guessing by Dr. S. Watanabe:

> "Yet an amateur has a fresh sense of 'amazement', a balanced bird's-eye view of tremendous scope, and a direct contact with the world of common sense which is the mother earth of all knowledge."

ALGORITHMS VS. BIOLOGICAL SOLUTION
TO THE PATTERN RECOGNITION PROBLEM

The solution of the scene analysis and pattern recognition problem is so natural to us that it does not even appear as a problem until we try to solve a similar problem with a computer. One reason for studying the "biological solution method" is thus obvious: there is a procedure to be discovered that actually works. The other, and much more important reason is that the algorithmic (computerized) solution will have to give similar results on the same problem as the biological one. How else are we to agree with our machines as to what a particular object is or what a scene depicts.

The human, and presumably animal, information processing systems, however, have evolved to facilitate survival and orientation in space. They supply quick answers to questions of the type: What might it be? What is it doing? These systems form hypotheses and make decisions based usually on very sparse evidence. They do not represent the world "as it really is" etc. [1].

We are trying to interpret a scene by mechanized means while at the same time the success of the interpretation is judged in terms of our own perception of it. Our opinion as to what a scene represents is the standard to which the algorithmic solution will have to conform. This constraint, of course, does not apply in situations where our own innate capabilities are insufficient (for example in image enhancement). It is amusing to observe that in such areas algorithmic procedures have made considerable advances, while in the pattern recognition area similar amounts of computational effort have produced scarcely anything.

THE "TWO WORLDS" OF PATTERN RECOGNITION

The "biological pattern recognition systems" have two eyes and are mobile. The computerized approach to scene analysis in most cases is to use a single gray level photograph or a TV image of the 3D scene. The data are further coarsened by a scanning (digitation) procedure before the analysis can be started, owing partly to computer architecture and our customary programming practices. In this process a large part of the information available to the biological system is lost.

Table 1

Cues to Depth [10]

Perspectives of position: (The observer is stationary, effect visible with one eye):

1. Texture perspective. (Texture gradient)
2. Size perspective (Object size vs. distance)
3. Linear perspective ("Parallel lines meet at infinity")

Perspectives of parallax:

4. Binocular perspective. (The skew of the image in one eye with respect to that in the other, stationary observer)
5. Motion perspective. (The change in binocular perspective when eyes are moved and the change in relative displacements of objects due to moving observer). Several aspects of the motion perspective are also observable by the moving one-eyed observer.

Perspectives independent of observer's motion or position:

6. Aerial perspective. (The haziness, blueness and desaturation of colours as a function of distance.)
7. The perspective of blur. (Variation in the quality of blur as a function of displacement from the center of clear vision.)
8. Relative upward location in the visual field. (The angular extent of background between the lower margin of the visual field and the object.)

"Depth at a contour"

9. Shift of texture density or linear spacing. (Sudden change of texture or texture gradient.)

10. Shift in the amount of double imagery. (Sudden change in the skew of texture over distance.)
11. Shift in the rate of motion. (Change in the displacement of texture elements on one side of a contour with respect to the other due to motion of the head.)

Table 1

Cues to Depth (continued)

Depth due to object shape:

12. Completeness or continuity of outline. (Complete
     objects appear closer)

Depth effects due to lighting:

13. Transition between light and shade.

Just as an example, Table 1 give 13 cues to depth perception.
The effects due to motion of the observer and the correlation
of the images in the two eyes figure prominently. A similar
situation exists on the "feature detector" (retinal field) level
[2]. Many of the feature detectors react to change in space
and time. The formulation of algorithms for detection of these
"missing" features does not appear to be very difficult, given
suitable sets of pictures. These problems, however, do not
appear to have been studied very intensively except in the case
of gray level gradients, contour followers, and edge [30, 31]
detectors. In general, however, the profusion of results obtained from these operations will need to be organized into
larger and more meaningful groups before a linguistic procedure
is attempted. There is rather interesting evidence available
on how the elementary features are combined into larger units
in the biological systems. (See Appendix A)

In computerized procedures each processing step is normally
carried to completion over the entire picture before the next
computing step is started. Even though selective processing
reduces the computational load significantly [32, 33, 34], biological systems use more elegant strategies. The procedures
according to which the biological system samples a scene may be
inferred from the studies of eye motion, but unfortunately much
pertinent information which computer programming requires is
still lacking. (See Appendix B).

The evidence on how or whether a biological system actually segments a scene needs qualifications as to what is meant by segmentation. If segmentation is to mean separation of a scene into meaningful objects, then there is a definite possibility that scene segmentation in the biological system is obtained after the analysis has been completed. However, segmentation on local feature level exists since, for example, moving and flickering "things" catch our attention immediately. The evidence in appendices A and B may also be viewed as segmentation of a scene. For further details see subsequent sections.

The, to linguists, most interesting aspect of the human information processing system concerns the existence of a picture language. There are hints that such a language exists. The clearest indications of its nature are obtained from studies on damaged systems where various aspects of the information processing strategy have failed. (See Appendix C)

The author is well aware of the dangers in trying to interpret such findings as hints to the nature of the underlying algorithms. In electrical engineering terms, the human information processing system is a very complicated "black box" with large memory. The inputs to this black box are to a degree controllable by the experimental setup: some output is measured, but one has no reliable control over the contributions to the output which came from memory.

THE PROBLEM

On the assumption that identification or recognition requires some form of prior knowledge in terms of which the unknown input (object, scene) is to be interpreted, one encounters in the general case a rather basic paradox. To identify an as yet unknown object in an unknown scene, the object will have to be extracted, described and compared with previously stored (known) descriptions. The unknown object, however, cannot be extracted before its identity is known. This fundamental difficulty is further complicated by the lack of exact match between objects which are classified as identical. The fine detail in particular may differ totally between the so-called identical objects.

This paradox can be sidestepped in numerous ways in particular situations. If the objects are distinct from the background, known to be non-touching and unbroken, contour following is often used. In case of touching or partially overlapping nontextured objects, object dependent algorithms are used (i.e., specific to the particular case). In the general case, however, where the picture represents an arbitrarily complex 3D scene, the paradox seems to be the major stumbling block to further advance. Yet our own visual system is able to handle this case without any apparent difficulty whatsoever! Possibly because of this apparent simplicity, in articles on picture languages, in linguistic and syntactic methods, etc., the problem is assigned to the area of "preprocessing", called a low-level problem, and the assumption is made that whatever the linguistic approach needs as "primitives" will be made available by some (simple) algorithm [3].

MORE ON THE PROBLEM

The scene analysis problem may be divided into two not entirely disjoint problems by asking:

1. How should a scene be segmented (fragmented)?
2. How should the fragments be described such that
    comparison operations with known data (recognition)
    can be carried out?

The answer to the second question is relatively simple, at least in principle. Table 2 lists the more obvious changes that an object in (or a segment of) a scene can undergo. It is clear that a procedure (such as mask matching) which requires a search through the entire variability space is totally impractical. The alternative is to arrange the form of the fragment description and to use parameters (features, primitives) that go into the description such that the description becomes:

a) invariant with respect to the entries in Table 2.
    If this fails for all or some of the table entries,
    then it should be
b) separable, i.e., the effect of each variability
    dimension should be decoupled. This allows a search
    only along the particular variability-axis, rather
    than through the entire space.

If neither of these conditions on the fragment description can be satisfied, the description is useless in a general case. To repeat, the primitives as well as the form of the fragment

description have to be normalizable before any comparison operation is attempted. One such example for a 2D case involving
table entries 1 to 7 is briefly described elsewhere [4].

Table 2

Variability Dimensions

		Number of Search Dimensions	
Type of Variability		2D case	3D case
1. Number of objects		n	n
2. Position in space (translation)		2	3
3. Rotation in space		1	3*
4. Size		1	1
5. Distortion (of shape)		?	?
6. Partial view (objects obscure each other)		$(n-1)^{n**}$	$(n-1)^{n**}$
7. Gray level		1	1
8. Texture		?	?
9. Color		3	3
10. Object flexibility (the relation between parts of a flexible or jointed object)		?	?
11. "Noise" (variability in smaller details, poor illumination in parts, etc.)		?	?

*6 faces minimum
**For fixed overlap between any two objects

The above conditions based on the segment descriptions assume that segments are individually recognizable and that they will have to be recognized. Under this assumption an object is an organized collection of segments. Such "atomic theory" (segment=atom) of pattern recognition was found in actual experiments to have limitations (see Appendix D). In these experiments the fragments ("atoms") were extracted by an algorithmic procedure without any reference to the object to which they were finally considered to belong. Such an "open-loop" procedure failed if the picture contained considerable amounts of detail.

The trivial answer to the first question, i.e., how should a scene be segmented is that the scene should be segmented into meaningful objects. (Background may also be considered to be an "object".) Such an answer requires the world to consist of uniquely definable objects, classes of objects, etc. This may also be a post-analysis abstraction derived from the need to describe the objects with a very large but still finite vocabulary.

The visual system seems to be entirely pragmatic in its approach to scene segmentation and analysis. It may be stated as follows:

a) Parts of the scene that can be **segmented** without recognition (i.e., on the feature level) are so segmented.
b) Prior knowledge is applied to analyze (segment?) the scene such that the needed information is abstracted with a minimum of effort.
c) A superficial analysis is completed very rapidly, and without any apparent fixed strategy.

Detectors for absolute and relative motion, the depth cues derived from the correlation of signals from two eyes, and the motion of the observer relative to his surroundings (the scene) are of great help in (partial) segmentation of the scene without the need to recognize the segments. Further clues to how the human observer appears to "segment" a scene are found in the studies of eye motion. (See Appendix B) In short, a person samples the scene as a function of picture content and of the problem to which an answer is sought.

Additional evidence on "segmentation" may be found in the works of artists. They reduce a complex scene to a rather limited set of lines, color combinations and so on. The caricature or cartoon artist in particular, specializes in representing a scene in a minimal set of lines. In the majority of cases we are satisfied with these representations. The few lines drawn by the artist apparently closely approximate the information we extract during a superficial examination of the original scene.

In general, in view of the complexity of a realistic scene and the evidence mentioned above, it must be concluded that scene segmentation is not a one-step open-loop process. The segmentation will have to vary as a function of the various recognition stages.

SOME THOUGHTS ON SEGMENTATION, RECOGNITION AND A PICTURE LANGUAGE FOR SINGLE GRAY LEVEL PICTURES OF 3D SCENES

At the start the scene will be assumed to be totally unknown, i.e., no prior information of any kind is available regarding the contents of the scene. Under this assumption, the processing of the scene can only proceed in stages where the results of one calculation may indicate which calculations are expected to be appropriate in the second stage, etc. It may be of interest to note that the single gray level photograph of a 3D scene is the hardest to segment since as was mentioned before, many "simple" feature (motion, parallax and depth) detectors cannot be used.

A specific object can be assumed to be a unique combination of measurable spatial as well as temporal characteristics. However, in general it cannot be assumed that an object possesses measurable characteristics which are unique to this object alone and computable in the absence of any prior knowledge. Not even a class of objects, it seems, can be defined in terms of uniquely measurable characteristics without prior knowledge. The exceptions occur on the "simple" feature level, where a class may be defined as "anything moving", "all flickering things", "areas of given color", etc. The acquisition of "prior knowledge" is a part of the recognition problem. However, if the system can perturb (move, or move relative to) an object in a scene, or if the object moves, it can be "segmented out" as one unit, based on "elementary feature detectors".

Scene analysis resembles an investigation by a detective where, it is claimed, quickest progress is made by finding answers to the following questions:

1. What to look for?
2. How to look for it?
3. Where to look for it?

Even though these questions help, the following arguments are based on what is feasible to compute under given circumstances. Two approaches are proposed, one on the macro and the other on the micro level.

Step 1

The purpose of the first set of calculations is only to determine the general nature of the scene. Answers to questions of the following type are sought:

a) Is the picture representing a world of straight edges? ("Block world", office scene, etc.)
b) How are the details in the picture distributed? (If there are uniform areas, where are they? Which areas are full of detail? Etc.)
c) Is there periodicity to the data in the picture?
d) Where are the more pronounced contours?
e) Any areas of uniform texture?

The above list is only intended as an illustration of the nature of questions to which answers can be found without need to know what the scene represents.

The requirements placed on the first set of calculations and the expected results are at the moment rather speculative due to lack of adequate experimental data. A properly selected "portfolio of scenes" and a judicious application of known algorithms should clarify the situation.

Given a scanned gray level scene $f(x,y)$ normally two kinds of operators are applied, the local operators (L) and the global operators (G). These operators retain the positional relationships between the picture elements. The third type of operator (H) reduces the dimensionality of the data but scrambles the positional relationships (Ex. L = Laplacian, G = Fourier transform, H = histogramming.) Since there are many other types of transformations, mappings, etc., the remainder will be labelled X.

Some Examples of Preliminary Computations:

1. $H_1(f(x,y))$: The ordinary (one-dimensional) gray level histogram is adequate for determining the range of significant gray levels and for scaling of parameters in subsequent calculations. If marked peaks or valleys in the histogram exist,

gray level-based segmentation may be tried [23].

2a. $H_1(L_1(f(x,y)))$, where L_1 = variation of the angular direction of the spatial gradient. The operator L_1 measures rapidly changing detail. Consequently, the high end of the histogram represents areas with much detail while the low end gives the uniform areas [5].

  b. L_2L_1f, where L_2 represents the local extremum (maximum) detector. The resultant maxima pinpoint the areas of greatly changing detail [5].

3. Lf, L = various textural features [6, 22].

4. $H_n(L_1f, L_2f, \ldots L_nf)$: An n-dimensional histogram, where the axes are $L_i(f(x,y))$, resembles a decision space. The classical techniques of decision-space manipulation apply. Some preliminary experiments on H_3 have produced interesting results, but as usual, the problem occurs in the selection of the measurements (i.e., "features" or L_if).

5. $L(f,f^*)$ where f = light intensity, f^* = color, $L(f,f^*)$ = distance in the (f,f^*) space between neighboring xy points [7].

6. LGf: local extrema of the magnitude values of the Fourier transform.

7. LGf': f' = specially illuminated scene, G = Fourier transform, L = local extrema of the energy vs. angle spectrum of $/Gf'/$ [8].

8. L_2XL_1f: L_1 = contour or edge detector, X = Hough transform, L_2 = local extrema [9].

In summary, a considerable amount of information can and should be extracted from the scene prior to recognition of specific objects. The scene can be segmented according to the nature of the information obtained from such calculations. However, the information derived and the resulting segmentation is in general not specific to any particular object in the scene, even though a classification of scene segments is now feasible.

Step 2

On the micro or local level in the scene a profusion of "features" are available from the local operations (Lf or LGf). To increase the confusion further, the operations in Step 1 may be applied to the segments, more specific algorithms based on the results of Step 1 may be used, etc. The multiplicity of results is further augmented by the "variability dimensions" (Table 2).

The biological systems have, of course, encountered this problem and rather than trying to form all the possible combinations of features, they have evolved a set of organization rules (see Appendix A). These rules operate on "extended-local" or "semiglobal" level, compete among each other and are overruled by any combination of features that makes up a meaningful object. In psychology literature these organization rules go under the names of "good continuation", "grouping by proximity and similarity", etc. Computer simulations of these "rules" do not seem to have been done, except possibly in following a contour or line which contains gaps.

Computer-manipulable representations of the "organized results" will, of course, have to be constructed such that as many of the variations (Table 2) as possible will be eliminated. The required mappings and transformations, however, are rather speculative at the moment [24].

COMMENT

The computations for "global features" (Step 1) do not interfere with the attempts to organize the features on the local level (Step 2). Both are necessary. However, the results of these calculations are too numerous and there are too many methods. These procedures will have to be guided by a picture language as soon as the first hypothesis can be formulated as to what an area in a scene might represent. The picture language will have to use primitives that are computable from a scene

  a) in the absence of prior information and
  b) in the presence of hypotheses provided by
      the language.

The picture language must be able to guide the search by providing tentative answers to the three questions: What to look for? How to look for it? and Where to look for it?

The rather general procedures described in the present article and the more detailed comparisons between human and computer vision [26] are essentially pointing out that a realistic picture language should try to employ the principles found in biological information processing systems. At present only specific instances of the operation of these principles are observed, some of which have been described in the present paper. The situation is similar to trying to elucidate the laws of aerodynamics by observing birds in flight. Furthermore, it is to be expected that biological information processing procedures are greatly influenced by the nature of the underlying "hardware" which is so different from the conventional computer hardware. Even if equipment for parallel processing were easily available, there still may exist many fundamental differences between biological and mechanical computing procedures [35].

CONCLUSIONS

The enormous amount of information available on "biological pattern recognition systems" has some relevance to computerized procedures. The few parallels drawn in this paper are tentative. The only real need to study biosystems is to make sure that computer interpretation of, for example, a scene agree with our own understanding of it. However, it is also interesting to know what the research and development on biological systems (evolution) has achieved in the past 10^9 years.

RESEARCH PROBLEMS

The motive for the present article has been the hope that the problem areas mentioned, and many that have been left out, will induce researchers trained in computer science to study such fields in terms of computational feasibility while not leaving themselves too open to criticism. Huge quantities of observational and experimental results are available in other fields which have direct bearing on the problems of pattern recognition, artificial intelligence, etc. The material, however, is descriptive, its terms and definitions lack the mathematical paraphernalia familiar to us, but the ideas are often far more advanced than what one normally encounters in, for example, pattern recognition literature.

Problem Areas Unrelated to Biology

a) How complex is our 3D world, i.e., can the "variability dimensions" (Table 2) be defined and subdivided in a logical manner?

b) What is computable from a scene in the absence of prior information, i.e., what can one expect from the so-called "preliminary computations"?

c) Can our 3D world be categorized in terms of results from (a) and (b)?

d) Which micro or local-level results allow normalization in the context of (a)?

e) In the context of results from (b) and (c), can the local-level results (d) be organized into "larger packages" which can serve as "features" for a linguistic procedure?

f) Could a "portfolio" of typical scenes be assembled?

Problem Areas Based on Findings in Fields not Traditionally Related to Computer Science or Engineering

1) To summarize the results from a variety of fields in a language comprehensible to researchers in computer science.

   a) What are the types of "local feature detectors" for given species?
   b) The cues to depth, can they be defined and programmed?
   c) The Gestalt laws, can they be arranged hierarchically and programmed?
   d) Can the results of eye motion studies be related to the information content and processing strategy? (Additional questions are in Appendix B).
   e) How are the effects of brain damage related to breakdown in information processing strategies?
   f) Can the stages in the development of structure in children's drawings be represented in "linguistic" terms? [36]

2) To construct and simulate models of the phenomena observed
    in biological information processing systems.

    a) Simulate the "local feature detectors". If the
        results appear "pleasing or artistic" it is likely
        that much of the relevant information is retained
        in the result [37].
    b) Simulate the Gestalt laws.
    c) Simulate eye motion, i.e., can an algorithm
        locate the same areas in the picture as are
        found in eye motion [5].
    d) Measure the information content of a scene as
        a function of observation time.

3) Arrange cooperative programs with experts in the various
    fields.

APPENDIX A: FEATURE COMBINATIONS

    The results from various local feature detectors (called
elements) will have to be combined into larger units, such as
parts of or even complete objects. In a general case, the
number of elements is very large, all the expected elements will
not be present while there are many extraneous ones. To try all
the possible combinations becomes impossible in practice.

The Laws of Organization

    Biological information processing systems seem to try to
avoid this problem by having evolved a set of processing strategies according to which individual feature elements are to be
combined. Such a procedure naturally reduces the number of
possible combinations that need to be compared against some
model (i.e., related to previous knowledge). Even though the
experiments from which the underlying procedures (laws) have
been elucidated have been done on simple figures, presumably
they carry over into scene analysis. The various laws seem
to compete with each other for predominance and are overridden
by the combination of elements which forms a recognizable object. Unfortunately the texts on these topics are very frustra-
ting to read, being mostly concerned with disproofs of opposing
theories, rather than reporting of experimental observations.

Some Examples of These Laws [1, 11, 12, 25]

1. Grouping by similarity. (Objects which look similar tend
    to be grouped together, Figure A1)

2. Grouping by proximity. (Close objects of approximately
    similar size but differing shape are grouped together,
    Figure A2)

3. Principle of good continuation. (A line or contour which
    has been cut (interrupted) is seen as a whole if the pieces
    form a smooth curve, Figure A3)

4. The law of closure. ("Closed objects are whole", Figure A4)

5. Many other laws are discussed in the texts on Gestalt
    psychology [12, 25].

The interaction between these laws is illustrated in
Figures A5 to A9. An amusing example of how a model impresses
organization onto even a few lines, or that conclusions are
based on very sparse evidence, is given in Figure A10.

Stabilized Images [13, 14]

During a fixation when one is under the impression that
eyes are stationary, our eyes actually are in rapid small-ampli-
tude motion. If, however, the image on the retina is stabilized
(i.e., made stationary) it has been found that the object being
observed falls apart into fragments or the object is segmented.
Only certain fragments are seen in a given instant of time, the
remainder of the figure having vanished. The picture becomes
very dynamic where in one instant a certain fragment combination
is seen, a different combination of fragments is seen in the
next instant, etc., only one combination being visible at any
instant of time. The recombination of fragments is topologically
correct, corresponding to the arrangement of fragments in the
original object. Whether these experiments indicate that frag-
ment-combinations are being formed before recognition is not
clear from the data.

Figures A1 to A10:   Some examples of the "laws of organization".
[1, 12, 25]

Figure A1:   Grouping by similarity. Columns of x-s and o-s may
be seen more easily than rows of xoxoxo.

Figure A2:   Grouping by proximity. Three columns of xo-s may
be seen more easily than other combinations.

Figure A3:   Principle of good continuation. Two crossing smooth
curves may be seen more easily than two v-shaped
curves joined at apices.

Figure A4:   Law of closure. Closed contours or "complete objects" appear as "wholes".

Figure A5:   Cooperation and conflict between grouping by similarity and proximity.

Figure A6:   Law of closure overrides grouping by proximity and
similarity.

Figure A7:   Law of closure overrides the principle of good continuation.

Figure A8:   Proper (b,c) and improper (d) methods of camouflag-
ing an object (a). Use of grouping, continuation
and closure laws to hide the original object.
"Principle of camouflage".

Figure A9:   Examples of camouflage:
a)   combination of script I and L,
b)   combination of script I and L,
c)   combination of b and q,
d)   combination of many p-s and q-s,
e)   combination of script 3, 4, E, S,
f)   what is the next term in this series?

Figure A10: Organization impressed by meaning:
a)   A soldier and his dog passing by a hole
in a picket fence.
b)   A washerwoman cleaning the floor.

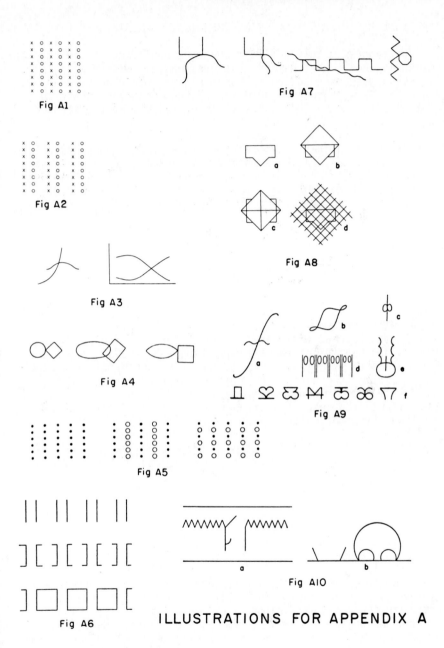

Fig A1

Fig A2

Fig A3

Fig A4

Fig A5

Fig A6

Fig A7

Fig A8

Fig A9

Fig A10

ILLUSTRATIONS FOR APPENDIX A

APPENDIX B: EYE MOTION DURING OBSERVATION OF PICTURES [15, 16,17]

For approximately the last 50 years equipment has existed for measuring how a person moves his eyes while studying a picture. It is assumed that the points on a picture where an observer focuses his eyes and the duration of that observation are related to the mental processes in identifying what the scene depicts.

It is found that the observer neither scans the picture like a TV camera, nor does he sample it at random. Rather, the sampling process is driven by picture content as well as the question to which an answer is sought in the picture, Figure B1. Areas which are not related to the problem at hand are practically ignored. The overall behaviour is what one would expect from a well-designed information retrieval system. No two persons' eye motions are exactly the same when observing the same picture, Figure B2, nor does a person, when tested on the same picture after intervals of time follow exactly the same eye motion pattern, Figure B3. However, there are interesting overall similarities [29]. Within any one experiment, an area of high interest is not inspected until exhausted of information, after which the next area is chosen; but rather, the attention alternates between the areas of high interest, with occasional excursions outside of these areas, Figure B4. Blank areas are seldom looked at. In pictures where there are no clear centers of interest, the observation sequence appears rather random. Crude attempts at contour following are apparent in some cases, but even in the case of written text the line of text is not followed systematically.

Overall statistics for many observers and many pictures are shown in the following table [15]. The pictures were divided into 16 rectangular areas, each table entry giving the percent of fixations in the corresponding area of the picture.

1.8	7.6	10.3	3.1
3.8	12.9	13.3	3.7
2.7	10.7	10.1	4.8
1.6	4.9	5.9	2.8

From the point of view of computerized analysis, these experiments have left many questions unanswered. In order to minimize the influence of subjects' memory, the pictures should be unknown to the observer, i.e., only presented once. This requirement is not mentioned by the experimenters. Some of the questions are:

a) What is the size of the area in the picture covered by one observation? It is conceivable that the observation of the motion of two eyes will indicate that the subject is not focusing onto the picture plane when attempting to get an overall impression of the scene.

b) How does the observer build up his impression of the scene, i.e., is there a sequence to the process, say from gross features to fine detail?

c) Are the areas with high information content examined first? Is the observation time proportional to information content in the area, etc.?

With computer displays it should be easy to frustrate the observer in many ways, for example by allowing him to observe an area only once, twice, etc. This might reveal whether new information is extracted at each observation of the same area.

Figures B1 to B4: Some examples of eye motion during observation of pictures [15, 16]

Figure B1: Eye movement dependence on the information to be extracted from the picture in the upper left corner during a 3 minute observation:

    1. free observation (no instruction)
    2. "Tell me, is the family poor or wealthy?"
    3. "How old are the people in the picture?"
    4. "What were they doing before the man entered the room?"
    5. "Try to memorize the clothing the people are wearing."
    6. "Try to memorize the placement of the furniture."
    7. "How long had the man been away from his family?"

Figure B2: Eye movement of 7 different observers.

Figure B3: Eye movements of the same observer at intervals of a few days.

Figure B4: The alteration of eye motion between areas of high interest. The fixation points are numbered, 1 being the first, 2 the second, etc. Observation times per fixation point are given below.

a) the original picture
b) example of eye motion of a subject
c) example of eye motion of another subject

Observation times per fixation point, (given as point number and observation time in 1/30th of a second).

Figure B4.b

1-15	10-7	19-40	28-12	37-10	46-6	55-43
2-4	11-18	20-5	29-2	38-7	47-6	56-7
3-6	12-5	21-21	30-5	39-5	48-5	57-8
4-5	13-9	22-6	51-18	40-4	49-5	58-20
5-12	14-11	23-11	52-6	41-4	50-31	59-5
6-5	15-5	24-5	33-5	42-16	51-6	60-4
7-6	16-7	25-6	34-6	43-7	52-6	61-6
8-16	17-12	26-26	35-16	44-6	53-4	62-27
9-5	18-4	27-9	36-16	45-5	54-6	63-9

Figure B4.c

1-5	11-9	21-9	31-10	41-8	51-25
2-4	12-5	22-6	32-4	42-6	52-10
3-19	13-8	23-11	33-11	43-5	53-8
4-5	14-7	24-6	34-7	44-22	54-8
5-6	15-5	25-7	35-11	45-8	55-31
6-7	16-6	26-6	36-8	46-11	56-18
7-7	17-12	27-6	37-6	47-6	57-11
8-8	18-6	28-7	38-6	48-6	58-9
9-6	19-6	29-9	39-8	49-6	
10-8	20-6	30-7	40-9	50-18	

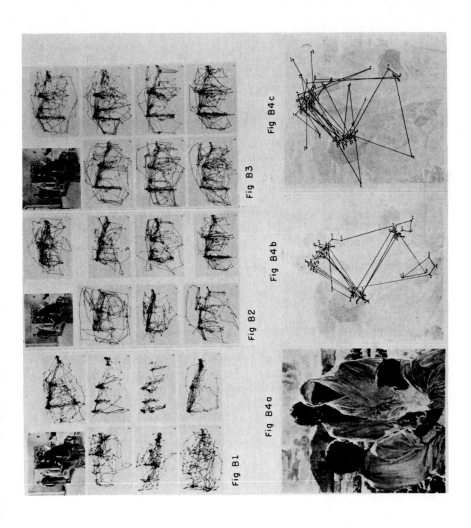

Fig B1

Fig B2

Fig B3

Fig B4a

Fig B4b

Fig B4c

APPENDIX C: EFFECTS OF BRAIN DAMAGE AND INCOMPLETE DEVELOPMENT [18, 19, 20]

The brain operates as a unit. Consequently damage to any of its parts may cause extremely varied disturbances in visual perception. This form of blindness is called "mental blindness" since the picture processing strategies disintegrate to some degree. The observed phenomena are very suggestive of a "picture language" which is failing in various ways. Most of the observed failures in perception are tantalizingly easy to interpret as, for example, a missing feature detector, a transformation not carried out, an incorrect classification, a forgotten positional relationship, analysis terminated too early, etc. On the assumption that such "algorithmic" interpretations are meaningful, the observed failures may be viewed as confirmations that the operational procedures used by the visual system are well within our computational knowhow. The observed phenomena, however, do not reveal how the now failing operations were used by the intact visual system.

The following examples are meant as illustrations:

Missing feature detector [20, 27, 28]

The well-known Hubel-Wiesel type feature detectors [21] seem to be developed as a response to environmental stimuli. Thus cats brought up in a world of vertical stripes did not possess horizontal line detectors and apparently did not see horizontal edges, since they refused to jump on top of chairs, but had no difficulties avoiding the legs of the chairs. Cats brought up in a world of horizontal stripes jumped onto chairs but did not appear to see the legs of the chairs since they kept running into them. Cats brought up in a world of dots only, had only dot detectors, something they do not have when brought up in normal environments. Persons who have been born blind due to nontransparent lenses in their eyes, do not learn to see properly if the nontransparent lenses are replaced later in life [19].

Loss of a "transform" [18]

In some cases of damage the significance of the angular orientation of, for example a letter, is either not understood or not seen. Thus M is confused with W, d with p, etc. A mirror image of a letter is confused with the letter itself (s = ƨ), etc.

Loss of interrelationship between parts of an object [18]

The effect of this type of damage is best noticed if the person is asked to draw something from memory or to finish an incomplete drawing. Thus, when asked to draw a picture of a man, he is unable to put the eyes, nose, arms, etc., in their correct positions.

Loss of some object parts [18]

In some cases of damage, for example, everything to the left of an object is forgotten.

Loss of object representation and superabstraction [18]

In certain cases, the person is unable to reproduce even the simplest drawing from memory or the drawing bears no resemblance to the desired object.

Loss of object classes

In some cases of damage the person may lose the ability to recognize objects belonging to certain object classes. In a rare case, a person lost the ability to recognize all animate objects, while the recognition of inanimate objects was intact.

Incomplete analysis of a scene [18]

The analysis process may fail in a variety of ways. One may jump to conclusions as to what a picture represents based on just a few or a single "feature". A pair of glasses may be called a bicycle because the round rims resemble the round wheels. The eye motion (fixation pattern) when observing a picture is erratic, i.e., not goal orientated and not related to the information to be extracted from the picture. Drawings obscured by extraneous lines cause great difficulties.

APPENDIX D: A SIMPLIFIED PICTURE LANGUAGE [4]

A rather simple picture language for two dimensional, monochromatic objects was formulated, programmed and tested experimentally. It illustrates how the first 7 variability-dimensions (Table 2) were handled. The language was based on the following premises:

a) Select local features (point features) which require no
    knowledge about picture content, in terms of which the
    objects can be described and for which a normalization
    procedure exists. These are, of course, spatial gray
    level gradients, contours, curvatures of contours, etc.

b) Fragment or segment the unknown objects (if complicated)
    such that reasonably coherent descriptions of the segments
    (atoms) can be obtained prior to any knowledge about the
    objects. The algorithm used the point features to pinpoint
    the atoms. (Translation problem eliminated.)

c) Form an atom description which can be normalized before
    knowing what it represents. A polar coordinate representa-
    tion of the atom allowed normalization for size and rotation.
    Since the as yet unknown atom is now described, its gray
    level is known.

d) Recognition of an atom is a comparison operation where the
    description of the unknown atom is compared with a list of
    known atoms and the best match is selected. The numerical
    value of this match is a measure of distortion.

e) A (complicated) object is a spatially organized collection
    of atoms. It may suffice to identify one atom only, if no
    ambiguity results (partial view).

The atoms were selected only by the computer (algorithm). The
online operator informed the machine which atoms belonged together to form a complex object. The spatial interrelationships
were computed automatically since the necessary data was available.

Besides numerous shortcomings the language behaved fairly
well. In retrospect, however, the greatest conceptual difficulty occurred in assigning atom priorities or in trying to
define which atoms were important in a given complex object.
The atom areas (segments) into which a complex object was fragmented were essentially mutually exclusive. The program had no
ability to disregard (i.e., not "see") elements in the picture
during the segmentation procedure. The problem is best illustrated with a very simple example: If the object is a circle with
a bar in it (like the letter θ) one could describe it as upper
semicircle ⋆ lower semicircle⋆bar, or circle=upper semicircle⋆
lower semicircle, object=circle⋆bar. An unrelated line through
this object (∅) ruins the description since the semicircles are
split into sectors. Basic difficulties arose due to irrelevant
details in a complex object.

REFERENCES

1. Kolers, P. A., *Some Psychological Aspects of Pattern Recognition, Recognizing Patterns*, The MIT Press, Koler, P.A. and M. Eden (eds.), 1968.

2. Dodwell, P.C., *Visual Pattern Recognition*, Rinehart and Winston, Inc., 1970.

3. Fu, K. A., *Syntactic Methods in Pattern Recognition*, Academic Press, 1974.

4. Kasvand, T., "Experiments With an Online Picture Language," *Frontiers of Pattern Recognition*, S. Watanabe (ed.), Academic Press, 1972.

5. Kasvand, T., "Segmentation of Single Gray-Level Pictures of General 3D Scenes," *Second International Joint Conference on Pattern Recognition*, August, 1974, pp. 372-373.

6. Haralick, R. M., et. al., "Textural Features for Image Classification, *IEEE Trans.*, Vol. SMC-3, No. 6, November 1973, pp. 610-621.

7. Yakimovsky, Y., Scene Analysis Using a Semantic Base for Region Growing, Stanford AI Lab., Memo AIM-209, June 1973.

8. Will, P.M. and K.S. Pennington, "Grid Coding: A Preprocessing Technique for Robot and Machine Vision," *Second International Joint Conference on Artificial Intelligence*, London, September 1971.

9. Duda, R.O. and P. E. Hart, "Use of the Hough Transformation to Detect Lines and Curves in Pictures," *Comm. of ACM*, Vol. 15, No. 1, January 1972, pp. 11-15.

10. Gibson, J. J., *The Perception of the Visual World*, Houghton Mifflin Co., 1950.

11. Koffka, K., *Principles of Gestalt Psychology*, Harcourt, Brace and World, Inc., 1963.

12. Osgood, C. E., *Methods and Theory in Experimental Psychology*, Oxford University Press, 1953.

13. Vernon, M. D., *The Psychology of Perception*, Penguin Books, 1962.

14. Evans, C. R. and A. M. Wells, "Fragmentation Phenomena Associated with Binocular Stabilization, *The British Journal of Psychological Optics,* 24, 1967, pp. 45-50.

15. Buswell, G. T., *How to Look at Pictures,* University of Chicago Press, 1935.

16. Yarbus, A.L., *Eye Movements and Vision,* Plenum Press, 1967.

17. Kolers, P.A., *Reading Pictures, Picture Bandwidth Compression,* T.S. Huang and O.J. Tretiak (eds.), Gordon and Beach, 1972.

18. Luria, A. R., *Higher Cortical Functions in Man,* Basic Books Inc., 1966.

19. von Senden, M., *Space and Sight,* Methuen and Co., Ltd., 1960.

20. Lewin, R., "The Brain: New Light on Seeing and Perceiving," *British Science News,* No. 117/1974/Spectrum/8.

21. Hubel, D. H. and T. N. Wiesel, "Receptive Fields, Binocular Interaction and Functional Architecture in the Cat's Visual Cortex, *J. Physiology,* Vol. 160, 1962.

22. Zucker, S. W., On the Foundations of Texture, A Transformational Approach, University of Maryland, TR331, Sept., 1962.

23. Hummel, R. A., Histogram Modification Techniques, University of Maryland, TR329, September 1974.

24. Bajcsy, R., Computer Identification of Textured Visual Scenes, University Microfilms Ltd., Ann Arbor, Michigan, 1973.

25. Wertheimer, M., "Untersuchungen zur Lehre von der Gestalt," *Psychologische Forschung,* 4, 1923, pp. 301-350.

26. Price, K., "A Comparison of Human and Computer Vision Systems," *Sigart Newsletter,* No. 50, February, 1975, pp. 5-10.

27. Blakemore, C. and G. F. Cooper, "Development of the Brain Depends on the Visual Environment, *Nature,* Vol. 228, October 31, 1970.

28. Creutzfeld, O.D. and P. Heggelund, "Neural Plasticity in Visual Cortex of Adult Cats After Exposure to Visual Patterns, *Science*, Vol. 188, June 1975, pp. 1025-1027.

29. Srinivasan, M. V., et. al., "A Probabilistic Hypothesis for the Prediction of Visual Fixations, *IEEE*, *SMC*, Vol. 5, No. 4, July 1975, pp. 431-437.

30. Ramer, E. U., The Extraction of Edges from Photographs of Quadratic Bodies, Part 1, New York University, Dept. of Electrical Engineering and Computer Science, TR403-29, April 1973.

31. Smith, M. W., On the Detection of Edges in Pictures, M.A.Sc. Thesis, Department of Computer Science, University of Alberta, Edmonton, Alberta, Fall 1973.

32. Kelly, M.D., "Edge Detection in Pictures by Computer Using Planning, *Machine Intelligence*, 6, B. Meltzer and D. Michie (eds.), American Elsevier Publishing Co., 1971, pp. 397-409.

33. Tanimoto, S. L. and T. Pavlidis, A Hierarchical Data Structure for Picture Processing, Princeton University, Dept. of Electrical Engineering, TR151, August 1974.

34. Tanimoto, S. L., Pictorial Feature Distortion in a Pyramid, Princeton University, Dept. of Electrical Engineering, TR176, February 1975.

35. Gibson, J. J., *The Senses Considered as Perceptual Systems*, Houghton Mifflin Co., 1966.

36. Arnheim, R., *Art and Visual Perception*, University of California Press, 1954.

37. Kasvand, T., "Iterative Edge Detection," *Computer Graphics and Image Processing*, 4, 1975, pp. 279-286.

ADDITIONAL READING

Nicolaides, K., *The Natural Way to Draw*, Houghton Mifflin Co., 1941.

Baird, M. L. and M. D. Kelly, "A Paradigm for Semantic Picture Recognition," *Pattern Recognition*, Vol. 6, No. 1, June 1974, pp. 61-74.

Uhr, L., "Flexible Linguistic Pattern Recognition," *Pattern Recognition*, Vol. 3, No. 4, November 1971, pp. 363-383.

Levine, M. D., et. al., "Computer Determination of Depth Maps," *Computer Graphics and Image Processing*, 2, 1973, pp. 131-150.

Rosenfeld, A. and J. S. Weszka, Pattern Recognition, University of Maryland, TR344, December 1974.

L.S. Davis, A. Rosenfeld and S. W. Zucker, General Purpose Models: Expectations About the Unexpected, University of Maryland, TR347, January 1975.

Rosenfeld, A., Picture Processing: 1974, University of Maryland, TR346, January 1975.

Discussions on "Vision", *Sigart Newsletter*, No. 52, June 1975.

A. L. Zobrist and W. B. Thompson, "Building a Distance Function for Gestalt Grouping, *IEEE*, C-24, No. 7, July 1975, pp. 718-728.

Ellis, W. (ed.), *A Sourcebook of Gestalt Psychology*, London, England, 1938.

ACKNOWLEDGMENTS

The author would like to express his sincere thanks to the Computer Graphics Section of NRC and the following publishers in particular: Oxford University Press, MIT Press, Plenum Publishing Company, Springer-Verlag, and University of Chicago Press, for granting permission to reproduce the illustrations referred to in the text.

FIGURES:

Permission to reproduce the following figures has been granted by:

Figures A1, A2, A3, A8a-d, The MIT Press, P. A. Koler and M. Eden (eds.), see Ref. 1

Figures A6, A10a-b, The Oxford University Press, See Ref. 2

Figures A4, A5, A7, A9a-e, Springer-Verhlag, see Ref. 25

Figure 9f, Private communication - Mr. E. Soomati, Sweden

Figures B1, B2, B3, Plenum Press, see Ref. 16

Figure B4, a-c, University of Chicago Press, see Ref. 15

Based on "Some Observations on Linguistics for Scene Analysis," from the 1975 Proceedings of the Conference on Computer Graphics, Pattern Recognition and Data Structure (75 CH 0981-1C). Copyright 1975 by The Institute of Electrical and Electronics Engineers, Inc.

DESIGN
DECISIONS

Data Management and
Pattern Recognition

CARL V. PAGE
Computer Science Department
Michigan State University*
East Lansing, Michigan 48824

ABSTRACT

Criteria which facilitate the design of an automatic data manager for a large data base are proposed. A syntactic pattern definition language provides a set of subdefinitions which can be
preprocessed. A total expected cost graph for a pattern definition set is used to define preprocessed sets for various costs.
The problem of the design of a preprocessor or automatic data manager is related to the specification of an appropriate adaptive
system.

1. INTRODUCTION

This paper deals with a framework for a theory of what
should be saved after access to a large data base and subsequent
computation and what should be redone. As Sammet has pointed
out, this problem goes back to the days when the classical decision was made to compute rather than store trigonometric functions [13]. The problem area which the issue of whether to
save a computation for future reference or to do it over if

*Part of this work was supported by National Science Foundation
Grant DCR74-19019 ORD 14377.

needed again is of course most important if the computation is very expensive and likely to be needed again, perhaps by another user. Although there are many types of large data bases to which the ideas to be presented will apply, in this chapter we will emphasize for purposes of concreteness, data bases which possess the following properties:

(1)   A large volume of geographically organized data.

(2)   A large group of users, generally unsophisticated in the use of computers and scattered around the country and the world.

(3)   Many different reasons for the users to access the data which prevents the development of a few standard application programs which serve all users. An example of such a data base might be remote sensing data accumulated from earth satellites and used by the agencies of states in one region for such purposes as land use, highway planning, etc.

We will be primarily concerned with the strategy of repeated data access rather than the tactics of how individual files are organized. Although file organization is important, we will be concerned with delineating an environment of data access in which an automatic data manager can exist and gather information which can lead to improved system performance at a higher level.

2.   A BASIS FOR THEORETICAL STUDY

We will describe some necessary properties of systems which can efficiently access such large data bases. These properties will assist in formulation of theoretical problems. First, we observe that full advantage must be taken of regularities and duplication in the needs of the community of users of the data. To accomplish this end, communication to the system by the users should not be in a language close to data definition at the system level. The language used to define pattern accesses should be at a high enough level so that users understand each others definitions. In particular they ought to be able to recognize equivalent formulations of the same pattern class in the language. Thus by sharing definitions of patterns, the users would not request the same thing expressed differently due to the opaqueness of a lower level language.

Second, use of a high level language close to the application allows opportunities for data independence. Preprocessing of the bulk data should allow additions to the data without disrupting the user programs. Likewise, improvements in the quality of data should increase the reliability of the users' results without making obsolescent the preprocessor of the programs.

Last, advantage must be taken of the fact that the users will seldom require a dense search of the whole data--such a search may be done from time to time to serve the needs of many users and to update preprocessed files. The preprocessor, using pattern definitions expressed in the higher level language can distinguish between relatively static patterns and those which need to be updated frequently. The preprocessor should keep statistics on user activity and model their intent so that the preprocessed pattern data reflects user needs.

3. PROPERTIES OF A PATTERN DEFINITION LANGUAGE

In the last section we have seen the desirable side effects of providing a higher level language for pattern access definition. Our main purpose in this paper is to study some properties of preprocessors of such data. The preprocessor and pattern language are intimately connected. However specification of a detailed pattern definition language for our concrete example of geographically organized data is outside the scope of this paper. Hence we will describe general properties of such languages which seem sufficient to allow the design of preprocessors. The basic assumptions which will be made concerning the structure of the question or pattern definition language are as follows:

(1) Pattern searches are defined from predefined patterns using system provided relations and functions in a syntactic manner.

(2) Top down pattern recognition seems more appropriate than bottom up because noise can be dealt with more easily. (It is easier to see a zebra in the sahdows if you know you are looking for one than to group the shadows (bottom up) to discern the form of a zebra.) The pattern definitions control a top down algorithm for pattern recognition.

(3) Patterns are two dimensional and occupy a region of bounded size.

(4) Gross simplification or summaries of the original data (with geographic relationships preserved) will suffice for many pattern searches. Such summary data can restrict the extent of search if organized in a hierarchical manner and selected according to user needs.

Now that some general properties of language for definition of patterns which facilitate the design of a pattern file pre-processor have been considered, let us present an example pattern language.

4. AN EXAMPLE OF PATTERN DEFINITION LANGUAGE

Let us proceed with a detailed example to provide the flavor of what such a pattern definition language might be like. The example is supposed to be suggestive but in no way claims to be practical in any sense. Suppose a community of users includes two individuals, one of whom is interested in finding plan sites and the other who is interested in finding camp sites. Both define their requirements in a pattern definition language which is represented graphically in Figure 1. The notation is based on the AND/OR trees found in Nilsson [12]. A slight generalization is the representation of arbitrary relations holding between the edges such as "next to" and "near". (The actual meaning of these relations could depend on the user and be determined by the preprocessor in dialog with the user.) In Figure 1, for instance, we note that the class of "dry woods" is to be "near" "shoreline" and "next to" "transportation". Likewise a "shoreline" here consists only of either a "river shore" or a "lakeshore" and so on. The pattern definition language need not be graphical in its presentation but could consist of context free productions which describe the branches of the tree. For example, such a production is

<Shoreline>   ←   <Rivershore> or <Lakeshore>

Representation of the elements of the necessary classes such as <Shoreline> can be by any of several means. It is helpful to think of the class <Shoreline> to be a data structure consisting of all <Rivershore> and <Lakeshore> coordinates with pointers back to either <Rivershore> or <Lakeshore> for each set of coordinates. This would allow items of <Shoreline> which possessed some property at a higher level to be examined at a lower level for some property such as temperature, which can be computed at a lower level. And if users frequently request temperatures of shorelines, the temperature data could be conjoined to the shoreline data. In the

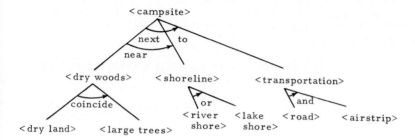

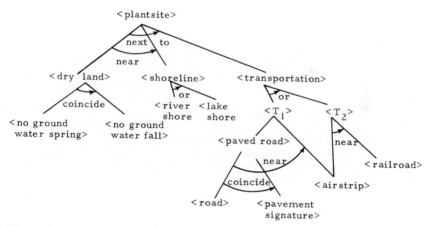

Figure 1.   Generalized and/or trees used to represent definitions of
<campsite> and <plantsite>. The pattern definition
language need not be graphical in its presentation but
might consist of BNF like productions which describe the
branches of the tree.

sections which follow, we make the simplifying assumption that whenever a pattern file is available, any subpatterns used to define it are available also, which has the same effect as combination of fields from different levels.

Definition 1: Any pattern class defined in the pattern definition language or pattern class combined with features available at lower levels in its definition will be called a data summary.

The task of preprocessing is to construct hierarchical data summaries relevant to user needs.

Definition 2: A pattern class will be called a subpattern or subcomputation of any node which is higher in some pattern definition tree.

Hence a data summary consists of a pattern and some of its subpatterns, depending on our viewpoint, a pattern will be identified with either its root node or the whole subtree which defines it.

5.   PREPROCESSING AND SELF-ORGANIZING DATA MANAGEMENT

A specific area, preprocessing of remote sensing data, has been emphasized as an example of a study which would have wider implications to large geographically organized data bases which must serve a variety of users. A preprocessor which possesses the properties which have been discussed is the key part of a self-organizing data management system. The pre-processor must organize and reorganize the hierarchical data summaries in a way which minimizes some statistical measure of pattern access cost. The maintenance of data bases, either by manual or automatic means, is a very difficult job in practice. Papers by Stocker and Dearney [3,15] contain an historical perspective and a discussion of some problems of data representation. A key idea in their work is that the system should be able to provide the users with cost estimates for various system requests prior to attempting them. A system which has such data on costs can also use them to examine the consequences of alternative degrees of preprocessing without actually doing it.

A recent thesis by Low [10] has dealt with some issues of automatic choice of representations for information structures. One point made in this work is that intelligent choices between alternative ways of representing information can be made only if there is a knowledge base containing properties of such representations. The most important factor in such considera- tion is cost.

Garvey at Stanford Research Institute reports [6] that his scene analysis program saves pattern computations which exceed a certain predetermined cost. These saved computations usually involve sets of points rather than functions of single points in the pattern space. The cost threshold was selected by hand based upon knowledge of the economics of the system on which the program was run.

6. COSTS

The user pattern access language defines both accesses to the data and computations on it. We shall assume that access to the bulk data is costly and that the cost can be expressed in some convenient measure such as dollars. We shall also assume that the cost of computation of a pattern definition can be express- ed in some simple way from the costs of arguments of the definition. However, this assumption is not crucial to most of what follows, although it generates the preprocessing example. The units of cost will be the same for both computation and main access.

We will suppose that preprocessing can be done either off- line or as a by-product of normal processing by saving some computations which had to be computed. We hope the reader is not confused by our use of the term preprocessing to mean both prior computation of files and retention of files which may have been computed to serve another purpose. Either way, practical limits must be placed on the amount of preprocessing allowed. Otherwise, a good strategy might be to save anything ever computed in hopes that someone might request it again. Hence costs will be used to restrict the amount of preprocess- ing that can be done on a particular set of pattern definitions.

Precomputed pattern classes will be assumed to be access- ible in zero cost. This assumption makes sense when the cost of accessing the precomputed patterns is negligible compared to the cost of searching the main data base. An example of this is a system possessing storage hierarchies in which the data base occupies the lower levels while preprocessed data occupies the higher levers. Or both types of data might occupy the same physical storage but the preprocessed data might be provided with keys or indices for rapid retrieval while the main data might be accessed only by search. Of course, any access costs

something and a more reasonable assumption might be a logari-
thmic reduction in cost. However, the zero cost assumption for
access to preprocessed data seems adequate at this early stage
of the theory.

Limitations to the amount of preprocessed material to be
retained for rapid access based on storage costs seems to lead
to issues found in paging theory. Of course, the data summaries,
although unequal in size in general, would play the role of
pages. We will not consider the relevance of paging theory to
design of preprocessors in this paper.

7. TOTAL COST DEFINITION GRAPHS

Suppose there are three user pattern definitions A, L, and
M which depend on patterns found in the basic data, namely, C,
E, F, G, H, and K as shown in Figure 2. We will assume that

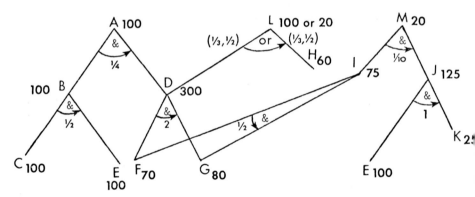

Figure 2: *Definition Graph for Patterns A, L, and M*

pattern recognition algorithms for carrying out the low level
access to the basic data depend linearly on the amount of basic
data. This assumption would be true if the patterns searches
were carried out using the methods suggested in Weiner's paper
[16] suitably extended to two dimensions. The number at the
nodes can then be viewed as relative costs per data item.
A word about notation. An arc connecting the branches of a node
means that the node depends on the lower nodes of the branches
for its definition. If all of the lower nodes must be computed,
(analogous to an 'and' node in Nilsson [12] no additional notation or sometimes an '&' is used. If being in the pattern class
defined by the node depends only on successful computation of

any of the lower nodes (analogous to an 'or' node in Nilsson) then an 'or' is used above the arc.

For an 'and' node we assume that the cost of the computation is a linear multiple of the sum of the input costs. In the example, this multiple is written near the arc. The multiple can be less than 1 or greater than or equal to 1 but it does not indicate whether the data at the node is either more or less extensive than its input data items. For an 'or' node, the cost of computation in reality depends on the relative frequencies of the occurrence of the input nodes as well as that fraction of them which also defines the higher level pattern class. Thus the notation for an 'or' node consists of two weights on each input, the first being the cost multiple and the second the probability of occurrence of the input. Although the expected cost depends on the order in which the tests are done, here it will be assumed that they are done in random order so that the cost of an 'or' node is just the weighted average of costs of the input nodes. The method of assigning costs to higher nodes is admittedly arbitrary. Subsequent work should consider cases in which costs are defined from lower nodes by polynomials or monotonic functions of some appropriate class.

Returning to Figure 2, observe that the graph of the pattern definition set is a forest of trees with some nodes identified. This of course, is true in general if the pattern classes are defined by means of trees. The identified nodes are depicted as single nodes in the figure. The total cost of computing a node is the cost associated with that node plus the costs of all nodes in the subtree defining it.

Definition 3: A total cost definition graph is obtained by labeling each node in the family of graphs defining all patterns with the total cost of computing that node.

In Figure 3 we have the total cost definition graph for this example.

In terms of this formulation, the key problem in the design of the preprocessor is the selection of a preprocessed set of nodes from the total cost definition graph. Several factors constrain the choice of the preprocessed set. First there may be a limitation on the storage available for the preprocessed data. Second there may be a limitation on how much time can be spent on off-line preprocessing. Whatever the real restrictions are, we assume they can be modeled by a bound on the total cost of preprocessing defined in this manner.

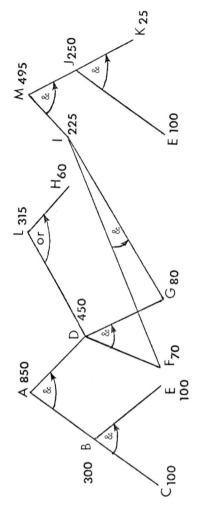

Figure 3. *Total Cost Definition Graph for Definition Graph of Figure 2.*

An important factor in the operation of the system is the relative frequency of occurence of requests of each of the pattern types. One might question why a pattern type might be requested more than once. A reason is that each user may wish to prepare special reports from the data in the pattern class. Another case of multiple accesses is when the system is displaying pattern classes graphically and the users prefer not to use any hard copy. Lastly in a situation in which the underlying data base changed slowly with time, it could be preprocessed regularly based on an access history which ignored small changes when estimating probabilities.

8. EXPECTED COST OF A FAMILY OF PREPROCESSED PATTERN DEFINITIONS

Given a preprocessed set R which contains some subset of the nodes of a total cost definition graph, we wish to compute the new (possibly reduced) cost of each defined pattern. Of course some subpatterns must be computed in order to obtain other subpatterns. If a subpattern and some of its subpatterns happen to be in the preprocessed set, we need to reduce the cost of the pattern in which they occur by the cost of sub-patterns which are maximal in a sense to be defined. We will assume that the reader is familiar with the concepts of tree, rooted tree, and subtree.

Definition 4: A node n of tree T is maximal with respect to a set of nodes R = {n(1),...,n(k)} if

(1)   All paths from the root of T to n(1),...,n(k) respectively pass through n.

(2)   The node n is the most distant node from the root with property (1).

Example: For the tree T of Figure 4, B is maximal for {B,D,J, M} while E is maximal with respect to {J,M}.

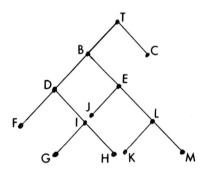

Figure 4

Definition 5:   Expected cost after preprocessing.   Given preprocessed result set R, a subset of nodes of the total cost pattern definition graph resulting from all pattern definitions and a specific pattern definition P: (Repeat (1) and (2) for each P)

(1)   Let P ∩ R denote nodes which are in common to both P and R.

(2)   Find all subtrees T' which cover P ∩ R such that the root r' of T' is maximal with respect to T'∩R and r' is in T'∩ R.   (Note that this set of maximal roots is unique and corresponds to the highest level subpatterns in R which can be used to compute P.)

(3)   The cost of each node in the total cost definition graph is reduced by the cost of each maximal node which is below it.

(4)   The expected cost is just the sum the costs obtained in (3) weighted by their respective probabilities.

Using the concept of maximal node, we can also make precise how the limitation on the total value of saved computations is defined.   We want to place a limitation on the total saved computation (total value of subpatterns computed) without counting shared computations more than once.   The principal problem occurs in cases such as shown in Figure 5

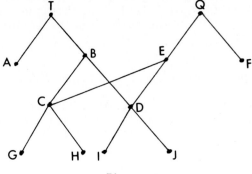

Figure 5

R = {B,C,D}.

Figure 5. Note that B, which is needed for T, requires the computation of C and D which are needed also for Q. Both C and D are maximal roots in Q while B is a maximal root in T. Furthermore, the subtrees with roots C and D are proper subtrees of the subtree with root T. We generalize from this case to define the total cost of the computations in R.

<u>Definition</u> 6: <u>The cost of a preprocessed set R</u> of nodes of the total cost definition graph is obtained by:

(1) Unioning into one set the subtrees, whose roots are maximal nodes, for each pattern.

(2) Deleting any subtrees properly contained in other subtrees in the set formed in step (1).

(3) Accumulating the costs of remaining subtrees.

This definition implicitly assumes that we know which of the subtrees that need to be computed for one pattern are also needed for other patterns. In effect, this assumption requires all definitions to be analyzed at once for dependencies. (Or else for them to be generated in order of lowest subtrees first.) As an alternative definition, we could assume the system never knew when a subpattern being computed for one user would be needed by some other. To compute the cost for this situation, we merely compute the sum all maximal nodes. Obviously, what would occur in practice would depend on the frequency of the introduction of new definitions of patterns. It would be closer to the alternative than the definition of cost of a preprocessed set if users tended to request complex patterns first, followed by requests for simpler subpatterns. However if the most users tend to go from the simple to the complex, which seems reasonable, then our definition of cost is more descriptive.

9. AN EXAMPLE OF EXPECTED COST AFTER PREPROCESSING

Table 1 displays the total expected cost for various pre-processed sets. Two cases are considered: Where class A is much more likely than the other two and when all are equal in probability.

TABLE I

Comparison of expected total costs for uniform probability over pattern classes and one which is mostly class A.

Preprocessed Set	Cost of Preprocessing	Expected costs $p(A)=.8$, $p(L)=p(M)=.1$	Expected costs $p(A)=p(L)$ $=p(M)=.33$
None	0	761	555.3
{F,G}	150	611	505.3
{E,F,G,K}	275	511	449
{C,E,F,G,K}	375	398.5	306.7
{D,F,G}	450	358.5	261.6
{D,K}	475	373.5	311.5
{J,B}	550	551	393
{D,E}	550	283.5	245
{D,I}	675	351	236.6
{D,J}	700	348.5	228.3
{D,B}	750	133.5	211.6
{A}	850	81	270
{A,D,F,G}	850	38.5	128.3
{D,B,J}	1000	108.5	128.3
{A,L,M}	1635	0.0	0.0

Table 1 illustrates how the expected cost of processing varies according to the amount of preprocessing. Note that the sum of the preprocessing cost plus the cost of computation exceeds the cost of computing with no preprocessing in all except the case {F,G}. This is because F and G are needed for all the pattern classes. Any other preprocessed set contains data which might not be needed at a particular instance. On the other hand, once a relatively infrequently requested pattern has been requested, the issue of whether to save the whole computation or even the most probable subtrees depends on storage costs. Another point illustrated by Table 1 is the sensitivity of the expected cost of computation after pre-processing to great changes in user request probabilities. A practical system would certainly require mechanisms to estimate these probabilities either explicitly or implicitly.

An appealing type of implicit estimation is to have changes in the probabilities change the chance that certain files will be stored. The rote memory file in the first Samuel checker player [14] operated in such a manner. The data items (previously encountered board positions together with some evaluation) were given an "age" when entered into the file and then "aged" at regular intervals. Whenever a record was used, its "age" was reduced. Only a fixed number of records, those which were lowest in "age" were retained at times when the file was reorganized. The need of more general techniques of this sort to apply to the preprocessing problem leads us to introduce the subject of adaptive systems in Section 13.

10. A SIMPLE MODEL OF WHEN TO PREPROCESS

There is a simple view of when retention of patterns or subpatterns ought to be done which will now be considered. The view essentially says to retain those patterns whose expected cost of recomputation exceeds the cost of storing them. Let us introduce some regretably elaborate notation to examine this view.

D - The underlying data base.

P(D) - The result of applying the search algorithm driven by the definition of pattern P on the data D.

C(P(D)) - The cost of computing the results P(D).

S(P(D),T) - Storage costs for results P(D) for time T.

n(P(D),T) - The expected number of times results P(D) will be requested by users in the time interval T.

Letting E[X] denote the expectation of random variable X, it is clear that it would pay to save the results of computation P(D) for time t if

$$E[S(P(D),T)] + E[C(P(D))] < n(P(D),T) * E[C(P(D))] \quad (1)$$

Or more simply if

$$E[S(P(D),T)] < \{n(P(D),T) - 1\} * E[C(P(D))] \quad (2)$$

Equation (2) provides some justification for considering preprocessing and retention of patterns to be essentially the same process. For preprocessing, we merely drop the -1 in the factor on the right side of the inequality.

The simple cost model is not very useful because the terms are difficult to obtain. For instance storage costs, S(P(D),T), may depend on system factors and arbitrary decisions. They may depend on the priority of access demanded by the users at various times. The cost of updating a file may be more important in deciding how it should be stored than the cost of storage itself. But once updating has been done, a less expensive form of storage may suffice for pattern search. As indicated in the inequalities above, the cost of storage needs to be treated as a random variable. Furthermore, the random variable seems to be defined by means of a stochastic process dependent on lots of detailed information inherent in the computer system in which the pattern recognition system resides. Moreover, the cost of processing of two identical jobs can vary on the same computer system because of subtle competition of other jobs being run at the same time, changes in the availability of certain parts of the system, and even small differences in timing. The difficult job of understanding the performance of computers has been undertaken by Grenander and Tsao [15]. Specific problems in assessing the performance of a data base system available from IBM, IMS/360, have been studied by Ghosh and Tuel [16]. In many systems, the user may affect the cost of his or her job directly by specifying a priority under which it is to be run. Hence an accurate model of cost would have to take into account both the system peculiarities and the needs in terms of priority usage of the users. Of course, n(P(D),T) is the expectation of a random variable which depends on the interaction of the class of users and may be the most difficult term to estimate for reasons which we will now consider.

Somewhat paradoxically, the simple model was proposed as a basis for deciding which subpatterns and patterns should be preprocessed but preprocessing changes the values of the terms on which the inequality is based. That is, the introduction of a preprocessor into the system invalidates subsequent conclusions which can be drawn with the simple model. The influence of feedback caused by the preprocessor needs to be modeled.

The main point is that the preprocessor changes the costs of some computations by accessing them rather than doing them. What the users do because of changing economics is clearly a factor of great importance. Those users whose costs go down are apt to run more jobs. On the other hand, any reorganization of the preprocessed files which results in increased costs for some important users will result in various political pressures on the staff of the system. It may cause such users to take their business elsewhere. In general, it seems desirable that reorganization of preprocessed data should not seriously degrade the performance of any user as measured by the cost parameter.

At any rate, users operate on a fixed budget for some accounting period and they are apt to use all the resources allocated to them. (Those who have resources left over at the end of an accounting period in a large organization tend to have them reduced which causes the assumption of full resource usage to be more accurate.) We will extend these ideas in the section which deals with a partial estimate of user needs using incomplete definition graphs.

11. PROJECTION OF USER NEEDS: INCOMPLETE DEFINITION TREES

A serious weakness in the cost model proposed in previous sections was the use of constant user pattern request probabilities. The demand for a "good" pattern definition is apt to be more like the demand for a "hit" record in the entertainment business than stationary over time. Thus the estimation of the pattern definition use probability is likely to be a very trendy business. However, most users are generally quite limited in the quantity of computer resources that they are allowed to use during an accounting period. Another factor of importance is that most users will be associated with projects involving users with similar aims.

We will assume that the users' aims can be described as the aims of a set of projects. Each project has a fixed amount of resource (again say in dollars) which must be spent in the period of interest. Let us further suppose that each project is able to specify a plan for its anticipated future activity described in terms of partially specified definition trees.

Definition 7: A partially specified definition tree is one in which some terminal nodes or some relations between any nodes are variables.

Our last of many assumptions is that the users know their problem areas well enough to be able to estimate about how much it will cost to compute the variable portion of the partially specified pattern definition tree. One appealing method we will use is to have them say in effect, "It will cost X% of cost of the known portion of the tree to do the unspecified part as well." (Here $X \geq 100$) The accuracy of such estimates may well be suspected. But as a practical matter, the managers of such projects must already do something equivalent to this estimation. It would be difficult to imagine a machine possessing enough knowledge of a programming project to extrapolate future costs as well as the managers unless the project itself depended heavily on automatic programming methods. The cost is, of course, the cost with whatever preprocessing is available at the time of the estimate. In addition, we conservatively ignore possible gains achieved by preprocessing after the unspecified portion is specified.

Example: Incomplete definition trees for a universe of four projects are shown in Figure 6. Variables to be defined later by the users are denoted by X,X',X",Y,Y', etc. whereas other symbols denote known definitions.

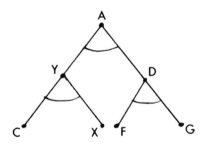

Project I. *Total Resources $8.500 Cost Estimate 200%*

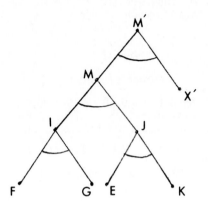

Project II. *Total Resources $17,000 Cost Estimate 120%*

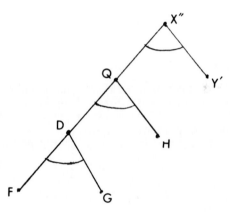

Project III. *Total Resources $1,000 Cost Estimate 150%*

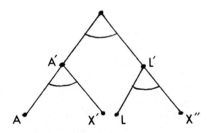

Project IV. *Total Resources $5,000 Cost Estimate 170%*
Figure 6. *Incompletely Specified Definition Trees*

In Table 2, we consider the influence of a few preprocessed sets on the total number of runs.

TABLE 2

Number of Runs

Project	No prep. Cost 0	{E,K} 125	{F,G} 150	{D,F,G} 450	{A,L,M} 1660
I ($8,500)	7.7	7.7	8.9	13.1	15.5
II ($17,000)	28.6	36.0	38.2	117.2	171.0
III ($1,000)	2.1	2.1	3.1	4.0	6.3
IV ($5,000)	2.5	2.7	2.7	3.2	6.1
Total number of runs	40.9	48.5	52.9	137.5	197.9

Table 2 shows that about 70% of the maximum number of runs can be obtained by using preprocessed set {D,F,G} which costs only about 27% of the cost of maximum preprocessing. The great benefits obtained by project II result from the low proportion of unknowns in its definition rather than the fact that is has more resources.

12. EXPECTED TOTAL NUMBER OF RUNS AS A FIGURE OF MERIT FOR PREPROCESSING

Once cost estimates have been obtained from the users, we can compute the influence of preprocessing various parts of the known portions of the definitions. If there is no preprocessing, the expected number of runs each project can afford is just the total resources divided by the expected cost. (We will not speculate on exactly what a fraction of a run means, it may or may not be useful to the user.) Even if all possible preprocessing is done, the users still must pay for the cost of the variable parts, so in this context there is a limit on what preprocessing can accomplish in terms of reducing cost. Consequently there is an upper limit on the expected number of runs after preprocessing which equals the total resources divided by the average cost of the variable part.

The issue we must now face is one closer to social values than to the technical matters with which we began. What should be a figure of merit for evaluating a preprocessed set R? A potential candidate figure of merit is the expected total number of runs for all users. Since a run is defined here means the completion of a pattern access by a user, increasing this number is clearly desirable. On the other hand, if a preprocessed set R was active and a new one R' were made active, it is possible that some users, say those with high costs might have their costs increase while the costs of other users decreased, resulting in the total number of runs increasing. But those users whose costs increased would certainly prefer to go back to using R or maybe R U R'. Whatever figure of merit is used, there is the possibility that some users will suffer from a preprocessing reorganization unless the system does not allow any user costs to increase. For the case of the expected number of runs as a figure of merit we have the following simple result.

Proposition: Let R and R' be two preprocessed sets of a total cost definition forest F and L a set of partially specified projects such that the expected number of runs using R' is greater than the expected number of runs using R and the cost for some users is greater using R' than using R. Then there is a preprocessed set S such that $S \subset R \cup R'$, the cost for each user is no greater using S than using R and the total number of runs for S is greater than or equal the total number for R'.

Proof: Let U be the set of pattern definitions whose costs are higher under preprocessing R' than under preprocessing R. For each pattern P in U, union to R' those nodes N of R such that $N \epsilon P \cap R$ and call the resulting set S. Under S, the cost of each P in U is now no more than it was under R. Likewise, the cost of each pattern not in U will not be increased by additional preprocessing. Consequently the total cost of each pattern definition under S is less than or equal what it was for R'. Any partially specified definition tree thus will have the costs associated with its nodes no higher than the minimum of what it had under R and R'. Consequently the total cost for the known portions is no more for any pattern and less for those patterns which depend on definitions in U. Since the total number of runs for each incompletely specified pattern type is inversely proportional to cost, the total number of runs increases if any members of U happen to be used to define the incompletely specified patterns. Otherwise, the total number of runs can not decrease, since no costs can increase under S.

It should be clear from the construction of S that the cost of S is bounded above by the sum of the costs of R and R'. The meaning of this result is that if the system is able to retain enough preprocessed data, there is no need to ever cause any user to incur increased costs from a reorganization of the preprocessor. However, if there is a bound on the cost of S, it seems unlikely that such a desirable state of affairs occurs.

13.   PREPROCESSORS AS ADAPTIVE SYSTEMS

In this section we will establish connections between preprocessor design and the specification of adaptive systems. The chief rationale for this is the formidable difficulty of computing preprocessing sets for large data definition sets and estimating necessary probabilities. A suitably formulated adaptive system adjusts to unknown factors in the environment as it gains information. It seems clear that a real environment of user access as we have described previously would not have stationary probabilities nor other properties which made the preprocessing example calculation possible. The reader is warned that this connection described herein is tentative and subject to further modification or refinement.

The following assumptions and notations will be established.

(1) The user pattern-question language will allow definitions of generalized relation trees (perhaps with a bounded number of resursions) similar to the previous examples. An arbitrary pattern definition tree will be symbolized by PT_i.

(2) The ensemble of users will have been assumed to have created an environment of pattern definitions which are available at time t:

$$E(t) = \{PT1, PT2, \ldots, PTn\}$$

At the next time step, a pattern request PT_{t+1} occurs whose definition is either within $E(t)$ or which possesses subtrees in $E(t)$.

(3) The hierarchical data summary file can at any time be described as a family of hierarchical graphs, the lowest level in the hierarchy being the resolution elements of the bulk data base. Data at each level can be considered be a homomorphism or transformation of data at a lower level which preserves the geometric properties. Notation to be used: H.D.S. for the set of all possible hierarchical data summary files and DS_i for an

arbitrary hierarchical data set. Thus:

$$H.D.S. = \{DS1,DS2,...,DSk\}$$

(4) A figure of merit or fitness criterion will be developed so that alternative elements of the H.D.S. can be compared taking into account the environment of user patter requests. An obvious choice is minimum expected cost if such cost
figures are available. A more general choice is the expected
number of bit comparisons needed for searching a typical mix
of patterns from E using a given hierarchical data summary.

(5) An adaptive strategy is a means for producing a tra-
jectory T each element of which is a set of hierarchical data
summaries.

We have now built up notation to characterize a self-organizing data manager of this type as an adaptive system. Modifying Holland [7] slightly, an adaptive system consists of a
quadruple:

$$\alpha = <D,E,T,X>$$

Here D is a set of descriptions of devices operating on an
environment E. The function X is a fitness criterion which eva-
luates the success of the devices in the environment. T is a
sequence of sets of devices. Each set is generated from the
previous set by an adaptive strategy which uses the ranking
provided by X to define the set. The preprocessor system described before is an adaptive system where the hierarchical
data structures together with a top down pattern search algorithm (fixed) constitute the devices. The environment supplies
both pattern definitions to be searched and the lowest level
data base. The fitness criterion X ranks the performance of
the pattern search on different hierarchical structures. The
adaptive strategy which generates T provides a new hierarchical data structure family based upon experience in searching
the previous family and knowledge of E. There could be systems
which had only one hierarchical data structure in the family
and systems with several of them corresponding to different
partitions on the system or to different times of operation.
We have thus identified the problem of the design of a preprocessor with the specification of an adaptive strategy.

The specification of an appropriate adaptive strategy is
by no means a trivial task. Some insight can be gained from
the work of Holland [7], Bosworth, Foo and Zeigler [9],
Cavicchio [10], Foo and Bosworth [11] and Franz [12]. Some con-

vergence properties of adaptive strategies defined as stochastic processes have been studied by Martin [13].

14. CONCLUSIONS

The problem of preprocessing large data bases to facilitate repeated pattern searches is examined. The main construct is a pattern definition language which allows a simple link between what must be computed and what must be stored. The question of which sets of subdefinitions (subtrees) should be saved or precomputed if there is a constraint on the total cost of processing is a key problem in the design of the preprocessor. This seems to be a lengthy computational problem for a large system even if all costs and probabilities are accurately estimated. Such costs and probabilities are usually hard to obtain and frequently are very time dependent. Hence the problem of specifying the preprocessor is recast in terms of adaptive systems.

Many problems remain to be solved before an automatic data manager can be routinely designed. Two issues only mentioned in this paper seem to be of great importance. The first is how the system in which the data resides is to be modeled. This was dealt with only in terms of one cost parameter which does not provide enough structure. The second is how future user activity is to be modeled. This is reflected only in terms of probabilities on the pattern requests and by partially specified pattern definitions. Both types of information are subject to rather great changes. This suggests that such models probably ought to be "table driven" as is the pattern recognition algorithm. Indeed, the preprocessor might treat the pattern definitions, the system model and the user intent model in the same manner. Although we have outlined what seem to be some of the principal issues and concepts in a theory of automatic data management, we recognize that there may be many other approaches to this problem area.

Based on "Outlines of a Theory of Automatic Data Management in a Pattern Recognition Environment," from the 1975 Proceedings of the Conference on Computer Graphics, Pattern Recognition and Data Structure (75 CH 0981-1C). Copyright 1975 by The Institute of Electrical and Electronics Engineers, Inc.

REFERENCES

1. Sammet, J. E. "Challenge to Artificial Intelligence: Programming Problems to Be Solved," *Second International Joint Conference on Artificial Intelligence Proceedings*, 1971, pp. 59-65.

2. Nilsson, Nils J. *Problem Solving Methods in Artificial Intelligence*, McGraw-Hill, 1971.

3. Stocker, P. M. and Dearney, P. A. "Self-organizing Data Management Systems," *The Computer Journal*, Vol. 16, No. 2, November 2, 1973, pp. 100-105.

4. Dearney, P. A. "A Model of a Self-organizing Data Management System," *The Computer Journal*, Vol. 17, No. 1, January 1974, pp. 13-16.

5. Weiner, P. "Linear Pattern Matching Algorithms," *IEEE Proceedings of the 14th Annual Symposium on Switching and Automata Theory*, 1973, pp. 1-11.

6. Samuel, A. L. "Some Studies in Machine Learning Using the Game of Checkers," *Computers and Thought*, ed. by Feigenbaum and Feldman, McGraw-Hill, 1963, pp. 71-105.

7. Holland, J. *Introduction to Adaptation in Natural and Artificial Systems*, University of Michigan Press, 1975.

8. Low, James R. "Automatic Coding: Choice of Data Structures," Stanford Artificial Intelligence Lab Memo AIM-242, August, 1974.

9. Bosworth, J., Foo, N., and Zeigler, B. P. "Comparison of Genetic Algorithms with Conjugate Gradient Methods," Computer and Communication Sciences, University of Michigan, 1972.

10. Cavicchio, D. J. "Adaptive Search Using Simulated Evolution," Ph.D. Dissertation, Computer and Communication Sciences, University of Michigan, 1970.

11. Foo, N. and Bosworth, J. "Algebraic, Geometric, and Stochastic Aspects of Genetic Operators," Computer and Communication Sciences, University of Michigan, 1972.

12. Frantz, Daniel R. "Non-linearities in Genetic Adaptive
     Search," Ph.D. Dissertation, Computer and Communication
     Sciences, University of Michigan, 1972.

13. Martin, Nancy "Convergence Properties of a Class of Adap-
     tive Schemes Called Sequential Reproductive Plans," Ph.D.
     Dissertation, Computer and Communication Sciences, Univer-
     sity of Michigan, 1973. (Also as Technical Report 210,
     Institute for Mathematical Studies in the Social Sciences,
     Stanford University, Stanford, Calif.)

14. Garvey, Thomas, Artificial Intelligence Center, Stanford
     Research Institute, Personal communication.

15. Grenander, U. and Tsao, R. F. "Quantitative Methods for
     Evaluating Computer System Performance: A Review and a
     Proposal," *Statistical Computer Performance Evaluation*,
     ed. by W. Freiberger, Academic Press, New York, 1972,
     pp. 3-24.

16. Ghosh, S. P. and Tuel, W. G. "A Design of an Experiment to
     Model Data Base System Performance," IBM Research Report
     RJ 1482, San Jose, Calif., December, 1974.

The Design of Satellite Graphics Systems

JAMES D. FOLEY

Bureau of the Census
Graphics Software Branch
Washington, D.C. 20233

The purpose of this chapter is to describe and evaluate the various general ways in which satellite graphics systems can be usefully integrated into a computing system. Two interrelated issues are addressed: design of the hardware, and design of the software. Basic methods of achieving good performance (response time) for two important classes of satellite systems are given, and a number of existing satellite systems are briefly described. Past and current research aimed at simplyfying the design problem is presented.

1. WHY SATELLITE GRAPHICS?

As a basic premise of this article, we presume the reader to already be persuaded that satellite graphics systems of the general type shown in Figure 1 are viable. Thus only a very brief summary of the advantages of satellite graphics is given here, abstracting and conglomerating numerous points found in the literature [9, 25, 27]. The advantages are:

1. Accessability - the satellite terminal is often conveniently located in the user's lab, office, or other work area, rather than some (possibly large) distance away at the computation center.

Supported in part by NSF grant GJ-34697 and NIH grant RR00898-02. Written while the author was at the University of North Carolina.

2. Control - the user has some larger degree of
   control over the graphics system. There is
   less contention for resources, less inter-
   user interference with the satellite, than
   with a display processor directly connected
   to a large time-shared or multiprogrammed
   host.

3. Minicomputer availability - given that a small
   computer is in the lab, it can often be used
   for other work.

4. Resource conservation - the host is unburdened
   of processing trivial user interactions which
   may occur frequently, require much operating
   system overhead for task-switching, but need
   very little actual processing.

5. Response - the satellite is able to give very
   fast response to many user actions, without
   depending on the host.

6. Economics - dollars can be saved by the above
   resource conservation, since use of the satellite for some classes of work is more cost-
   effective than use of the host.

7. Independence from host - even though the host
   may be unavailable, it may be possible to do
   some interactive work on the satellite, saving
   the picture changes for later transmission to
   the host.

8. Compatibility - the satellite's minicomputer
   can be used to emulate other terminal devices,
   such as storage tube displays.

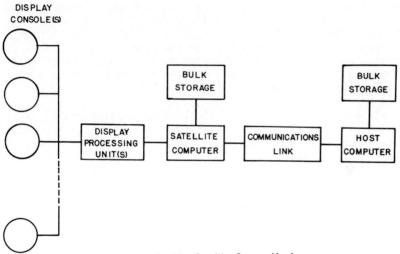

Figure 1.   Satellite Graphics System Hardware.

2.   DESIGN PROBLEMS AND GOALS

The design of a satellite graphics system is a complex process, requiring many decisions concerning both the hardware and
software configurations. Each of the hardware subsystems shown
in Figure 1 must be selected. Those subsystems, and salient
characteristics which affect their use in a satellite, are:

Subsystem	Characteristics
1. communications link	speed, half/full duplex
2. satellite computer	instruction set power
3. satellite main store	size, speed
4. satellite backing store	size, speed
5. display processor (DPU)	instruction set power

Excluded from direct consideration here are the host computer
and its backing store, as these are usually beyond the satellite
system designer's control.

Just as important as choosing a hardware configuration is designing an appropriate software configuration. A graphics satellite and its host constitute a two-computer network, with one or both computers having a hierarchy of storage devices, from main store to fixed and moving-head disks. Thus processes (programs and subprograms) must be assigned to the two processors, and data must be allocated to storage devices. In essence, a "division of labor" between the host and satellite must be established.

This is a long-standing issue. Many researchers [4, 7, 8, 17, 27, 30] have raised the question of how to divide processing tasks between the host and satellite, but no one has asserted that a single division of labor is best for all applications. Myer and Sutherland [17] argue against this view, and the author [7, 8] has in fact demonstrated the converse.

In making these decisions, the designer of a satellite graphics system is generally faced with two constraints which in large part dictate the basic alternative designs to be considered. These constraints are performance and cost.

Performance has several dimensions, the most important of which is response time. Response time requirements differ greatly for interactions at the lexical, syntactic, and semantic levels. Wallace proposed this terminology, described in [10]:

"The the lexical level are those things which are done by reflex, either natural or trained. It appears that our time to perform such actions goes down to about 50 ms, which approximates the period between key depressions for a very fast typist (this figure loosely corresponds to one provided by Miller). To be useful, system response to lexical actions must be within the same time interval, since human psychology does not tolerate interruption of reflex actions.

At the syntactic level are the semiconscious actions by which sentences, or complete thoughts, are constructed. The basic elements meaning "add a 5 ohm resistor between this node and that node" would be constructed more deliberately than the lexical construction, because the user is forming his "idea" as he works. Time intervals of approximately 1s seem most characteristic of syntactic actions. The system's responses to them are

correspondingly less exacting with a half-
second delay being entirely adequate, while
often even 2s to 4s delays are tolerated.

The semantic level involves requests of major
import for which the user expects "thoughtful"
answers. Semantic actions are completely conscious actions, and may take tens of seconds
and more. The tolerable response time appears
to be highly variable. If the action were the
sentence "Hello, I'm Joe", it would be dis-
concerting to wait more than 2s for the response, "Hi". On the other hand, a request to
display the minimal energy bond in a complex
molecule could take 10s or more without a user
losing this train of thought."

Other dimensions of performance involve the display processor itself, and factors such as screen resolution, screen
addressability, intensity levels, flicker-free display capacity,
and capability for dynamic rotation of large images. Any display processors which meet performance criteria for all these
factors can be considered for inclusion in the satellite graphics system. These factors do of course have a direct bearing on system cost, but have only a secondary influence on response time. For instance, increasing screen addressability
from 10 bits to 11 bits may mean that slighly more time will be
taken to process an interaction if DPU programs are sent over
the communication link or are held on bulk store. These factors,
however, are common to all graphics system designs, while response time plays more of a central role with satellite systems
than with other type systems.

There are still other factors which have a direct bearing
on performance, such as reliability, maintainability, and the
satellite's operating system capabilities. These too are most
conveniently thought of as screening factors to determine
whether specific subsystems are even considered for use in the
overall system.

Choosing a hardware and software system are not orthogonal
activities; they are intimately interwined. A division of labor
which places a heavy processing burden on the satellite requires
a large satellite; conversely, a minimal satellite with little
main store and no backing store dictates against assigning it
much processing or data.

To summarize, the satellite system designer considers only subsystems which meet essential basic requirements, and must then structure a hardware and software system meeting cost and response time requirements.

3. PROGRAM STRUCTURES

Figure 2 represents the structure of a typical interactive graphics application program. The lexical processing functions are separated from the mainline interaction monitor, and are further divided into those handled by the graphics support package and those handled by the application program. This subdivision of lexical processing tasks will be very important when discussing the division of labor in some types of satellites. Lexical processing includes light pen tracking, dragging, sketching, text input/echo/edit, and cursor movement: a more complete list is given in section 4.4. However the lexical processing is done, it may require access to the correlation table, to routines which modify the DPU program, and perhaps to the transform/clip routines as well. The correlation table, or symbol table, identifies specific sequences of DPU code with a name provided by the application-program. Any user actions not handled by the subroutine package's lexical processing are queued and passed on to the application program, where additional lexical processing and syntactic and semantic processing are performed.

Syntactic processing may include prompting, enabling of input devices, interpretation of values from input devices in the context of the application, and simple modifications to the data base and DPU program. Operations which call for new views of displayed objects, or display of new objects may require traversal of the picture data base. On the other hand, semantic processing usually requires accessing much of the data base and performing significant processing, as typified by analysis of an electrical network or of a ship's hull design. Typical consequences of the semantic processing are display of a single number or a graph, modifications to the data base, or modifications of the previously displayed image.

Details of the application program's structure may vary from application to application, and from one display processor to another. If a DPU which directly executes from the picture data base is used, the lexical processing functions will make modifications to the displayed image by modifying this data base. Of course some applications (drafting) have no semantic functions.

The buffer management process is charged with responsibility for allocating, freeing, and compacting the memory area used by the DPU program.

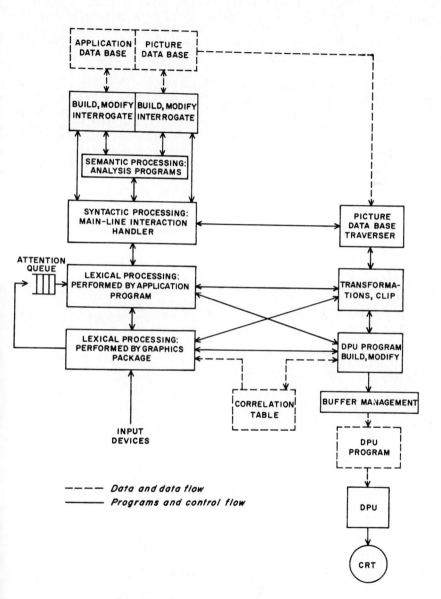

Figure 2.   Graphics Program Organization.

The satellite system designer must decide which processor will be assigned each of the processing tasks and which memory device will store the various data bases. The possibilities for distributing processing tasks between the satellite and the host are nearly endless, but two major categories have been identified. They are descirbed at length in sections 4 and 5.

Briefly, the two are the fixed function satellite and the programmable satellite. Some writers call these the intelligent terminal" and "intelligent satellite", respectively. The fixed function satellite, so named in [14], is seen by the host's application program as a "black box" whose behavior is essentially fixed and unvarying. In some cases, the application program has some very limited control of the satellite's behavior by enabling or disabling various functions, or by setting parameters used by algorithms executing in the satellite. But still, the satellite can perform only a certain predetermined set of functions, and the application programmer must live with them. The programmable satellite of course remedies this problem. The application programmer has direct access to the satellite by means of an assembler-level language, or preferably a procedural language. The application programmer, rather than the graphics systems designer, has at least partial control over the division of labor.

4. FIXED FUNCTION SATELLITES

In a fixed function satellite graphics system the application programmer has no control over the software configuration. Rather, the satellite is accessed from the host-resident application program via a graphics subroutine package. The division of labor is bound at the time the subroutine package is written, and can usually be changed only by a sophisticated graphics system programmer. Only those functions performed by the graphics package can potentially be assigned to either CPU, or to special purpose DPU hardware.

With the application program executing exclusively on the host, large amounts of picture description/modification information will be sent across the communications link. This can be time-consuming. For instance, the transmission time for a 2000 line picture, described by 4 bytes or 32 bits per line, would take about half a minute on a 2400 bit per second communications link. Decreasing this to 2 bytes per line would still yield a 15 second transmission time.

Thus whatever can be done to minimize the amount of picture description sent across the communication link can have an important influence on response times. This minimization, or compression of transmitted data will be a major criterion used in evaluating various fixed function satellite software configurations.

A second consequence of the application program executing exclusively on the host is that many user actions may need to be reported to the host. Before the application program actually receives the report, delays from one or more of the following are likely: operating system task scheduling and switching, waiting for higher-priority tasks to release the CPU, and program roll out/roll in or page swapping. Such delays can be debilitating and are best avoided whenever possible. Ideally, host operating systems should be structured to eliminate most such overhead for at least a majority of interactions. But since this is often not the case, the alternative is to maximize the number of user actions which can be processed by the satellite, thereby minimizing the number of actions processed by the host. User actions processed by the host will be called "significant events"; their number is to be minimized, especially for user actions involving lexical actions, all of which require quite rapid response.

The purpose of this section, then, is to explore several different ways of effectively constructing software for fixed function satellites. The order in which various alternatives are discussed will be (approximately) by increasing complexity of the satellite's software. Basic design goals are compressing the amount of picture description sent to the satellite and minimizing the number of significant events. Examples of existing software systems will be presented when appropriate.

4.1 The Minimal System

Any satellite must have resident a certain minimum set of programs and data in order that it function at all. The data required is just the DPU program, which is of course viewed as data only by the CPU, not by the DPU. The necessary programs are device drivers for the display, communication link, and operator interaction devices, and a simple executive with the following basic functions:

1. Pen tracking, if a lightpen is available.
2. Cursor positioning in response to movements of mouse, joystick, tablet's pen, or key strokes, if any of these devices exist.

3. Accept new DPU programs or portions thereof from host, to be stored in satellite's memory at locations specified by host.

4. Start DPU execution at host-specified location in satellite's memory, and stop DPU execution.

5. Give host, when asked, status information such as the current tracking cross, cursor, mouse, or joystick position.

6. Report to host each significant event's use of interaction devices, and associated status.

Figure 3 shows the software division for this type of satellite. The host builds and modifies the DPU program, allocates memory in the satellite, and is informed of many, but not all, user actions. The specific significant events and status reported to the host would include:

1. Pen detect (other than tracking), and the contents of the DPU's instruction counter when the detect occurred, for use with the host-resident correlation table.

2. Loss of pen tracking, and the tracking cross' position.

3. Key strokes on the alphanumeric keyboard and on other devices such as programmed function keyboards.

The only user actions not reported to the host are those involving movement of the tracking cross or other cursor(s). These are, however, actions which can occur quite frequently.

A system very similar to the one described here was implemented by Kilgour [14] on a mini with 8K of 18-bit words, and a 300K bps link to the dedicated host. The system, called SPINDLE, manages its own memory and can store DPU programs on its own bulk memory and reload them for later display. Rubberbanding and dragging are relegated to the host. Because the host is dedicated to graphics and there is a high-speed communications link, the system is nevertheless viable.

Kilgour describes an interesting experiment in which the effective communications link rate was reduced to 2400 bps. The overall elapsed time required for an application program's

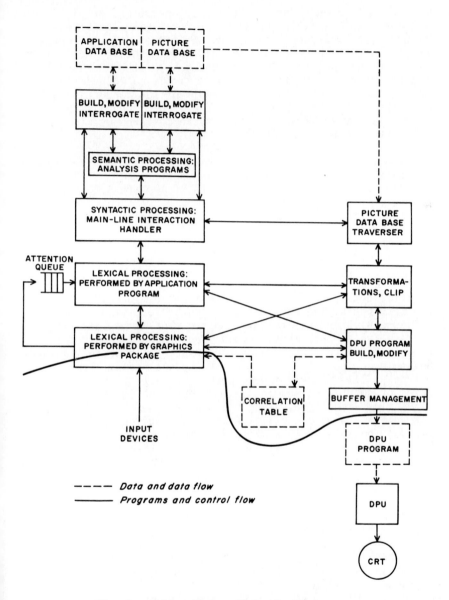

Figure 3.   Division of Labor: Minimal Satellite System.

user to go through a fixed sequence of operations tripled! Delays were "tolerable if occasionally irritating, and the lag in dragging labels around was not too noticable". In this experiment the user's think time was presumably relatively invariant. Then assuming that think time in the case of the 300K bps link accounted for 80% of elapsed time, a simple calculation shows that response time with the 2400 bps link was more than 10 times worse than with the faster link. The point, then, is that a fast link is needed for this type system, if the user's productivity is not to be affected.

A next step in improving the responsiveness of fixed function satellites, and at the same time permitting satisfactory performance with communications links of less than 300K bps, is to move more function to the satellite, decreasing the amount of information transmitted from host to satellite. Several techniques are useful.

4.2 Data Compression

Efficiently encoded information is transmitted, and expanded into DPU code by the satellite, giving the division of labor in Figure 4. For instance, graphs are sent as an initial (X,Y) location, an X increment, a point count N, and then N data values. Arcs are sent as a center point, and starting and ending angles or points. A circle is a special case. Text is sent as ASCII or EBCDIC codes, then if necessary expanded into series of short line segments. A dashed line is sent as end points plus a code indicating the line's type. Many DPUs have instructions to handle exactly these and similar sorts of situations. The instructions exist as a means to shorten DPU programs, decrease the DPU's load on the satellite's memory bus, and to increase the DPU's flicker-free drawing capacity. In the case at hand, satellite software can be used to simulate DPU instructions not actually available.

The choice of which such features to implement in hardware, and which in software, is itself a subject for considerable discussion, but is not unique to satellite systems, and thus will not be pursued at length here. References [7, 22] consider this issue in more detail. The basic tradeoff is between higher hardware cost and performance on the one hand versus lower cost and performance coupled with software complexity on the other. In any case, software can be used to enhance the DPU's apparent capabilities.

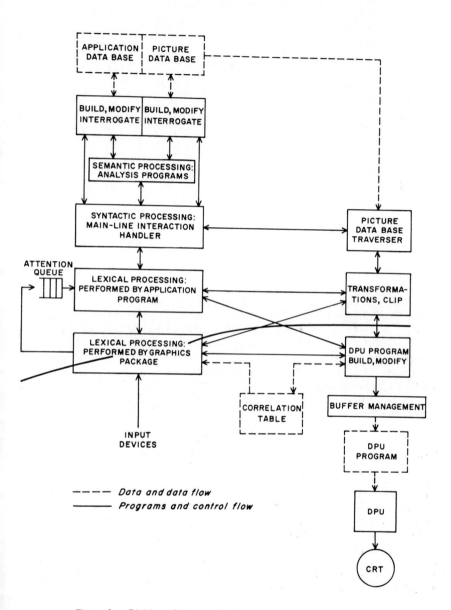

Figure 4. Division of Labor: Satellite Generates DPU Program.

A partial list of ways in which data compression might be effected follows:

1. Graphs.
2. Graph grids.
3. Conic sections (includes circle as special case), splines, etc.
4. Character strings.
5. Line structure encoding (dot, dash, etc.)
6. Parametric representation of surfaces.
7. Subpicturing.

For any of these concepts to be used, the graphics package must actually make them available to the application programmer. There is thus a very strong and close relation between the design of fixed-function satellites and the design of the graphics subroutine package (or other language) used to drive the satellite. This relation has often been neglected in the past.

4.3 Eliminate Redundant Transmissions

The subpicturing mentioned above can be considered as one means to eliminate transmission of redundant data to the satellite. A description of the subpicture is sent just once. Then for each instance of the subpicture, only a reference to the subpicture and the instance's position, scale, orientation, and other attributes need be transmitted. This can also be done with picture macros, with the difference that already displayed instances of the macro are not changed if the macro's definition is changed.

The same basic concept can be extended beyond the scope usually associated with picture subroutines or picture macros. Any picture or picture part which is likely to be displayed more than once during a user session need really be sent to the satellite only once, at the sessions' start. The information can be retained in the satellite's main or backing store for display whenever needed. Even better, with some single-purpose satellites, the picture pieces might be stored permanently at the satellite. Candidates for such treatment are menus, prompts, error messages, and templates such as electrical symbols (for circuit designs), flow chart symbols (for program documentation) or office furniture (for office layout).

A common and effective technique used with segmented DPU programs is to permit the application program to turn individual segments on and off. Turning a segment off causes it to be removed from the refresh cycle; turning it back on cause it to be placed back in the cycle. The practical limit on use of the technique is usually satellite main memory, although there is no conceptual reason not to write segments which are "off" onto backing store.

Another fundamental approach is for the application program to build the picture description in a segmented or hierarchical fashion, so that when picture modifications are to be made only a few segments or a subtree in the picture hierarchy need be retransmitted to the satellite. This eliminates the redundant retransmission of unchanged portions of the picture.

This is particularly a concern with direct-view storage tubes, since many graphics subroutine packages for using them do not allow the picture to be segmented. Placing a small computer with the storage tube creates a satellite graphics terminal. By then using a segmented or hierarchical DPU program graphics package and by storing a picture description in the satellite, redundant retransmission is avoided. This approach was used in the Bell Labs G101 system [21].

The division of labor used with this concept is essentially that of Figure 4, with a bit more intelligency built into both the host and satellite to eliminate the redundant transmission.

In summary, there is a significant potential for decreasing data transmitted from host to satellite. However, the graphics subroutine package used by the host's application must be structured so that the potential can be realized. Unfortunately, much contemporary fixed function satellite system software either is not appropriately structured or else is structured to only take advantage of one DPU's actual hardware. The notion of hardware -software tradeoffs is not exploited. The only nearly universally used concept is that of temporarily removing segments from the refresh cycle.

4.4 Servicing User Interaction in Satellite

The final major way in which the performance of fixed-function satellites can be enhanced is by using the satellite to service as many user actions as possible, thereby reducing the number of such actions reported to and serviced by the host. In the introduction, this was referred to as significant event reduction. Lexical actions by the user are primary candidates for satellite servicing. They occur frequently, need fast response time, usually require few resources in terms of memory space and CPU time, and, significantly, can most always be structured in a way which is completely independent of the syntax or semantics of any particular application program. Indeed, the name "lexical" was chosen by Wallace partially in recognition of this separability. The implication of the term is that the very same system software can be used to handle simple actions and feedback for all applications.

With a fixed-function satellite, only those lexical capabilities built into the graphics support package can be considered for implementation on the fixed-function satellite. This means that the support package's design is of critical importance, if the suggestions of this section are to be implemented. If the graphics package's lexical processing is performed by the satellite, we have the division of labor shown in Figure 5.

Precisely what is the scope of lexical interactions? A partial list follows:

1. Pen tracking.
2. Cursor movement.
3. Control of object's scale, position, orientation, or other attributes dynamically by use of knobs, dials, pens, styli, etc., as locators and valuators.
4. Automatic intensification of the object being detected by pen or other pick.
5. Rubber band line drawing.
6. Constrained rubber band line drawing (horizontal, vertical, oblique).
7. Sketching (inking).
8. Creation of gravitational field to attract cursor or tracking cross near line end points.
9. Simple text entry -- keystroke feedback on screen, character delete, and line delete.
10. On-line character recognition.
11. Light Handle [19].
12. Continual display of potentiometer values.

Most existing systems provide at least a few of these capabilities. Several systems provide a reasonable selection. For instance, the GINO [30] satellite's lexical functions are automatic intensification of an entity when detected by the pen, pen tracking, and intensifying and deintensifying picture entities. Optional functions, provided if so instructed by the

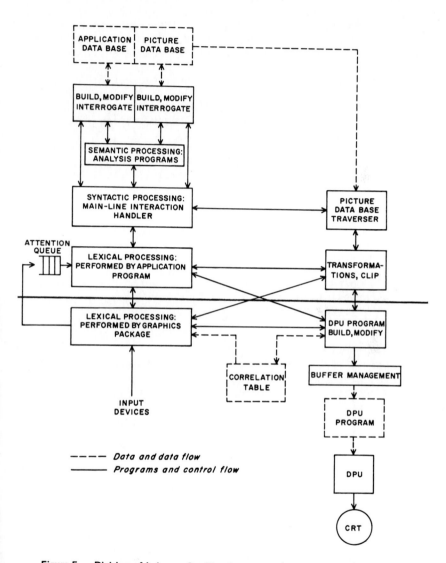

Figure 5.   Division of Labor: Satellite Generates DPU Program, Does all of Graphics Package's Lexical Processing.

application program, are displaying supplementary material when an entity is detected, rubber band line drawing, drawing lines constrained to be horizontal or vertical, and creating gravitational fields around points to attract the tracking cross. Other satellite functions are correlation table processing, memory management, and adding and deleting picture entities.

The main CPU used with GINO is a multi-access ATLAS-2. Two satellites are supported. One is an 8K (18 bits/word) PDP-7; the other, a 16K (18 bits/word) Elliot 905. Communications link speeds are 20K bps and 4.8K bps, respectively.

The fixed function satellite described by Dill & Thomas [5] implements pen tracking, pen detect feedback, dragging, sketching, rubber-banding, and simple text editing. The satellite, an 8K (16 bits/word) PDP-11, also contains the correlation table, and manages its own memory space. The host, a time-shared IBM 370/168, creates DPU program segments and sends them to the satellite via a 1200 bps link. Because actual DPU code is transmitted, and the DPU has relatively modest capabilities, little data compression is achieved. Although the communications link speed "is acceptable for a limited number of applications, especially to new users, it is not sufficient for experienced users of current major applications".

4.5 Summary

A minimal fixed-function satellite requires a (potentially expensive) high-speed communications link to provide satisfactory responsiveness. The communications load can be reduced by bringing more fixed functions to the satellite, by compressing data, eliminating redundant transmissions, and servicing lexical interactions in the satellite.

Whether these steps can be taken is determined primarily by the structure of the graphics package in use, and secondly by the economics of buying satellite main memory to support these additional functions.

5. PROGRAMMABLE SATELLITES

No matter how capable a fixed-function satellite system may be, it is intimately tied to the host, where some lexical and all syntactic and semantic processing is performed. Programmable satellites (also called intelligent satellites) offer a means of bringing some (or perhaps all, in special cases) of the syntactic and semantic processing to the satellite. There are several reasons for wanting to do this.

The reliability of the overall system is no greater than the joint reliability of the communications link and host computer, which unfortunately can sometimes be rather low. Programmable satellites provide the potential for at least some productive work to be done stand-alone on the satellite, should the host or link be unavailable.

Fixed function satellites may not be able to provide satisfactory responsiveness to user interactions, especially for experienced users or advanced applications. The bottlenecks are usually the link and/or time-sharing swapping on the host. These bottlenecks are partially avoided by moving more processing to the satellite. The rapidly developing packet switching communications networks will soon have an impact on communications link reliability and speed, so the communications link may cease to be so important in this respect. Another perspective is that fixed function satellites provide very little flexibility in controlling the software configuration (division of labor). The configuration is bound at system design time, and no application - dependent functions can be assigned to the satellite. Programmable satellites avoid this problem.

If a powerful satellite already exists, fixed-function software will not fully use the satellite's resources. Instead, host resources will be used, incurring usage charges which would have been lower, were more processing being performed on the satellite.

5.1 Basic Divisions of Processing and Data

In a programmable satellite, functions incorporated into the graphics package are all implemented in the satellite. The application programmer controls the distribution of application code between the two computers. The major consideration, then, is how the application program is divided between the two processors. Referring back to Figure 2, the first component of application code likely to be moved to the satellite is the lexical processing not done by the graphics package. This increases responsiveness by decreasing communications link traffic. Next to be moved to the satellite would be some or all of the main-line interaction handler.

This now presents a problem. The data base is accessed by 3 programs: syntactic processing, semantic processing, and the picture data base traverser. The first of these programs is now satellite-resident; the other two, host-resident. Where should the data be: at the host, at the satellite, duplicated in whole or in part, or part at each computer?

There is no one answer to the question: answering it requires a thorough familiarity with the application program, and
knowledge of how often each of the 3 programs accesses the data,
and how much data is transferred on each access. This knowledge, plus speed specifications for the communications link and
bulk storage devices in use, form the basis for some simple computations to estimate lower bounds on response time for each of
the alternatives.

Several general comments can be made, however. In one typical division, the picture data base might be stored at the satellite, the application data at the host. However, the two data
bases are typically not disjoint, so some duplication of information will occur. The application programmer must take care
that all updates of this duplicate information are performed on
both data bases. This is sometimes referred to as the synchro-
nization problem: two data bases must be kept in synchronism
one with another, if not continually, then at certain critical
points in time. The converse problem, that of two programs
concurrently trying to modify the same data base element, can
occur whenever concurrency (parallelism) exists between the
host's and satellite's application program modules.

The "data structure distillate" method is often used. Information is sent to the satellite describing only that portion
of the picture currently being displayed. The satellite can
send user-caused changes back to the host as they occur or in
batches, or it can send the entire modified distillate back to
the host, to be used in updating the permanent data base.

So long as the picture data base is at the host, the picture data base traversal process and the transform/clip process
should be host-resident as well. This avoids sending over the
communication link picture elements which are subsequently discarded as being outside the viewing window. At the same time,
though, the very same data compression techniques of section
4.2 can be used to further decrease the communications link
load. In this case, the division of labor will likely be similar to that of Figure 6.

By moving the picture data base to the satellite, we produce the division of labor shown in Figure 7. Many real applications are so structured, since the link to the host is much
less crucial than with most other divisions of labor. Further,
it is possible to give faster response to all lexical and syntactic interactions, unless moving function and data from the
host to the satellite forced programs or data which were core-
resident at the host to be disk-resident at the satellite.

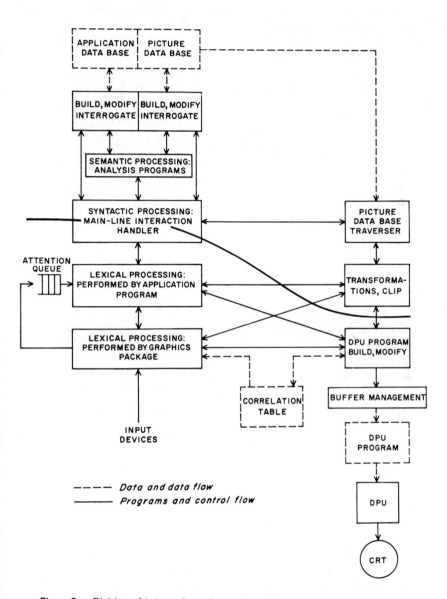

Figure 6.   Division of Labor: Some Syntactic, all Lexical Processing at Satellite.

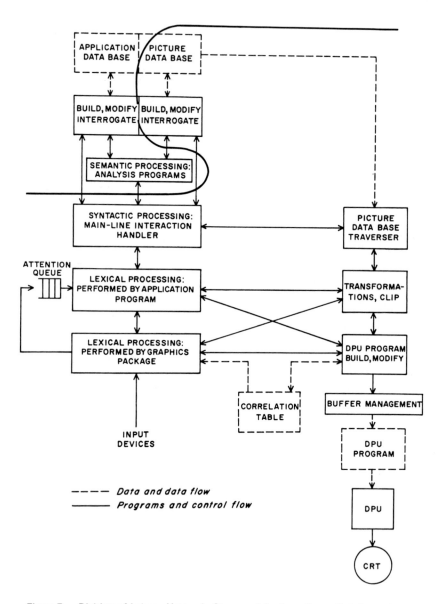

Figure 7.   Division of Labor: Host only Stores and Analyzes Semantic Information.

With a sufficiently powerful mini and/or a well circumscribed and limited application, all semantic processing and data bases can be moved to the satellite. The transformation of a satellite into a full stand-alone system is reminiscent of Myer and Sutherland's "Wheel of Reincarnation" [17]. "For just a little more money one can" add more main store, add more backing store, etc.. Indeed, decreasing minicomputer prices make stand-alone operation more and more attractive. But computing activities have a way of always expanding to need more than the available resources. Also, many applications need to access a large common data base. It is reasonable to expect that many graphics applications will continue to need both a host and a satellite.

5.2 Existing Systems

Programming a satellite graphics system can be a nontrivial task. The programmer may have to learn two operating systems, two or more languages, and communications protocols. In light of this and the preceeding discussion, it is therefore appropriate, when examining and contrasting the various extant systems for programming satellites, to apply the following criteria [9]:

1. How effectively the host is unburdened of lexical processing tasks, and how capable the system is of providing fast response to lexical user interactions.

2. How easily the application programmer can distribute and redistribute processing tasks and data between the host and satellite.

3. How easily the programmer can learn to use the system.

It is the purpose of this section to briefly describe and evaluate several systems meant to ease the task of programming host satellite systems. Note that we are not discussing applications implemented with a programmable satellite: rather we discuss systems meant to simplify the implementation process.

At the very lowest level, such a system might be just a communications package for inter-processor communications. At a slighly higher level are packages such as IBM's processor-to-processor (PTOP) routines for 360-to-1130 communications [23], which provide not just a communications interface but data conversion capabilities as well. More recently, the inter-process

communications protocols for use on the ARPA net [29] hide the
need for explicit communications line handling, and provide some
data description capabilities.

A very general system of this type has been outlined, but
not fully implemented, by Ross, et. al. [24], in which a Display Interface System (DIS) is described. The DIS consists of
basic executives in both the satellite and host processors.
These executives act in conjunction to provide attention and
program-handling mechanisms in both machines. Additional features, such as satellite storage management and DPU program
handling, are available in the form of standard system-provided
routines which can be allocated to either processor. Thus the -
division of labor can be controlled within the context of the
prewritten standard system routines.

Cottong and Greatorex [3,4] describe a system for UNIVAC
1557 (graphics support CPU) and 1558 (DPU) linked to a UNIVAC
1108 (main CPU). The main application program is written in
FORTRAN, and subroutine calls are used to build a hierarchical
data structure. At any time the structure can be clipped, and
a distillate transmitted to the satellite. The same hierarchical structure is maintained by the satellite. The satellite
can do additional clipping, and can create a DPU program.

The satellite is accessable to the application programmer
via an interpretive language whose syntax is similar to assemb-
ler language, but with more powerful semantics. It is called
ICT (for Interactive Control Tables). The language operates on
65 registers plus a stack holding a maximum of 15 entries.
Some registers have permanently assigned meanings: for instance,
registers 8 and 9 always contain the tracking cross's current
position.

The language is capable of providing user feedback and interaction of any sort, including but not limited to rubber-banding,
intensification of detected entities, prompts, and constrained
line drawing. It can interrogate and modify the satellite's
hierarchical data structure, can perform logical and arithmeti-
cal computations, can compose messages to be transmitted to the
main CPU, and can effect transfers of control and subroutine in-
vocations. Hence the language is powerful. A large number of
pictures changes can be made without main CPU intervention.

When messages are sent to the main CPU, the application program decodes them, and either updates the data base as required, or performs some analysis of the data base. In the former case the user can continue his interactions, as the satellite's data base has already been updated. In the latter case he will normally wait for the results before proceeding.

The UNIVAC system has many advantages. A lot of work can be done by the satellite, so the user can receive fast responses to most of his actions. Communication link traffic can be kept low. There is some flexibility in dividing processing between the two computers, although semantic analysis must be done on the host. But the programmer must be bilingual, so there are learning difficulties. The syntax of the interpretive language could easily be considerably improved at rather low cost, thereby reducing some of the learning problems. Finally, the programmer is forced to be very conscious of the dual CPU configuration.

The GRAPHICS-2 system developed at Bell Telephone Laboratories and reported on by Ninke [18] and Christensen and Pinson [2] is in most wasy similar to the UNIVAC system. GRAPHIC-2's hardware is a GE (now Honeywell) 645, and the satellite is an 8K (18 bits/word) PDP-9, and a DEC 343 DPU. The communication link transmits at 2000 bps.

An interpretive language, GRIN, is used. Its capabilities are interaction handling, data structure interrogation and modification, and control over which parts of the data structure are displayed. As with Cotton's system, a dual data structure is used. The difference is that all data structure modifications performed at the satellite are automatically applied to the main data structure. No explicit messages need be composed and sent to the main CPU. This is possible becuase the GRIN program is interpretively executed on both the satellite and the main CPU, with the communications task absorbed by the interpreters. The two CPUs can in general operate asynchronously: the main CPU usually need not update its data base before the user continues.

The GRIN programmer does not have to compose messages for the main CPU. Thus the dual CPUs are invisible to him. On the other hand, all data base changes, even those which may be temporary, are always transmitted: the programmer has lost control over this function.

GRIN's syntax, like ICT's, is wanting, but more importantly, based on the brief published description, its semantics appear less powerful. Programmers must be bilingual because analysis programs for the 645 are not written in GRIN, but in one of the 645's compiler languages. The interface between the GRIN program and the analysis program is the main CPU's hierarchical data structure, which the application program accesses via subroutine calls.

The semantic processing programs need not be concerned with decoding messages from the satellite to update the data base: it need only decode requests for analyses which are to be performed. In most other respects, the GRAPHICS-2 and UNIVAC systems are similar in concept, if not in detail.

THEMIS [15] uses an RCA Spectra 70/46 host and an 8K (12 bits/word) DEC 338 satellite display, connected by a 2400 bps link. All semantic processing must be done on the host, but interaction processing can be done on either host or satellite. Two different languages for specifying interaction handling are provided; one for the host, the other for the satellite. While the languages are nearly semantically equivalent, they are syntactically different. Interprocessor communications are explicitly programmed.

THEMIS does unburden the host of lexical processing, but gives only partial control over the distribution of processing since semantic processing is fixed at the host. Redistributing processes requires recoding to a new language, and changing calls to communications routines.

5.3   Systems for Configurable Programming

All of the systems described in section 5.2 represent important advances in satellite graphics, but do lack ease of learning and convenient redistribution of processing between the host and satellite. Two on-going research projects have built on this earlier work to develop systems which eliminate these two problems. The projects are van Dam's at Brown University [26, 27, 28], and Foley's at the University of North Carolina [9, 11, 12]. While there are important differences in technique, the similarity of purpose is more important.

Both projects' goal is to allow an application programmer to write in a single language as though for two computers sharing a common memory and then assign programs and data to either the host or satellite. Further, this initial configuration (division of labor) can be later "reconfigured" with no re-programming. The programmer never explicitly deals with inter-processor communications.

The Brown system (ICOPS, for Interconnected Processing Sys-tem) allows interprocess communication by means of subroutine calls and passed parameters. It is currently used with a macro-level language, and will be eventually used with LSD, Language for System Development [1]. The hardware is an IBM 360/67 host, a 50K bps link, a 32K byte microprogrammed Digital Scientific Meta 4 satellite, with disk and a display processor consisting of a second Meta 4 driving a Vector General.

The UNC system (CAGES, Configurable Applications for Gra-phics Employing Satellites), permits programs to be written in a PL/1 subset called PLCD [6, 13], and supports interprocess communications not only by calls and parameters, but also by signalled PL/1 conditions and references to variables known on both host and satellite. Hardware is an IBM 360/75 host, a 2M bps link, a 56K byte PDP-11/45 with disk, and a Vector General display processor.

Both ICOPS and CAGES have resident run-time systems to pro-cess references to procedures or data on the other computer, and to apply needed representational conversions to procedure parameters or data, such as converting from ASCII to EBCDIC.

This "configurable programming" approach to the use or pro-grammable satellites has a number of desirable attributes as pointed out in [12]. First, a single programming language is used. The language processors can produce executable code for either the host or satellite.

Second, the application programmer does not explicitly pro-gram inter-CPU communications. Such communications are auto-matically provided by the run-time system whenever a reference to a non-resident procedure or data element is made. The pro-grammer continues to use the familiar subroutine call or data reference to implicitly initiate the communication.

Third, performance data can be used to fine tune the divi-sion of labor to minimize response time, host usage charges, or some other metric.

Fourth, the programmer can conceive of and write the entire application program as a whole, as if it were going to be exe-cuted only on one computer, without knowing its eventual con-figuration. This should be helpful in conceiving of the application as a whole. For execution efficiency, however, he may want to be aware when designing the program structure that it will eventually be distributed. He may also want to optimize performance for what he considers to be likely configurations.

Fifth, program configurability is a necessary (but not sufficient) condition for program portability among dissimilar host-satellite systems. This is because, when moving to another satellite graphics system, the size of the host and satellite computers may change drastically. Some parts of the application program may have to be moved from the satellite to the host due to memory or other restrictions on the satellite.

5.4 Guidelines for Writing Configurable Programs

As more and more attention is paid distributed processing in computer networks, we are beginning to see systems like CAGES and ICOPS available for production use. The use of such systems raises an important question for the application programmer: How shall the application program be structured so that it will execute efficiently for a number of different arbitrary configurations? Efficient execution is achieved mainly by modularizing the program so that communications link traffic can be kept within reasonable bounds. In addition to building CAGES at UNC, Hamlin [11] also addressed this question. His conclusions form the basis for this section.

First, data base access routines should be used to search, read, write, and modify the data base. This means that a program which accesses a data base need not be resident on the same computer as the data base. In particular, the data base can be accessed from the satellite without first bringing the data base to the satellite. Parnas [20] has described the successful use of this approach in another context.

Second, top-down programming can produce efficient program structure, because it emphasizes both modularization and localization. The latter effect means that all processing related to a specific function (user action) is likely to be coded in just a few modules, which communicate chiefly among themselves and the data base access routines.

Third, Hamlin experimentally demonstrated the importance of separating lexical, syntactic and semantic processing into different modules, using Figure 2 as a model. Since semantic processing is often constrained to the host, lack of a clean modularization will force the lexcial and syntactic processing

there as well. In one case Hamlin studied, average response
time decreased from 3.2 seconds to 1.7 secons when all lexical
and some syntactic processing were moved to the satellite. In
this case, though, the communications link could transmit at a
quarter million bytes per second. With a more conventional link
in the 300 byte per second range, the response time would have
been decreased from 6.2 to 3.4 seconds: an important improvement, based on response time requirements described by Miller
[16] and mentioned briefly in section 2.

5.5 Summary

Programmable satellites can improve performance beyond that
of fixed function satellites, by moving function and data to the
satellite. Unfortunately, most existing systems for using satellites suffer deficiencies. The use of systems such as ICOPS,
CAGES, and other network distributed processing systems alle-
viate the deficiencies, and give considerable flexibility to the
application designer.

6. THE HARDWARE CONFIGURATION

Thus far we have concentrated on the software division of
labor. What about the hardware? How much is needed to support
a fixed function satellite? A programmable satellite? What is
the appropriate balance between the satellite's main and bulk
store sizes?

Some questions can be answered by the examples of real systems given in the preceeding sections. Fixed function satellites typically use a small mini with 8K or 16K bytes of main
store, have no bulk store, and use a communications link in the
100 to 1000 byte per second range, although this is sometimes
not fast enough for all applications. Programmable satellites
use more powerful minis with at least 32K bytes of main store,
a disk and a communication link in the same general speed range.
(Some of the experimental systems use much higher speed links,
but this is very expensive and not usually economically viable.)

If the performance of an existing system is to be upgraded,
which subsystem(s) should be made more powerful? The only
rigorous study of this question [7] provided the following
guidelines:

"A satisfactory inexpensive display system
uses a voice grade link, no bulk storage,
little or no core storage beyond the absolute minimum, and the least expensive
satellite computer-display processor.
For a little more money, the addition of
...bulk storage will provide better response time. Inexpensive increases in the
satellite computer-display processor (such
as extended instruction sets, limited picture scale-translate) are also helpful.
Further response time decreases are
achieved with broadband data link speeds
and more bulk storage. Additional response time improvements are obtained (at
high cost), first, by enhancing the satellite and display (with capabilities such as
floating point hardware, fast subroutining,
general dynamic picture transformations,
subpicturing, transformation compounding,
windowing) and then by adding more core
storage (beyond the minimum needed, to
eliminate overlaying or trashing on the
satellite, or to move more functions there)."

7. CONCLUSIONS

We began by reviewing the justification for satellite graphics, then described the system designer's task as choosing a
hardware and software configuration to meet cost and performance requirements. Two basic software approaches, the fixed
function and programmable satellite, were described and compared.

A fixed function satellite and the graphics package used to
access it should be designed to allow compression of transmitted
data, avoid redundant transmission, and minimize significant
events. Several divisions of labor for programmable satellites
were described: the data base placement is an important concern.

Programmable satellites are best used in an operating system environment which provides distributed processing capabilities and a common programming language, with the actual application program structured according to Hamlin's guidelines.
This permits easy reconfiguration to improve system performance
or resource utilization characteristics.

The hardware needed by satellites ranges from a small 8K byte micro or mini processor with no bulk store on up to a 64K byte or more processor with large bulk store.

References

1. Bergeron, D., et. al., "Systems Programming Languages,"
   Advances in Computers, 12, (1972), Academic Press.

2. Christensen, C. and E. N. Pinson, "Multi-function Graphics
   for a Large Computer Syste," *Proc. 1957 FJCC,* 697-711.

3. Cotton, I.W., "Languages for Graphic Attention Handling,"
   Proc. Computer Graphics Symposium, Brunel University,
   1970.

4. Cotton, I. W., and F. S. Greatorex, "Data Structures and
   Techniques for Remote Computer Graphics," *Proc. 1968 FJCC,*
   553-544.

5. Dill, J. D. and J. J. Thomas, "On the Organization of a
   Remote Low Cost Intelligent Graphics Terminal," *2nd Annual
   Conference on Computer Graphics and Interactive Techniques,*
   Bowling Green, Ohio 1975, pp. 1-8.

6. Dunigan, T., PLCD-PL/1 for the DEC PDP-11/45, Master's
   Degree Thesis, Department of Computer Science, University
   of North Carolina, Chapel Hill, N.C., 1973.

7. Foley, J.D., Optimum Design of Computer Driven Display
   Systems, Report 34, Systems Engineering Laboratory, Uni-
   versit of Michigan, Ann Arbor, 1969.

8. Foley, J. D., "An Approach to the Optimum Design of Computer Graphics Systems," *Comm. ACM 14,* 280-290, (1971)

9. Foley, J. D., "Software for Satellite Graphics Systems,"
   Proc. of the ACM 1973 Annual Conference, pp. 76-80.

10. Foley, J. D. and V. L. Wallace, "The Art of Natural Gra-
    phic Man-Machine Conversation," *Proc. IEEE 62 (4),* April
    1974, 462-470.

11. Hamlin, G., Configurable Applications for Satellite Gra-
    phics, Ph.D. Dissertation, Department of Computer Science,
    University of North Carolina, Chapel Hill, 1975.

12. Hamlin, G. and J.D. Foley, "Configurable Applications for
    Graphics Employing Satellites (CAGES)," *Proc. 2nd Annual
    Conference on Computer Graphics and Interactive Techniques:*
    9-19, Bowling Green, Ohio, 1975.

13. Kehs, D., Extensions to the PLCD Compiler, Master's Degree Thesis, Department of Computer Science, University of North Carolina, Chapel Hill, N.C., 1974.

14. Kilgour, A.C., "The Evolution of a Graphics System for Linked Computers," *Software Practice and Experience, 1,* 259-268, 1971.

15. Kulick, J. H., THEMIS -- A Distributed Processor Graphics Systems, Ph.D. Thesis, University of Pennsylvania, 1972.

16. Miller, R. B., "Response Time in Man-Computer Conversational Transactions," *1968 FJCC, AFIPS Conf. Proc., Vol. 33,* Monvale, N. J., AFIPS Press, pp. 267-277, 1968.

17. Myer, T. H., and I. E. Sutherland, "On the Design of Display Processor," *Comm. ACM 11, 6,* 410-414, 1968.

18. Ninke, W. H., "A Satellite Display Console System for a Multi-Access Central Computer," *Proc. IFIP Congress,* E65-E71, Edinburgh, 1968.

19. Newman, W., "A System for Interactive Graphical Programming," *1968 SJCC, AFIP Conf. Proc., Vol. 32,* Montvale, N.J., AFIPS Press, 1968, pp. 47-54.

20. Parnas, D. L., "On the crtieria to be Used in Decomposing Systems into Modules," *Comm. ACM,* 15, pp. 1053-58, December 1972.

21. Pardee, S., P. Rosenfeld, and Dowd, P. G., "G101- A Remote Time Share Terminal with Graphical Output Capabilities," *IEEE Transactions on Computers, C-20, 8:* 878-881, August 1971.

22. Puk, R., Personal Correspondence, August 1975.

23. Rapkin, M.D., and O.M. Abu-Gheida, "Stand-Alone/Remote Graphic System," *FJCC 33,* 731-746, 1968.

24. Ross, D.T., et. al., "The Design and Programming of a Display Interface System Integrating Multi-Access and Satellite Computers," *Proc. ACM/SHARE 4th Annual Design Workshop,* June 1967.

25. Rundle, A. R., "Software for Satellite Graphics," *Proceedings Computer Graphics Symposium,* Brunel University, 1970.

26. Stabler, G. M., A System for Interconnected Processing, Ph.D. Thesis, Brown University, Providence, R. I., 1974.

27. van Dam, A., et. al., "Intelligent Satellites for Interactive Graphics," *National Computer Conference*, 1973, pp. 229-238.

28. van Dam, A., et. al., "Intelligent Satellites for Interactive Graphics," *Proceedings of the IEEE*, 62, 4, pp. 483-492, April 1974.

29. White, J. E., *The Procedure Call Protocol*, November 1974, unpublished.

30. Woodsford, P. A., "The Design and Implementation of the GINO 3D Graphics Software Package," *Software-Practice and Experience*, 1, 1971, pp. 335-365.

Interactive Image Segmentation:
Line, Region and Semantic Structure

R. A. JARVIS
The Australian National University
Department of Computer Science
Canberra, A.C.T. 2600

ABSTRACT

This paper presents a number of ideas concerned with the problem of generalized image segmentation; in particular, the proposal of combining line, region and semantic structure as a powerful approach to a working solution is examined in detail. The interactive system for image processing, pattern recognition and graphics utilized for this work is briefly described. The graph theoretic representation of image segmentation structure is explored and the thorny question of visual texture analysis (in relation to the segmentation problem) is commented on. Some general remarks are made about the role of high level semantics in facilitating meaningful segmentation for images from well known environments, perhaps at the cost of generality. Preliminary implementation results for several fragments of the total proposal are given for a number of simple scenes.

INTRODUCTION

Image segmentation is that part of image analysis that concerns itself with the spatial definition of the various 'objects' constituting a visual scene. In many pattern recognition contexts this operation, whether manual or automatic, is regarded as being a form of preprocessing prior to object feature extraction, selection and ultimately, classification. Often 'ad hoc' methods are employed at the segmentation stage; mostly, and very sensibly, the known characteristics of the physical phenomenon associated with the image are invoked and generally a successful direct attack is made on the problem if these characteristics are well defined and not too complex.

This paper presents another approach to the segmentation problem; its aim is by no means to dissuade researchers from direct approaches when success can be found in them; rather a more generalized approach is explored as a means of better understanding how parts of a scene make up the whole and what is it about an element of a picture that defines its membership to that group of elements making up a part of an identifiable 'object'.

The types of images commonly encountered differ in complexity in terms of the spatial configurations and gray level fluctuations to be anticipated. In simple binary pictures, associations based on connectedness definitions are sufficient to solve the segmentation problem; subsequent boundary extraction is trivial. In some multigray level images, spatial partitions based on gray level homogeneity and adjacency links are sufficient for meaningful segmentaion; in others, where some degree of gray level gradation is acceptable within the same segment, tolerances have to be built into the element clustering procedures and various merge techniques based on shared borders, perimeter and area measurements etc., come to mind. It is where the question of texture enters the arena that a new level of difficulty is encountered.

Visual Texture Analysis has enjoyed a considerable amount of attention lately amongst researchers in the pattern recognition/scene analysis arena [7, 8, 9, 11, 14, 15]. A clear definition of 'visual texture' appears elusive. Pickett [7] suggests that the salient features of visual texture can be associated with a large number of visible elements, arrayed densely and evenly over a field of view. Haralick, et. al. [9] point out that spectral, textural and contextural features are among the fundamental pattern elements utilized in human interpretation of color photographs; they go on to comment on the way in which tone (based on the varying shades of gray values among pixels) and texture (related to spatial distributions of gray values) are not independent concepts but are interrelated in an 'inextricable' way. Hayes, et. al. [11] tackle the property of texture referred to as 'coarseness' and indicate that Fourier and Autocorrelation methods, spatial co-currence probabilities and the number of edge points per unit area have been proposed as texture coarseness measures and go on to suggest a 'best size' approach to texture coarseness based on spot detectors of various sizes; one type of spot detector used step like aperture masks while a second type used Gaussian distribution weighted apertures. The above mentioned attempts at

texture analysis seem to be directed towards providing discrimi-
natory evidence for classifying textures in a pattern recognition
sense. The structural attributes of texture are exploited only
indirectly, with statistical integrative estimators perhaps
masking structural attributes including fragment shape, placement, orientation etc. This statement is not made as a criticism of the work cited above but to emphasize that one must be
careful to distinguish those cases where the analysis of texture is of prime importance to the overall study (as in rock
or metal surface analysis, for example) from those in which texture is regarded as a microstructure which can be considered to
identify meaningful regions in an image but is not itself the
direct object of analysis. In as much as one is concerned with
discovery of interfaces between texturally distinct regions but
not primarily the description of the textured region in terms
of shapes, sizes and spatial configurations of the component
parts, it may be possible in many cases to side-step the issue
of defining texture in any exact way. Where this is not the
case one is faced with a micro scene analysis problem which is
itself to be solved before the macro scene analysis can be
attempted.

Most image pattern recognition and scene analysis is haunted
by some type of 'parts/whole' paradox: the dilemma that arises
when a fragment can more easily be detected and recognized by
its relationship to the whole but the whole cannot be sensed
except as the structural integration of the previously detected
fragments. Texture edge detection has its own special version
of this dilemma: - as texture manifests itself over a spatially
spread field, the attributes of individual textured regions necessary for edge discrimination cannot be reliably extracted
before the edge itself is declared. This implies that features
extracted from regions known to be of unmixed texture, though
quite capable of discriminating between candidates in a pattern
recognition sense, may not always be of value in finding texture
edges between two differently textured regions. In some cases
(particularly in man-made visual environments) it may be that
the 'edge effects' associated with visual truncation of textural
fragments may be detected more easily than that different textures exist on each side of the edge.

Another general idea is perhaps worth exploration at this
point. It concerns the use of high level semantics relating
the world as we know it to restricted classes of images from
known visual environments. To supply to an image analyzing
system 'a priori' knowledge about both expected and unacceptable
image component relationships which our own visual and physical
experience has, over a considerable span of time, taught us

seems like an extremely reasonable thing to do. Specifying such
information in a structured way is often difficult. Apart from
this difficulty, however, are there other problems associated
with this approach? There appears to be at least two objections
or at least warnings associated with this approach. One concerns
the diminishing generality of an image analyzing system which
is dominated by high level semantic direction and constraint
specifically designed for a particular visual environment. This
objection can certainly be brushed aside where meaningful results can be reliably obtained in a restricted visual environment of considerable importance, e.g. biological cell visual
analysis, fingerprint recognition etc. Further, this objection
can be met rather than brushed aside by providing a large data
base of knowledge about the world deemed helpful in image analysis for a wide range of image classes; no doubt, this would
be a difficult and expensive exercise but could be justified
for cetain visual environments. The second possible objection
could be that, in providing a great deal of high level semantic
information to a visual image analyzing system, researchers
might neglect the richness of the raw image data material itself
in providing low level cues as to its structural organization;
discovery of such structure would still be guided by human intuition in relation to the goals of the analysis but the problem
specific information could in many cases be less dominant.
Both ends of the spectrum of image analysis methodology need
attention so that specific practical solutions can be arrived
at reliably and efficiently and at the same time, the tools of
image analysis may be sharpened.

   In the majority of complex images containing multigray
level textured components, it would be anticipated that simple
edges based on gradient measures would be inadequate in defining
meaningful segment boundaries. On the other hand, sophisticated
region clustering techniques adequate to combine a texturally
similar image protion to a larger segment might have difficulty
in defining sharp edges. Line and region growth structures can
be used in a complementary fashion to help solve the general
segmentation problem. Finding lines by combining edge fragments
is a string like clustering problem, perhaps operating in a
gradient vector field derived from the original image. Clustering regions can be considered a more globular and spatially
diffuse procedure. Note also that, whereas regions always have
closed borders, lines derived from linking fragmentary edges
may not be closed; known line structure can be used to constrain
region growth and known regions to help close some lines and
delete others as inconsequential.

This paper presents a case for combining the line, region and semantic structure of a general class of images in the pursuit of meaningful segmentation. It is proposed that fragmentary line extracts and region pieces might interact in refining each in a structured way with the semantic component entering both at the low level of defining the acceptable linkage processes for combination of line and region fragments and also at the high level of human interpretation of the results and interactive feedback aimed at improving the computational processes invoked. In particular, well defined lines can act as border constraints for region growth while as yet undiscovered lines (in the gradient sense) might be defined in terms of the analysis of adjacent or even overlapping regions. Also, sophisticated merging procedures can utilize both fragmentary line and region structures, allowing for complex assessment of line and region adjacency relations in the general neighborhood of merge candidates. The concept of an adjacency map indicating all the adjacency conditions between region fragments is introduced as a data base for intelligent merge procedures. A line structure map derived from the gradient vector field of the original image is refined as information of regions and merges come to hand; the region map is developed in conjunction with the current line structure map and is refined through the merge procedures. The overall approach of the paper is the creation of a framework within which line, region and semantic structures of a general class of images might be manipulated with mutual interactions semantically supervised by the experimenter with the goal of meaningfully segmenting the image.

OVERALL SEGMENTATION STRATEGY

The raw image data is considered to be made up of a rectangular matrix of elements of pre-specified dimension, each element consisting of a smaller matrix of image intensity values. These elements constitute the basic fragments of the image mosaic which are to be analyzed to determine element associations leading to meaningful image segmentation. Region and line growth processors utilize features of the above mentioned elements and produce preliminary region and line maps, respectively, together with lists of corresponding line lengths, region sizes, line strengths and region strengths. An adjacency map giving region border interrelationships is derived from the intermediate data output by the region growth processor. Also, at this stage, a line link is derived from the intermediate data output from the line growth processor. All the information so far extracted constitutes an image data base which is the raw data for the region and line refinement processor. This data base includes

the preliminary region and line maps, the region and line
strength lists, region sizes, line lengths, the region adjacency map and the line link list. The region and line refinement
processor is responsible for interpreting semantically based
guide lines, conditions, constraints supplied by the operator
in prescribing region merges, divisions, appendages and line
joins, breaks, deletions. The ultimate outputs are the refined
region and line maps. (See Figure 1.)

SYSTEM CONFIGURATION

Figure 2 shows the equipment configuration of the mini
computer laboratory used for this study. Details are given in
reference [1,2,3] and only an overall description will be given
here. General purpose interfaces are used to communicate between the computer and image related equipment. A video interface allows the computer access to television camera images
which can at the same time be monitored by the operator. The
television camera can be attached to a high quality general
purpose optical microscope or can be used for imaging natural
scenes. A joystick and a graphics tablet are available as
alternative means of graphics input and a storage display screen
is capable of displaying line graphics, alphmeric and gray tone
images. Both flying spot photographic transparency and flying
spot microscope scanning equipment is provided. The microscope
slide stage is also position controllable remotely by the operator either directly or via the computer. Focus adjust is also
under computer control. The system can be easily reconfigured
for a variety of experiments in the image processing, pattern
recognition and graphics areas and has to date been used for
work on adaptive optimization, cluster analysis, convex hull
identification, isometric and contour plotting, handwritten
character recognition, biological cell analysis, signature verification, colinearity detection and focus optimization studies
in addition to the work reported in this paper.

For the experiments associated with this project it was decided that the flying spot transparency scanner be utilized as
the image data source, the graphics tablet for interactive input and the storage C.R.T. for image display. Core restrictions
and the inefficiency of existing disc storage random access
software made it necessary to consider the transparency itself
as the secondary memory source and the flying spot scanner as
the random access probe. Though extremely slow by comparison
with core access (if it were available in sufficient quantity)
this mode of operation did have the advantage of allowing the
investigator to directly view the scan and region/line growth

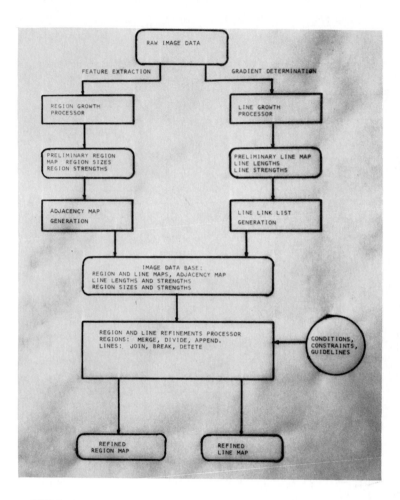

FIGURE 1. OVERALL IMAGE SEGMENTATION STRATEGY

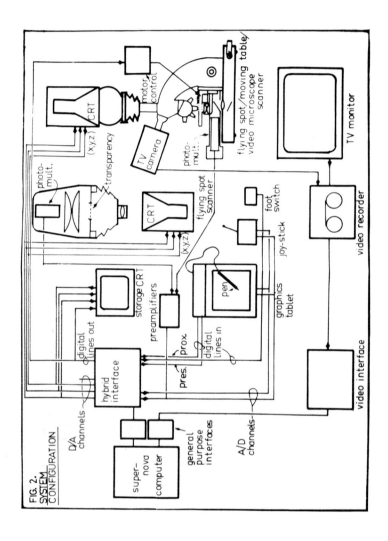

FIG. 2.
SYSTEM CONFIGURATION

process on the storage screen. The storage screen was slaved to the scanning C.R.T. and video data allowed to modulate the intensity; at the same time, the processor could mark the screen to indicate the acceptance of elements in the current growth sequence.

REGION GROWTH

The process of converting the raw image data array of gray level (intensity) values to a region map, where each element associated with predefined groups of original image points is labelled to indicate segment membership, can be viewed as a two stage mapping process. The first process is the substitution of each group of image points constituting a predefined element by the feature vector considered appropriate for capturing the properties of the elements important for classification. The second process is the classification or labelling stage, one label being associated with each feature vector to indicate image segment membership.

A 'classical' supervised pattern classification approach could be used if a sufficient set of representative feature prototypes were available or if a representative set of labelled samples were on hand or if either the exact statistics or means of estimating the statistics of the probability density distributions of all the active generating sources were known.

However, to the extent that the above types of information would not normally be available for the large variety of possible picture objects (assuming we wish to generalize as much as possible) the problem becomes one of unsupervised classification and various clustering procedures immediately came to mind as possible tools in this stage of the segmentation process. Clearly, for a restricted set of pictures some degree of supervision can be introduced; as always, the proper introduction of 'a priori' information can both simplify and improve the reliability of the decisions made.

Two important pieces of 'a priori' information that should be used when applicable (and this is so for a large range of pictures) are that elements in close spatial proximity have intuitively a greater chance of belonging to the same object than elements far apart and that spatial association linking the parts of an object together plays an important role in the image context.

In a previous paper [4] an associative growth procedure was emphasized and a simple euclidean metric used to measure 'distances' between spatially adjacent vectors; the decision to include an element spatially associated with a partially grown object within that object was made on the basis of the 'distance' between an as yet unclassified element and any associated element already in that object being less than a preselected threshold while at the same time the 'distance' of the candidate from a vector representative of the growing object (in a running average sense) was less than a second preselected threshold. Figure 3 shows typical results of the above approach.

The above approach, though moderately successful in relatively simple case, has a number of drawbacks on close re-evaluation.

Firstly, the associative growth procedure is strictly sequential in nature, i.e., at each stage of the process the two class decision of whether a candidate belongs or does not belong to the current growing picture object is made without reference to the possibility that the candidate picture element might better be placed in another as yet undeveloped object. There is no turning back and each new setting of the experimental values chosen for the thresholds mentioned above requires the entire sequential procedure to be repeated. Secondly, the use of a simple euclidean metric and preselected threshold is an extremely crude decision mechanism and does not properly take subtle vector variations into consideration; the measure is absolute and unrelated to the relative distances of other candidates. Finally, as a consequence of the clumsiness of the metric and the intuitive selection of thresholds, the large number of repetitions of the calculations required before acceptable results are obtained leads to a computationally expensive analysis procedure.

It was thought that the use of the more powerful clustering technique using a similarity measure based on shared neighbors [5,6] would avoid a number of the short-comings of the previous method. The results were disappointing and the investment in the considerable increase in processing effort not adequately repaid. Figure 4 shows typical results of the shared neighbor clustering approach with a spatially constrained circle of influence used to reduce processing effort. These results can be compared with those of Figure 3. The superiority of the more elaborate approach is clearly not evident. The method of reference [4] was reconsidered and minor variations were made for the region growth component of the current study. The features extracted were average gray level, variance, population entropy

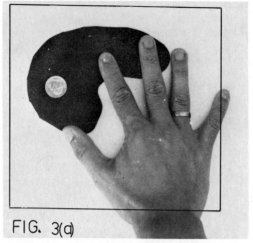

FIG. 3(a)

Figure 3(a)   Hand, Vinyl Shape and Coin
Original Image

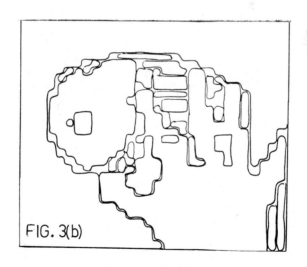

FIG. 3(b)

Figure 3(b)   Hand, Vinyl Shape and Coin
Previous Segmentation Results

Figure 3(c) *Family Group
Original Image*

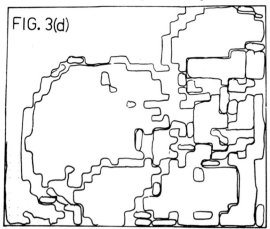

Figure 3(d) *Family Group
Previous Segmentation Results*

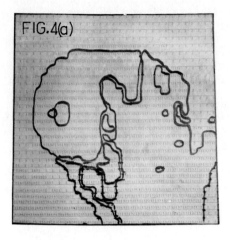

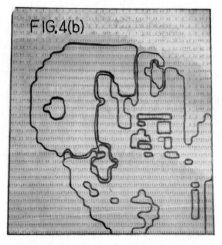

Figure 4(a) and 4(b) *Hand, Vinyl Shape and Coin-*
Previous Segmentation Results Using Shared
Near Neighbor Clustering in Feature Space

and components of the frequency histogram of the gray level distribution. The variance, population entropy and frequency histogram components were thought to have some importance in linking texturally similar elements; obviously more complex features should be investigated [7,8,9]. To reduce computational effort, any element initially discarded in any region growth sequence is not reconsidered if it was sufficiently different from the appropriate adjacent member on the first pass.

This meant the possibility of answering "yes", "no" or "maybe later" to the question "should the candidate element be labelled as belonging to the current segment?". The region growth method adopted can be summarized as follows:

(1)   Scan image elements in standard raster fashion till first unlabelled element is located; mark element (labelling and marking taking place in integer matrices of same dimension as image element grid).

(2)   Test for current segment membership any element in the adjacent neighborhood (8 neighbor interpretation) of the marked element, provided that such an element is neither already labelled nor has been discarded from consideration of membership as indicated below. (Weighted euclidean distances between the candidate elements feature vector and that of the marked element and between the candidate elements feature vector and the running average feature vector representing the segment at its current state of growth, are used as dissimilarity measures, separate tests being made against prespecified thresholds). Any candidate element sufficiently dissimilar from the marked element is discarded from any future consideration of membership in the current segment. (A different mark is used for this purpose).

(3)   Repeat (2) for any marked element, advancing repeatedly in standard raster scan, until no further elements eligible for marking can be found.

(4)   Label all marked elements with an as yet unused symbol.

(5)   Remove element marking (activity marking) but not labels.

(6)   Return to (1) and repeat (1) to (6) till all elements are labelled.

A second innovation was tested and then discarded as not being sufficiently advantageous to justify extra processing effort. It was thought useful that the sequence dependency of segment growth on the strict raster order of selection of candidate elements should be broken by randomizing selection using a "digital space filling" random sequence. The technique is worth a brief mention as it may prove useful in future work. A maximal length pseudo random binary sequence generator [8] was used and the content of the bits in the "shift register" interpreted as an integer pointer to an element of the image array. This method guarantees "space filling" without repetition within any one scan and needs very little memory space to implement.

It became clear that line structure and semantic based supervision are needed for more satisfactory segmentation results. Intuitively, in viewing Figures 3 and 4 one can see how knowledge of line structure could help refine the result.

The work by Horowitz and Pavlidis on the segmentation problem using a directed split-merge procedure [20] is valuable, not because it displays insight into the mysteries of image element "cohesion" in defining "objects" of interest, but because it provides an elegant and efficient framework within which to explore hypothesized cohesion rules.

In this work reported in [20], in addition to spatial association, only the simple constraint of gray level variation range was put on the elements constituting an image segment. It is not difficult to extend the representation of a basic image element from a single gray level value to a feature vector capturing tonal and textural properties (and others) of the group of resolution cells associated with each basic element as has already been described.

LINE GROWTH

The main approach for line growth explored in this paper is the attempt to discover adequate concatenation constraints to piece together image edge fragments detectable in a gray-level gradient vector field (calculated as shown in Figure 5a). The constraints so far used incorporate both gradient magnitude and direction. A two pass technique has been devised which shows some promise but needs refining and linking with a higher level structural approach which would allow both deletion of "spurs" and the "filling in" of small breaks between approximately co-linear line fragments. The first pass allocates gradient

direction to those image elements whose gradient magnitude
exceeds certain specified thresholds. If a fixed gradient magnitude threshold is used, it is difficult to recover both low
and high contrast edges without spurious noise like effects.
What is needed is a method of adaptively modifying the threshold
in response to local average gradient magnitude in the vicinity
of elements one would perceive as being on an edge. As a first
attempt to investigate adaptive thresholding, both a fixed
threshold and one evaluated by calculating the running average
of all previous gradient magnitude of elements not accepted were
used. An element is accepted in the first pass if its gradient
magnitude either exceeds the fixed threshold or exceeds by a
specified factor, the running average threshold. The sequence
dependency of this technique is one obvious flaw. A local
sphere of influence adaptive threshold would be expected to be
more effective and will be explored in the near future.

Elements accepted by the first pass are candidates for concatenation in the second. Three types of concatenation constraints, used in various combinations, were investigated with
some success.

(i)   Elements constituting a line must be linked by simple
      adjacency connectedness (8 neighbor interpretation).

      Considering two adjacent elements as possible parts of
      the same line

(ii) both candidates must have gradient tangent (edge direc-
      tion 90° to gradient vector direction) directions suf-
      ficiently close to the direction associated with the
      geometry of their relative adjacency positions as shown
      in Figure 5b,
and
(iii) both candidates must have their gradient vectors in
      the same direction within a specified angle of tole-
      rance.

(iv) Line fragments of less than a specified length are dis-
      carded.

The extrapolation of fragments in search of approximately co-
linear fragments across a gap should be investigated.

The effects of spatial quantization in distorting detectable
line structures are evidenced in Figure 8c, which shows the detected lines for a high contrast white triangle against a black
background.

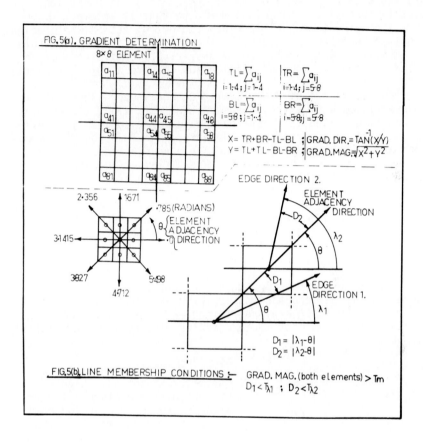

FIG.5(a). GRADIENT DETERMINATION
8×8 ELEMENT

$$TL=\sum a_{ij} \quad i=1:4; j=1-4$$

$$TR=\sum a_{ij} \quad i=1-4; j=5-8$$

$$BL=\sum a_{ij} \quad i=5-8; j=1-4$$

$$BR=\sum a_{ij} \quad i=5-8; j=5-8$$

$$X= TR+BR-TL-BL \quad ; GRAD. DIR.= TAN^{-1}(X/Y)$$
$$Y= TL+TL-BL-BR \quad ; GRAD. MAG.=\sqrt{X^2+Y^2}$$

2·356   1·571   ·785 (RADIANS)

3·1415   θ { ELEMENT ADJACENCY DIRECTION   0

3·927   5·498

4·712

EDGE DIRECTION 2.

ELEMENT ADJACENCY DIRECTION

D_2 λ_2 θ

D_1 EDGE DIRECTION 1.   θ λ_1

$$D_1 = |\lambda_1 - \theta|$$
$$D_2 = |\lambda_2 - \theta|$$

FIG.5(b). LINE MEMBERSHIP CONDITIONS :—

GRAD. MAG. (both elements) $> T_m$
$$D_1 < T_{\lambda_1} \quad ; \quad D_2 < T_{\lambda_2}$$

Some preliminary results of the above line growth procedure are shown in Figure 8 and are discussed in a later section. An overall comment on the method would be that it attempts to detect line structure by balancing gradient direction and gradient magnitude constraints against one another; its local "aperture of activity" is too small to be properly effective, but it is a valuable core for more sophisticated attempts at line extraction.

The estimation of gray level gradient vector components for a general class of images needs careful attention; the simple method illustrated in Figure 5a can be improved upon in a variety of different approaches. Rosenfeld and Thruston [8] recognize and elegantly meet the need for providing edge detectors with varying image domain size over which they operate to correspond to the variety of "edge widths" encountered in images. They propose a search for "best" edges based on computing over edge detectors applied to a set images derived from the original with various degrees of local overaging. The method has both a strong intuitive appeal and can be efficiently structured to be of computational complexity linearly related to the number of modified images used and their size. A related approach which could be termed the "distributed stochastic gradient estimate" approach is being investigated by the author; early experiments suggest it to be computationally expensive but still of sufficient interest to be explored further. A specified number of spatially Gaussian distributed samples of gray level are taken with known mean and variance. The mean is taken as the point on the image with which the resulting distributed gradient estimates is associated and the variance as the "spread" of the spatial domain over which the estimator is active. Each possible group of three points in this set define a plane. The gradient of each such plane is evaluated and the vector components averaged to provide the gradient vector for the locality about the specified mean.

Using several variance values for the random sampling around a specified mean, a set of gradient vectors distributed over corresponding domains can be searched for maximum magnitude and the appropriate gradient estimate used in subsequent analysis. This approach lends itself more to flying spot scanning of image data with immediate estimation of gradient values rather than the examination of digitized values over a quadruled grid (previously collected). No doubt there are other more efficient methods of achieving similar results, but the general idea is perhaps worth retaining. Huekel [12,13] presents a rigorous analysis of edge detection and offers a convincing, if computationally complex, method of edge detection. Circular image apertures of gray level values are examined and the intercepts of a dominant edge line through the aperture and the average gray levels on each side of the line are evaluated. Yakimovsky [21] presents a novel edge detector which searches about each point, on an expanding connected neighborhood basis, for the best evidence of the existence of an edge and the search is aborted on the lack of sufficient sequentially collected supporting evidence; an unaborted search returns a value indicative of confidence in the starting point being an edge point.

IMAGE DATA BASE

As each region or line is grown, a count is kept of the number of elements constituting the region or line. For regions these are called areas, for lines these are called lengths. Each region and line will have the corresponding number associated with it. In addition, again as each region or line is grown, a measure called its "strength" is accumulated. For regions, the strength is the inverse or negative of the average euclidean distance between a feature vector of a candidate element and the feature vector of that adjacent element, already a member of the current segment, associated with the successful membership test of the candidate. For lines, the strength is the average of the magnitude of the gradients of its member elements.

After the preliminary region and line maps have been generated (refer back to Figure 1), an adjacency map and a line link list is generated to complete the image data base which constitutes the input to the region and line refinement processor.

The adjacency map can be thought of as a square matrix with as many rows as there are regions in the region map. The (I,J) element of the matrix contains the number of elements touching the mutual border between the Ith region and the Jth region. Clearly, only a triangular matrix, including the main diagonal, is needed to store this information. The average strength between adjacent elements of different regions for each pair of regions is stored in the (J,I) element. If the self border lengths of the main diagonal are kept in a separate list, the main diagonal elements can be displaced by the self strengths of the borders. The resulting adjacency map is a very compact and powerful data base upon which to base region merge evaluations. The procedure to calculate the components of the adjacency map is as follows:

(i)   Find the bordering elements of each region of the pre-
       liminary region map by finding those elements not
       entirely surrounded by elements of the same region
       membership.

(ii)   For each pair of region borders (NxN/2 for N regions)
       count adjacent pairs of different membership and ave-
       rage corresponding strengths as the search proceeds,
       remembering to keep the number of elements in each
       self border in a separate list so that the main dia-
       gonal of the adjacency map can be used for self border
       strengths.

It is appropriate, at this stage, to discuss the underlying
concepts associated with the evaluation of the adjacency map.
An important structural view of the region interrelationship
is concerned. Suppose each element of the image (each of specified size in terms of image points) were to be considered as
"leaves" of a linkage tree. (See Figure 6d.) A bottom up
clumping view of the clustering procedure to produce segments
(or a hierarchy of segment groupings) would allow us to clump
"leaves" with "twigs", "twigs" with "minor branches", "branches"
with "main branches" and "main branches" with the "trunk". The
relationships are strictly non interactive between nodes at the
same level and the interpretation unrealistically simplistic.
Each piece of an image at any level is made up of other pieces
and is part of a bigger piece; this is not ambiguous but says
nothing about the complex border interrelationships. The adjacency map provides the information related to a more useful
view of segments in an image - the nodal graph interpretation.
(See Figure 6a, 6b, 6c.) Each segment is associated with a
node. Nodes have labels, region sizes and region strengths.
Branches between nodes are associated with border sharing between the linked nodes and border sharing is associated with
length and strength of the shared border. If a segment is to
be merged into another, all its links with other nodes are also
affected and the graph should be readjusted. In this way one
has a method of evaluating both the reasonableness of a region
merge and the disruption it will produce and can use this information for more subtle approaches to the refinement process.

The duality relationships between nodal graphs with nodes
representing segments and branches relating to mutual borders
and those where nodes represent border junctions and branches
are associated with border components may be exploited where
appropriate. Graphs with border fragment nodes and region related branches are a third variation. Horowitz and Pavlidis
[23] discuss some aspects of graph analysis for picture processing.

Evaluations such as the "order of connectedness" [22] of each node (the number of connected components into which the graph is divided if the corresponding node and the branches emanating from it are deleted) can easily be computed.

Borrowing from Finite State Machine analysis using Gill's [24] terminology and thinking of borders as the vehicle of transitions between regions (undirected in this sense), proper path high order matrices can be evaluated by matrix "multiplication", to formally clarify region interconnectedness of any order desired. Retaining order information in multiple transitions (as is normally preserved in F.S.M. analysis), all paths between specified regions can be enumerated. If only the skeleton matrices (connection matrices) are manipulated, the number of such paths can be calculated with less complexity than necessary for the symbolic concatenations associated with the higher order matrices themselves. Extending still further into the realm of probabilistic automata, border transitions can be allocated probabilities related to border weaknesses and image segment merge strategies can be based on higher order analysis of the probability matrix structures. Care would need to be exercised to exploit only those aspects of the "ready-made" formal methodology that properly reflected meaningful image cohesian mechanisms; allowing formal development to dominate and perhaps overwhelm the "sense" of the data would be counter-productive.

The line link list is the complementary structure for lines that corresponds to mutual borders for regions. The image coordinates for adjacent points on different lines is evaluated; these points can become the focus for possible line joining actions at a later stage of refinement.

REGION AND LINE REFINEMENT

This part of the paper is very tentative and only primative concepts of how the image data base (as described in the previous section) might be used have so far been entertained. So far, only a list of guidelines has been compiled; these are meant to reflect (rather simplistically) semantically based information related to how man views the world of two dimensional images. It was intended that considerable interactive facility would be needed at this stage to provide a flexible framework for manipulating the image data base in pursuit of meaningful segmentation. This aim appears rather too ambitious at this stage of development but it is felt that the rationale of the approach is basically sound, though implementation is bound to cause serious difficulties.

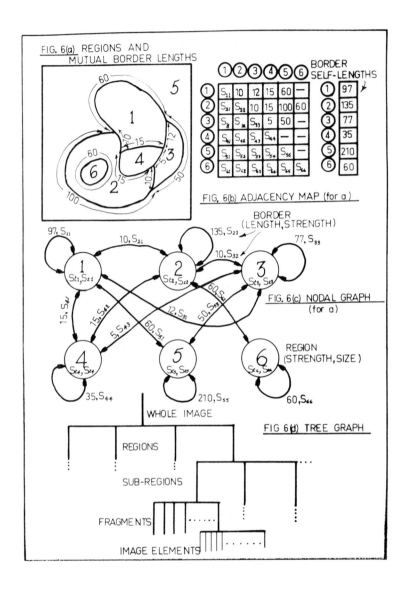

FIG. 6(a) REGIONS AND MUTUAL BORDER LENGTHS

FIG. 6(b) ADJACENCY MAP (for a)

FIG. 6(c) NODAL GRAPH (for a)

FIG 6(d) TREE GRAPH

The guidelines, conditions, constraints, whatever, are meant to provide means of assessing the reasonableness of merging, dividing and fragment appending for regions and of joining, breaking and deleting for lines. Some guidelines are:

(1) Look first for small weak regions with weak borders with few border links with other regions. Test mutual border strengths and merge when appropriate (interactively supplied thresholds) conditions exist.

(2) Look for regions with small area/border length ratios with few links with other regions. Test as in (1).

(3) Break weak regions with strong lines cutting almost entirely across them, especially where lines are in the vicinity of narrow "necks".

(4) Merge fragments if there is little evidence of strong line structure in vicinity.

(5) Join line pieces if there is good correspondence with mutual border between two strong regions and line gap is small.

(6) Prune (delete) lines if they are short, weak and/or do not correspond to a border between two or more strong regions whose mutual border strengths are weak.

Obviously, testing order and readjustment of the image data base must be carefully considered. Some guidelines here are:

(1) Change first only those things which disrupt the rest of the structure least.

(2) Use simple size weighted averages for strength calculations after merges and joins.

(3) Border lengths are easily re-evaluated after region merges by referring to border lengths in adjacency map.

(4) Recheck data from scanner when in doubt about a local property; finer scans can be used where appropriate (e.g. thin lines).

It is envisaged that interactive guidance be given to the region and line refinement process; the experimenter can point out regions and lines of particular interest or of critical importance and provide thresholds for various tolerance requirements, whilst

the processor provides quantitative information about the relevant regions and lines. Eventually, it is hoped that by this
cooperative venture, insight might be gained into the important
interrelationships that define regions and lines as we interpret
them. Of course, one would not expect to discover simple correspondence between perceptual and sensory edges and regions;
these matters are context dependent to a degree outside the
scope of this study and involve a complex restricted world model which assigns meaning to anticipated visual components and
which constrains the relationships such objects may have consistent with the reality of human experience.

PRELIMINARY IMPLEMENTATION RESULTS

Actual implementation has proceeded to the generation of
the preliminary region and line growth stage, including calculation of region sizes and strengths, line lengths and strengths.
The source code to develop the other components of the image
data base, including the adjacency map and line link list, have
been written but not yet tested. It is anticipated that some
headway into the realm of interactive region and line refinement with semantic based supervision will be made in the near
future. It is felt that the concentration of implementation
effort in developing the preliminary region and line maps is
not misplaced, as these represent the data for the subsequent
stages; the quality of the final result is critically dependent
on the quality of the intermediate data. Also, the "preliminary" maps are of significance in themselves and worth looking
at critically in the hope of better understanding the important
cohesive properties of elements constituting regions and lines.

A brief discussion of the preliminary studies presented in
Figures 7 and 8 follows:

Figure 7a depicts a number of simple objects in juxtaposition. This "innocent" assemblage, as it turns out, presents
quite a number of interesting problems in terms of image segmentation. The kidney shaped object is a piece of vinyl which is
line textured to a greater degree than is evident in the print
(far from homogenous); there are light fluctuations across the
coin due to the relief stamped upon it; the block of wood is
visually textured in quite a complex way as also is the scrap
of printed paper. Only the remaining two objects, one a lens
cap, are homogenous, as also is the background except for some
shadows near the block of wood. Figures 7b and 7c represent
the sort of tests which are helpful in interactively determining the types of element features that might prove useful in

Figure 7(a)   *Miscellaneous Assembly*
              Original Image

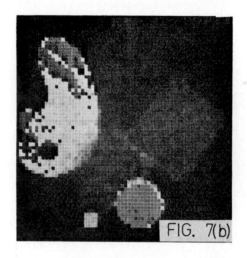

Figure 7(b)   *Gray Level Variance Plot*
              for Figure 7(a)

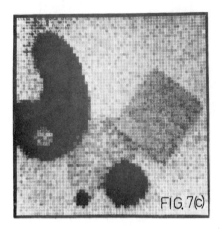

Figure 7(c)   *Gray Level Average/Variance Plot*
for Figure 7(a)

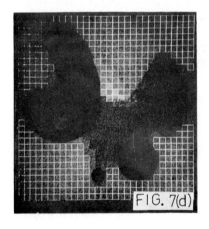

Figure 7(d)   *Growth of Background Segments*
for Figure 7(a)

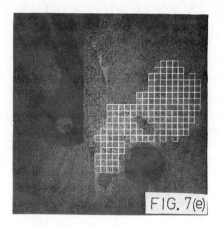

Figure 7(e)   *Wooden Block and Scrap of Printed Paper Grown
as Merged Segments Later in the Same Run as Figure 7(d)*

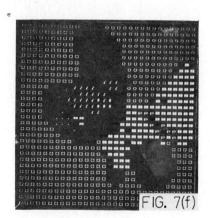

Figure 7(f)   *Labelled Segmentation Plot for Typical Run*

discriminating between regions whilst retaining cohesiveness
between elements of the same region. 7b is a scan of the original image showing the variance of the elements as brightness;
the high variance in the vinyl material is quite surprising and
distinct and a line caused by light catching a slight fold is
clear in the top portion. Light catching the top edge of the
lens cap also causes increased element variance in that vicinity. The printed scrap of paper and the wooden block tend to be
lost against the background. Figure 7c shows a similar scan,
but with average/variance modulating the image intensity. The
three dark objects stand out clearly with the variations in the
vinyl material suppressed. The wooden block and the printed
material are relatively easily detected visually. Figures 7d
and 7e show two stages of a single image region growth run using
all the extracted features (average gray level, variance, population entropy, frequency histogram components) but with strong
emphasis on average gray level and population entropy (using
feature weighting factors). Figure 7d shows the background detected as two regions (top and bottom) without any object broken
into. Figure 7e shows a single region corresponding to the
printed scrap of paper and the wooden block (developed later in
the same run). The joins between the printed material and wooden
block are thin and are a good example of a situation where line
structure and region strength calculations could be effective
in breaking the links. In this particular run, the vinyl region
was fragmented; this could indicate that features effective in
some region growths are totally ineffective for others. This
in turn suggests that perhaps a multipass technique using different features and weighting might provide better results; for
example, no doubt the dark objects could easily be detected by
emphasizing the feature (average/variance) as Figure 7c would
seem to indicate. Figure 7f shows a similar result as plotted
using distinct labels to indicate different regions.

Figure 8 is a group of line structure studies; 8c illustrates
the spatial quantization effects in distorting line structure
(for a high contrast triangle image), whilst the other figures
are various line studies of the source image of Figure 7a. In
Figures 8a, 8b, 8d, 8e, 8f, the images are intensity modulated
by the gradient direction for elements accepted by the gradient
magnitude thresholding pass.

Figure 8a shows how, with a high fixed gradient magnitude
threshold, high contrast edges can be found but lower contrast
edges are lost; for comparison, Figure 8b indicated how unwanted details appear when the fixed threshold is lowered.
Figures 8d and 8e, 8f are atempts at capturing both high and
low contrast edges using the mixed fixed and running average

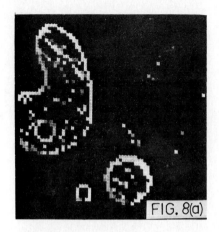

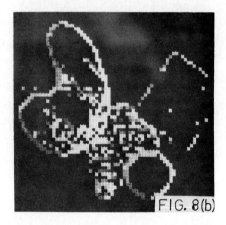

Figure 8(a) and 8(b) *Line Structure Studies: Images Intensity Modulated by Gradient Direction Indicator for Elements Accepted by Gradient Magnitude Thresholding Test.*

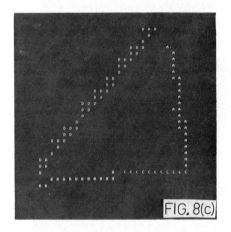

Figure 8(c)   *Illustration of Spatial Quantization Effects*
in Line Structure Detection

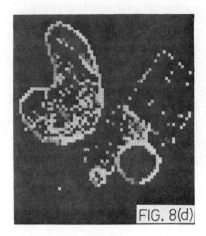

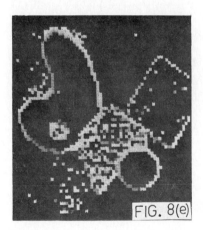

Figure 8(d) and 8(e) *Line Structure Studies: Images Intensity Modulated by Gradient Direction Indicator for Elements Accepted by Gradient Magnitudue Thresholding Test.*

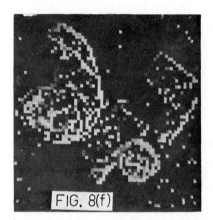

Figure 8(f) *Line Structure Studies: Images
Intensity Modulated by Gradient Direction
Indicator for Elements Accepted by Gradient
Magnitude Thresholding Test.*

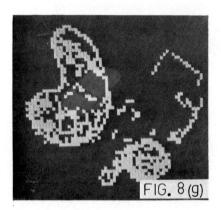

Figure 8(g) *Detected Line Structure Results Using
Gradient Direction and Line Fragment Length Constraints.*

gradient magnitude thresholds as discussed in the line growth section. In Figure 8e, the lack of detail in the body of the vinyl material was brought about by inadvertant video signal clipping for the dark regions by the flying spot scanner. Figure 8g is the result of applying element concatenation gradient direction constraints ((ii) and (iii) of line growth section) and discarding fragments smaller than 3 elements ((iv) of line growth section).

CONCLUSIONS

The combination of line, region and semantic structure in images would seem to have advantages over attempts at image segmentation restricted to one of the first two domains. As the project is far from complete no firm conclusion can presently be drawn. All one can say is that the direction of analysis proposed seems intuitively sound, if posing difficult problems in implementation. Time will tell if these intuitions prove fruitful.

Based on "Image Segmentation by Interactively Combining Line, Region and Semantic Structure," from the 1975 Proceedings of the Conference on Computer Graphics, Pattern Recognition and Data Structure (75 CH 0981-1C). Copyright 1975 by The Institute of Electrical and Electronics Engineers, Inc.

REFERENCES

1   Jarvis, R. A. "A Interactive Minicomputer Laboratory for Graphics, Image Processing and Pattern Recognition," *Computer,* October 1974, pp. 49-60.

2   Jarvis, R. A. "A General-Purpose Hybrid Interface for a Minicomputer," *Simulation,* Vol. 22, No. 4, April 1974, pp. 107-112.

3   Jarvis, R. A. "Computer Controlled Scanning Optical Microscope," *The Microscope,* Vol. 22, No. 3, July 1974, pp. 247-258.

4   Jarvis, R. A. and Patrick, E. A. "Picture Segmentation by Pattern Recognition," *Proc. N.E.C.,* 1970, Vol. 26, pp. 476-479.

5   Jarvis, R. A. and Patrick, E. A. "Clustering Using a Similarity Measure Based on Shared Near Neighbours," *IEEE Tran. on Computers,* November 1973, pp. 1025-1034.

6   Jarvis, R. A. "Clustering Using a Similarity Based on Shared Near Neighbours: Visual Image Experiments," *Proc. Workshop on Pictorial Organisation and Shape, C.S.I.R.O. (Aust.), 29-30 November, 1971,* pp. 90-97.

7   Pickett, R. M. "Visual Analysis of Texture in the Detection and Recognition of Objects," *Picture Processing and Psychopictorics,* ed. by Lipkin and Rosenfeld, Academic Press, 1970, pp. 289-308.

8   Rosenfeld, A. and Thurston, M. "Edge and Curve Detection for Visual Scene Analysis," *IEEE Trans. on Computers,* Vol. C-20, No. 5, May 1971, pp. 562-569.

9   Haralick, R. M., Shanmugan, K. and Dinstein, I. "Textural Features for Image Classification," *IEEE Trans.,* Vol. SMC-3, No. 6, November 1973, pp. 610-621.

10   Chow, P. E. K. and Davies, A. C. "The Synthesis of Cyclic Code Generators," *Electronic Engineering,* April 1964, pp. 253-259.

11   Hayes, K. C. Jr., Shah, A. N. and Rosenfeld, A. "Texture Coarseness: Further Experiments," *Correspondence IEEE Trans. SMC,* September 1974, pp. 467-472.

12   Hueckel, M. H. "An Operator Which Locates Edges in Digitized Pictures," *Journal of the ACM,* Vol. 18, No. 1, January 1971, pp. 113-125.

13   Hueckel, M. H. "A Local Operator Which Recognises Edges and Lines," *Journal of the ACM,* Vol. 20, No. 4, October 1973, pp. 634-647.

14   Rosenfeld, A. and Troy, E. "Visual Texture Analysis," Computer Science Center, Univ. of Maryland, Tech. Report 70-129, September 1970.

15   Troy, E. B., Deutsch, E. S. and Rosenfeld, A. "Gray-level Manipulation Experiments for Texture Analysis," *IEEE Trans.,* Vol. SMC-3, January 1973.

16   Tenenbaum, J. M., Garvey, T. D., Weil, S. and Wolf, H. C. "Research in Interactive Scene Analysis," SRI Artificial Intelligence Group, Technical Note No. 84, March 1975.

17   Duda, R. D. "Some Current Techniques for Scene Analysis," SRI Artificial Intelligence Group, Technical Note No. 46, October 1970.

18   Yakimovsky, Y. and Feldman, J. A. "A Semantics-Based Decision Theory Region Analyser," *Proc. 3rd Joint International Conference on Artifical Intelligence,* August 1973, Stanford University, pp. 580-588.

19   Bajcsy, R. and Lieberman, L. I. "Computer Description of Real Outdoor Scenes," *Proc. 2nd International Joint Conference on Pattern Recognition,* August 1974, Copenhagen, pp. 174-179.

20   Horowitz, S. L. and Pavlidis, T. "Picture Segmentation by a Directed Split-and-Merge Procedure," *Proc. 2nd International Joint Conference on Pattern Recognition,* August 1974, Copenhagen, pp. 424-433.

21   Yakimovsky, Y. "Sequential Decision Based Edge Detection," *Proc. Conference on Computer Graphics, Pattern Recognition and Data Structures,* May 14-16, 1975, Beverly Hills, Calif., pp. 290-291.

22   Rosenfeld, A. and Pfalz, J. L. "Sequential Operations in Digital Picture Processing," *Journal of the ACM,* Vol. 13, No. 4, October 1966, pp. 471-494.

23 Horowitz, S. L. and Pavlidis, T. "Picture Processing by Graph Analysis," *Proc. Conference on Computer Graphics, Pattern Recognition and Data Structures,* May 14-16, 1975, Beverly Hills, Calif., pp. 125-129.

24 Gill, A. *Introduction to the Theory of Finite State Machines,* McGraw-Hill, 1962.

Interactive Audio-Graphics
for
Speech and Image Characterization

JOHN P. RIGANATI
Rockwell International
Anaheim, California 92803

MARILYN L. GRIFFITH
Rockwell International
Anaheim, California 92803

INTRODUCTION

Purpose of This Chapter

At the current state-of-the-art, high performance inter-active graphics systems for specific engineering design appli-cations require custom tailored software and hardware configu-rations. A prospective architect of such a system is faced with a wide variety of options, none of which address his particular problem. The purpose of this chapter is to discuss, retrospectively, the considerations which were (or, alas, in some cases, should have been) paramount in structuring one such system and to, cautiously, generalize these considerations.

Our "Credentials"

The system upon which this discussion is based has evolved in a group doing signal processing and pattern recognition research and advanced development in a variety of contexts at Rockwell International. This system is not a general one; in fact, it is what Newman and Sproull, in a special IEEE Pro-ceedings' issue on Computer Graphics [1], have described as just another "unique configuration." However, it is one which has been and is being used with success for research and de-velopment on problems of significant economic interest. It consists of an interactive graphics system with bi-directional audio capability for use in classifying and describing (or cha-racterizing) speech and image data. The use of an interactive system allows human inspection of intermediate steps in algo-rithm development, easy modification of parameters, and imme-diate examination of the results. The graphics portion of the system used a keyboard, joystick, opaque and transparent image

309

scanners, and control panel for data input and has access to
a Tektronix 611 memory scope, an electrostatic printer/plotter,
a Calcomp plotter, and a high-resolution CRT with a camera
attachment for data output. As many as three different files
may be processed concurrently and may be stored either on magnetic tape or disc. A history file which maintains a record
of all or selected operations, may be viewed directly or on
hardcopy. The system has been used to generate a labelled
speech data base of 35,000 tokens for use in semi-automatic
speaker identification, to perform design of a low-cost alphanumeric character recognition algorithm capable of MOS/LSI rea-
lization, to analyze imagery for bandwidth reduction studies,
to research classification and matching algorithms for use in
fingerprint processing, and to develop electronic identification
systems based on several different parameter sets.

Who is Addressed?
      The chapter has been organized to address the reader who
is interested in constructing such a system from several points
of view. The following sections cover the system engineer's
worries on system configuration, the programmer's worries on
effective interactive procedures, and, by means of examples,
the user's worries on whether or not all of this is really
going to help solve his specific application problem. For
those interested in producing more general systems, we hope
that our attempt at candor has been successful and that the
importance to at least one operating environment of a system
which is continuously useful may be appreciated.

Why Audio-Graphics?
      Hearing and vision are the most powerful of man's senses.
Any determination of which of them is more useful is a function
of the application. Who would be content to merely watch
a symphony orchestra? Or, given a choice of television without
audio or audio without imagery (radio!) which would survive?
In another context, the utility of the hearing sense in crossing a busy street is usually underestimated.

      The blend of audio and graphics used in this system evolved
quite naturally from work on speech and speaker recognition.
The concept, of course, is not new [5,6] but it does seem to
us, from reading the literature, that the addition of audio is
a man-machine communication link which has not been properly
nor extensively exploited outside of the speech processing
community. Perhaps this is a result of the fact that while
audio communications are ephemeral, graphic communications may
be perused at the leisure of the experimenter. For communications which require extensive operator consideration, or in

the poor noise environments which characterize many computer
facilities, audio isn't very appropriate. To ease the burden
on an already overcrowded graphics display, for simple communications which may be perceived by the experimenter even when
his attention is diverted, or to enhance the experimenter's
intuitive grasp of his data, audio communication seems to us to
be indispensable. A trivial example is the use of an audio
signal, be it a word or a beep, at the end of a long computational cycle. This has been found to significantly lower the
frustration level since the experimenter does not have to constantly be looking at the screen and can freely divert his
attention to other matters. Another possibility for long communications is to provide a number of status reports. For example,

    "Phase One completed"
    "Overlay 08 rolled in"
    "Sorry, disc I/O error"
is quite an informative sequence even to the experimenter who
is distracted and is contemplating what to do with the expected
results.

    Less trivial, perhaps, is the use of audio output to extend
the range of or enhance the appreciation for information obtained
from the graphics display. Given a seven gray level image,
for example, the relative intensities of two points or regions
can be refined by positioning a cursor at each and converting
the true unquantized intensity into a tone. The effective dynamic range of the display is thus greatly extended. The
experimenter who is involved in an intuitive design process has
available another dimension in which he can perceive his data.
Pairs of point or area cursor also yield useful results. For
more than two cursors sounded simultaneously, the resulting
cacophony might be of interest to those bent on creating new art
forms which "speak" to each observer in a unique way, but we
have not found them useful.

    In a research environment in which the number of experi-
menters is small and the noise conditions controllable, the
addition of even a simple audio input link, with perhaps only
half a dozen commands, can contribute considerably to the ease
of operation. The operator who misses a status report, for
example, can request "Repeat" or "Status." Such verbal communications may also be appropriate in general purpose computer
environments to avoid the necessity of constantly running to
the teletype to obtain system directives. To date our prime
use of the audio input link has been for speech and speaker
recognition studies, where it plays a natural role. We have
just begun to exploit the potential of this bi-directional

audio link and feel this approach will be both fascinating
and economically fruitful for our applications.

DATA CHARACTERIZATION

The objective of data characterization consists of two
elements:
- classification using the classical measurement, feature extraction, class membership model

- description in sufficient detail to allow one to
  generate patterns belonging to a class

We know of no rigid dichotomy between the two that is suitable
for generalization. For specific applications, the distinctions
become obvious and perhaps even trivial. In our work we have
tended to shy away from formal models so that an "heuristic"
or "ad hoc" description properly describes our intended approach.
The descriptive act is related to the "linguistic" or "syntactic"
model, to "structural pattern recognition" and to the older
"analysis by synthesis" concepts. It differs primarily in the
degree of ambiguity permitted, a degree which is very much
problem dependent. The definition of characterization given
above differs also from what is ususally understood by the term
pattern analysis by the fact that it does require a dual
approach, even when this duality is not appropriate. Of course,
in such a case a more general pattern analysis is performed.
Since this characterization process is inevitably iterative,
it has become clear to a large number of workers in the field
that an interactive graphics approach is a very natural structure with which to perform it. The computer system performs
tasks such as cluster analysis, analysis of variance, or
histogram or scatter plots and presents the results in forms
suitable for uncovering the structure and irregularities of the
data. The designer is usually very familiar with the data and
observes nuances and properties which have not been embedded in
the general routines. This much is obvious and has been very
clear to both industrial and academic workers for a number of
years. What is less obvious, perhaps, is the magnitude of the
burden this puts on the man-machine communication links. This
smooth interactive approach to evolving a solution simply falls
apart if the data is not presented in a manner suitable for
exploration by the human's gestalt, if the system response
characteristics are annoying or distracting, if the system down
time is excessive, or, perhaps most significantly, if the system costs are not low enough to allow sufficient time for the
very unspecified iterative process to work. Hence, data cha-

racterization in an interactive environment involves both careful problem definition and the availability of a system which
has been well designed with that or a similar application in
mind.

Figure 1   illustrates the importance of perceptual considerations. Both portions of the figure illustrate the same
data derived from a fingerprint and explained in more detail
below. However, the second method of display includes a set of
dots at the center of the line segments. For most observers
the data in part (b) looks "smoother" than that of part (a)
despite the fact that exactly the same information is displayed.

Another example of the importance of perceptual effects is
shown in Figure 2,   which illustrates Roberts' phenomenon.
Part (a) shows an original photograph displayed to 32 shades of
gray; part (b) shows the same photograph limited to four shades
of gray. The contouring is quite evident. The second portion
of the figure shows the effect of corrupting the original by
additive white noise and again displaying the result at 32
shades of gray, part (c), and 4 shades of gray, part (d). Not
only has the contouring disappeared but many observers prefer
version (d) to version (c) despite the fact that it contains
less information in the formal sense.

In an operational environment the choice of features and
descriptors is inevitably restricted by constraints which are
tangential to the "pure" problem definition. The "time and
cost" arguments have been stated so often that to the uniniti-
ated they sound like lame excuses (which they may well be) for
a poor problem formulation. The fact that they are essential
ingredients in that formulation in a non-academic environment
is often misunderstood by those bent on exhaustive problem
understanding in an artificial environment. The initial representation employed for any particular problem usually results
from a combination of problem knowledge, intuition, analogous
experience and equipment availability, sometimes abetted by a
modicum of investigation. Clearly, any theoretically "optimal"
procedures applied to such a formulation must be interpreted
with considerable care and if their results are not in accord
with intuition they must either be modified or discarded.

We believe firmly that "quick and cursory explorations
usually result in quick and useless results," and that "a poor -
plan well executed is better than a good plan poorly executed."
The sheer joy that comes from a successful solution to an under-
specified problem cannot be adequately appreciated vicariously.
The search for total understanding and optimal criteria in the

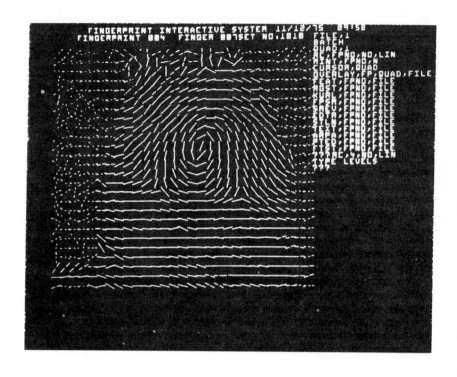

Figure 1a: *Ridge Flow Display Illustrating
Detailed Structure*

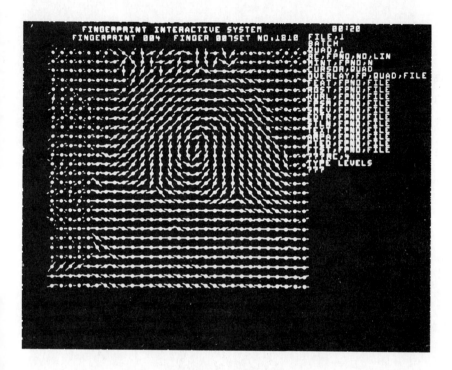

Figure 1b: *Ridge Flow Display Illustrating
Smooth Overall Structure*

Figure 1:   *(a) and (b) Illustrate the Same
Data Displayed Without and With
Central Dots*

(a) *Original 1200 x 1500 with 32 Shades of Gray*   (b) *Original Limited to Four Shades of Gray*

(c) *Original Corrupted by Additive White Noise (±40%) (Full-Scale)*   (d) *Corrupted Original of (c) Limited to Four Gray Levels*

Figure 2:   *Illustration of Roberts' Phenomenon*

academic world may be replaced by one very simple non-academic criterion: is the result economically viable? This viewpoint makes the feature design process one of challenge rather than one of frustration. Our view is that the complexity of the initial representation cannot be considered independently of the classification and description structure and these, in turn, are closely tied to the objectives of the investigation. The interactive system provides the ties.

SYSTEM CONFIGURATION

Design Considerations

An interactive system for pattern recognition problems combines the superior pattern recognition of the human with the superior data manipulation and mathematic capabilities of the computer. For many years computer users were besieged by stacks of paper with more numbers than they could begin to thoroughly examine. The stereotype computer user is often pictured sitting at a desk buried in listings. With interactive capability the researcher can rapidly examine a significant amount of data using various alternate algorithms and qualitatively reach conclusions as to validity or applicability to the problem without analyzing pages of numbers.

A good system design must begin with an understanding and familiarity with the problems to be solved and an identification of the intended users needs and human nature. This has been described succinctly by the KNOW THE USER dictum of Hansen [2] and Foley and Wallace [3]. Any system designer is plagued with the need to compromise in some areas in order to satisfy other requirements. Compromise in our interactive system was most often caused by the need to get results using the system within a minimum time from original definition of the problem. This often necessitated taking a path of specificity rather than generality in the design. Despite the limited and simple character of the system structure imposed by these typical industrial constraints, our system has become surprisingly versatile and powerful for our pattern analysis and classification problems in a developmental research environment.

These constraints of time and manpower led to a simple system with a high degree of modularity and very simple communications between researcher and computer. As many general capabilities for a useful interactive system as were possible with limited manpower and time available were implemented. An excellent summary of these capabilities is outlined by Kanal [32]:

. "Communication and control of the system through simple procedures ...." This was achieved with a menu of available commands displayed on the CRT, with short often 1 or 2 character inputs and default options. The users of this system are familiar with computers and with pattern recognition terminology. This sophisticated user community made the design of the menu and communication much simpler since education of the user was not necessary.

. "Quick response in an online mode, allowing rapid formulation, insertion and testing of alternate methods." With rare exception the system responds within 10 seconds. When a longer time is required for computation the use of audio signals and display of previous results on the CRT allow the researcher to become involved in contemplating the next experiment.

. "Easy online generation and modification of algorithms and programs ...." Due to the limited manpower and financial support for the interactive design task this capability was not feasible to develop. The only feature implemented which relates is complete flexibility of parameter specification for all previously defined algorithms. Also because the system was structured in a very modular fashion using separate subsystems and separate programs (overlap) installation of new algorithms was very simple using FORTRAN.

. "Ability to go forward and back to any option available in the system, to temporarily store and compare results of applying various optional procedures on a data set; to obtain intermediate and end results while sequencing through options." This goal was partially fulfilled by a variety of methods. The system is essentially a sub-operating system with most communication directing the analyses occurring between the executive program and user. This allows virtually any pathway through the system to be taken. The ability to save and compare intermediate and end results by two methods of obtaining a hardcopy of the CRT face at user's discretion.

Available Hardware
One of the most important factors in an initial design of a system is the available hardware. The bi-directional audio link is only one aspect of what we consider to be the interesting features of this system. Our research efforts are directed toward describing and classifying, or characterizing, data for a variety of applications. Dixon and Tappert [6] have observed a "need in experimental work involving machine proces-

sing of large data bases taken from the natural world" for "the development of techniques for online observation and data manipulation by the experimenter." The experimenter must be able to process a significant amount of data without losing intuitive involvement and to retain control at each stage of the inevitably iterative design process. An interactive system capable of calling powerful statistical routines, displaying intermediate results and, when desired, of giving a complete hardcopy of the experimental session, is an invaluable tool. The joint use of a binary storage scope and a graphics line printer enables this system to produce a hardcopy of the screen simply by copying the core image to the dot line printer without having to correct symbols or otherwise produce an interpretation of the screen. The storage scope itself is addressed through a special purpose dual line-drawing/image controllers so that line drawings and gray scale imagery, in both store and write-through modes, are efficiently available. A more complete description of data characterization in a variety of contexts is given below.

The pattern recognition interactive system shown in Figure 3 is developed on a Systems Engineering Labs (SEL) 8600. Its basic configuration consists of 32K words of core, a 24 megabyte disc, 3 tape units, a card reader, an electrostatic line printer and a special I/O controller -- the acquisition and control system (ACS) which handles all the I/O devices directly used by the interactive system. The ACS allows for rapid data input and output of 100,000 16-bit halfwords per second and can be easily expanded.

The usual graphic communication between man and machine takes place using a keyboard input and a Tektronix 611 CRT memory scope. Our memory scope has a special controller which gives flexibility not normally associated with a memory scope. Writing can be done in a store mode or in a write-thru mode which is used for cursors and small arrays superimposed on stored arrays. A gray level display can be achieved by using a matrix of dots to obtain several gray levels. The line drawings can be done either from point-to-point or from a point with displacement in x and y. The special interface has a fast output time for a full screen display to minimize frustration of the user.

Using the electrostatic printer, a high quality hardcopy of the memory scope screen can be generated easily since the information going to either device is similar. The electrostatic printer is very useful in our laboratory for fast output of gray level images, sonagrams or any gray level representation

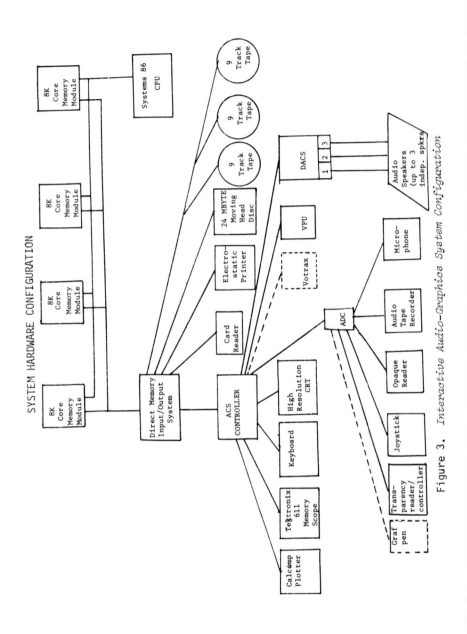

Figure 3. *Interactive Audio-Graphics System Configuration*

320

we may want to display. Graph plotting routines exist for the
electrostatic printer to enable any line drawings to be done
either on the printer, which is very fast, or on the Calcomp
incremental plotter, which is better for some applications.

Other devices associated with the interactive system are
an Analog-to-Digital Converter used for speech input from
analog tape or microphone and image input from either an opaque
or a transparency scanner. Three Digital-to-Analog Converters
are available for audio output. For image output we have a
high resolution CRT with polaroid and 70 mm movie camera attach-
ments.

The ability to save intermediate results can be achieved
by the hardcopy feature for putting CRT screen image to the
electrostatic printer of by taking a polaroid picture of the
CRT screen. Also the use of a history file of operations performed by the user aided in documentation of the intermediate
results. The current menu and operator responses were also
listed on the side of the CRT screen with the intermediate or
final results.

By examining the figure of the hardware system a multi-
tude of paths for data input are evident: data input
may be from disk, tape, audio input, image input devices, or
any other hardware added to the system at a particular time.
The researcher initially specifies the source of the input data
and then may forget where the data came from since the executive
system maintains this information. If the researcher later decides to change the source of data it is also very easy to do.
This flexibility of input data residency is very amenable to
further hardware expansion without major software change.

System Structure

The system design feature that has been found to be of
most utility and benefit is the sub-operating system or executive structure. This structure has been found useful by many
other designers. The executive program is minimal in size and
has as its main task directing the execution and loading of
specific applications programs in response to the researchers'
commands to the system. The executive is always resident and
is returned to upon completion of a specific application in
speech processing, image processing or any of the other modules.
Each application program is basically a stand-alone system
itself composed of many overlay programs.

Figure 4 shows the independence of each subsystem with interface to the executive. Each of the subsystems may also have an subexecutive which has special applications program.

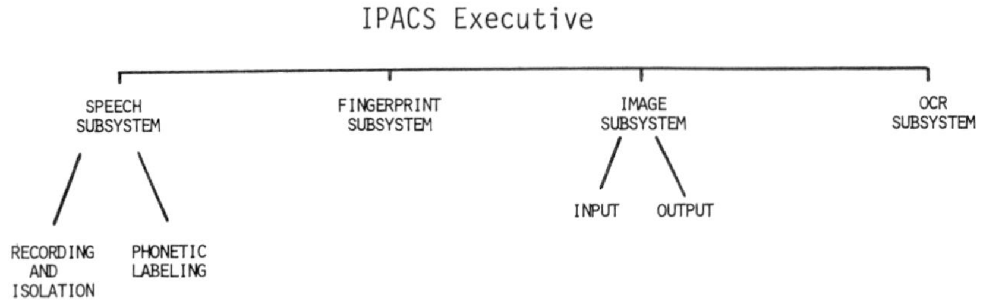

IPACS Executive

Figure 4. *Executive System*

The overlay structure is dictated by the amount of core available but has been found to have the additional advantage of modularity. Therefore easy addition of new modules when required is possible with little modification of the existing system. It also allows multiple programmers to add to the system without possessing knowledge of the total system structure and with little if any impact on each other or on users of the currently existing system. The only significant problem that has been found is a potential duplication of program functions in two or more subsystems since communication between subsystems is not possible. In our experience this has not been a serious disadvantage.

This system evolved as needs arose and began with a requirement for image input and output. The input and output had a number of associated parameters which were subject to variation for each image. An interactive system seemed to be the optimal solution. The original design was small in scope because the input/output capability was desired immediately. Based on the success of the interactive approach other problems were found to be very amenable to interactive processing and a total interactive system was evolved as the need for other pattern recognition projects arose. Resources were not available for dedication to the interactive system so it had to evolve as contracts or funding for the specific applications arose. This led to an evolutionary development and the described subsystem approach. It is very gratifying to see this structure be as versatile, powerful and applicable to our environment as it has been.

General Interactive Procedures
   Newman and Sproull [1] define a minimal set of functions
for a graphics system. The following are the functions we have
found useful for our specialized applications.

A. Output Procedures

   1. CURSOR. This routine sets up the cursor position and
   length, and starts a timer to activate the program which
   refreshes the cursor at a programmable rate.

   2. LINESCOPE. Draws lines on the scope from point A(x,y)
   to B(x,y).

   3. YSCOPE. Draws lines on the scope from an array of x, y
   values.

   4. DENSCOPE. This is used in character output and also for
   the gray level display. The individual gray level patterns
   are to be previously defined but they may be expanded in
   multiples of 8 x 8 bits. The array may start anywhere on
   the screen and may be any length in both vertical and horizontal directions.

   5. CHAROUT. This gives full character output to the screen
   of variable size (in multiples of 8 x 8 bits or .8 mm).
   The characters can be written wither vertically or horizontally at any point on the screen.

   6. PLAYBACK. Produces output words and tones from a stored
   lexicon using double buffering.

B. Input Procedures

   1. KEYBOARD. For input from the keyboard for user communication. This routine also references CHAROUT for a display of the user input.

   2. RECORD. This routine uses double buffering to facilitate continuous data recording without gaps due to I/O
   waiting. The recording can be done with a minimum of 30
   microseconds to a maximum of 65 milliseconds between samples. Data may be recorded for any length of time until
   one magnetic tape has been filled.

   3. JOY. This routine gets the joystick values for positioning the cursor.

4. LISTEN. Recognizes a small set of command utterances.

C. Miscellaneous Procedures

1. ARADNSTY. This routine quantizes a 1 or 2 dimensional array using input quantization levels to densify codes for the gray level display in PENSCOPE.

2. IASCBIN-IBINASC. For efficient ASCII-to-binary or binary-to-ASCII conversion for keyboard input and scope output.

3. FEATURE. This is actually a separate overlay which can be used to extract features from any data.

4. HARDCOPY. This allows copying of the memory scope screen to the electrostatic printer.

The interactive system is structured with overlays. This provides two main advantages: minimal core usage and convenient segmentation of blocks for use by more than one main segment. The minimal core usage is of prime importance to permit simultaneous use of the interactive system and other program functions with only 32K of core under control of the multiprogrammed Real Time Monitor. In one use, in six months over 3600 hours were logged on the speech labelling system described below. This program resides in 5600 words of core, leaving about 10,000 words for batch processing.

SUBSYSTEM ARCHITECTURE

All of the subsystems have a similar architecture but differ in complexity and structure. The fingerprint subsystem is an example of a tree structure and the OCR subsystem of an executive with many options at the same level. The worries of the programmer are addressed by discussion of these two subsystems.

Optical Character Recognition
This developmental effort was done very effectively with an interactive subsystem, allowing a high degree of human gestalt to operate with a rapid examination of large amounts of data. Figure 5 shows the OCR subsystem structure from data input to the adaptive learning and recognition program. The basic steps are familiar to anyone involved in OCR; thresholding analog data to binary data, enhancement of the data, segmentation of the data. At this point there exist a number of options;

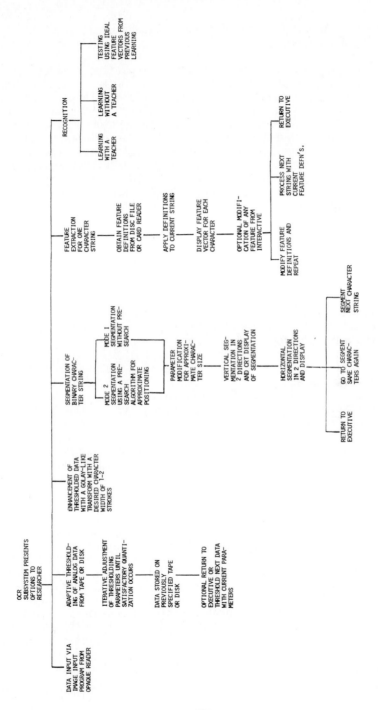

Figure 5: *OCR Subsystem Detail*

we chose to use a feature approach followed by an adaptive
learning algorithm.

The user would typically begin by inputting a number of
character strings and saving the data in a file. The data input
module remains in control until the user specifies a return to
the executive for further processing. This might be a termina-
tion with the data remaining for another session or a continuation to the following steps. The total control was given to
the user in that he could execute one module, until the results
were satisfactory, in his opinion from an intuitive analysis, or
execute the complete system to evaluate the total algorithm
rather than the individual parts. Most often the researcher
would iterate within an application program until satisfactory
parameters were established and then process a small representative amount of data with the parameters selected. These results might be held in a file until another session with the
next application program or transferred immediately to the next
step.

Two options for permanent data display are available at
intermediate and final stages: the image output subsystem can
be used as well as a feature which copies the CRT screen to the
electrostatic printer.

The main concerns for the programming task were the typical
interactive concerns of quick response time, processing or rather
not processing user's input errors, allowing maximum flexibility
and parameter adjustments, and not overburdening the user with
input requirements.

Quick responses are not a significant problem until the
feature extraction and recognition phases. At the feature step,
although a complete character string is processed, the feature
vector for each character is displayed as it is computed. Thus,
although the feature extraction for a character string is relatively long, the user's enthusiasm is held by the use of intermediate results. The output of intermediate results is a general philosophy of the system for the minimization of boredom
and, more importantly, as a tool to enable the researcher to
have a more thorough understanding of the final results. The
problem of user errors is often neglected by the systems designer who is deeply enmeshed in the beauty and efficiency of
the system and ignores the problems of the end-user. Hansen [2]
has defined the term "error-engineering" for this concept. He
notes that it is important to the user for the system to recognize errors and allow the user to act on them or recover
rather than terminating the run with the resulting loss of time,

loss of data, and user frustration and, maybe, eventual abandon-
ment of the system. Since in our application the programmer/
designer is also often the user it is of much concern to the
programmer to make the system "idiot-proof" as defined by
Wasserman [66]. The "idiot-proofing" in our system is quite
effective although not very elegant. If the user input did not
conform to any of the acceptable inputs at that time the user
is so informed and asked to correct and repeat the input. The
user also has the ability to erase the current input if he notices a mistake. The effects of unavoidable program termina-
tions due to hardware malfunction or an undebugged loop are
minimized by an adherence to the principle of saving intermediate results. Flexibility wityout undue requirements for user
input is achieved by defining default parameters, displaying
them to the user and allowing the user to modify none, any, or
all of them. Thus when one segment of the system has been defined the user need only activate that segment and it will
essentially run automatically without further interaction.

Flexibility is also achieved in this system by allowing
the researcher to begin processing at points for which data is
permanently stored: input from tags, analog data (data before
thresholding), enhanced binary data, segmented data and feature
vectors. Small amounts of data are stored on disc. However,
the reservoir is primarily magnetic tape. With an executive
the researcher may also go from any program to any other program assuming that the input data to the module had previously
been computed. This capability allows dynamic modification of
parameters and examination of the effects on one or all of the
subsequent steps. By special direction to the executive, the
loop from thresholding to learning or testing can occur on a
large amount of data, suppressing interactive communication and
giving only final statistical results. Thus, this system serves
two functions: an intuition training function and a testing or
evaluation function.

Fingerprint Subsystem
This subsystem is the last interactive system to evolve
and is currently being developed. At completion it will be a
complete classification system for use either as an interactive
research tool or as a processing algorithm for a significant
number of fingerprints requiring user interaction only at the
beginning steps for parameter and procedure specification. The
capability for the same software system to act interactively
and in a batch mode has been found to be very valuable. In
pattern recognition it is important to use both an intuitive
or heuristic approach and then to apply the resulting algorithms to a statistically significant data base and evaluate

Figure 6.   Fingerprint Subsystem Detail

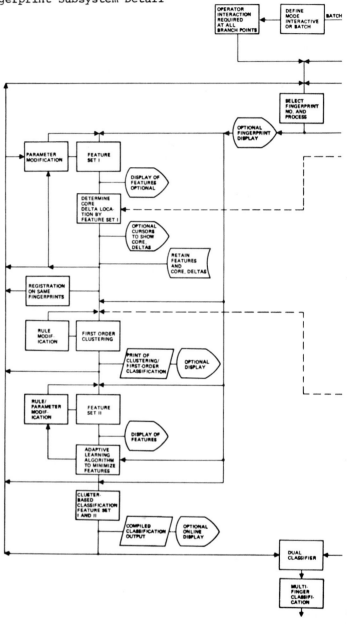

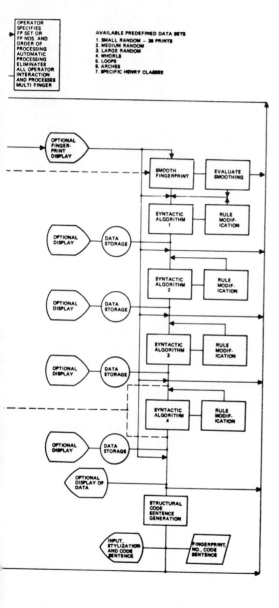

OPERATOR
SPECIFIES
FP SET OR
FP NOS. AND
ORDER OF
PROCESSING
AUTOMATIC
PROCESSING
ELIMINATES
ALL OPERATOR
INTERACTION
AND PROCESSES
MULTI FINGER

AVAILABLE PREDEFINED DATA SETS
1. SMALL RANDOM – 30 PRINTS
2. MEDIUM RANDOM
3. LARGE RANDOM
4. WHORLS
5. LOOPS
6. ARCHES
7. SPECIFIC HENRY CLASSES

OPTIONAL
FINGER-
PRINT
DISPLAY

SMOOTH
FINGERPRINT

EVALUATE
SMOOTHING

SYNTACTIC
ALGORITHM
1

RULE
MODIF-
ICATION

OPTIONAL
DISPLAY

DATA
STORAGE

SYNTACTIC
ALGORITHM
2

RULE
MODIF-
ICATION

OPTIONAL
DISPLAY

DATA
STORAGE

SYNTACTIC
ALGORITHM
3

RULE
MODIF-
ICATION

OPTIONAL
DISPLAY

DATA
STORAGE

SYNTACTIC
ALGORITHM
4

RULE
MODIF-
ICATION

OPTIONAL
DISPLAY

DATA
STORAGE

OPTIONAL
DISPLAY OF
DATA

STRUCTURAL
CODE
SENTENCE
GENERATION

INPUT,
STYLIZATION
AND CODE
SENTENCE

FINGERPRINT,
NO., CODE
SENTENCE

the results. Although for clarity this flow diagram is drawn
in a linear pattern - Figure 6, as in the OCR sybsystem, data is
saved at intermediate points and a session can use the intermediate results and continue the processing in either batch or
interactive mode. In addition to this capability there is a
combination for a semi-automatic processing where the researcher
is expected to be interacting and examining. Instead of specifying each fingerprint and all the steps to be processed, the researcher initially selects a predefined data set and defines all
the algorithms each print of the set is to undergo with associated parameters. This option is used very frequently to quickly
sequence through a specific set of fingerprints and see how the
algorithm being examined is performing.

APPLICATIONS

     In a brief summary paper (Griffith, Riganati, 1975) [4] we
conclude that an industrial user involved in application of
interactive pattern analysis techniques ought to take the aged
admonition KNOW THYSELF very much to heart. We know of no more
effective way to illustrate this dictum and our belief in it
than to discuss some of the practical applications in which our
system has found use. In presenting this synopsis of some of
the projects carried out at Rockwell International's Electronics
Research Division over the past five years we have attempted
to emphasize those design considerations which had most influence on the evolving interactive system.

     The major projects in which the evolving interactive sys-
tem has played a central role have included isolated word recognition, keyword recognition in continuous speech, continuous
speech recognition, language discrimination, speaker identification, optical character recognition, image bandwidth compression, image restoration and enhancement, and various electronic
identification systems including fingerprint processing. The
discussions below present background concepts and discussion
in some detail in three of these areas: speaker identification,
optical character recognition, and electronic identification
systems. Since we recognize that few readers will be interested in the details of any particular problem, the discussions
are kept broad and conceptual except where specific algorithmic
details are either necessary to a general understanding or are believed to be novel. A careful definition of the problems which
have been economically interesting and the constraints under
which reasonable solutions have been attained is required to
appreciate the structure of the interactive system which has
played and is playing a central role.

The applications we have addressed have been oriented
toward development of electronic hardware from individual LSI
chips to complete multicomputer installations. Our interests
have not generally been related to service applications or
feasibility studies on theoretical but economically non-viable
problems. Studies have product goals and are not merely "academic demonstrations that suggest the relevance of the methodology" (Kanal, 1974). Accordingly, we have selected three specific applications, for discussion at some length, in which
the pattern recognition methodology coupled with an interactive
system have resulted in products. One of these has been in
production for several years and the other two currently undergoing field tests prior to production commitment.

Optical Character Recognition

One of the earliest commercial applications of pattern recognition was in optical character recognition systems. Given
the existence of a collection of successful recognition strategies, a natural consequence was the design of a very low cost
structure for high volume restricted format data. This work
has led to a pair of MOS/LSI chips capable of realizing piece-
wise-linear decision surfaces and to a complete microprocessor
with concurrent bit and word manipulations designed especially
for binary pattern recognition processing.

A. An Embossed Credit Card Reader (ECR)

The MOS chip develpment was carried out in conjunction
with the design of free standing unit to read the embossing
on standard in-pocket credit cards (without imprinting the
card). The paramount constraint was to develop a system whose
cost was compatible with the projected applications. All
aspects of the desired unit from the initial sensor to the mechanical transport to the final recognition logic required development. The key area in which interactive processing played
a role was in clarifying the design tradeoffs involved in
matching the data quality obtained from the sensor to the quality which could be handled, with acceptable accuracy, by a
recognition algorithm whose complexity was compatible with the
cost constraints and suitable for use in other recognition
problems. Since the design of both the sensor and the recognition algorithm was carried out over the same time period, the
close connection of the two subelements of the unit was mandatory. The computer system provided this connection.

The hardware results for the recognition of the embossing
on credit cards are shown in Figures 7 to 10.

Figure 7 shows a photograph of the patented sensors employed in the unit. An optical wheel covered with a rubber-like membrane is brought into contact with the raised characters. A high contrast binary image results which is insensitive to height and background variations. A linear array of photocells, shown being held in the hand in Figure 7, was also designed and developed to read the image produced by the optical wheel. At the time no such sensors were commercially available. The read wheel/photocell characteristics were optimized using the recognition algorithm, described below, as the "judge".

Figure 8 shows the optical wheel and photo array interconnected to an electronic assebly which contains the pair of MOS/LSI chips which perform the recognition process. Figure 9 shows a complete mechanical unit including the mechanical drive. Figure 10 shows one installation where the credit card reader is employed. In this application the pump monitor is online to a credit verification computer which both approves the purchase and carries out an automatic billing.

The recognition algorithm employed in the Embossed Card Reader, shown above, evolved with the optical and mechanical portions of the unit. This is a typical example of what might be termed a "design-before-data-base" situation in which all elements of a solution to a particular problem must evolve simultaneously, even though each element is quite dependent on the final form and performance of all other elements. Experience has shown, time and time again, that successful new developments inevitably require an iterative design approach. It is simply unreasonable to expect to anticipate all of the problems without running some experiments. The apparent contradiction between this fact and a design-before-data-base situation may be resolved by simulating various portions of the system. When this is done interactively the various system elements may evolve smoothly from an initially ill-defined form to the final successful result. For systems involving speech and image characterization, the algorithm employed in "judging" the input's acceptability during the design process is of considerable importance. An important very general class of decision surfaces are described by piecewise linear discriminant functions, where the discriminant function for any category $i(i=1,\ldots,R)$ is determined by selecting from L_i subsidiary

discriminant functions, each of which is linear. Explicitly,

$$g_i(\underline{x}) = \max_{j=1,\ldots,L_i} \left[g_i^j(\underline{x}) \right], \quad i=1, \ldots, R .$$

Figure 7: *The Optical Read Wheel Produces
a High Contrast Binary Image
Which Is Sensed by the Linear
Photocell Array Shown*

Figure 8:   *The Read Wheel Assembly and*
            MOS/LSI Recognition Electronics

Figure 9: A Complete Assembly for Reading
Embossed Credit Cards

Figure 10: *A Typical Application, For the*
Embossed Card Reader, Performs
Automatic Credit Verification
and Billing

Each $g_i(\underline{x})$ is thus piecewise linear over the pattern space E^d, and the classification regions are convex sets. This particular description is actually subsumed by the more general piecewise linear but not necessarily convex surfaces. However, the convex case is of particular interest since a minimum distance classifier with respect to finite point sets is of this form. This is intuitively the correct form for the case of multimodal distributions within each category -- i.e., where a single "typical pattern" does not reasonably characterize a category but a set of typical patterns does. The fact that a minimum distance classifier with respect to point sets is indeed a piecewise linear machine with convex regions is easily demonstrated. For $i = 1, \ldots,$ R categories, L_i points per category, $\mathcal{D}_i$ denoting the set, and a Euclidean metric; the minimum distance classifier is

$$\min_{i=1,\ldots,R} \left[d(\underline{x}, \mathcal{D}_i) = \min_{j=1,\ldots L_i} |\underline{x} - \overline{P}_i^{\,j}| \right]$$

but $|\underline{x} - \overline{P}_i^{\,j}| = \sqrt{\underline{x} \cdot \underline{x} - 2\underline{x} \cdot \overline{P}_i^{\,j} + \overline{P}_i^{\,j} \cdot \overline{P}_i^{\,j}}$

so the solution to the minimization is equivalent to

$$\max_{i=1,\ldots R} \left[\max_{j=1,\ldots L_i} \ (\underline{x} \cdot \overline{P}_i^{\,j} - 1/2 \, \overline{P}_i^{\,j} \cdot \overline{P}_i^{\,j}) \right]$$

let this define $g_i(\underline{x})$, a piecewise linear function of $\underline{x}$.

Hence, the solution is

$$\max_{i=1,\ldots R} \ [g_i(\underline{x})]$$

which is a piecewise linear machine with strictly convex regions.

If we restrict attention to a binary space, the Hamming distance is equivalent to the Euclidean distance squared; monotonicity assures that minimizing with respect to Hamming distance produces the same results as minimizing with respect to Euclidean distance.

The algorithm implemented in the MOS/LSI chips designed for the Embossed Card Reader is a minimum distance classifier with respect to point sets -- a subset of the more general non-convex region piecewise linear decision machines. This algorithm has been referred to in the literature as a "modified" template match -- a description which is somewhat misleading unless the precise meaning of the "modification" is understood. The function implemented is

$$\sum_{i=1}^{N} w_i \cdot \left[d_i \oplus r_i \cdot c_i \right]$$

where c_i = 0 (don't care) or 1 (care)

w_i = 1 or 2 (with some restrictions)

r_i = 1 or 0 (reference)

d_i = 1 or 0 (input data)

N = dimension of the input vector

The "match" is actually formulated as a weighted mismatch between the binary input and the reference cluster. A zero mismatch represents perfect similarity.

The asymmetry or wasted state which appears to be mandated when an n bit weight includes zero is particularly disturbing for n = 2. This has been avoided by interpreting the two ROM bits allowed per position in the following manner:

ROM State	c_i	w_i	r_i
01	1	1	0
11	1	1	1
10	0	-	-
00	1	2	F_i

F_i is the state of an auxiliary flip-flop which is set to 1 when a 11 ROM state is encountered and to 0 when a 01 ROM state is encountered. This implies that the use of the double weight position is contextually restricted. The effect of this restriction is a minor for a large class of data since the regions available for double weighting are precisely those which have the highest information content. This approach yields a reasonable ROM size versus algorithm capability tradeoff at the very low cost end of the OCR spectrum.

Several ROM design procedures have been used. In general, the contents of the software "ROM" are initilized to a known sample point of each category. Features extracted from a labelled data base consisting of known samples of each category are presented to the algorithm. Its thresholds are initially set to include a reasonable number of these among its correct recognition responses. These are used to modify the contents of the ROM in an adaptive learning process. Typically, the references are modified to include an increasing number of points in the pattern space at a decreasing rate as successive new versions are presented to the algorithm. Eventually, the requirements for each category will become so "loose" than confusion between categories begins to appear. The adaptive procedure, learning with a "teacher" (the labelled data base), recognizes this situation and adds additional requirements to the erroneously responding reference. This process of successively loosening the requirements for recognition and then strengthening them when confusion results is continued until no reasonable amount of additional training produces a significant change in the references. The result is a set of references which are near optimum for the given training data and the given initial condition.

Unfortunately, the effect of initilialization often does not decrease fast enough to be insignificant at the point of "convergence." A second algorithm examines the cluster points which have been derived (exclusive of the double weights) and chooses a subset of points from each category which carries the maximum amount of discriminating information; i.e., only those points from category i are selected which effectively discriminate against category j. These new references are used to initialize the ROM and the training process is repeated. The result of the two steps is a set of two references for each category. They differ in their response to perturbations of other categories than itself. The second has less strict requirements resulting in poorer discrimination against perturbation of other categories but better response to perturbed (but not "trained-on") versions of itself. The final choice of references is made by subjective judgement using the two sub-optimal forms for inspiration.

The software algorithm is then fixed so no further adaptation occurs and a set of labelled testing data is classified. The result is a characterization of the performance of the algorithm on the given data with the references designed above. The "surprises" at this stage are usually rare enough to convey a large enough amount of information to determine specific changes in the references. The process is repeated until sa-

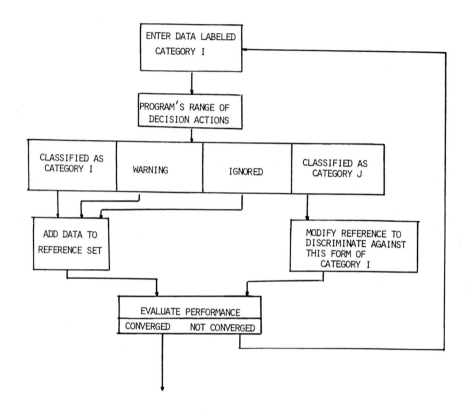

Figure 11:   *Adaptive Design Decisions*

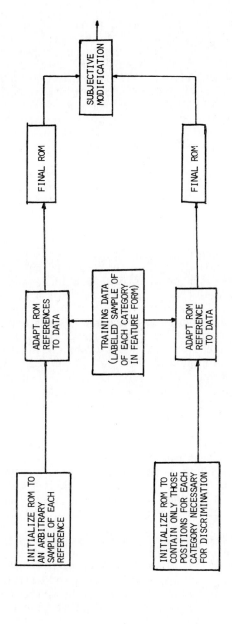

Figure 12: *Reference Design Procedure for Recognition of Categories*

tisfactory performance is achieved. These adaptive design decisions are illustrated in Figures   11 and 12.

B. Inadequate Data
    Tacit in any training procedure is the assumption that the
available data is "representative" of the totality of pattern
forms. In practice, the training set is never large enough to
do anything but represent the patterns for which the probability
density function has an area of "local concentration" in pattern
space. Including a "sampling" of other points is not useful
and can be detrimental. For example, a single extraneous point
which nullifies the linear separability can cause the diver-
gence of certain iterative algorithms which would otherwise
converge. What is required of the algorithms is the additional
power to make "no decision" decisions -- i.e., guard bands,
majority logic, or threshold regions. The separating surfaces
in the pattern space, while still piecewise linear (or capable
of being so approximated), are no longer easy to visualize for
the more general cases. A guard band region modification of
the minimum distance classifier with respect to point sets is
a simpler example than most and yields to intuitive visualization. The points are clusters ("galaxies") in pattern space.
Within a surface surrounding the cluster, a point is classified
as a perturbed member of the cluster. Within a band outside
the first surface but within a second surface, a pattern point
is considered to be a very corrupted version of the category
and is rejected. (The decision response is "it looks like category i but don't force me to guess.") Outside the second
surface the points are classified as not belonging to this category. Points which are outside the second surfaces for all categories are classified as "noise" inputs. This gives the
classification part of the recognition algorithm the ability to
search for patterns within a stream of unedited data (a "self-
editing" scheme).

    Concisely, the modified minimum distance classifier with
respect to point sets has three responses: 1) if a pattern
point is "close enough" to category i, it is classified as i;
2) if it is "close but not close enough," it is classifed as
marginal i; 3) if it is "not close enough to any category,"
it is classified as noise (ignored).

    The metric used to measure "close enough" is a key factor
in the success of the algorithm. As mentioned above, the
cluster of representative points may be viewed as a maximum
region of the probability density function in pattern space
($p[\underline{x} \ \varepsilon$ cluster/category i]). Of course, the points in the
cluster are not equiprobable and the visualization of a

"gaussian* puffball" riddled with "swiss cheese type" holes is
a reasonably accurate one. The holes are caused by the truncation of very low probability density values to zero -- i.e.,
very unlikely patterns are not explicitly included. This
notion also makes the use of a recognition "deadband" extremely
reasonable -- points in the holes are "close" to the cluster
but not actually members of it. As the penetration into a hole
or the distance outside the entire cluster gets larger, the
probability density should monotonically decrease (according
to the visualization). The algorithm implements this decision.
Although it is not always in accord with the human gestalt
sense of "correctness," especially for the lower order algorithms, (i.e., the probability density function is not monotonically decreasing, by subjective judgements) the mechanization
is a reasonable one (the performance/cost ratio is acceptable).

C. A Hand Held OCR Wand
     A large number of variables affect the design of any re-
cognition system. For the design of a low cost hand held wand
the interactive graphics system allowed exploration of a large
range of data quality variations. This design was performed
concurrently with the development of a CCD sensor for reading
an entire line of data without any wand motion. Close space
lines, interfering marks, connected characters, grid cell size,
serial/parallel processing architectural considerations and
their effect on clock rates are illustrative of the variables
which must be examined and appropriately characterized. Three
of the steps in this design are shown in Figure 13. Figure
13a shows the gray level data displayed to seven gray levels
and the output of a thresholding algorithm which was designed
interactively on this system. It also shows the binary threshold data before and after a Golay-like transformation whose parameters were designed statistically. Isolation of these binary
characters is shown in Figure 13b. The interactive system permits either monitoring the results at the completion of each
step in the processing or the performing of a long run on a
large section of data with either a detailed or a summary hardcopy of the results.

Image Processing
     A significant portion of our image processing work has
clustered around systems in which the observer is part of an
image communication link. The considerations for such systems

---

*The distribution is not actually "gaussian," but this is
a convenient visualization.

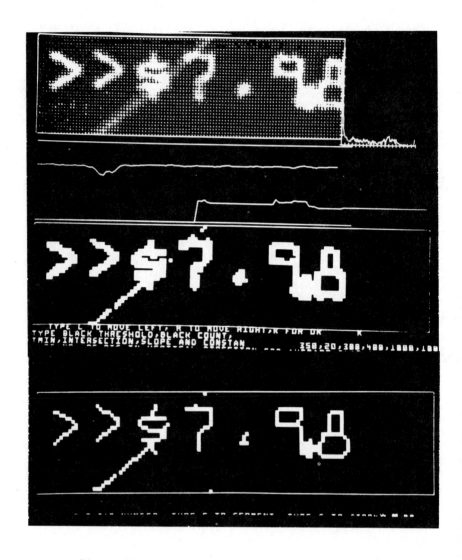

Figure 13a: *OCR Display of Seven Gray Levels,
Thresholded and Enhanced Binary*

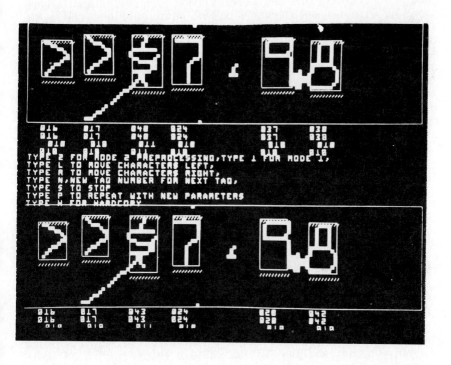

Figure 13b: *OCR Display of Character Segmentation*

may be grouped into three areas: 1) display of information which is more intelligible to the observer; 2) quantitative analysis of the trade-offs required to conform to channel limitations, power constraints, and desirable decision functions and use of these to direct the observer's attention to portions of the scene having a high probability of interest. Efficient transmission implies sending only that information which is useful to the observer. Extracting such information requires understanding and careful use of both the redundancy inherent in the imagery and in man's eye-brain perception system. This processing must be in consonance with the cost, complexity and flexibility requirements of practical systems. The interactive image subsystem procedures have been constructed as a tool to aid in these investigations.

Since quantitative specification of image quality remains such an elusive goal for all but the most narrowly defined classes of imagery, direct and rapid viewing of the effects of processing is a prime requirement for work in the area. Desirable supporting features include a class of histogram normalizations, transforms, thresholding, automatic labeling, gamma and distortion corrections and automatic zoom. Figure 14 shows a zoom sequence on a 1500 x 1200 element original with labeling. With movie film and still camera output capability, the system can be operated wither interactively one image at a time or in a batch mode with automatic output to movie film.

Image Input. The input procedure is very simple. Parameters controlling speed of input, size of picture, black/white/gray levels and labeling information are entered using a simple command language with computer prompting. Input may take up to 15 minutes, depending on the picture size.

Image Output. To facilitate black/white level adjustment, a histogram of the levels for each image may be used to quantize to any number of gray levels or to set black and white levels with gray being distributed linearly between the two levels. The number of gray levels, the black and white levels, the picture size and portion of picture displayed are controlled by a simple user command language. If movie film is used, the film is automatically advanced.

Figure 2-14.   Imaging System Illustration of the Zoom Feature

Figure 14:   *Imaging System Illustration of the Zoom Feature*

347

Electronic Personal Identification

A. Introduction

Electronic identification systems offer a means of providing control over access to and creation of personal data files, of virtually eliminating the many fraudulent transactions which plague our private and governmental business, of permitting rapid and reliable selective access to restricted areas ranging from apartment dwellings to military bases, and, perhaps most significantly, of safeguarding the rights of the individual by drastically reducing false identifications. Any successful personal identification technique must rely on one or more non-transferable attributes which are functions of either anatomical or learned characteristics or both. Systems which are based on codes, passwords, cards, keylocks, psychological deterrent, or human monitoring have been successfully and economically employed for a considerable number of years. A large number of these are in the process of being replaced by this new class of electronics identification systems because of their superior performance, lower total system costs, totally new capabilities or some combination of these factors. Law enforcement agencies and the military have provided the chief impetus for the development of these systems and have played a significant role in making ready the paths down which this technology will travel to commercial markets.

Of the many possible approaches to automated identification, three have emerged as the most promising for solving the very practical problems facing society.

These are based on fingerprints, speech, and handwriting. Table E-1 shows a qualitative tabulation of the degree of dependence of these three approaches on either anatomical or learned characteristics. No judgement concerning the merits of the different dependencies can be made without considering a complete system and none is intended to be implied by Table E-1.

Table E-1

Approach	Dependence on Anatomical Characteristics	Dependence on Learned Characteristics
Fingerprint	complete	none
Speech	high	moderate
Handwriting	low	high

The fingerprint technique relies on measuring pattern structure and ridge ending and bifurcation minutiae from one or more fingers. The speech based approach utilized measurements from the acoustic wave to infer both anatomical information, such as vocal cavity resonances, and particular learned characteristics which are distinctively individual, such as the way each person uses his lips, tongue or teeth to form words. The handwriting approach extracts, from the dynamic pressure-as-a-function-of-time signal, elements of style and flourish which are lost in the static orthographic representation of the word or signature. The dynamics are influenced to some extent by the hand size and musculature.

Non-technical factors significantly influence the choice of an approach for a particular application. The banking industry has long relied on signatures on checks even though they are rarely examined manually. Signature verification appears to the industry to be a natural technique to employ if the costs and error performance are commensurate with the needs. The data storage per individual appears to be the least. Law enforcement agencies, on the other hand, have been using manually processed fingerprint cards since the turn of the century and no real question of choice of techniques arises except for crimes involving verbal threats or forgeries. The fine details of the fingerprint ridge structure form the basis for the manual fingerprint systems, which have come to be universally accepted as legal evidence of identification. This history and the very large amount of reliable data available from an individual support the fingerprint systems' claim to the lowest theoretical error rates. The speech based systems are well suited for convenient human interaction and, of course, are solely applicable when only voice information is available (through the ubiquitous telephone, for example). Hence, each system appears to have a primary sphere of applications where it is the natural system of choice and a secondary sphere where it competes with the other approaches.

B. Speaker Identification
     One of our largest efforts has been the use of the interactive system in conjunction with studies on a Semi-Automatic Speaker Identification System (SASIS) [7,8,13]. The speech processing group at Rockwell International has created the largest labeled speech data base (5640 sentences) known to exist, to the best of our knowledge, by using this interactive procedure. Because of the large number of hours this required, it was essential to avoid inefficient ineffective man-machine communications.

Background

Speech is usable for indentification because it is a product of the speaker's individual anatomy and linguistic background. When air is expelled from the lungs, it passes through the glottis, which is the opening bounded on either side by the vocal folds. When the vocal folds are drawn together and air from the lungs is forced through them, they vibrate, making a buzzing sound. This sound is modified as it passes through the vocal tract, which is the tube formed principally by the pharyngeal cavity and the oral cavity. The shape of the vocal track serves to concentrate sound energy at certain frequencies and reduce it in others. During speech, the shape of the vocal track serves to concentrate sound energy at certain frequencies and reduce it in others. During speech, the shape of the vocal track is continuously modified by movements of the tongue, lips, and other vocal organs. Thus, the quality of the speech sounds a speaker produces represents the sizes and shapes of his vocal organs and the way he uses them in speaking. Therefore, speech characteristics vary from speaker to speaker. The effect is termed interspeaker (between speakers) variability. Speech analysis also reveals variability when the same speaker utters a given sound several times. This is called intraspeaker (within speaker) variability. Intraspeaker variability arises because the physiological activity necessary to make speech sounds need not be exactly controlled to effect adequate communication.

The speech signal produced by a given individual is affected by both the organic characteristics of the speaker (in terms of vocal tract geometry) and learned differences due to ethnic or social factors.

Research leading to the conception of the SASIS can be divided into two broad categories, one treating manual spectrographic comparison (voiceprint) techniques and the other treating automatic or semi-automatic computer-assisted speaker identification techniques.

It is generally acknowledged that voice spectrograms (voiceprints) contain significant information about speaker identity. The spectrographic comparison method has been used extensively in forensic applications but has been recently under increasing criticism from the linguistic community [19,20,21]. The primary deficiencies in the voiceprint technique are subjectivity on the part of the voiceprint examiner and lack of continuous training of the examiner's discriminant ability. A labelled spectrogram is shown in Figure 15.

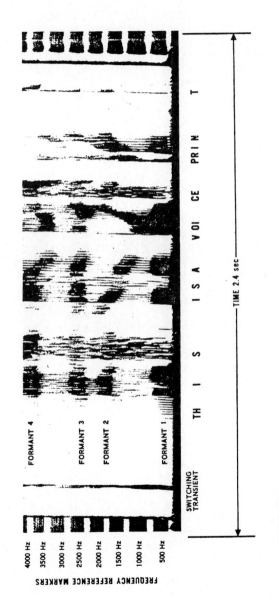

Figure 15: A labeled Spectrogram of: "THIS IS A VOICEPRINT"

351

The voiceprint research has contributed to the conception of the SASIS in establishing a definite need for the system's objectivity and introducing the concept of voice identification to the investigative and forensic application areas. The methodology of voiceprint comparison is poorly documented in the published literature, but basically attempts to match relevant areas of corresponding spectrograms for an identification decision. This method differs significantly from the SASIS in that it relies primarily upon the dynamic properties of the spectrum, whereas the SASIS approach analyzes steady-state segments of phonetic events.

The computer-assisted approach to speaker identification has also been investigated, and several systems have been proposed [5]. Most techniques developed prior to SASIS have attempted to be completely automatic, based on digital spectrographic comparison of samples of speech from groups of speakers. Typically, such systems require the speakers to say a sequence of specified words, which are automatically segmented and compared using Fourier LPC or analog filter measurements. Such automatic segmentation techniques are not yet advanced to the state where these systems can deal with the kind of unconstrained speech found in criminal utterances. Therefore, the emphasis by the law enforcement community has been on techniques such as in the SASIS, which make use of the best and most dependable capabilities of both the human operator and the computer.

A number of factors were taken into consideration in selecting the candidate phoneme set. Vowels were selected in nonnasalized, stressed positions since they have been shown to have good discriminating ability and are easily labeled. Fricatives and stop releases were not selected because they show less intraspeaker variability and are difficult to analyze. Diphthongs and glides were not selected due to the lack of steady-state intervals for analysis. The events which are used are shown in Figure 16.

The problems that had to be solved and the tasks that had to be carried out in the SASIS analytical studies included:
1. Design of phonetically and statistically valid speech data bases and recording procedures;.
2. Recruitment, screening, scheduling, and recording of over 250 speakers;
3. Processing of the data bases to examine, analyze, label, extract, and catalog over 35,000 phonetic tokens;
4. Research on the effects of coarticulation on speaker comparison;

Event	Example
i	eve
I	it
ɛ	met
a	ask
a	father
Λ	up
ɝ	bird
ɔ	all
ʊ	put
u	boot
m	me
n	no
ŋ	sing
ə	the (schwa)

Figure 16: *Phoneme Event Set for Speaker Identification*

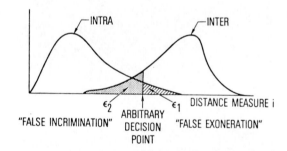

Figure 17: *Intraspeaker and Interspeaker Normalized Histograms*

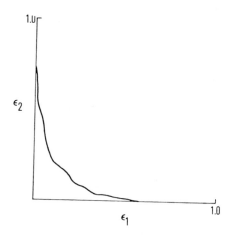

Figure 18:   *SOC (SASIS Operating Characteristics)*

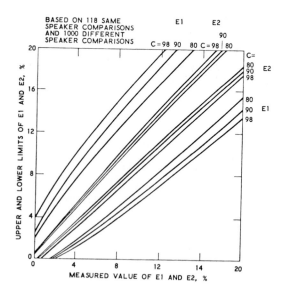

Figure 19:   *Example of Confidence Estimates on SASIS Statistics*

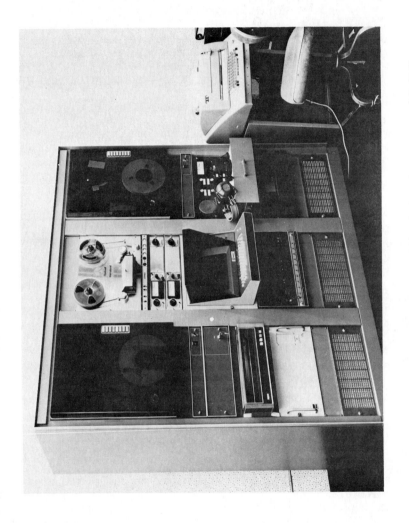

Figure 20: *Semi-Automatic Speaker Idnetification System (SASIS)*

5. Development of a large set (162) of candidate fea-
    ture measurements and refining of that set down
    to the 30 best features for each phonetic type.
6. Research on the effects on speaker comparison of
    the channel over which the speech is transmitted
    and the acoustic surroundings at the speaker lo-
    cation;
7. Development of optimum techniques for combining
    features into distance measures, and distance
    measures into similarity measures;
8. Development of statistically valid system perform-
    ance testing techniques.

These are discussed at length in references 8 and 18.

Various measures were evaluated based on comparisons of
SASIS operating characteristic curves (SOC curves). The curves
represent the cumulative error distribution that would result
if specific values of similarity measure were used in making
decisions regarding whether two voice samples came from the same
or different speakers. Figure 17 and 18 indicate how the
SOC curves are derived. The SOC curves are used as an evaluation
figure of merit that indicates sensitivity in the ε_1 and ε_2
overlap region.

The speaker data base used in the SASIS development is the
largest of its type in existence. The fact that it is a sample
of the total population, however, results in some statistical
uncertainty in applying the results to the general population.
Standard statistical techniques were used to compute the confidence levels of the performance statistics, using worst-case
assumptions. Figure 19 shows the upper and lower limits to
the ε_1 and ε_2 error probabilities at three different confidence
levels. These error limits indicate to the operator the stati-
stical uncertainty associated with the measurements made by the
system. This data allows the operator to assign a "weight" to
the system results when he is using these results to arrive at
a decision regarding the voice samples under consideration.

The prototype system is shown in Figure 20. The interactive system being described here was used to design the algorithms which are implemented in this prototype system. The prototype is dedicated to the speaker identification function and
is, in fact, a deliverable item which is currently undergoing
field testing. The interactive labeling system portion is described below. Further details may be found in references
[7,8,18].

Speech Interactive Labeling System (SPIL)

The labeling system operates in two modes consisting of a detailed description of the command language for prompting a new user and a cryptic prompting for the experienced user. The system had to be immune to user mistakes. There is probably no frustration greater than losing control of the system or losing data. Whenever any option was requested which affected previous results, a reconfirmation was required before any action was taken. Since response times varied from 10 ms to 5 sec, there was a potential for considerable boredom. This was partially alleviated by allowing previous outputs to remain on the screen while processing was being done.

The interactive graphics procedure was developed to permit analog-to-digital conversion (digitizing) of the recorded speech sentences, selecting and labeling candidate phonetic events within the sentences and segmenting three pitch periods of the steady-state portion of each selected phonetic event. A total of over 35,000 events were labeled and segmented.

The first phase of this procedure involved digitizing the prerecorded spoken sentences. The audio from the telephone channel was passed through the combination of a C-2 telephone channel simulator and a 3.2 KHz low-pass sampling filter. The resultant audio was sampled at 6.8 KHz. The sentence digitizing was controlled by an operator at the interactive graphics console. He first instructed the computer to sample 10 seconds of speech after which a display of the smoothed energy in the digitized signal was displayed on the CRT. The operator next isolated the sentence with a set of cursors. He then verified the sentence using digital-to-analog playback between the cursors and judged whether to accept or reject the utterance. Upon acceptance, complete speaker and sentence identification information was entered, and the isolated sentence was automatically stored on a digital output tape.

The digital sentence tape was then processed by the labeling and segmentation program in order to identify and extract candidate phonetic events. Each sentence on the tape was transformed to a digital voice spectrogram (voiceprint) via the Fast Fourier Transform and displayed on the CRT. The spectrographic display frame on the CRT was limited to 1100 milliseconds. The operator advanced the display a frame at a time until the entire sentence was labeled. Phonetic labeling is done with two phases: the macrophase and the microphase. The macrophase is used to isolate the desired phonetic event from the spectrographic display; the microphase uses this event as input and enables the operator to isolate three pitch periods.

Macrophase. Figure 21 shows the display of a spectrogram of 1.1 seconds of speech used for the isolation of a desired phoneme. A cursor under joystick control is used to select the desired phoneme. To verify the phoneme, two choices for audio output are available: playback of 100 milliseconds of speech or 300 milliseconds of speech. One hundred milliseconds would playback essentially the phoneme, while 300 milliseconds includes some surrounding context. This audio feedback may be repeated continuously for any number of times for more clear discrimination by the operator. If the operator is content with the position of the cursor, he may compute and display the correlation with a set of reference spectra. The highest five correlations will be displayed; the operator chooses the correct phoneme using prior knowledge of phonetic sonagraphic characteristics and the audio playback. The surrounding 100 milliseconds of speech is saved for use in the microphase.

Microphase. Figure 22 shows the time waveform for each phonetic event displayed on the CRT screen. Two cursors are provided to isolate three pitch periods from the isolated phonetic event with the aid of an automatic zero-crossing algorithm. This section will be about 75 milliseconds; for verification of the correct labeling it can be played back concatenated 10 times. If the labeling is correct, the three-pitch periods and respective labels are initially saved on the disk and stored permanently on tape at a later time. Three separate verifications of the labels associated with the isolated event are required to minimize incorrect labels.

Fingerprint Processing
    Background
    Fingerprints have been widely used as a positive means of identification by the law enforcement community since the turn of the century. A typical 10-finger card is shown in Figure 23. The automation of the classification and matching of individual fingerprints and of individual cards has lead to a ridge flow shown in Figure 24 and minutiae description shown in Figure 25. Production equipment now exists for reading this data from the cards which are currently in files. One configuration of this equipment is shown in Figure 26.

    The most prevalent manual classification system in use today is a modified form of the same 10-finger Henry system which first came into use in the early 1900's. One significant reason for the success of the Henry system is its inclusion of an ever branching decision tree structure with sufficient depth to resolve whatever clustering results from lack of a priori knowledge about the relation of the data to the classification scheme.

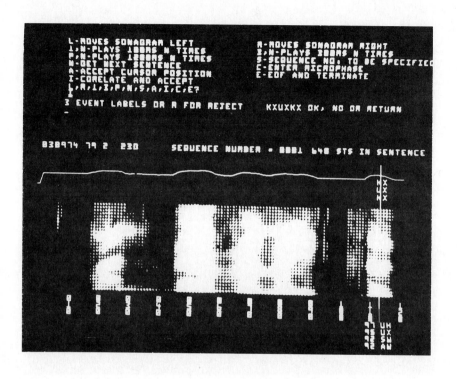

Figure 21: *Speech Labeling Macrophase Display*
Showing Spectrogram of:
"When Beverly Cooks..."
With /u/ in "Cooks" Labeled

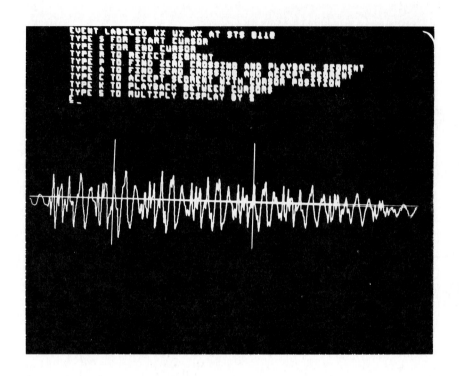

Figure 22:   *Speech Labeling Microphase Display Showing Cursor Isolated Three-Pitch Period Segment from /ü/ of "Cooks"*

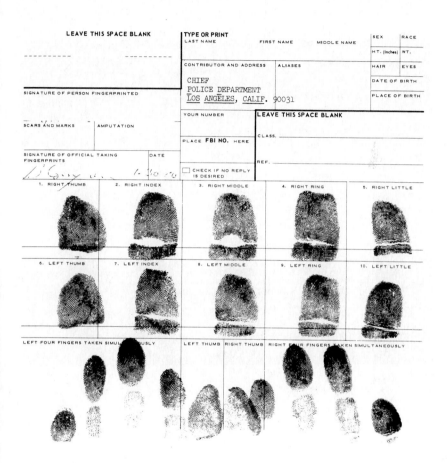

Figure 23: *A Standard 10-Finger Fingerprint Card*

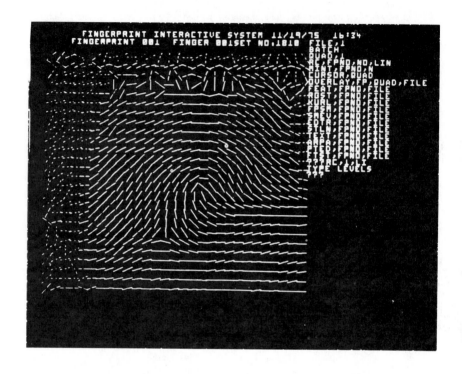

Figure 24:   *A Fingerprint Ridge Contour Plot
for a Loop Pattern*

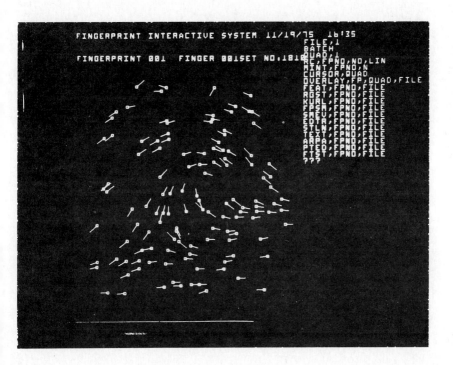

Figure 25: *A Fingerprint Minutiae Plot (for the Same Loop Pattern) Representing the Position and Orientation of the Ridge Endings and Bifurcations*

Figure 26: *An Automated Fingerprint Reading System*

This highly successful system is designed for human talents (good complex observation and judgement) and limitations (poor memory for many fine details) and makes good use of these qualities to desensitize the primary descriptors in the tree structure to input variations. For example, the presence or absence of a whorl may be accurately determined even for extremely poor quality input. This successful manual classification system relies fundamentally on pattern characteristics related to the presence or absence of deltas (or triradii) and the specific relation of these to the center of the pattern or core. The transition from one pattern type to another is essentially a continuum which the specific rules of procedure must quantize. Reliance on primary features (the deltas) which are inherently quantized greatly facilitates the specification procedure. The details of descriptions following the initial characterization may be attained by a very large number of equivalent formulations. For example, Bridges (Bridges, 1963) tabulates 46 variations on the basic pattern characterization of the patterns.

Although any automated classification system must rely on the same topological notions which have been fundamental to the manual systems, the details of the characterization will be different largely because the capabilities and limitations of automated processing are inverse to those of the human. Thus, memory for many fine details is an automated algorithms' forte, while attainment of any significant gestalt is essentially beyond the state-of-the-art.

The initial automated description is thus concerned with ridge flow direction and ridge and valley ending minutiae. Minutiae-based classification has been considered at Rockwell (internal letters only) but has not been reported in the literature. The problems associated with distortion and false and missing minutiae are large and appear to be beyond the capabilities of the current state-of-the-art. Ridge-flow-based-classification is much less sensitive to variations in the input and is the approach which has been considered by a number of research workers in the field. It offers the capability to emulate a number of the characteristics of successful manual system while retaining the advantages of automated processing. The basic notion is to perform a classification on the ridge flow based information and to search within a classification bin using the minutiae data in a matching algorithm. Figure 27 shows the ridge contour and minutiae data from two different impressions of the same finger.

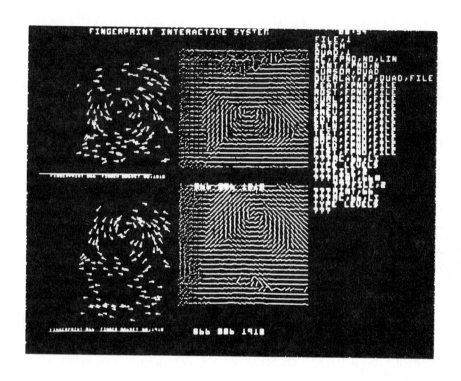

Figure 27a: *Ridge Flow and Minutiae Data for a Pair of Whorls*

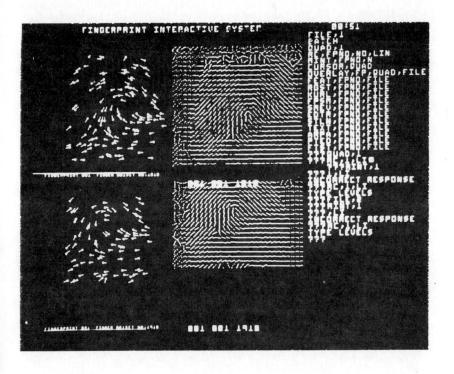

Figure 27b: *Ridge Flow and Minutiae Data*
               for a Pair of Loops

Figure 27:   *Ridge Contour and Minutiae Data*
               for Two Impressions of (a) Whorl
               and of (b) a Loop

Fingerprints may be characterized by topological (deformation independent) or leptomorphic (fine structural) features. Examples of the former are pattern types, ridge ending and bifurcation minutiae, or the number of cores and deltas; examples of the latter are core-delta distances, minutia interrelationships, or detailed connection path descriptions. The interactive procedures permit display and manipulation of such information. They have been used to develop automatic classification and matching algorithms. Additional work is in progress.

A Latent Fingerprint Identification System

Latent or crime scene prints are admissable in court as evidence of identity. A print fragment lifted from a backporch screen frame is shown in Figure 28. Its mate, taken from a 10-finger card and used to demonstrate that the suspect had been in contact with that screen door, is shown in Figure 29. Ten of the many points of correspondence are identified with arrows. Since the typical latent print is not suitable for automated reading, a semi-automated latent system has been developed to allow manual entry of minutiae from low quality images. These minutiae, together with auxiliary descriptors, may then be searched against a file of 10-finger cards which have been automatically read. A photograph of this system, which is currently undergoing field tests, is shown in Figure 30. The algorithms used and man-machine interface were developed on the interactive graphics system described above.

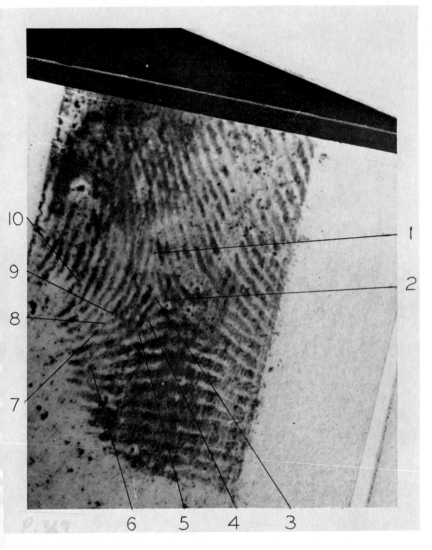

Figure 28: *A Fingerprint Fragment Lifted
from a Backporch Screen Frame*

Figure 29: *The Mating Print to Figure F-5 Taken from a Standard 10-finger Card*

Figure   30:   *A Latent Fingerprint Identification
System*

PROBLEMS

1. Consider a 512 x 512 image representable as:

   (1) an image with 8 shades of gray
   (2) the image of (1) with audible tones with a 3 octave range (approximated as 32 levels) extractable from any pair of points.

   (a) What is the maximum information (in bits) representable in each case?

   (b) Each of the twelve notes in an equal tempered octave has a frequency of $[2]^{1/12}$ times the preceding note. This interval is 100 cents (centisemitones). A relative error of 20 cents is readily detectable even to the untrained ear.

   What subjective factors must be considered in the design of system (2)?

2. Given a 4096 x 4096 point addressable binary storage display scope with write through capabiliton, draw a functional block diagram of a controller which will accept a sequence of 16-bit instructions of data and allow display of an 8 gray level image of 256 x 256 points with vector and point displays superimposed.

3. (a) List the significant variables which should be taken into account in the construction of an OCR system. Which may reasonably be included in a data base?

   (b) Assume you are faced with a design-before-data base OCR system definition. What interactive data display and processing capabilities would you desire to perform a system analysis and design and what specific variables would you explore with this interactive system?

4. (a) What are the objectives of an image enhancement or bandwidth reduction system? What are the criteria by by which a successful approach may be measured?

   (b) Given an interactive system with the capability for both immediate display and photographic output, how would you approach the evaluation of a technique which you conceived for enhancing or reducing the bandwidth of a class of images?   What specific results would you document to convey your presumed success to others? What role would the interactive system play in this documentation?

5. What properties are desired for measurements to be used in a personal identification system? How do the characteristics of fingerprints, speech and handwriting relate to these desired data? Which characteristics are common? Which differ? How can an interactive system be utilized to clarify the merits and deficiencies of any specific approach? The interaction of several approaches?

6. You are assigned the task of determining the feasibility of an automated approach to measuring facial characteristics for the purpose of personal identification. No automated sensors are available but an interactive system similar to that described above is available.

What is your approach to ascertaining the economic viability of the basic idea? How do you factor in the existence of competitive approaches? Estimate a time frame for a specific investigation and list the tasks to be performed and the approximate amount of effort to be devoted to each. Assume you are available full time and a total of two other people are available (more than two people each part time if this is appropriate). What form will your conclusions take and what role will the interactive system play in reaching them and preparing the results for discussion with others?

7. Considerations important for an interactive system are highly dependent on the application. What are important considerations for a research design tool? What are important considerations for a production system?

8. Design an interactive system to allow design testing, and interactive modification of a feature set for an optical character reader.

9. How can audio be used to enhance the user's perception of non-audio data?

10. Consider a 10x10 square array of points. Consider a particular subset of these points obtained by randomly drawing the coordinates of 50 points with replacement so that the actual number of distinct points may be as many as 50 or as few as 1. Define this set of N points to be set X. From the remainder, again with replacement, draw as many addi-

tional point coordinates as are required to obtain a total of 50 unique points and define the set of M points as Y, where N+M = 50. Y may be the null set if N = 50. From the set X+Y draw M points without replacement and define the remainder as the set W, which, like X, consists of N points. Eliminate the 50 points in sets X and Y and from the remaining 50 draw M times, with replacement, to obtain $L \leq M$ unique points. Define this as set Z. The original 10x10 array of 100 points is thus divided into four sets

No. in the Set	Set	Criteria
N	X	$1 \leq N \leq 50$
M	Y	$N + M = 50$
N	W	$W \supset X + Y$
L	Z	$1 \leq L \leq M$

Let U = X + Y - W.

Repeat the process on the same 10x10 array to form sets X^1, Y^1, Z^1, W^1, and U^1.

a) Consider the following interpretation of the sets defined above. V = X + Y is a set of 50 points; X and W are subsets of V of N points each with M points missing. Z is a set of L additional points which are not members of V (noise). The sets X+Z and W+Z each represent an "observation" of V with N missing and L extra points. Construct a similarity measure, S, preferably with the formal properties of a metric, such that

$$S(\{X+Z\}, \{W+Z\}) \geq S(\{X+Z\}, \{X^1+Z^1\})$$

$$S(\{X+Z\}, \{W^1+Z^1\})$$

$$S(\{W+Z\}, \{X^1+Z^1\})$$

$$S(\{W+Z\}, \{W^1+Z^1\})$$

b) Why can't this be done for all sets X^1, Y^1, Z^1, W^1, V^1?

c) What is a reasonable set of criterial for evaluating the relative success of two or more trial similarity measures?

d) How might an interactive system be used to develop the measure and evaluate it?

e) What affect will points misplaced by, for example, a shearing distortion have on the measure you have proposed?

f) Examine Figure 27 above and attempt to ascertain how this simplified model may be related to the "best match" problem for minutia arrays representing finger-prints.

REFERENCES

1   Newman, W. M. and Sproull, R. F. "An Approach to Graphics System Design," *Proc. IEEE,* April 1974, pp. 471-483.

2   Hansen, W. J. "User Engineering Principles for Interactive Systems," *1971 Fall Joint Computer Conference, AFIPS,* 1971, pp. 523-532.

3   Foley, J. D. and Wallace, V. L. "The Art of Natural Graphic Man-Machine Conversation," *Proc. IEEE,* April 1974, pp. 462-471.

4   Griffith, M. L. and Riganati, J. P. "Interactive Audio-Graphics for Speech and Image Characterization," *Proc. of the Conference on Computer Graphics, Pattern Recognition and Data Structure, May 14-16, 1975,* IEEE Cat. No. 75-CH-0981-1C, pp. 163-169.

5   Anderson, R. H. "An Introduction to Linguistic Pattern Recognition," RAND, P-4669, July 1971.

6   Dixon, N. R. and Tappert, C. C. "Toward Objective Phonetic Transcription -- An On-Line Interactive Technique for Machine Processed Speech Data," *IEEE Trans. on Man-Machine Systems,* December 1970, pp. 202-210.

7   Broderick, P. K., Paul, J. E., and Rennick, R. J. "Semi-Automatic Speaker Identification System," *1975 Carnahan Conference on Crime Countermeasures, University of Kentucky, Lexington, Ky., May 7-9, 1975,* IEEE Cat. No. 75-C-CHO-958-9-AES, pp. 29-37.

8   Paul, J. E., Rabinowitz, A. S., Riganati, J. P., and Richardson, J. M. "Development of Analytical Methods for a Semi-Automatic Speaker Identification System," *1975 Carnahan Conference on Crime Countermeasures, University of Kentucky, Lexington, Ky., May 7-9, 1975,* IEEE Cat. No. 75-CHO-958-9-AES, pp. 52-64.

9   Riganati, J. P. and Griffith, M. L. "An OCR Media Reader: Design Approach for the Recognition Process," TM521-010-006, Electronics Research Division, Rockwell International, Anaheim, Calif., August 1974.

10   Riganati, J. P., Vitols, V. A., and Griffith, M. L. "Minutia-Based Fingerprint Matching," *1971 IEEE Conference on Decision and Control, Miami Beach, Fla.,* Dec. 1971, pp. 217-2

11   Swanlund, G. "On-Line Digital Imagery Pattern Recognition,"
      *Conference on Near Future Prospects for Image Pattern Re-
      cognition, Silver Spring, Md., Nov. 11-13, 1974.*

12   Underwood, W. and Kanal, L. N. "Problems and Prospects
      for Pattern Analysis of Diagrams," *Conference on Near Fu-
      ture Prospects for Image Pattern Recognition, Silver Spring,
      Md., Nov. 11-13, 1974.*

13   The SASIS development was sponsored by the Law Enforcement
      Assistance Administration (LEAA) through the National In-
      stitute of Law Enforcement and Criminal Justice under
      contract J-LEAA-025-73 and was performed by the Electronics
      Research Division of Rockwell International under subcon-
      tract to the Aerospace Corporation.

14   Hecker, M. H. L. *Speaker Recognition - An Interpretive
      Survey of the Literature,* Jan. 1971, American Speech and
      Hearing Association, Monograph No. 16.

15   Papcun, G., Ducoff, G., and Smith, R. D. "Voiceprint
      Application Manual," July 1973, TOR-0073(3654-06)-1, The
      Aerospace Corporation, El Segundo, Calif.

16   "Voiceprint Identification," *Georgetown Law Journal,* Feb.
      1973, Vol. 61, Issue 3.

17   Hair, G. D. and Rekieta, T. W. "Speaker Identification
      Research," August 1972, Final report, Texas Instruments,
      Inc., Dallas, Texas.

18   "Semi-Automatic Speaker Identification (SASIS)," Dec. 1974,
      Final report No. C74-1185/501, Rockwell International Corp.,
      Anaheim, Calif.

19   "People vs E. D. Law," Opinion expressed in Appellate Re-
      port, Aug. 13, 1974, Court of the State of California,
      5 Crim. No. 1516 (Swp. Ct. No. 26331).

20   Papcun, G. and Cadeferged, P. "Two 'Voiceprint' Cases,"
      1973 Acoustical Society of America 86th Meeting, Los Ange-
      les, Calif., LL15.

21   Poza, F. "Voiceprint Identification: Its Forensic Appli-
      cation," *Proceedings of the 1974 Carnahan Crime Counter-
      measures Conference, University of Kentucky, Lexington, Ky.*

22   Becker, R. W., Clarke, F. R., Poza, F., and Young, J. R.
     "A Semi-Automatic Speaker Recognition System," 1972, SRI
     Project 1363 - prepared for Michigan Dept. of State Police,
     East Lansing, Michigan.

23   Pruzansky, S. and Mathews, M. V. "Talker-Recognition Pro-
     cedure Based on Analyses of Variance," *JASA 1964*, 36:11,
     pp. 2041-2047.

24   Baker, R. A. and Jones, T. A. "ACID - A User-Oriented
     System of Statistical Programs," *AFIPS Conference Procee-
     ding*, 1973, Vol. 42, p. 621.

25   Riganati, J. P. "An Overview of Electronic Identification
     Systems," *WESCON 1975, Session 31, San Francisco, Calif.*,
     Sept. 16-19, 1975.

26   Stock, Robert M. "Present and Future Identification Needs
     of Law Enforcement," *WESCON 1975, Session 31, San Fran-
     cisco, Calif., Sept. 16-19, 1975.*

27   Rennick, R. J. and Vitols, V. A. "MUFTI - A Multi-Function
     Identification System," *WESCON 1975, Session 31, San Fran-
     cisco, Calif., Sept. 16-19, 1975.*

28   Doddington, G. R. "Speaker Verification for Entry Control,"
     *WESCON 1975, Session 31, San Francisco, Calif., Sept. 16-
     19, 1975.*

29   Sternberg, J. "Automated Signature Verification Using
     Handwriting Pressure," *WESCON 1975, Session 31, San Fran-
     cisco, Calif., Sept. 16-19, 1975.*

30   Kanal, L. N. "Patterns in Pattern Recognition: 1968-1974,"
     IEEE Trans. Info. Theory, Nov. 1974, pp. 697-722.

31   Kanal, L. N. "Interactive Pattern Analysis and Classifi-
     cation Systems: A Survey and Commentary," *Proc. IEEE*,
     Oct. 1972, pp. 1200-1215.

32   Sammon, J. W., Jr. "Interactive Pattern Analysis and
     Classification," *IEEE Trans. Computers*, July 1970, pp.
     594-616.

33   Herbst, N. M. and Will, P. M. "An Experimental Laboratory
     for Pattern Recognition and Signal Processing," *Communi-
     cations of the ACM*, April 1972, pp. 231-244.

34   Anderberg, M. R. *Cluster Analysis for Applications*, New York, Academic Press, 1973.

35   Bellman, R., Cooke, K. L., and Lockett, J. *Algorithms, Graphs and Computers*, New York, Academic Press, 1970.

36   Bridges, B. C. *Practical Fingerprinting*, New York, Funk and Wagnalls, 1963.

37   Clerici, R. "Fingerprints: A New Classification Scheme," *Nature*, Vol. 224, P. 779FF, 1969.

38   Elliott, J. "Automatic Fingerprint Recognition," *Ferranti Journal*, Spring 1968.

39   Fu, K. S. *Syntactic Methods in Pattern Recognition*, New York, Academic Press, 1974.
FBI, *The Science of Fingerprints*, U.S. Department of Justice.

40   Grasselli, A. *Automatic Interpretation and Classification of Images*, New York, Academic Press, 1969.

41   Grasselli, A. "On the Automatic Classification of Fingerprints - Some Considerations of the Linguistic Interpretation of Pictures," *Methodologies of Pattern Recognition*, ed. by S. Watanabe, New York, Academic Press, 1969, pp. 253-273.

42   Hopcroft, J. E. and Ullman, J. D. *Formal Languages and Their Relation to Automation*, Reading, Mass., Addison-Wesley, 1969.

43   Harkley, W. J. and Tou, J. T. "Automatic Fingerprint Interpretation and Classification via Contextual Analysis and Topological Coding," *Pictorial Pattern Recognition*, ed. by G. C. Cheng, R. S. Ledley, D. K. Pollock, and A. Rosenfeld, Thompson Book Co., 1968, pp. 411-456.

44   Harkley, W. J. "Automatic Fingerprint Interpretation and Classification via Contextual Analysis and Topological Coding," Ph.D. Thesis, Ohio State University, 1967.

45   Jacobs, R. A. and Rosenbaum, P. S. *English Transformational Grammar*, Waltham, Mass., Blaisdell Pub. Co., 1968.

46   Levi, G. and Sirovich, F. "Structural Description of Fingerprint Images," *Information Sciences*, October 1972.

47   McGinty, L. "Fingerprint - The Next Data in the Bank,"
New Scientist, 31 October 1974, pp. 320-323.

48   Meisel, W. S. *Computer Oriented Approaches to Pattern Recognition,* New York, Academic Press, 1972.

49   Millard, K. "An Automatic Retrieval System for Scene of
the Crime Fingerprints," *Conference on the Science of
Fingerprints,* September 1974, London.

50   Moayer, B. and Fu, K. S. "A Syntactic Approach to Fingerprint Pattern Recognition," *First International Joint Conference on Pattern Recognition, Oct. 30 - Nov. 1, 1973,
Washington, D.C.,* pp. 423-432 (IEEE Computer Society Publication 73 CHO 821-9C).

51   Nilsson, N. J. *Problem-Solving Methods in Artificial Intelligence,* New York, McGraw-Hill, 1971.

52   Ohteru, S., Kobayashi, H., Kuto, T., Noda, F., and Kimura, H.
"Automated Fingerprint Classifier," *Second International
Joint Conference on Pattern Recognition, August 13-15, 1974,
Copenhagen, Denmark,* pp. 185-189, (IEEE Computer Society
Publication 74 CHO 885-4C).

53   Rabinowitz, A. S. "On the Value of the Fano Algorithm in
Establishing the Graphemic Form of Machine-Derived Phone-
tic Strings," Ph.D. Thesis, University of North Carolina,
March 1972.

54   Rao, C. V., Prasada, B., and Sarma, K. R. "An Automatic
Fingerprint Classification System," *Second International
Joint Conference on Pattern Recognition, August 13-15,
1974, Copenhagen, Denmark,* pp. 180-184, (IEEE Computer
Society Publication 74 CHO 885-4C).

55   Sgall, P., Nebesky, L., Goralcikova, A., and Zajicova, E.
A Functional Approach to Syntax, Elsevier, 1969.

56   Shelman, C. B. and Hodges, D. "A Decimal Henry System,"
*First International Conference on Electronic Crime Counter-
measures, Edinburgh University, Edinburgh, Scotland, July
18-20, 1973.*

57   Shelman, C. B. "Machine Classification of Fingerprints,"
*Proceedings of the First National Symposium on Law Enforce-
ment Science and Technology,* New York, Academic Press, 1967.

58   Shelman, C. B. and Hodges, D.   "Fingerprint Research at Argonne National Laboratory," *1975 Carnahan Conference on Electronic Crime Countermeasures, University of Kentucky, April 25-27, 1975.*

59   Van Emden, B. M.   "Advanced Computer Based Fingerprint Automatic Classification Technique," *Law Enforcement Science and Technology,* New York, Academic Press, 1967.

60   Wegstein, J. H. and Rafferty, J. F.   "Machine Oriented Fingerprint Classification," *Law Enforcement Science and Technology,* New York, Academic Press, 1967.

61   Wegstein, J. H.   "Manual and Automated Fingerprint Registration,"   NBS Technical Note 730, U.S. Government Printing Office, Washington, D.C., 1972.

62   Wegstein, J. H.   "The Automated Classification and Identification of Fingerprints," *Conference on the Science of Fingerprints, September 1964, London.*

63   Stock, R. M.   "Automatic Fingerprint Reading," *1972 Carnahan Conference on Electronic Crime Countermeasures, April 1972, University of Kentucky, Lexington, Ky.,* BULUKY98, pp. 16-28.

64   Agrawala, A. K.   "Learning with Various Types of Teachers," *Proc. First International Joint Conference on Pattern Recognition, Oct. 30 - Nov. 1, 1973,* IEEE Cat. No. 73CH0821-9C, pp. 453-461.

65   Kanal, L. H.   "Prospects for Pattern Recognition - Workshop and Survey Report - 1975,"   Automatic Imagery Pattern Recognition Committee, Electronic Industries Association, Washington.

66   Wasserman, A. J.   "The Design of 'idiot-proof' Intetactive Programs," *AFIPS Conference Proceedings,* Vol. 42, 1973, pp. M34-M38.

67   Sclabassi, R. J., Buchness, R., and Estrin, T.   "Interactive Graphics in the Analyses of Neuronal Spike Train Data," *Computer Graphics, Pattern Recognition and Data Structures Conference, 1967,* pp. 47-50.

Special issues:

Proc. IEEE, October 1972, Digital Pattern Recognition

Proc. IEEE, April 1974, Computer Graphics

Proc. IEEE, June 1975, Interactive Computer Systems

Proc. IEEE, October 1975, Laboratory Automation

ACKNOWLEDGEMENT

The authors are pleased to acknowledge the significant contributions of Drs. J. E. Paul, A. S. Rabinowitz, V. A. Vitols,
M. A. Caloyannides, J. M. Richardson, and S. A. White; Messrs.
G. W. Kephart, D. Perlman, R. J. Rennick, and Ms. M. M. Kimura.
Portions of the speaker identification section, including Figures 15 - 20, were extracted from references 7, 8, and 18 and
were written by Dr. Paul. Portions of the electronic identification section were extracted from reference 25, copyright
WESCON '75, used by permission.

RESEARCH
ASPECTS

Modifying Graphics Images*

MICHAEL L. RHODES

and

ALLEN KLINGER

Computer Science Department
University of California, Los Angeles
Los Angeles, California

ABSTRACT

This paper reports on the development of a text understanding program for a minicomputer with 8K memory to facilitate modifying graphics images. Two versions of an interactive language are described. An early system used a non-linguistic method for picture variation. Later emphasis was placed on conversational linguistic structure. The early language used regular decomposition to approximately locate standard display templates. The later language allowed conversational dialogues between the user and image modification routines. We present an implementation of it that retains context during a dialogue and enables relational adjustments of facial features. Imprecise feature judgements issued by the user are used to modify images. Ambiguities encountered by the program are resolved by interrogating short term memory buffers and hash table data. Language and hardware features are combined by data structures that interface display processor instructions and requests generated by the interpreted text. Updating these structures is discussed in terms of relationships between structure elements.

*Research partially sponsored by the Air Force Office of Scientific Research, Air Force Systems Command, USAF, under Grant No. AFOSR-72-2384.

385

1. INTRODUCTION

Humans easily recognize faces. We can use verbal descriptions and form mental pictures. Though only a few of us can sketch these visualizations with accuracy, with the help of an artist most can describe our visual memory 'pictures' in sufficient detail so that reasonable facsimilies are generated. This paper describes cooperative interactions to use both human recognition and descriptive powers and computer capabilities for generating facial images and modifying more general graphics displays. Text understanding programs to facilitate this task are described.

Repositioning nonfacial templates was used in a prototype system where interactions were based on rough geometric relations rather than text commands. The interactive potential of the underlying regular decomposition structure used here is presented. The improved program system modifies facial line drawings using a text understanding control structure.

These programs simplify communication between user and machine display facilities. The later provides a conversational medium to allow a dialogue to be established, where the central processor can "understand" both the display screen contents and user's descriptions. In operation, the user gives descriptions to generate a facial image, and the computer-program system serves as an 'artist'. A sketched interpretation of the description appears on the graphics display. The 'artist' is called 'SKETCH', a program written for an IMLAC PDS-1 display processor and minicomputer with 8K of 16 bit/word memory. Users can modify the screen contents via the interactive language and in some cases teach the machine an interpretation of their descriptions.

The computer inputs to SKETCH are imprecise, subjective feature judgements. Goldstein et al [1], and Harmon [2] established limits of performance for persons isolating faces from a population using such feature descriptions. Their experiments provide measures of feature reliability for identification, utility for establishing similarities, and sufficiency of sets of features for file retrieval[1]. Work by Bledsoe [3] and Sakai et al [4] attempted to sort [3] and classify [4] facial images by working with their features. By contrast, this work allows use of imprecise feature judgements in generating facial images. The prototype version of SKETCH used regular decompo-

---

[1]Their model predicts that for a population of 4×10^6 only 14 feature desciptors are required to isolate a face [1, pp. 757].

sition to allow relocating arbitrary templates. Nonfacial
images were repositioned according to approximate and imprecise
geometric locators in this version of the work. Using imprecise
descriptors in the early SKETCH program lent impetus to design
a more robust program to understand conversational descriptors.

The user communicates with SKETCH through a keyboard
console in a limited natural language. The machine replies are
changes in image displayed or text messages presented on the
CRT. Previous work [5,6] was used as a model, but SKETCH was
built around a police identification technique [7]. (Details
of our implementation are based on a concept relating linguistic variables to numerical codes [10,11]. For an overview of
limited natural language computer processing see [12,13].)

The language is severely restricted due to the size of the
machine but it is sufficiently flexible to be conversational.
Command instructions provided allow numerous modifications to
facial images. A key contribution is the way SKETCH facilitates
processing relational information. Gillenson [5] cited airline
reservation systems as examples of mechanical interaction and
Winograd's program for Understanding Natural Language [6] as
"intelligent" interaction. SKETCH processes relational phrases
concerning faces: this enables interaction like [6] with facial
images: in its domain, SKETCH is an "intelligent" graphics aid.
We can compare commands and display in the sequence of pictures
shown in Figure 1 to demonstrate this.

The first photograph in Fig. 1 shows the introductory
frame that begins a user-SKETCH dialogue. The five following
pictures illustrate a few typical commands. Photograph 2 shows
the HAIR drawn. In photograph 3 a new word, FULLER, is defined
and in the subsequent picture the new word is used to enlarge
the HAIR. Immediately after the command in photo 4, the
command in 5 demonstrates the maintenance of context during
the dialogue. Photograph 6 shows the NOSE made wider.

Our purpose is to present the data structures and program
organization used for this bridge between language and graphics
displays. This is done by focusing on the system; illustrations
of its use are also given. In order to describe the SKETCH
program, the paper is divided into two main parts. The first
section specifies the language including an early version of
SKETCH that uses picture decomposition terminology for locating
image features [14,15,16], and the second presents data structures used for the implementation.

Figure 1. *A Series of Six Photographs Showing Typical User Commands.*

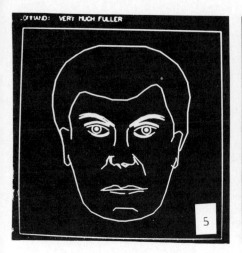
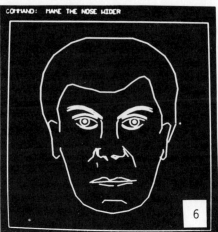

Figure 1. *Continued.*

2. LANGUAGE SPECIFICATION

Overview

The power of SKETCH depends on how easily and naturally the user can express his modifications to the IMLAC CRT and have them understood. SKETCH can function conversationally because its scope of discourse is very small. Display facilities are also constrained to a finite number of image types, each a facial feature.

Eleven features are in the current language:

FACE	CHIN	JAW
NOSE	EYES	EYEBROWS
HAIRLINE	HAIR	CHEEKLINES
EARS	MOUTH	

Each can be modified in position, size, and relative location to other features. All are individually addressable; alterations to one feature may be made relative to another. For instance, eyebrows may be moved closer to the eyes: if this is done the eyebrows will be repositioned relative to the current location of the eyes. Global alterations are also possible where the entire face is subjected to modifications.

SKETCH is modeled on the Penry Facial Identification Technique [7,8,9], also known as Photo FIT, and Gillenson's interactive program, WHATSISFACE [5]. The Phot-FIT kit is a police identification aid which consists of transparencies: 162 pairs of eyes, 151 noses, 159 mouths, 112 chin and cheek lines, and 261 foreheads with a variety of moustaches, beards, spectacles and headgear. There are over 12,000 million possible combinations of features.

SKETCH enables a similar assembly of faces from features on the display screen, so that a computer could be an aid in the Penry identification process. This gives the investigator added power and convenience, since a single line drawing can be altered in many ways, reducing the number of basic features needed. For instance, we estimate that the 162 pairs of eyes could be realized by 20-25 basic eye templates in the computer display library. The library could be stored on auxiliary storage and accessed via system commands issued by the user[2].

WHATSISFACE [5] provided seventeen basic features for the user to modify while forming the facial image, and involved user communication via analog devices or one-character keyboard symbols. SKETCH adds to this natural discussion between the user and the display processor. However the earlier program [5] possessed superior graphic display capability: hardware facilities for rotational transformation and variable intensity were made available to WHATSISFACE users. No such facilites were available at the IMLAC minicomputer used by SKETCH when it was written.

Language Description

Figure 2 describes the SKETCH language in context-free Backus Normal Form notation. Brackets, "<" and ">", are used to distinguish metalinguistic variables defined either in terms of others or in symbol strings. The symbols "|" and ":=" denote "or" and "defined as" respectively.

The SKETCH syntax has several message structures. The two basic message types allowed are: <DEFINITION> and <DESCRIPTION PHRASE>. In order for these messages to be inter-

---

[2]Although this is not currently available, the program could support such access at a later time.

```
<USER MESSAGE>:= <USER PHRASE> CARRIAGE RETURN |
            CARRIAGE RETURN
<USER PHRASE>:= <DEFINITION> | <DESCRIPTION PHRASE> |
            <USER PHRASE> AND <USER PHRASE>
<DESCRIPTION PHRASE>:= <COMMAND WORD> <TEMPLATE PHRASE>
            <MODIFIER PHRASE> | <COMMAND WORD>
            <TEMPLATE PHRASE>
            <IMBEDDED RELATIONAL PHRASE> |
            <SUBSEQUENT COMMAND PHRASE> | REMOVE
            <TEMPLATE PHRASE>
<COMMAND WORD>:= MAKE | DRAW | MOVE | BRING
<IMBEDDED RELATIONAL PHRASE>:= <ARTICLE><IMBEDDED
            COMMAND> | <ARTICLE><IMBEDDED
            COMMAND><TEMPLATE PHRASE>
<IMBEDDED COMMAND>:= CLOSER | FURTHER
<SUBSEQUENT COMMAND PHRASE>:= <ARTICLE> <VERY>
            <DEGREE PART> <SUBSEQUENT COMMAND>
<SUBSEQUENT COMMAND>:= <ARTICLE><IMBEDDED COMMAND> |
            <ARTICLE><ADD-SUB> |
            <ARTICLE><ADD-SUB><MODIFIER> |
            <ARTICLE><ADD-SUB><IMBEDDED COMMAND>
<DEGREE PART>:= <EMPTY> MUCH | LITTLE
<ADD-SUB>:= MORE | LESS | <EMPTY>
<TEMPLATE PHRASE>:= <ARTICLE><PRONOUN> |
            <ARTICLE><TEMPLATE>
<PRONOUN>:= IT | THEM
<MODIFIER PHRASE>:= <ARTICLE> <VERY> <DEGREE PART>
            <ADD-SUB> <IMBEDDED COMMAND>
<ARTICLE>:= A | THE | TO | EVEN | OVER | THAN | BE |
            SAME | AS | JUST | LIKE | <EMPTY> |
            <ARTICLE><ARTICLE>
<TEMPLATE>:= FACE | NOSE | HAIRLINE | EARS | CHIN |
            EYES | HAIR | MOUTH | EYEBROWS | JAW | SCAR
<MODIFIER>:= FAT | WIDE | THIN | BIG | LARGE | SMALL |
            HIGH | LOW | RIGHT | RIGHTWARDS | LEFT |
            LEFTWARDS | TALL | SHORT | UP | DOWN |
            UPWARDS | DOWNWARDS | SLENDER | NORTH |
            SOUTH | EAST | WEST
<VERY>:= VERY | <EMPTY>
<EMPTY>:=
<DEFINITION>:= DEFINE<ANY WORD><ARTICLE><LEXICAL
            MEMBER> | DEFINE <ANY
            WORD><ARTICLE><LEXICAL MEMBER> AND
            <LEXICAL MEMBER>
<LEXICAL MEMBER>:= <COMMAND WORD> | <TEMPLATE> |
            <IMBEDDED COMMAND> | <ADD-SUB> | <PRONOUN>
            | <MODIFIER> | VERY | <ARTICLE>
```

Figure 2. *SKETCH Syntax.*

preted, a carriage return must be hit on the keyboard to begin processing.

Word Order

SKETCH uses sentence normalization in parsing user messages. Only one basic sentence structure must be recognized by the interpreter after normalization has taken place. Normalization does not rearrange the user message, it simply deletes superficial words.

Users are constrained to follow the specified word order in constructing messages. However flexibility is incorporated within each sequence to allow for conversational phrasings of messages. For instance, the following messages have exactly the same meaning for SKETCH:

(1) DRAW EYES LITTLE WIDE
(2) MAKE THE EYES A LITTLE WIDER
(3) DRAW THE EYES JUST A LITTLE WIDER
(4) DRAW EVEN THE EYES A LITTLE WIDER

The essential elements of the message are in (1). DRAW (or MAKE) signals the parser that the ensuing message is a descriptive phrase. The occurrence of EYES as the next non-<ARTICLE> signals the parser to expect a message of the form: <COMMAND WORD> <TEMPLATE PHRASE> <MODIFIER PHRASE>, <COMMAND WORD> <TEMPLATE PHRASE> <IMBEDDED RELATIONAL PHRASE>, or <COMMAND WORD> <TEMPLATE PHRASE>.

When LITTLE is encountered the parser expects a <MODIFIER PHRASE> to complete the message. The word LITTLE by itself is a <DEGREE PART> that is interpreted to be a multiplicative factor of 1/2. This factor is then used as a multiplicand times the standard change associated with EYES when made WIDER. WIDER is a <MODIFIER> that means: "increase the horizontal stretch lines of the template referenced in the message."

When applied to EYES, WIDER has the effect of increasing the vertical but not the horizontal stretch vectors in the EYE display templates. "WIDE EYES" are interpreted "wide open", not "wider in terms of distance between pupils." For most other templates, like NOSE and JAW for instance, WIDE will mean an increase in the actual horizontal stretch vectors of the referenced templates. A command like, MOVE THE EYES CLOSER TOGETHER, will bring the eyes closer together horizontally (pupil to pupil).

Messages (2), (3) and (4) above are variations of (1) with
<ARTICLE>s interspersed to achieve a more conversational tone.
<ARTICLE>s can appear in a variety of places depending on the
message construction chosen by the user. If there is room for
essential parts of a user's message, then whenever on <ARTICLE>
is permitted, the number of <ARTICLE>s that can fit in the keyboard queue is allowed. An irregular message like:

DRAW THE JUST EYES THE LIKE EVEN LITTLE WIDE

would appear perfectly acceptable to SKETCH and equivalent to
the four messages (1), (2), (3), and (4) seen earlier.

SKETCH expects a sympathetic user who will most likely use
common expressions in his commands. Messages which seem non-
sensical will be interpreted to program action if no violation
of the language syntax is detected. The user must be careful
not to misuse his liberty with <ARTICLE>s.

On the other hand, some messages may be sensible but not
understood by SKETCH. The user is not expected to ask:

DRAW A LITTLE WIDER THE EYES

since word order is violated. This message will not be understood and the error message processor would reply to the user.

Predicate Modifiers for Variable Adjustment

Messages sent to an early version of SKETCH included
approximate, inexact requests for picture modification. Phrases
such as "MOVE RIGHT AND DOWN" were interpreted using regular
decomposition to determine target locations. However single
commands were often inadequate to relocated display templates
exactly where desired. A subsequent command like "A LITTLE MORE,"
"MUCH LESS," or "VERY MUCH MORE" was then added to the grammar
making SKETCH responsive to a series of approximate adjustments.
These subsequent commands generally take the form of predicate
modifiers, <VERY> <DEGREE PART> <ADD-SUB>, which form a set of
"hedges", or "words whose job it is to make things fuzzier or
less fuzzy [10]." Lakeoff [10] describes hedges in the context
of fuzzy sets (developed by Zadeh [11]). One such fuzzy set
could be the set of all wide pairs of eyes. A degree of membership (real number between 0 and 1) would be attached to each
pair of eyes in the fuzzy set indicating just how "WIDE" each
pair is considered to be. Any pair of eyes with degree of
membership of .9 or 1.0 are "WIDE". The membership function for

the set of wide pairs of eyes is illustrated in the graph shown in Figure 3.

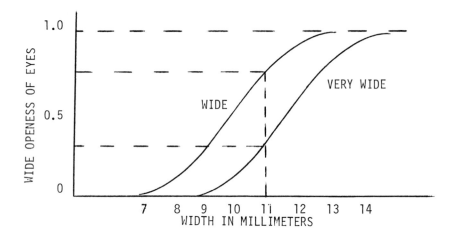

Figure 3. *Membership Function for Wide Pairs of Eyes*

Although the "WIDENESS" curves quantify the qualitative text term, the function chosen is subjective. Adding the hedge VERY defines a new set: very wide pairs of eyes. The membership function for this set is also shown in Figure 3: in effect a shift of values to the right has occurred. Pairs of eyes that were "wide" to degree .75 now are only "very wide" to degree .25.

The <VERY> <DEGREE PART> and <ADD-SUB> predicate modifiers affect features by causing SKETCH to use new functions to describe membership classes.

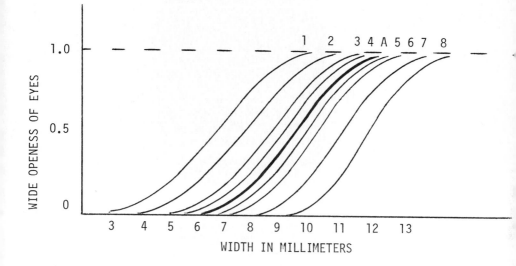

(A)   DRAW THE EYES WIDE
(1)   MAKE THEM VERY MUCH LESS WIDE
(2)   DRAW THEM MUCH LESS WIDE
(3)   DRAW THE EYES LESS WIDE
(4)   MAKE THE EYES A LITTLE LESS WIDE
(5)   MAKE THEM A LITTLE MORE WIDE
(6)   DRAW THEM WIDER
(7)   MAKE THE EYES MUCH WIDER
(8)   DRAW THEM VERY MUCH WIDER

Figure 4. *New Membership Classes*

Figure 4 illustrates the correspondence between the original
membership function for "WIDE EYES" and the various functions
resulting from <VERY> <DEGREE PART> <ADD-SUB> commands. Each
numbered modification command is issued in the context of
screen (A); the numbered graphs reference the commands listed.
The plots show the relative sizes associated command (A) and
the new command, when each numbered command immediately follows
(A).

In Figure 5, photographs 8, 9, and 10, show actual display
results for commands (A), (2) and (8) respectively. The commands
in Photographs 9 and 10 were each issued directly following the
display shown in Photograph 8.

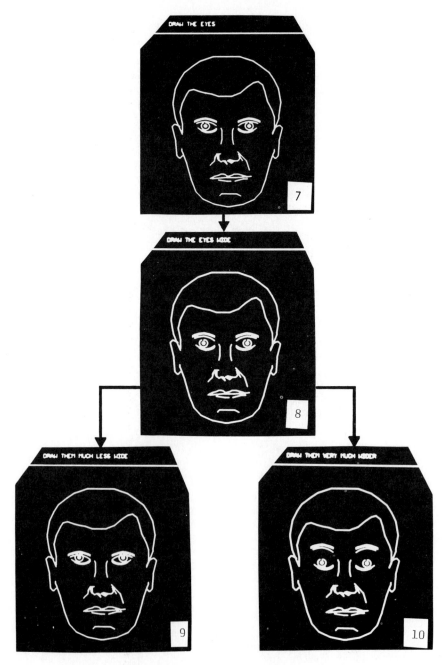

Figure 5. *Adjustment of Features Using Hedges.*

By adjusting a modification in a series of commands the user can reach detail equivalent to 1/2 the resolution of the CRT. The predicate modifiers multiply the standard increment by one of eight factors (-4, -2, -1, -1/2, 1/2, 1, 2, 4). Since each command is relative to the current image, successive modifications are able to reach half of the 1024 screen points in each direction, i.e., EYES could be separated by any amount using a series of commands like:

COMMAND	EFFECTIVE ADJUSTMENT
BRING THE EYES FURTHER APART	CIPD + 1(SI)
MUCH MORE	CIPD + 2(SI)
A LITTLE BIT LESS	CIPD - 1/2(SI)
VERY MUCH LESS	CIPD - 4(SI)
MORE	CIPD + 1(SI)

where CIPD = current inter-pupil distance
SI = standard increment for horizontal EYE changes

The preceding discussion concerns modifications that change feature size. Predicate modifiers can also be used to qualify reposition commands. Increments associated with each template for reposition are the same as the standard value in feature size and shape adjustments.

Dictionary Additions

The <DEFINITION> phrase allows extensions to the dictionary. For example, the new word TUBBY can be defined to be the same as known words (dictionary members) or as a combination of some of them.

DEFINE TUBBY TO BE THE SAME AS FAT AND SHORT

This can also be done in the more natural way:

DEFINE TUBBY LIKE FAT AND SHORT

If we keep only the essential elements in this it becomes:

DEFINE TUBBY FAT AND SHORT

Each message results in a dictionary element with the meaning "combination of FAT and SHORT." Notice the string of

<ARTICLE>s, "TO BE THE SAME AS" is only used to "naturalize"
the user's message. During the interpretive process these
<ARTICLE>s are stripped from the message and ignored.

Regular Decomposition

Several workers in computer graphics, scene analysis and
pattern recognition independently proposed use of regular decomposition of two-dimensional arrays:
  (a) to obtain a condensed and approximate version of a
      raster scan picture record to fit into fast memory, and
  (b) as a tool for writing programs which access, modify, or
      display portions of such arrays.
Warnock [17] used successively finer squares in his hidden-line
-elimination algorithm (for displaying a solid figure given the
overlapping lines from a stick-drawing planar projection).
Analogous methods were proposed in [18,19,14]; programs described
in [16] used decomposition to isolate informative areas of
digitized pictures.

Preliminary versions of SKETCH allowed less flexible interaction with users: the natural language interface was added to
a format based on regular decomposition. The earlier input
language used the partitioning convention of [16] to locate
points on the display. The remainder of this section first outlines the addressing scheme for picture zones (based on [14])
and then presents use of regular decomposition addresses for
graphics interaction. The convention of [14,16] follow.

Every entire array has four subquadrants located as the
four quadrants of a Cartesian coordinate system. If "entire
array" refers to a scanned picture P stored as a matrix of
picture elements $P[i,j]$ (i^{th} row, j^{th} column element), for an
array of size 512 x 512 we call the quadrants P.a, P.b, P.c,
and P.d, where

$$P.a = \{P[i,j]: 1 \leq i \leq 256, 1 \leq j \leq 256\}$$
$$P.b = \{P[i,j]: 1 \leq i \leq 256, 257 \leq j \leq 512\}$$
$$P.c = \{P[i,j]: 257 \leq i \leq 512, 1 \leq j \leq 256\}$$
$$P.d = \{P[i,j]: 257 \leq i \leq 512, 257 \leq j \leq 512\}$$

These symbols correspond to the '"Dewey decimal" notation
for trees' [20] since we can now apply the same subquadrant
procedure to any one of these quadrants as an "entire array,"
finding:

P.a.a = {P[i,j]: 1 ≤ 128, 1 ≤ j ≤ 128}

.
.
.

P.b.a = {P[i,j]: 1 ≤ i ≤ 128, 257 ≤ j ≤ 384}

.
.
.

P.d.d = {P[i,j]: 385 ≤ i ≤ 512, 385 ≤ j ≤ 512}

The genralization to square arrays of length k is immediate and there is a useful method for locating the center of such regular decomposition regions. Let any decimal encoding of a region of picture P be called a subquadrant and denote it or its center point by $P.X_1. X_2. \ldots X_i. \ldots X_n$ (context will show which - set or point - is intended). While X_i takes values a, b, c or d for convenience of representation, the following computations interpret these values as ordered pairs: a = (-1,1), b = (1,1), c = (-1,-1), and d = (1,-1). For an arbitrary symbol in i^{th} decimal position $X_i = (X_{i1},X_{i2})$, where the first numeral relates to x-direction offset and the second to y-direction offset. The subquadrant center position (X,Y), can be specified in terms of picture center position (P_x,P_y) and picture square array size k by the pair of equations:

$$X = P_x + \sum_{i=1}^{n} X_{i1} \, (k/4^i)$$

$$Y = P_y + \sum_{i=1}^{n} X_{i2} \, (k/4^i)$$

This observation can be easily extended to locate subquadrant centers for any regular recursive decomposition of a square array. For example, successive partitioning into nine subpictures of P, P.1, P.2, ..., P.9 was proposed in [14] (where P.1 is upper left, ..., P.4 center left, P.5 center, ..., P.9 lower right). Encoding the numerals 1, 2, ..., 9 as X_{i1}, X_{i2} that take on -1, 0, +1 values (-1,-1), (0,-1), ..., (+1,+1) and replacing 4 by 3 in the pair of equations suffices.

The creation of four-successor trees to represent a picture permits a significant number of distinct structures to be described by only a finite depth decomposition scheme. A complete tree with root-node P and successors P.a, ..., P.d which terminates at level seven (nodes P.a.a.a.a.a.a.a, ,,,, P.d.d.d.d.d.d.d) has $1 + 4 + 16 + \ldots + 4096 = 5461$ nodes. There are sixteen distinct two-level trees, and hence $16 = 2^4$ ways to refine any single node in the tree; thus there are $2^4 \times 2^{4096}$ ways to refine a six-level tree into a seven level tree. Specific cases which possess useful symmetries can be distinguished and grouped. One such group has the downward diagonal as symmetry axis. Here trees with paired nodes which have both elements present or basent describe a structural class. Two downward diagonal symmetric trees pair: P.b and P.c; and, at level three, P.a.b and P.a.c, P.b.a and P.c.a, P.b.b and P.c.c, P.b.d and P.c.d, P.d.b and P.d.c.

The regular decomposition subquadrant scheme enables generation of roughly similar pictures from standard templates. For example, a given geometric shape can be used to obtain a sequence of pictures which differ only in template position. Vertical, horizontal, and diagonal lines through several subquadrant centers are partitioned into a templete-location-grid by the subquadrant method of addressing. A quadrant decomposition to tree level seven (six values of letters, e.g., as in P.a.a.b.c.a.d) has $\sum_{i=1}^{6} 2^i = 126$ subquadrant center points specified by all the available decimal codes. Hence a program which describes locations in pictures by a six-tuple of four-level elements is 1) sufficient for generating a large number of similar pictures, and 2) suitable for an iterative correction or repositioning of a template to get picture structure that "looks right."

Figure 6 shows a circular template positioned in several locations on the IMLAC videographic console. The command shown is "DRAW CIR 2, P.B.A.D.D.C.A, 1"; it causes the template "CIR 2" to be drawn at the given location with size 1. It is also shown drawn at standard size 2 at nine other locations: P (picture center), P.c, P.c.b.c.c, P.c.b.c, P.c.b.c.b, P.c.b, P.c.b.c, P.c.b.b, and P.c.b.b.b. Automatic adjustment of a template location can also be accomplished by interpreting higher level commands and the current template location six-tuple: e.g., "MOVE UP" takes a template centered at P.c.b.b.b and puts it at (P.c.b.b.b.a + P.c.b.b.b.b)/2, i.e., the next refinement level's upper two subquadrant centers x-y locations averaged, "MOVE UP AND RIGHT" puts it at P.c.b.b.b.b, etc.

Figure 6. *Series of Circles Using Six-tuple Locators*

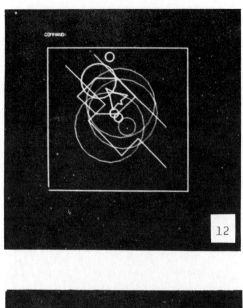

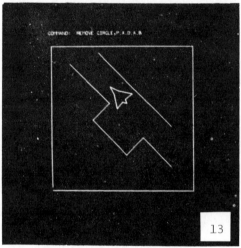

Figure 7. *Stylized Plane and Runway with and without Simulated Clouds*

Figure 7 shows two views of an airplane template on a runway: one with simulated clouds and one without. The "clouds" are eight circles of various sizes and they were generated by the use of center locations. One important picture generation sequence is illustrated by Figure 7: the step-by-step elimination of unwanted objects from a scene. Here a picture which has had a template removed from the original scene is the generated picture. In the figure, the circles may not all be clouds and they may not all be solid (obscuring the plane and runway). A person interacting with the picture data-base via a videographic terminal display would choose one or more circles to be deleted. An important round ground feature such as a missile silo might become apparent in the reduced scene. Note that only a rough judgement of circle size and location is needed to initiate the reduction. Imprecise specifications are used to find most likely candidates for modification. Cursor markings showing major subquadrant boundaries with software to interpret commands ("MOVE UP AND RIGHT") or hardware to convert keyboard inputs to "refine one level" ("add a coordinate") can facilitate this. The result is an interactive system at low cost since sophisticated interaction hardware: lightpens, joysticks, etc.; can be avoided. Thus image generation can be accomplished relatively cheaply: regular decomposition facilitates introducing computer power into picture interpretation.

3.   SKETCH IMPLEMENTATION

The implementation of SKETCH is best described from the viewpoint of the SKETCH supervisor. Only a few program segments are actually coordinated by the supervisor but they represent the brunt of all SKETCH processing. Three logical partitions are made in SKETCH which closely correspond to program operational modes: the Interpreter section to handle user messages; the Message Processor to compose messages sent to the user; and the Display Files to maintain bookkeeping and display processor instructions. Portions of these three partitions are called in sequence by the supervisor.

At the supervisor level SKETCH is uncomplicated. The supervisor simply passes control down a sequence of routines: to invoke any, all its predecessors must have been successfully executed. Whenever a routine is unsuccessful, control is passed to the reply message processor to identify the error and notify the user. If all routines are successful, the supervisor returns to a waiting state for a new user message.

Any routine invoked by the supervisor could update one or more of the three program partitions. While a user message is being parsed by an interpretive routine, information is gathered for the reply message processor. A trace is made of the interpreter's flow of control to help locate errors. If an error is encountered, the message processor portion of the program can reply.

In Figure 8, photograph 14, an error message was sent since SCRATCH in the user message was not in the dictionary. SCRATCH was then defined to be "same as REMOVE." Photograph 15 shows SCRATCH used successfully.

Figure 8. *Photograph 14, 15. Error Message.*

Five program modules are employed by the SKETCH supervisor. Each involves specialized routines for modifying and maintaining specific data structures. The five accomplish the following tasks:
1. Hash-dictionary look-up.
2. Message normalization.
3. Normalized-message processing.
4. Feature table modification.
5. Table interpretation.

The schematic in Figure 9 illustrates the interconnection of these utility routines and their relevant data structures.

As a user's message is entered on the keyboard, the keyboard queue retains the order and identity of each word for the interpretation phase. Each character is displayed and misspellings can be corrected before sending the message to the interpreter.

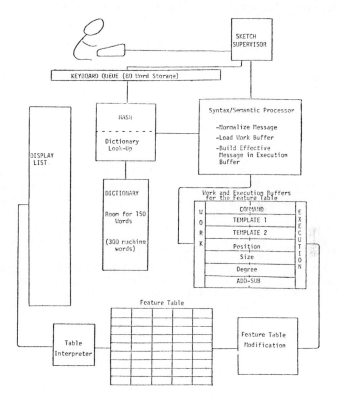

Figure 9. *Program Schematic.*

Once a carrieage return key is hit the supervisor enters the interpretive mode.

The first task undertaken by the supervisor is a left to right examination of each word in the user's message. Each word is hashed and the corresponding interpretation is looked up in a dictionary. The hash routine is a very simple one that currently has no collision safeguards but introduces considerable economy of core. If the retrieved interpretation conforms to the semantic restrictions of the language, the next word in the message is then considered. Before hashing the next word, the interpretation of the last is stored in the work buffer. Hash-dictionary look-up continues until either a violation of the language is detected or the keyboard queue is exhausted. At successful conclusion the work buffer will store the relevant information of the user's message.

Alternatives available to the hash look-up routines depend on the message semantics. These alternatives correspond to possibilities in interpreter parse trees. Messages are normalized: they are first filtered for informative elements and then condensed to a standard representation. Message filtering involves ignoring <ARTICLE>s and condensation by reducing information in some phrases to more convenient encodings. For example, the predicate modifier phrase, <VERY> <DEGREE PART> <ADD-SUB>, has a condensed interpretation represented in just two machine words. There are many variations of the standard representation so that the user has a wide range of allowed messages.

The work and table execution buffers are software data structures containing standard representations of user messages. After a message has been normalized and is resident in the work buffer, it is examined again. The second examination yields a message which is given to the table execution buffer and then put into effect. This is called the effective message. Indefinite context-sensitive relations appearing in the normalized message of the work buffer are given definite interpretations in the execution buffer. For instant, arguments for <PRONOUNS> are assigned during this type of processing. In addition, <SUBSEQUENT COMMAND PHRASE>s that do not reference <TEMPLATE>s explicitly are given implicit assignments. Both types of binding interrogate the execution buffer to "remember" which <TEMPLATE>s are in context. This contextual information is available since the execution buffer still contains the prior effective message.

The message that is actually executed is a composite of the user's message in the work buffer and information extracted from the execution buffer. Once formed, the effective message is entered into the execution buffer itself and feature table modification can then proceed.

Feature table modification is controlled by the arguments found in the table execution buffer. The encoding of the COMMAND word interpretation selects table modification routines that are candidates for execution. From these candidates POSITION and SIZE isolate the modification to be done while TEMPLATE1 and TEMPLATE2 specify features (or records in the feature table) to be addressed.

The table modification procedures respond to relational information encoded in the feature table. This relational information identifies paired features (eyes, ears, eyebrows, etc.) and also controls the incremental changes associated with each feature. Modifications to the eyes, for instance, are done in smaller increments than those made to a hairline or jaw. Spatial relations such as ears being on the same horizontal are also maintained by the feature table and its traversal routines.

The (feature) table interpreter is the last utility invoked by the SKETCH supervisor. After the feature table is interpreted the supervisor enters a waiting state for subsequent user messages.

All the features listed in the feature table correspond to display list templates. When a change is made to HAIR, for example, the record for HAIR in the feature table is altered then the corresponding display list segment, or template, is modified by the table interpreter. The table interpreter changes the display list to reflect the size and position of templates as specified in the feature table. By using pointers that are elements of the record for each feature, the table interpreter can locate the place in the display list where changes corresponding to record entries should be made.

Figure 10 illustrates the pointer fields in each feature table record. The pointers, TABLPNTR, ENTRYPTR, CURLOCAT, and DISPTRGT are all work pointers used by the table interpreter to locate display instructions in the display list. Using the information in the feature table the feature display instruction locations are found and subsequently modified. The type of modification made is also specified in the features table record.

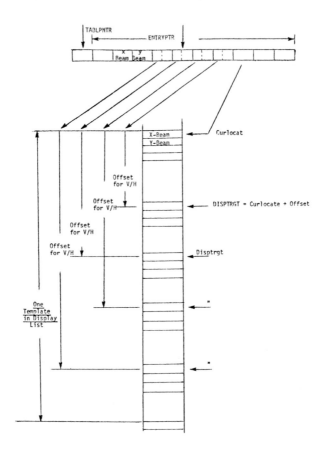

Figure 10. *Pointer Fields for each Record in the Feature Table.*

4. CONCLUSION

The SKETCH program is a vehicle for man-machine interaction to generate and modify facial images. Earlier versions explored how arbitrary nonfacial templates could be repositioned with relocation-ease rather than placement-accuracy stressed. In this, special equations were developed from regular decomposition of general pictures. We discussed translation from text input to display processor instructions, and how this was accomplished by the program using data structures for modularity and contextual association. The interface of the display processor and minicomputer was discussed in detail.

A variety of structures were used to retain relational information between features and contextual association during a user-SKETCH dialogue. Retention of this data is made possible by encoding relational information for each feature and storing keywords from user messages.

The SKETCH program was designed to be modular so that extensions could be realized by adding new feature display code or by exploiting other display processor hardware features as they become available. Feature rotation or variable beam intensity, for instance, would have their own settings represented in the Feature Table (see Figures 9 and 10). Changes to these settings could be made through an expanded user language.

The language itself has not been awkward to use but many enhancements have been suggested. Some require minor additional code or simply revisions of existing software. The majority of the suggestions are possible only after additional core storage is made available to our mini-computer. The SKETCH program now uses 7.5K of the 8K available.

The quality of the CRT displays depend only on the detail in the facial features addressable by SKETCH. Once a library of features is accessible to the program accurate sketches of a large number of faces can be made. Figure 11 shows how SKETCH could be used to draw the suspect police sketches published in a newspaper[3].

SUSPECT—Two views of Los Angeles' slasher suspect by police artist based on common elements that were reported in hundreds of police views. "This guy's a jackal," one officer

Figure 11. *Police Sketches and Computer Image.*

[3]Los Angeles Times, January 31, 1975, p. 1.

ACKNOWLEDGEMENT

This research was sponsored by the Air Force Office of Scientific Research, Air Force Systems Command, USAF, under Grant No. AFOSR-72-2384. The United States Government is authorized to reproduce and distribute reprints for Governmental purposes notwithstanding any copyright notation hereon.

The authors would like to express their appreciation for this support.

REFERENCES

1. Goldstein, A., Harmon, L., Lesk, A. "Identification of Human Faces," *Proceedings of the IEEE*, Vol. 59, No. 5, May 1971, pp. 748-760.

2. Harmon, L. "Some Aspects of Recognition of Human Faces," *Pattern Recognition in Biological and Technical Systems*, ed. by O.-J. Gruesser, New York, Springer, In Press.

3. Bledsoe, W. "Man-machine Facial Recognition: Report on a Large-scale Experiment," Panoramic Research Inc., Palo Alto, Calif., Report PRI:22, August, 1966.

4. Sakai, T., Nagao, M., Kanade, T. "Computer Analysis and Classification of Photographs of Human Faces," *Proceedings of the First USA-Japan Computer Conference*, 1972, pp. 55-62.

5. Gillenson, M. L. "The Interactive Generation of Facial Images on a CRT Using a Heuristic Strategy," Ph.D. Dissertation, Ohio State University, Columbus, Ohio, March 1974.

6. Winograd, T. *Understanding Natural Language*, Artificial Intelligence Laboratory, M.I.T., 545 Technology Square, Cambridge, Massachusetts 02139.

7. Hopper, W. R. "Photo-FIT, The Penry Facial Identification Technique," *Journal of Forensic Science Society*, Vol. 13, 1973, pp. 77-81.

8. Della Riccia, G. "Automatic Recognition of Identi-Kit Pictures of Human Faces," Ben Gurion University Technical Report, Beer-Sheva, Israel, MATH-48, June 1973.

9. Della Riccia, G. "An Attempt to Identify Human Faces with Only a Few Available Features," Ben Gurion University Technical Report, Beer-Sheva, Israel, MATH-58, June 1973.

10. Lakeoff, G. "Hedges: A Study in Meaning Criteria and the Logic of Fuzzy Concepts," *Journal of Philosophical Logic 2*, D. Reidel Publishing Co., Dordrecht, Holland, 1973, pp. 458-508.

11. Zadeh, L. "Fuzzy Sets," *Information and Control*, No. 8, pp. 338-353.

12. Klinger, A. "Natural Language, Linguistic Processing and Speech Understanding: Recent Research and Future Goals," Rand Corporation, Technical Report No. R-1377-ARPA, Santa Monica, Calif., December 1973.

13. Klinger, A. "Recent Computer Science Research in Language Processing," *American Journal of Computational Linguistics,* Vol. 12, No. 3, July 1975, pp. 2-25.

14. Klinger, A. "Patterns and Search Statistics," in *Optimizing Methods in Statistics,* ed. by J. S. Rustagi, Academic Press, New York, 1971.

15. Klinger, A. "Regular Decomposition and Picture Structure," *Proceedings 1974 IEEE Systems, Mand and Cybernetics Conference,* October 1974, pp. 307-310.

16. Klinger, A., Dyer, C. "Experiments on Picture Representation Using Regular Decomposition," UCLA-ENG-7494 Technical Report, December 1974.

17. Sutherland, I. "Computer Displays," (*Scientific American,* June 1970), in *Computers and Computation,* ed. by R. R. Fenichel and J. Weizenbaum, W. H. Freeman and Company, San Francisco, 1971, pp. 52-69.

18. Eatman, C. "Representation for Space Planning," *Communications of ACM,* Vol. 13, No. 4, April 1970, pp. 242-250.

19. Rosen, C., Nilsson, N. "Applications of Intelligent Automata to Reconnaissance," SRI Project 5953, Third Interim Report, Rome Air Force Development Center, Griffiss A.F.B., New York, December 1967.

20. Knuth, D. *Fundamental Algorithms* (Volume 1 *The Art of Computer Programming*), Addison-Wesley Publishing Co., Reading, Mass., 1968.

Surface Representation for
Computer Aided Design

R. E. BARNHILL
Department of Mathematics
University of Utah
Salt Lake City, Utah

R. F. RIESENFELD
Computer Science Department
University of Utah
Salt Lake City, Utah

ABSTRACT

This article surveys curve and surface representation and approximation. The topics discussed include B-splines, tensor products, rectangular and triangular Coons patches, Shepard's formula, and surfaces under tension.

1. INTRODUCTION

Computer Aided Geometric Design is the representation and approximation of curves and surfaces. The use of computer graphics, particularly if they are <u>interactive</u>, introduces certain constraints. Representations need to be "local" rather than "global", which means that a change in one part of a surface must not induce a change far away. Another constraint concerns "hard" and "soft" data, to which interpolation must be exact and approximate, respectively. These and related concepts are discussed more fully in [14].

2. TENSOR PRODUCTS

a. Bilinear Interpolation

We begin with the humble but useful linear interpolant. Given the two positional values f_0 and f_1, then

$$P_1 f = (1-x)f_0 + xf_1 \qquad (2.1)$$

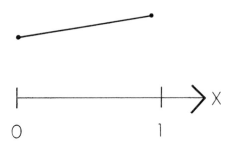

Figure 2.1: *Linear Interpolant*

interpolates to these data. If f is replaced successively by
the coordinate functions x, y, and z, then a parametric line
segment in space is obtained.

The bilinear interpolant to the four positional values F_{00}, F_{10},
F_{01}, and F_{11} is

$$PF = (1-x)(1-y)F_{00} + x(1-y)F_{10} + (1-x)yF_{01} + xyF_{11} \quad (2.2)$$

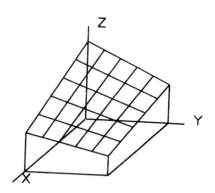

Figure 2.2: *The Bilinear Interpolant (2.2)*

By direct substitution, $(PF)(0,0) = F_{00}$ etc. PF is said to be
bilinear because it is linear in each of the variables x and y.
This property is also expressed by saying that PF is linearly
ruled, parallel to the coordinate axes x and y. If F is replaced
successively by components x, y, and z, then a parametric surface
in space is obtained.

PF can be built up from one-dimensional schemes as follows: for $f = f(x)$, $f_0 = f(0)$, and $f_1 = f(1)$, let $P_1 f$ be defined by (2.1). For $g = g(y)$, $g_0 = g(0)$, $g_1 = g(1)$, let

$$P_2 g = (1-y) g_0 + y g_1 \qquad (2.3)$$

Then $F = F(x,y)$, $F_{00} = F(0,0)$, etc. implies that

$$PF = P_1 P_2 F = P_2 P_1 F \qquad (2.4)$$

by direct calculation. Schemes formed as in (2.4) are called tensor product schemes. They were the first surface approximations devised and are still used more than any other class of schemes.

b.   Bicubic Spline Interpolation

The linear interpolant (2.1) can be generalized in two ways: (1) piecewise linear and (2) higher order. The piecewise linear interpolant $P_L f$ to the positions $\{(x_i, f_i)\}_{i=0}^{n}$ is simply illustrated by its graph:

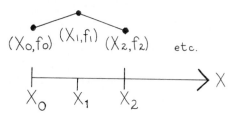

(X_0, f_0) (X_1, f_1) (X_2, f_2) etc.

X_0 X_1 X_2 $\longrightarrow X$

Figure 2.3: *Piecewise Linear Interpolant*

$P_L f$ has the distinguishing characteristic that it minimizes

$$\int_{x_0}^{x_n} [h'(x)]^2 \, dx \qquad \text{among all functions h interpolating to the}$$

data $\{(x_i, f_i)\}_{i=0}^{n}$. A spline is a function that minimizes a variational principle and so $P_L f$ is called the piecewise linear spline. It minimizes the length of a curve obtained if $f(x)$ is replaced by $x(t)$ and $y(t)$ successively, and (x_i, f_i) by

(t_i, x_i, y_i), where we recall that the length of $\begin{pmatrix} x(t) \\ y(t) \end{pmatrix}$ between

t_0 and t_n is $\int_{t_0}^{t_n} \{[x'(t)]^2 + [y'(t)]^2\}^{\frac{1}{2}} dt.$

Notice that $P_L f$ has local support, as defined in the Introduction. $P_L f$ will come up later in this article in connection with "splines under tension".

$P_L f$ is continuous (c^0). Visual smoothness requires at least a continuous derivative, i.e., a continuous tangent, and preferably continuous curvature as well. In short, a c^2 interpolant is desired. Given f_0, f_0^1, f_1 and f_1^1, the cubic Hermite interpolant is

$$P_C f = \phi_0(x) f_0 + \phi_1(x) f_0^1 + \psi_0(x) f_1 + \psi_1(x) f_1^1, \quad (2.5)$$

where

$$\phi_0(x) = (1-x)^2(2x+1),$$

$$\phi_1(x) = x(1-x)^2, \text{ and}$$

$$\psi_i(x) = (-1)^i \phi_i(1-x), \text{ i = 0, 1.}$$

The corresponding piecewise cubic Hermite interpolant provides a c^1 function interpolating to positions and directions, but it is not a c^2 function. An equivalent number of parameters can be made to yield a c^2 interpolant, which can be illustrated as follows:

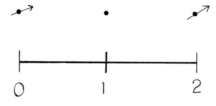

Figure 2.4: *Data for a Cubic Spline*

Let $C_i(x)$ be a cubic function defined only on $[i, i+1]$, $i=0, 1$, respectively. C_0 is to interpolate to f_0, f_0^1, and f_1, whereas C_1 is to interpolate to f_1, f_2, and f_2^1. Moreover, the smoothness constraints

$$C_0'(1) = C_1'(1)$$

$$C_0''(1) = C_1''(1)$$

are imposed. Two cubics have eight degrees of freedom (i.e., 4 coefficients each to be determined). The six interpolation conditions and two smoothness constraints yield eight equations for the eight unknowns and it can be shown that they have a solution. The resulting interpolant is called a cubic interpolatory spline. Similarly to the linear interpolatory spline, the cubic interpolatory spline has the distinguishing character-

istic that it minimizes $\int_{x_0}^{x_n} [h''(x)]^2 \, dx$ among all functions h

interpolating to the data

$$f_i, \ i = 0, 1, \ldots, n; \quad f_i^1, \ i = 0, n.$$

That is, the "linearized curvature" is minimized.

The tensor product of two univariate cubic interpolatory splines is the bicubic spline to the data:
(1) Function values F_{ij} at the mesh points.
(2) Normal derivatives at the mesh points along each side of the defining rectangle.
(3) Twist derivatives at the corners of the rectangle.
The cubic interpolatory spline does not have local support. However, it turns out that local support can be obtained, and the smoothness of the splines preserved, whilst giving up the interpolation properties. This is achieved by "B-splines".

c. Bézier Curves and Surfaces

P. Bézier of Renault, Paris, developed a technique [5] for designing curves and surfaces interactively which applies an approximation method, namely Bernstein approximation, instead of a traditional interpolation scheme like the previously described ones. In his investigations of interactive methods,

Bézier discovered that control points that were near the curve, but not on the curve itself, were more tractable for controlling the shape of the curve. In his curve form he uses interpolation and tangency at the end points with approximation of shape at the intermediate control points to attain a computationally simple method of designing a curve that meets certain "hard", or fixed, end conditions while achieving "soft", or flexible, interior requirements on shape and position.

Connecting the control points P_i of a Bézier curve produces a polygonal line, simply called a (Bézièr) polygon, which can be implemented to generate the (Bézier) curve defined by

$$\gamma(s) = \sum_{i=0}^{n} P_i \ \theta_i \ (s) \tag{2.6}$$

where $\theta_i(s) = \binom{n}{i} s^i (1-s)^{n-i}$, $0 \le s \le 1$.

As the parameter s varies over the interval $[0,1]$, a smooth, easily controlled curve $\gamma(s)$ is drawn [see Figure 2.5].

Figure 2.5: *Bézier Polygon and Curve*

We see from (2.6) that $\gamma(s)$ is a linear combination of polynomial blending functions having degree n, the number of polygonal vertices less 1. Thus the degree of the curve increases with the addition of extra vertices, a situation leading to higher degree polynomial evaluations than is normally desirable. Since $\gamma(s)$ is a polynomial curve changing any vertex P effects a global perturbation of $\gamma(s)$, albeit diminishing with distance on the curve away from P. Similarly, a polynomial that is linear in any open interval must be entirely linear, so Bézier curves cannot encompass linear segments without being linear throughout. It is also a shortcoming that these curves do not have a periodic closed form that responds to each vertex in an identi-

cal manner. Finally we note $\theta_i(s)$ in (2.6) is always nonnega-
tive, so that $\gamma(s)$ is a <u>convex</u> combination of the P_i, that is,
$\gamma(s)$ is in the <u>convex hull</u> of $\{P_i\}$. This very important geometric property ensures that the curve does not overshoot or
otherwise elude the control of the designer. The simplicity in
implementation and the geometric intuitiveness in its use have
led to widespread use of these Bézier curves and their tensor
product surfaces given by

$$S(u,v) = \sum_{j=0}^{m} \sum_{i=0}^{n} P_{ij} \; \theta_i(u) \; \phi_j(v) \qquad (2.7)$$

where
$\qquad \theta_i(u)$ is defined in (2.6)
$\qquad \phi_j(v) = \binom{m}{j} v^j (1-v)^{m-j}$

and $\qquad \{P_{ij}\}_{i=0,j=0}^{n,\;m}$ forms a polyhedral (Bézier) net [see
Figure 2.6] that serves to determine the associated bipolynomial
surface in a way exactly analogous to the curve generation in
(2.6).

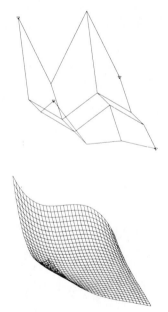

Figure 2.6: *Bézier Polyhedral Net and Surface*

d. B-spline Curves and Surfaces

   B-spline approximation is a proper spline generalization
to Bernstein approximation which can be employed to yield an
interactive design scheme analogous to Bézier's which produces
spline curves, called B-spline curves, instead of polynomial
curves. This extension to B-splines overcomes many of the
objections raised about Bézier curves, but they are somewhat
more complicated to implement. Essentially, the B-spline curve
has the same form as (2.6), except that the $\theta_i(u)$ are taken to
be an appropriate B-spline basis, where much freedom is allowed
in choosing the degree, parametric spacing, as well as the form
(open/closed). The deBoor/Cox Algorithm is a very general algorithm that can be employed as a single, compact and efficient
procedure for computing the curve specified by any of the stated
variations. The details of this implementation are reported
elsewhere [9,13], and therefore are omitted in this survey
article.

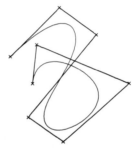

Figure 2.7: *Polygon and B-spline Curve*

3. COONS PATCHES

   a. Rectangles

   For a bivariate function $F = F(x,y)$, the linear interpolant
(2.1) yields
$$P_1F = (1-x)\ F(0,y) + x\ F(1,y) \qquad (3.1)$$

   This is a "lofting" interpolant to the curves $F(0,y)$ and
$F(1,y)$. Similarly
$$P_2F = (1-y)\ F(x,0) + y\ F(x,1) \qquad (3.2)$$

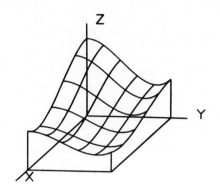

Figure 3.1:
Bivariate Function F

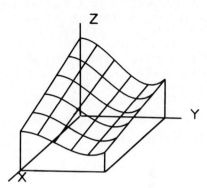

Figure 3.2:
Lofting Interpolant P_1F

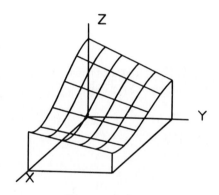

Figure 3.3:
Lofting Interpolant P_2F

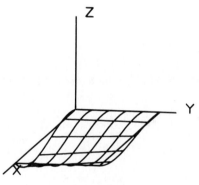

Figure 3.4:
Remainder $F-P_2F$

From Figures 3.1 - 3.4, it appears that $P_2F + P_1(F - P_2F)$ interpolates to F all around the boundary of the square. This is true
and can be verified algebraically from the formula

$$P_1F + P_2F - P_1P_2F = (1-x) F(0,y) + x F(1,y) + (1-y) F(x,0)$$

$$+ y F(x,1) - [(1-x) (1-y) F(0,0) + x(1-y) F(1,0)$$

$$+ (1-x)y F(0,1) + xyF(1,1)] \qquad (3.3)$$

Interpolants of this type were initiated by Coons [6]. (3.3) is called the bilinear Coons patch and the "weighting" or "shape" functions $(1-x)$, $(1-x)(1-y)$, etc., are called the "blending" functions. They "blend" together the information $F(0,y)$, $F(1,y)$, etc. Gordon [8] calls this a "transfinite element", because whole curves of information are used. He has also developed the algebraic structure of such interpolants, beginning with the observation that $P_1F + P_2F - P_1P_2F$ is a Boolean sum, which is written $(P_1 \oplus P_2)F$. When such interpolants are discretized along the sides, e.g., $F(0,y)$ is replaced by its quadratic interpolant to $F(0,0)$, $F(0,\frac{1}{2})$, and $F(0,1)$, etc., then the resulting interpolant is called a "serendipity finite element" in the engineering literature.

The bilinear Coons patch (3.3) interpolates to position all around the square and so it also interpolates to all tangential derivatives, e.g., $(\frac{\partial F}{\partial y})(0,y)$, as well. If additional derivatives, e.g., normal derivatives like $(\frac{\partial F}{\partial x})(0,y)$ are also to be interpolated, then P_1 and P_2 can be redefined to do it. For example, if just the function and first derivatives are desired, then P_1F in (3.1) can be replaced by P_cF from (2.5) etc.

Blending schemes of the form $(P_1 \oplus P_2)F$ include the tensor products as the special discretization P_1P_2F.

b. Triangles

Triangles are more flexible than rectangles for subdividing regions. Coons patches for triangles were initiated by Barnhill, Birkhoff, and Gordon [2]. These interpolants involve rational functions. Barnhill and Gregory [3] overcame this difficulty by inventing triangular Coons patches with polynomial blending functions. These interpolants are especially suitable for the direct (nonparametric) treatment of interpolation over a triangle with one curved side. A summary of triangular patches is given by Barnhill in [1].

Example. Triangle with one curved side.
Let the curved side of the triangle have the parametric representation $x = f(t)$, $y = g(t)$, $0 \leq t \leq 1$. This is the form of the curve that is usually encountered in practice.

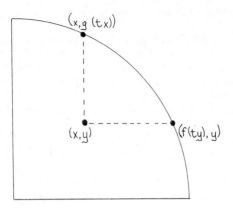

Figure 3.5: *Standard Curved Triangle with One Curved Side*

The interpolation problem is to interpolate to function values
(position) all around the boundary of the curved triangle. For
(x,y) in the curved triangle, let $t_x = f^{-1}(x)$ and $t_y = g^{-1}(y)$.
Then the following function solves the above interpolation
problem.

$PF = yF(x,g(t_x)) + [1 - g(t_x)]F(f(t_y),y)$

$+ F(0,y) + F(x,0) - F(0,0)$

$- y[F(0,g(t_x)) + F(x,0) - F(0,0)]$

$- [1 - g(t_x)][F(0,y) + F(f(t_y),0) - F(0,0)]$

The interpolation properties

$$[(P_1 \oplus P_2)F](x,0) = F(x,0)$$
$$[(P_1 \oplus P_2)F](0,y) = F(0,y)$$

are easily checked. For (x,y) on the curved side, i.e.,

$(x,y) = (f(t),g(t))$ for some t; $t_x = t = t_y$ implies that

$$[(P_1 \oplus P_2)F](f(t),g(t)) = F(f(t),g(t)).$$

$$(3.4)$$

3.4 Additional Surface Methods

a. Shepard [15] has recently introduced an interpolation scheme for arbitrary data in the plane. It has global rather than local support and employs rational weighting functions. Shepard's formula has recently [4,12] been combined with an interpolant of Barnhill and Gregory over triangles to produce a continuously differentiable interpolant to arbitrary position data.

b. "Splines under tension" are interpolatory functions that minimize $\int[f''(x)]^2 \, dx + \sigma^2 \int[f'(x)]^2 \, dx$, σ a constant (the "tension") to be chosen. This variational principle is a combination of the ones for cubic and linear interpolatory splines: $\sigma = 0$ yields the cubic interpolatory spline and σ large yields a spline near to the linear interpolatory spline. Splines under tension involve exponentials. Nielson [10] has introduced polynomial alternatives with similar properties, the so-called "ν-splines." Pilcher [11] introduced "surfaces under tension", with a two-dimensional variational principle. An alternative type of surface under tension has been introduced by Dube [7]. These schemes have the common feature that the tension permits a degree of local control.

ACKNOWLEDGEMENTS

This research was supported by The National Science Foundation with Grant DCR 74-13017 to The University of Utah. REB's research was also supported by the United Kingdom Science Research Council with Grant B/RG/61876 at The University of Dundee, Scotland and by The University of Utah Research Committee.

REFERENCES

1   Barnhill, R. E.   "Smooth Interpolation over Triangles,"
    Computer Aided Geometric Design, ed. by R. E. Barnhill and
    R. F. Riesenfeld, Academic Press, 1974, pp. 45-70.

2   Barnhill, R. E., Birkhoff, G., and Gordon, W. J.   "Smooth
    Interpolation in Triangles," *J. Approx. Theory* 8, 1973,
    pp. 114-128.

3   Barnhill, R. E. and Gregory, J. A.   "Polynomial Interpo-
    lation to Boundary Data on Triangles," *Math Comp* 29, 1975,
    pp. 726-735.

4   Barnhill, R. E., Poeppelmeier,C. C., and Riesenfeld, R. F.
    "An Interpolation Scheme for Arbitrary Data for Computer
    Aided Geometric Design" (To appear).

5   Bézier, P. *Numerical Control-Mathematics and Applications,*
    John Wiley, London, 1972.

6   Coons, S. A.   "Surfaces for Computer-Aided Design of Space
    Forms," MIT Project MAC TR 41, June 1967.

7   Dube, R. P.   "Local Schemes for Computer Aided Geometric
    Design," Ph.D. Dissertation, University of Utah, 1975.

8   Gordon, W. J.   "Distributive Lattices and the Approximation
    of Multivariate Functions," *Proceedings of the Symposium
    on Approximation with Special Emphasis on Splines,* ed. by
    I. J. Schoenberg, University of Wisconsin Press, 1969,
    pp. 223-277.

9   Gordon, W. J. and Riesenfeld, R. F.   "B-spline Curves and
    Surfaces," *Computer Aided Geometric Design,* ed. by
    R. E. Barnhill and R. F. Riesenfeld, Academic Press, 1974,
    pp. 95-126.

10 Nielson, G. M.   "Some Piecewise Alternatives to Splines
    Under Tension," *Computer Aided Geometric Design,* ed. by
    R. E. Barnhill and R. F. Riesenfeld, Academic Press, 1974,
    pp. 209-235.

11 Pilcher, D. T.   "Smooth Parametric Surfaces," *Computer
    Aided Geometric Design,* ed. by R. E. Barnhill and R. F.
    Riesenfeld, Academic Press, 1974, pp. 237-253.

12   Poeppelmeier, C. C. "A Boolean Sum Interpolation Scheme
      to Random Data for Computer Aided Geometric Design,"
      Master's Thesis, University of Utah, 1975.

13   Riesenfeld, R. F. "Applications of B-spline Approximation
      to Geometric Problems of Computer Aided Design," Ph.D.
      Dissertation, Syracuse University, 1973.

14   Riesenfeld, R. F. "Aspects of Modelling in Computer Aided
      Geometric Design," *Proceedings of National Computer Confe-
      rence*, AFIPS Press, 1975, pp. 597-602.

15   Shepard, D. "A Two-Dimensional Interpolation Function for
      Irregularly Spaced Data," *Proceedings of 23rd National
      Conference of ACM*, 1968, pp. 517-524.

Automatic Detection of Suspicious
Abnormalities in Breast Radiographs

CAROLYN KIMME
BERNARD J. O'LOUGHLIN
JACK SKLANSKY

*School of Engineering and
Department of Radiological Sciences
University of California
Irvine, California 92664*

The National Cancer Institute has estimated that 88,000 new breast cancers **and** 32,600 breast cancer deaths will be reported this year (1975) [3]. Early diagnosis may yield a 75 percent five-year survival rate for cases where no axillary metastases are involved. Mass screening has been widely proposed as a means of achieving such early diagnosis.

Motivated by the large case load which would result from mass screening, we are investigating the feasibility of computer-aided systems for diagnosing breast radiographs. In such systems radiologists, paramedical aids [2], and computers would work jointly and interactively. We believe that such a system is likely to be more cost-effective and achieve fewer errors than non-computer systems [1]. In this paper we report some of the recent results that support us in this belief.

We describe, in particular, some of the techniques we employ in processing xeromammograms so that abnormal regions of the breast can be detected automatically. We restricted our computing to a minicomputer with 8,000, 16-bit words of core memory, thereby stimulating the construction of cost-effective algorithms.

Our methods proceed as follows. First we identify the boundaries of the image of the breast tissue in the xeromammogram. Then we partition it into at most 144 sections per breast in such a way that a particular section on the right breast has

a similarly placed section on the left breast. We next compute
10 statistics for each section to use as features representing
texture. The features are normalized and then selected or eliminated by evaluating how well they separate abnormal from normal tissue on a small training set of sections. The training
set is also used to devise simple classification rules for the
selected features. The complete classification of 2,270 sections for eight patients takes less than 2 minutes of minicomputer time and yields a false positive rate of 26 percent and a
false negative rate (for cancerous sections) of .6 percent.

PRELIMINARY PREPARATION

The medical images we are presently using are lateral view
xeromammograms obtained from Dr. Gloria Frankl of the Kaiser
Permanente Hospitals. After initial experiments on a data base
of four patients, we chose a data base of eight patients. These
eight were collected from different sized breasts, different
ages, and different diagnoses. Three patients had breast cancer; three were normal; one had benign cysts; and one was normal but appeared abnormal enough to be checked regularly. We
refer to the last patient as "follow-up".)

Since our scanner accepts only transparencies or negatives,
we photograph the xeromammograms before scanning. Very careful
control and some experimentation with film, exposure, filters,
and development are necessary. We divide each xeromammogram
into two parts because of limitations in the size of the image
our digitizer can scan.

Our scanner produces a matrix of numerical values of optical
density. Each element of the matrix (a "pixel") is approximately the average optical density in a 0.12 mm. x 0.12 mm. square
of the original xerogram. Each patient file has four matrices
since each breast is divided into a top half and a bottom half.
At full resolution, each half xeromammogram is represented by a
matrix of 900,000 pixels, i.e., 3,600,000 pixels per patient.
To reduce the amount of computation and stroage these matrices
require, we reduce the size of these matrices by 1/4 and 1/16,
replacing 4 x 4 and 16 x 16 submatrices by their averages. We
achieve still further efficiencies in data handling through restricting high-resolution analysis to areas of the breast identified by the computer as "suspicious abnormalities".

BREAST TISSUE OUTLINING

Our computer algorithms find the breast tissue by detecting
the boundaries of the breast: the skin and chest wall. Our algorithms are a blend of traditional edge enhancement and heuristic methods based on the appearance of the skin and chest wall
of the xeromammograms. Since the skin is denser than the background, the xerogram toner is pulled away from the background
near the skin, leaving a white halo along the skin. A layer of
fat separates the skin from breast tissue and also leaves a
light area on the other side of the skin (Figure 1).

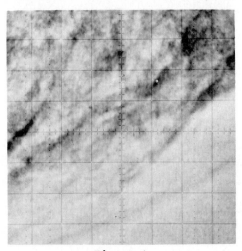

Figure 1
Detail of Digitized Skin
on a Photographed Xeromammogram

These physical characterisitics are used in programming the
computer to recognize skin pixels. Since some areas of skin will
be missing, and since the computer program may select some
breast tissue pixels as skin, a smoothing of the computed skin
boundary is necessary. The chest wall image pulls toner away
from breast tissue because of increased density in the chest
wall and ribs. The dark line (in the negative) allows us to use
a modified ridge following algorithm similar to a heuristic
graph search. Both the skin and chest wall algorithms use the
1/16 reduced images and integer arithmetic, even on skin smoothing, so they are very economical of computer storage and execution time.

BREAST PARTITIONS

The right and left breasts of the same woman are not always
the same size, although the tissue itself, if normal, will match
a similar section of tissue in the opposite breast. To insure
that we only compare similar regions, some care is taken to
partition the breasts correctly. The slope of the skin halfway
between the nipple and edge of the picture is computed and then
extended so that each half breast is enclosed in a triangle,
(Figure 2).

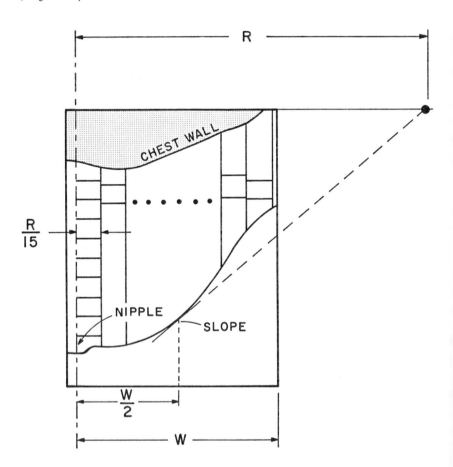

BREAST PARTITIONING

Figure 2

The base of the triangle is divided equally into fifteen segments, defining the bases of fifteen strips. Each of these
strips is divided into a specified number of squares, the number of such squares depending on the position of the strip.
Each square represents a partition ranging in size from 24 by
25 elements to 15 by 16 pixels. These pixels refer to the pictures reduced by 1/4 from the original scan. Usually no more
than 9 strips appear on the photograph and are used in our
classification method.

Each partition is represented by four histograms from which
texture statistics are later computed. The first histogram, H,
represents the distribution of the optical densities in the
partition. It is limited to a spread of 40 grey level values
centered at the mean density of the strip that the partition is
on. The second histogram U, ranges over 20 values and is the
distribution of the maximum density differences between adjacent pixels. The third and fourth histograms, V and W, have
four possible values each. Histogram V represents the distribution of the directions of maximum density differences between
adjacent pixels and W is the distribution of the differences
between the directions computed in V. Both V and W are defined
in more detail in the section on "Feature Selection".

TEXTURE STATISTICS

We use some of the inspection techniques of mammographers
as clues in implementing our automatic search. These radiologists speak of unilateral increases in ducting, increased
vascularity, and dense areas with spiculated edges as symptoms
which induce them to examine an area of the breast in more detail [5, 6]. Ducting in xeromammograms appears as irregular,
high-contrasted, convoluted regions where some pattern of ducts
can be seen, but the edges of the ducts are blurred and irregu-
lar-- unlike the veins which are easily identifiable. These
texture changes are the preliminary reasons for a radiologist
to examine a xeromammogram in greater detail Since most textures can be represented by statistical measures, we felt that
the variance of the numbers in a partition would measure the
amount of contrast in the partition. Similarly the third moment
about the mean would measure whether the variance is due to
dark or light areas in the partition. We also form measures of
the differences between adjacent elements in the partition.
Each of these statistical measures we call a _feature_. We form
10 features for each partition.

Since radiation dosage, photographic exposures, and patient physiognomy cause each set of xeromammograms to differ from one another, we normalize each patient's breast sections. This normalization technique is very critical to the success of our method. Each section is normalized in two steps. Suppose a section in the upper right breast is to be normalized. Then the matching section in the upper left breast of the same patient is found. This section and all the adjacent sections form an area that we can use to normalize the right breast's section (Figure 3).

LOWER LEFT BREAST   LOWER RIGHT BREAST

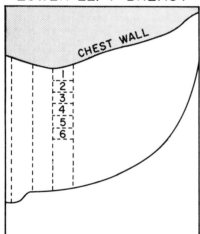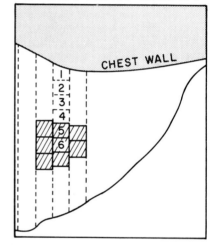

Figure 3

INITIAL NORMALIZATION

Let the sections be numbered as follows: section (i,j) is the jth section in the ith strip, where the sections in each strip are counted from chest wall to skin. Let $N(i,j)$ denote the set of neighbors (i.e., neighboring sections) of section (i,j) entering into the normalization for section (i,j). The number of neighbors, N_{ij}, can vary from 2 to 8, depending on the position of section (i,j). (Figure 3 illustrates the neighbors belonging to section $(3,6)$ where $N_{ij} = 8$. In order to normalize the kth feature, x_k, of the section (i,j) on the right breast, we compute

$$\mu_k^L (i,j) = \frac{1}{N_{ij}+1} \left[\sum_{(m,n)\in N(i,j)} x_k^L(m,n) + x_k^L(i,j) \right]$$

where superscript L identifies left breast data. Then initial
normalization consists of computing

$$\hat{x}_k^R(i,j) = |x_k^R(i,j) - \mu_k^L(i,j)|$$

When all the sections of the breast have been normalized this
way, we have a measure of unilateral differences. The range of
values of a single feature in a patient's upper breast differs
from the range in that patient's lower breast. This variation
in range, as well as the variation among patients, compels us to
normalize each of the sections. We normalize each feature by
its variance over the half breast. For example, to complete the
normalization of a particular patient's right upper breast,
U^R, compute

$$\bar{x}_k^R(i,j) = (\hat{x}_k^R(i,j))/\sigma_k^R$$

where

$$\sigma_k^R = \frac{1}{N_R} \sum_{(i,j)\in U^R} (\hat{x}_k^R(i,j) - \hat{\mu}_k^R)^2$$

$$\hat{\mu}_k^R = \frac{1}{N_R} \sum_{(i,j)\in U^R} \hat{x}_k^R(i,j)$$

and N_R is the number of sections in U^R.

We use the $\bar{x}\,^R_k(i,j)$'s as data points in our classification process. An example of the result of this normalization is illustrated in Table 1.

Table 1

Section From	I RAW DATA	II SUBTRACT MEAN OF OPPOSITE NEIGHBORHOOD	III DIVIDE ENTRY II BY VARIANCE OF II OVER A HALF BREAST
Upper Right	255	171	1.07
Upper Left	628	228	1.48
Lower Left	987	860	5.58
Lower Left	153	366	3.00

NORMALIZATION EXAMPLES

(Feature is Variance of the Densities)

FEATURE SELECTION

For our classification procedure, we selected seven features from an initial group of ten features. We selected the seven features by evaluating how well small subsets of the ten features distingusih normal from abnormal tissue. In this evaluation, we used a training set of three patients. Each of their 832 sections was labeled normal or abnormal on the basis of visual examination by a trained layman. Twelve percent of the sections required structure evaluation or magnification and so were labeled abnormal.

Since feature selection is a one-time computation, we did not need to restrict the search to inexpensive algorithms. We used an iterative cluster classifier [4] on four features at a time. The classifier assigns each section to a cluster on the basis of the mean and radius of the clusters. Since new assignments change the means and radii of the clusters, the classifier continues until it has either iterated six times or until no more than 10 percent of the sections are reassigned on the preceding iteration.

We scored the effectiveness of candidate subsets of features by computing the fraction of false positives and false negatives obtained by each subset. Since about 12 percent of the training set contined sections believed to be suspicious abnormalities ("abnormalities" for short), we first adjusted the threshold T of the classifier to T = 12 percent so that if 12 percent or more of the training-set sections in a cluster were abnormal, then the entire cluster would be labeled abnormal by the classifier. We found that this threshold yielded a false positive rate of over 30 percent. Hence, we adjusted the threshold upward from 12 percent to 14 percent, thereby achieving a false positive rate below 30 percent while maintaining a low false negative rate (less than 10 percent).

By repeating this classification on combinations of four features at a time, three features were eliminated as poor descriptors of abnormal texture. Core restrictions allowed us to use the cluster classifier on only six of the seven remaining features. The clusters obtained by using the first six features yielded a false positive rate of 28 percent and a false negative rate of 10 percent. We used the parameters of the abnormal clusters as starting values when we defined our classification rules.

At the present time, the texture features, x_k, that we use are x_1, ten times the variance of the optical density, $f(\underline{y})$ in each section, and x_2, the third moment about the mean of $f(\underline{y})$. These are computed from histogram H.

Features x_3, x_4, x_5, and x_6, are computed from the modulus and direction of $g(\underline{y})$ which is an estimate of the gradient of the picture function $f(\underline{y})$ in each section.

Let

$$D_1 = f(\underline{y}) - f(\underline{y} + (0,1))$$
$$D_2 = f(\underline{y}) - F(\underline{y} + (1,1))$$

$$D_3 = f(\underline{y}) - f(\underline{y} + (1,0))$$

$$D_4 = f(\underline{y} + (0,1)) - f(\underline{y} + (1,0))$$

Then we define

$$g(\underline{y}) = \underset{i}{Max} \, |D_i|$$

where $g(\underline{y})$ is an estimate of the modulus of the gradient of $f(\underline{y})$.

Features x_5 and x_6 are the variance and mean of $g(\underline{y})$ in each section and are computed from histogram U. Features x_3 and x_4 depend on $\phi(\underline{y})$, our estimate of the angle of the gradient of $f(\underline{y})$. Let I denote the value of i at which $|D_i|$ is a maximum. Define $\phi(y)$ in terms of I and sgn (D_i) in accordance with Table 2. Note that we quantize ϕ into eight angles spaced at intervals of $\pi/4$.

	$Sgn(D_I)$	
I	+	−
1	π	2π
2	$3\pi/4$	$7\pi/4$
3	$\pi/2$	$3\pi/2$
4	$\pi/4$	$5\pi/4$

Table 2

Values of ϕ

We form x_3 as follows: for each pixel where $g(\underline{y}) > 4$, form a histogram $V_i(i = 1, \ldots, 4)$ on the number of threshold pixels which have direction π or 2π, $3\pi/4$ or $7\pi/4$, etc., let

$$V_j = \{\underset{i}{Max}\ V_i\}$$

we define

$$\mu = 1/3 \sum_{i=1}^{4} V_i - V_j$$

and

$$x_3 = \frac{|V_j - \mu|}{N}$$

where N is the number of pixels in the section.

We compute the fourth feature by counting the number of thresholded pixels whose $\phi(\underline{y})$ differs from neighboring $\phi(\underline{y})$ by $3\pi/4$, the third value of histogram W. This count is divided by the total number of pixels in the section.

The bimodality feature, x_7, is computed from the histogram H_i of the optical densities in the breast section. We find the maximum

$$M_1 = \hat{H}_j = \underset{i=1,255}{Max}\ \{H_i\}$$

and a second maximum

$$M_2 = \hat{H}_k$$

such that

$$\hat{H}_k = \underset{i=1,255}{Max}\ \{H_i\ |\ i \neq j, |k-j| > 4,\ \hat{H}_k > \frac{\hat{H}_j}{2}\}\ ,$$

and there exists at least one H_l such that $H_l < H_k$ and l falls between j and k.

If an H_k which satisfies these conditions cannot be found, then the section is not considered bimodal, and $x_7 = 0$. Otherwise $x_7 = |j-k|$.

This feature is a measure of the difference between the two most frequently occurring optical densities in a section.

A section of breast with high values of x_3, x_4, and x_7 is illustrated in Figure 4. This is the underside of a fibrocystic breast. An example of a section with large values of x_1, x_5, and x_6 is illustrated in Figure 5, the nipple area of a cancerous breast. The dark area at the bottom of the photograph is thickened skin. The example of a skin section shown in Figure 1 also illustrates large values of features x_3, x_4, x_5, and x_6.

CLASSIFICATION

We classify the 2,270 sections of the eight patients by applying the following four rules:

1. At least two of x_1, x_2, x_4, or x_5, must exceed 100.

2. Either x_3 or x_4 (or both) must exceed 50.

3. The sum of $x_1 + x_2 + x_5 + x_6 + 50x_7$ must exceed 600.

4. If a patient's matching right and left sections satisfy Rules 1, 2, and 3, then we check the unnormalized x_1 for the right and left sections.

   If one side's value is more than two times the opposite side's, the larger value's section is retained as a positive. Otherwise, both are retained. In Table 1, the upper left and lower right sections would be classified as abnormal.

We developed these rules by examining the ratio of false positives and false negatives as we changed the rules and parameters on our training set of three patients. We began developing a number of rules and first approximations of their parameters by using the coordinates and radii of the clusters described under "Feature Selection". By counting the number of true positives and true negatives identified by each rule, we

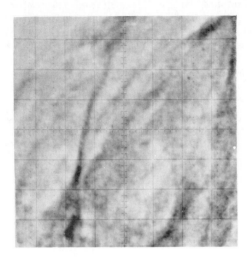

Figure 4
Detail of the Lower Portion of a Fibrocystic Breast

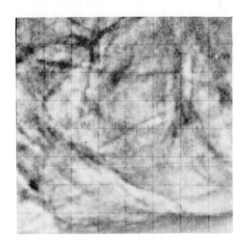

Figure 5
Detail of Tissue Changes Behind the
Nipple in a Cancerous Breast

eliminated redundant rules. We refined the values of the parameters by incrementing them through a range of values and counting the resulting range of false positives and false negatives.
Our final selection of rules and parameter values yielded the
minimum false negative rate with a false positive rate below
30 percent.

RESULTS

   This classification detected all three cancerous areas as
well as all the cysts. It labeled about 4 percent of the breast
sections as positive even through they are clearly normal.
Table 3 lists the results of our classification.

Table 3

Classification Results

Diagnosis	Areas	FP	FN/OK	FN/CA
1. Normal, Fibrocystic	21	6	4	0
2. Cancer, 2 cm.	22	7	2	0
3. Asymetry, Adenosis	19	3	2	0
4. Normal	27	9	2	0
5. Normal, Different Size	22	6	2	0
6. Cancer, Small	26	6	3	0
7. Cancer, Interductal	24	5	5	1
8. Cysts, Normal	22	0	9	0

   Note that the results are by areas, not breasts or sections.
An area can be as small as one section or as large as eight sections. Figure 6 is a photograph of the upper breast listed as
Case 7 of Table 3. Seven areas are shaded. The one cancerous
false negative section appears on this photograph in the middle
right. An elargement of the cancer is shown in Figure 7.

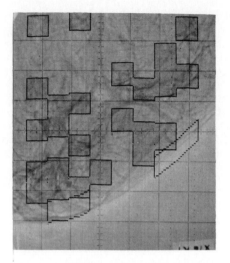

Figure 6
Result of Classification on a Cancerous Upper Breast
Shaded Areas are Labeled Abnormal

Figure 7
Detail of Figure 6 at the Cancer Site

DATA STRUCTURE

Because each mammogram must be digitized into large numbers of bits and because the size of our core memory is small, it was essential to build our algorithms on an efficient data structure. Furthermore, becuase the ultimate users are radiologists, our data structure also reflects the physiological and diagnostic environment.

The limited size of our core memory stimulated us to organize the pictorial data in a hierarchical structure.

Gross descriptors of the picture, such as the chest wall and the skin, were computed from a coarsely digitized picture: a 16-to-1 reduction in linear size was used.. The partitioned breast images were reduced by a factor of 4. The pixels of each partition in this reduced picture occupied from 240 to 600 words of core memory. Further data reduction was obtained by replacing the histograms by the seven features derived from these histograms. Further reduction is obtained by eliminating from the stored data all of the partitions classified as "normal". These systematic reductions of core storage requirements gave us the core space needed to examine the abnormal partitions at full resolution.

Physiological considerations required that each breast image be partitioned in a manner facilitating comparison of left against right breast. Since microcalcifications of 0.25 mm. are diagnostically significant, our data structure was constructed to facilitate analysis of full-resolution data when requested by the algorithm. Thus physiological and diagnostic considerations led us to a data structure that reflects the partitions of the breast image and that has hierarchic access to several pictorial resolutions.

CONCLUSIONS

We have demonstrated on a data base of eight patients that abnormal areas of scanned xerograms of breasts can be identified by texture statistics. A very low false negative rate encourages us to further refine our classification rules on a larger data base. Under more sophisticated decision rules, isolated sections calssified positive can probably be reclassified as negative. We believe that further reductions in the number of false positives can be achieved by applying algorithms that are sensitive to structural features, such as blood vessels and cysts, as contrasted to the present statistical features.

ACKNOWLEDGMENT

   This research was supported by the National Institute of
General Medical Sciences of the U.S. Public Health Service under
Grant No. GM-17632.

EXERCISES

1. In the following Example of Digitization, the photograph
    and digitization of the chest wall illustrates the import-
    ance of data structures in algorithm development. In this
    example, the chest wall begins between the 12th and 13th
    pixels of the first column. It ends between the 10th and
    11th pixels of the last column (at the right).

    a) Complete the delineation of the chest wall without
        reference to the photograph. Check your decisions
        with the photograph.

    b) Construct a rule for finding the chest wall.

    c) In what way would the rule change if the data
        were stored by rows and not more than three rows
        could fit in the computer's main memory? Would
        you construct a different rule if the data were
        stored by columns and only three columns at a time
        could be stored in the computer's main memory?

2. Figure 3 shows the neighborhood configuration used for the
    initial feature normalization. Suppose we wish to normalize
    feature 6 (the mean of $g(y)$) at section (3,6) on the lower
    left breast. If $X_6^L(3,6) = 5$ and the right breast values
    for $X_6^R(i,j)$ are:

i

j	1	2	3	4	5	6	7	8	9
1	8	7	4	4	3	5	7	8	7
2	3	4	4	5	6	4	3	9	8
3	6	5	5	4	1	0	6	7	6
4	5	4	2	1	3	8	4	2	1
5	2	3	1	4	5	6	5	3	2
6	4	6	2	7	4	3	4	4	3
7	3	7	0	6	5	4			
8	0	8	4	4	3	2			
9	1	5	3						
10	2	1	2						

a) Compute $\mu_6^L(3,6)$ and $X_6^L(3,6)$ given that

   $N(3,6) = (2,5),\ (2,6),\ (2,7),\ (3,5),\ (3,7),\ (4,4),\ (4,5)$

b) Note that the 4th and 7th columns extend downward so that the skin at section (3,10) is contiguous to skin at section (4,8). With this in mind, enumerate the neighbors of sections (3,7), (7,5) and (4,2).

c) Design a data structure for the 72 sections' features so that the neighbors of a given feature can be obtained easily.

ANSWERS

2(a) $\mu_6^L(3,6) = 3,\ \hat{X}_6^L(3,6) = 2$

(b) $N(3,7) = (2,6),\ (2,7),\ (2,8),\ (3,6),\ (3,8),\ (4,5),$
          $(4,6)$

     $N(7,5) = (6,6),\ (6,7),\ (7,4),\ (7,6),\ (8,5),\ (8,6)$

     $N(4,2) = (3,1),\ (3,2),\ (3,3),\ (4,1),\ (4,3),\ (5,1),$
          $(5,2),\ (5,3)$

(c) HINT: Classify the different neighborhood configurations which can occur: such as those near columns 3, 4 or 6,7; those on the skin, chest wall, etc.. Then assign a configuration number to each section. When a section is to be normalized, the configuration number of the section identifies the table entries containing the N(i,j)'s.

EXAMPLE OF DIGITIZATION

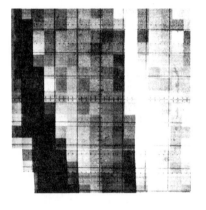

CHEST WALL and RIB at 1/16 REDUCTION

```
81  98  94  96  94 100  99  98 100 106 117 108 105 110 123 119
80  91  93  95  93 100  99  98 106 118 105 108 114 120
79  85  97  94  99  99 100  97  99 119 100 110 106 103 114
80  79 100  93  96  97  99  96  94  92 117  97 111 105 120 106
79  80  94  94  95  96  96  94  95  93 121 105 109 108 112 107
87  80  86  97  96  96  96  95  96  90 117 112 107 109 110 104
93  74  80 100  94  98  95  95  93  92 107 116 103 105 106 107
95  73  80  96  93  97  93  96  95  94  98 121 104 104 104 105
96  76  77  88  96  96  94  93  93  94  98 122 108 108 109 108
98  79  73  81  98  95  93  94  93  90  95 118 111 107 107 112
92  85  72  75 100  95  94  93  93  92  89 116 112 110 104 110
91  95  69  77  88  95  97  92  92  90  90 110 116 117 107 100
113 93  72  79  82  93  97  93  92  90  88 108 114 111 102 108
134 91  77  80  77  93  95  93  91  90  87  98 117 107  99 109
134 108 75  77  76  87  93  93  91  89  86  99 107 106 100 105
132 128 71  77  76  83  90  92  87  89  84  95 104 108 108 104 106
```

446

REFERENCES

1. Ackerman, L. V. and Gose, E. E.,"Breast Lesion Classifica-
    tion by Computer and Xeroradiographs," *Cancer, Vol. 30,
    No. 4,* pp. 1025-1035.

2. Alcorn, F. S., O'Donnell, E. R., and Ackerman, L. V., "The
    Protocol and Results of Training Nonradiologists to Scan
    Mammograms," *Radiology, 99,* pp. 523-529, 1971.

3. "Cancer Statistics, 1975," *Ca-A Cancer Journal for Clini-
    cians, Vol. 25, No. 1,* pp. 10-11.

4. Sebestyen, G. and Edie, J., "An Algorithm for Non-Parametric
    Pattern Recognition," *IEEE Transactions on Electronic Com-
    puters, Vol. EC-15, No. 6,* pp. 908-916.

5. Wolfe, J. N., "Analysis of 462 Breast Carcinomas," *American
    Journal of Roentgenology, Radium Therapy and Nuclear Medi-
    cine, Vol. 121, No. 4,* 1974, pp. 846-853.

6. Wolfe, J. N., *Xeroradiography of the Breast,* Charles C.
    Thomas Publishers, Springfield, Illinois, 1972.

Error-Correcting Parsing For
Syntactic Pattern Recognition

K. S. FU
School of Electrical Engineering
Purdue University
West Lafayette, Indiana

1. INTRODUCTION

Syntactic approach to pattern recognition has recently received an increasing attention [8]. In syntactic pattern recognition, a pattern in a class is described by a sentence (a
string of pattern primitives) in a language, which, in turn, is
generated by a (pattern) grammar. Syntax analysis or parsing
algorithms are then used as recognition procedures. When a pattern is represented by a sentence, it will be parsed with respect to the grammars characterizing different pattern classes.
The grammar which accepts the sentence will identify the class
assignment of the pattern and the parse of the sentence provides
the structural information of the pattern.

In practical applications, pattern distortion and measurement noise often exist. Misrecognitions of primitives and/or
subpatterns will lead to erroneous or noisy sentences rejected
by the grammar characterizing its class. With such a limitation, syntactic methods have often been regarded as only effective in dealing with abstract or artificial patterns. At least
three approacheds have been proposed to attack this problem.
They are: (1) the use of approximation [16], (2) the use of
stochastic languages [4-7], and (3) the use of transformational
grammars [11]. Recently, the use of error-correcting parser as
a recognizer of noisy and distorted patterns has been proposed
[9, 18]. In this approach, a pattern grammar is first expanded
to include all the possible errors into its productions or re-
writing rules. The original pattern grammar is transformed into

This work was supported by the National Science Foundation Grant
ENG-74-17586.

a covering grammar that generates not only the correct sentences but also all the possible erroneous sentences. If the pattern grammar is non-stochastic the minimum-distance criterion proposed by Aho and Peterson [1] for error-correcting parser can be applied. On the other hand, if the grammar is stochastic, the maximum-likelihood criterion can be used. A priori class probabilities, if available, can also be included in the decision criterion (e.g., the Bayes criterion).

In this chapter, both the minimum-distance and the maximum likelihood error-correcting parsers are described. They are then applied to the recognition of noisy and distorted patterns characterized by context-free grammars or transition network grammars. We first briefly introduce some basic notations and definitions of context-free grammars (CFG) and stochastic context-free grammars.

A CFG is a 4-tuple $G = (N,\Sigma,P,S)$ [10] where

N is a finite set of non-terminal symbols
Σ is a finite set of terminal symbols
P is a finite set of production rules, each of which is of the form $A \rightarrow \alpha$ where A is in N and α is in $(N \cup \Sigma)^*$
S is the start symbol

The context-free language generated by the CFG

G is $L(G) = \{x \mid x \in \Sigma^* \text{ and } S \overset{*}{=>} x\}$.

A stochastic CFG is a 4-tuple $G_S = (N,\Sigma,P_S,S)$, where N, Σ, and S defined as in CFG and P_S is a finite set of stochastic productions each of which is of the form:

$$A_i \xrightarrow{P_{ij}} \alpha_{ij}, \quad j = 1, 2, \ldots, n_i; \quad i = 1, 2, \ldots, k$$

where $A_i \in N$, $\alpha_{ij} \in (N \cup \Sigma)^*$ and P_{ij} is the probability associated with the application of this production:

$$0 < P_{ij} \leq 1 \text{ and } \sum_{j=1}^{n_i} P_{ij} = 1$$

The stochastic context-free language generated by G_S is

$$L(G_S) = \{(x,p(x)) \mid x \in \Sigma^*, S \overset{p_j}{\underset{*}{\Rightarrow}} x, j = 1, 2, \ldots, k \text{ and } p(x) =$$

$\sum_{j=1}^{k} p_j\}$ where k is the number of all distinctly different

derivations of x from S, and p_j is the probability associated with the jth distinct derivation of x.

II. MIN-DISTANCE ERROR-CORRECTING PARSER AS A SYNTACTIC PATTERN RECOGNIZER

The most common errors on symbols of a noisy sentence or string can be classified into substitution error, deletion error and insertion error. We may describe these errors in terms of three transformations, T_S, T_D, and T_I, respectively. For any x, y $\in \Sigma^*$

(1) substitution error: $xay \overset{T_S}{\vdash\!\!-\!\!-} xby$, for all a $\neq$ b,

(2) deletion error: $xay \overset{T_D}{\vdash\!\!-\!\!-} xy$, for all a in Σ

(3) insertion error: $xy \overset{T_I}{\vdash\!\!-\!\!-} xay$, for all a in Σ

Where the notation $\vdash\!\!-\!\!-\!\!-$ represents error productions, $x \overset{T_i}{\vdash\!\!-\!\!-} y$ means y $\in T_i(x)$ for some i $\in \{S,D,I\}$.

The distance between two sentences x and y in Σ^* could be defined by letting d(x,y) be the smallest integer k for which $x \overset{k}{\vdash\!\!-\!\!-} y$, i.e., the least number of transformation rules that are used to derive y from x. For example, given a sentence x = cbabdbb and a sentence y = cbbabbdb, then the distance is

d(x,y) = 3. Since x = cbabdbb $\overset{T_S}{\vdash\!\!-\!\!-}$ cbabbbb $\overset{T_S}{\vdash\!\!-\!\!-}$ cbabbdb $\overset{T_I}{\vdash\!\!-\!\!-}$ cbbabbdb = y, i.e., $x \overset{3}{\vdash\!\!-\!\!-} y$. The minimum number of transformations required is three.

Given a CFG $G = (N, \Sigma, P, S)$, an error-correcting parser is a parsing algorithm that with any input string $y \in \Sigma^*$ will generate a parse for some string x in $L(G)$ such that $d(x,y)$ is as small as possible.

Based on the above three types of errors, we first construct a covering grammar G' by adding error productions to G such that $L(G') = L(G) \cap \{x | x \in T_\delta (L(G)), \delta \in \{S, D, I\}^+\}$, the following is an algorithm that constructs $G' = (N', \Sigma', P', S')$.

<u>Algorithm 1</u>: A CFG $G' = (N', \Sigma', P', S')$

Step 1: For each production in P, substitute all terminal symbols $a \in \Sigma$ by a new non-terminal symbol E_a and add these productions to P'.

Step 2: Add to P' the productions

    a. $S' \rightarrow S$

    b. $S' \rightarrow SH$

    c. $H \rightarrow HI$

    d. $H \rightarrow I$

Step 3: For each $a \in \Sigma$, add to P' the productions

    a. $E_a \rightarrow a$

    b. $E_a \rightarrow b$ for all b in Σ, $b \neq a$

    c. $E_a \rightarrow Ha$

    d. $I \rightarrow a$

    e. $E_a \rightarrow \lambda, \lambda$ is the empty string.

Here $N' = N \cap \{S', H, I\} \cap \{E_a | a \in \Sigma\}$ and $\Sigma' = \Sigma$.

The production set P' obtained from Step 1 and $S' \rightarrow S$, $E_a \rightarrow a$ for all a in Σ, will give $L(G)$; $S' \rightarrow SH$ will insert errors at the end of a sentence; $E_a \rightarrow Ha$ will insert errors in front of a. Where productions of the form $E_a \rightarrow b$, $b \neq a$; $I \rightarrow a$; $E_a \rightarrow \lambda$ introduce substitution error, insertion error, and deletion error in a sentence respectively. We call them "terminal error productions".

The minimum-distance error-correcting parser is a modified Earley's algorithm [3]. It keeps counting the number of terminal error productions used and updates parse lists with the least number of terminal error productions. A flow chart of this parsing algorithm is given in the appendix.

Example 1: Consider the example of using a minimum-distance error-correcting parser as pattern recognizer to distinguish two different types of chromosomes, median and submedian. Two CFG's are developed. Each describes one class of chromosomes [13]. Also, they are disjoint from each other, that is, at most one grammar can accept a given string. If a string is not accepted by any of the two, then the pattern it represented can not be classified without using error-correcting parser. A minimum-distance pattern recognizer contains a minimum-distance error-correcting parser for each pattern grammar and a selector. The selector chooses the parse with the minimum number of terminal error productions used. A block diagram of the two-class pattern recognizer is given in Figure 1. In this example,

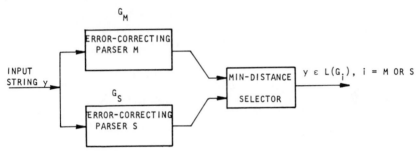

Figure 1: Block Diagram of the Min-distance Pattern Recognizer

Parser M represents the parser for median class, and Parser S represents the parser for submedian class.

Typical median and submedian chromosomes are shown in Figure 2(a) and (b). Grammars that used to describe median and submedian chromosomes are as follows:

Primitive: $\{$ —— , $\curvearrowright$, $\smile$, $\sim\!\!\smile$ $\}$
           b   a   c   d

Median $G_M = (N_M, \Sigma_M, P_M, S)$

$N_M = \{S, A, B, D, H, E, J\}$

$\Sigma_M = \{a, b, c, d\}$

P_M:
1.	$S \to AA$	5.	$D \to EDE$
2.	$A \to cB$	6.	$D \to d$
3.	$B \to EBE$	7.	$E \to b$
4.	$B \to JDJ$	8.	$J \to a$

Submedian $G_S = (N_S, \Sigma_S, P_S, S)$

$N_S = \{S, A, B, D, J, E, W, G, R, K, M, N\}$

$\Sigma_S = \{a, b, c, d\}$

P_S:
1.	$S \to AA$	11.	$R \to RE$
2.	$A \to cM$	12.	$R \to JNJ$
3.	$B \to EBE$	13.	$G \to EG$
4.	$B \to EL$	14.	$G \to d$
5.	$B \to RE$	15.	$W \to WE$
6.	$D \to EDE$	16.	$W \to d$
7.	$D \to EG$	17.	$M \to EBE$
8.	$D \to WE$	18.	$N \to EDE$
9.	$L \to EL$	19.	$E \to b$
10.	$L \to JNJ$	20.	$J \to a$

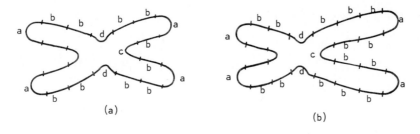

Figure 2a: *Median, string representation is*
cbabbdbbabcbabbdbbab

2b: *Submedian, string representation is*
cbabbdbbbabbcbbabbbdbbab

Let's consider substitution, deletion and insertion errors on b and d only. By following Algorithm 1, G_M and G_S can be converted into covering grammar G_M' and G_S' which are given in Table 1 and Table 2, respectively. In Table 1 and Table 2, the column entitled with "probability" is for the discussion of stochastic grammar that will be used in the next section.

TABLE 1

Covering Grammar G_M' for Grammar of Median Chromosome G_M

Rule No.	Production Rule	Probability	Rule No.	Production Rule	Probability
1	$S \rightarrow AA$	1.00	8	$J \rightarrow a$	1.00
2	$A \rightarrow cB$	1.00	9	$Ed \rightarrow d$	.95
3	$B \rightarrow EBE$	.20	10	$Eb \rightarrow b$	.80
4	$B \rightarrow JDJ$	.80	11	$Ed \rightarrow Hd$	.005
5	$D \rightarrow EDE$	.80	12	$Eb \rightarrow Hb$	.01
6	$D \rightarrow Ed$	.20	13	$H \rightarrow HI$	.1
7	$E \rightarrow Eb$	1.00	14	$H \rightarrow I$	.9

Table 1
(continued)
Covering Grammar G_M' for Grammar of Median Chromosome G_M

Rule No.	Production Rule			Probability
15	Ed	→	b	.03
16	Eb	→	d	.15
17	Ed	→	λ	.015
18	Eb	→	λ	.04
19	I	→	b	.9
20	I	→	d	.1

Table 2

Covering Grammar G_S' for the Grammar of Submedian Chromosome G_S

Rule No.	Production Rule	Probability	Rule No.	Production Rule	Probability
1	S → AA	1.00	14	G → Ed	.80
2	A → cM	1.00	15	W → WE	.20
3	B → EBE	.60	16	W → Ed	.80
4	B → EL	.20	17	M → EBE	1.00
5	B → RE	.20	18	N → EDE	1.00
6	D → EDE	.80	19	E → Eb	1.00
7	D → EG	.10	20	J → a	1.00
8	D → WE	.10	21	Eb → b	.80
9	L → EL	.20	22	Ed → d	.95
10	L → JNJ	.80	23	H → HI	.10
11	R → RE	.20	24	H → I	.90
12	R → JNJ	.80	25	Eb → Hb	.01
13	G → EG	.20	26	Ed → Hd	.005

Table 2
(continued)
Covering Grammar G_S' for the Grammar of Submedian Chromosome G_S

Rule No.	Terminal Error Production Rule	Probability
27	Eb → d	.45
28	Ed → b	.03
29	Eb → λ	.04
30	Ed → λ	.015
31	I → b	.9
32	I → d	.1

Listed in the following are examples of input strings, the outputs of the minimum-distance pattern recognizer, i.e., the parse of the input string, and the output strings derived from eliminating the terminal error productions used in the parse.

Case 1: Input String - cbbabbdbbabcdabbdbbbabb. Its parse is as follows:

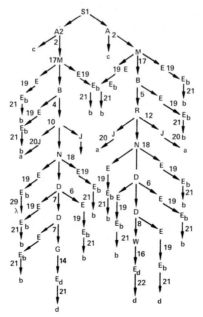

There has been one terminal error production used in this parse; that is the production rule no. 29, $E_b \rightarrow \lambda$ which represents a deletion error. After replacing it by the production rule $E_b \rightarrow b$, we obtain the string cbbabbdbbabcbabbdbbbabb. The above parse is selected from the output of Parser S; therefore, the pattern it described after the error correction is a sub-median chromosome as shown in Figure 2(b)

Case 2: Input string - cbabdbbbabcbabdbbab

Parse: S $\xrightarrow{1,2,17,19,21}$ AcEBb

$\xrightarrow{4,10,20,18,19,21}$ AcEEJEDbab

$\xrightarrow{8,19,21,16,22,19,21,20}$ AcEEabdbbab

$\xrightarrow{19,21,19,29}$ Acbabdbbab Let β = cbabdbbab

$\xrightarrow{2,17,19,21,5,19,29}$ cERbβ

$\xrightarrow{12,20,18,19,21,8,19,21}$ cEJEWbbabβ

$\xrightarrow{8,19,21,16,22}$ cEJEdbbbabβ

$\xrightarrow{19,21,20,19,21}$ cbabdbbbabcbabdbbab

In this parse, there are two deletion errors. After replacing the two production rules 29 by production rule 21, we obtain the string cbabdbbabbcbbabdbbab. This parse is also selected from the output of Parse S.

Case 3: Input string - cbabdbbabcbbabbdbbab

Parse 1. The parse from the output of Parser M is:

S $\xrightarrow{1,2,3,7,10}$ AcEBb

$\xrightarrow{4,8,5,7,10,5,7,10}$ AcEJEEDbbab

$\xrightarrow{6,9,7,10,7,10,8}$ AcEabbdbbab

$\xrightarrow{7,12,14,19}$ Acbbabbdbbab Let γ = cbbabbdbbab

$\xrightarrow{2,3,7,10,4,8}$ cEJDabγ

$$\underline{5,7,10,5,7,10,6,9} \rightarrow cEJEEdbbab\gamma$$

$$\underline{7,10,7,18} \rightarrow cEJbdbbab\gamma$$

$$\underline{8,7,10} \rightarrow cbabdbbabcbbabbdbbab$$

Parse 2. The parse from the output of Parser S is:

$$S \xrightarrow{1,2,17,19,21} AcEBb$$

$$\xrightarrow{4,10,20,18} AcEEJEDEab$$

$$\xrightarrow{19,25,31,7} AcEEJEDbbab$$

$$\xrightarrow{7,14,22,19,21,19,21,20,19,21,19,21}$$

Acbbabbdbbab

$$\xrightarrow{2,17,19,21,5} cEREb\gamma$$

$$\xrightarrow{19,29,12,20,8} cEJEDEab\gamma$$

$$\xrightarrow{19,21,8,19,21,16,22,19,21,20,19,21}$$

cbabdbbabcbbabbdbbab

Both Parse 1 and Parse 2 have one deletion error and one insertion error. Replacing them by their corresponding correct production rules, we obtain, correspondingly, the string cbabdbbabcbabbdbbab which represents a median chromosome and the string cbabdbbabbcbbabbdbab which represents a submedian chromosome. In this case, the minimum-distance selector gives both answers as correct classification. Either one could be chosen as the answer.

III.   STOCHASTIC (MAXIMUM-LIKELIHOOD) ERROR-CORRECTING PARSER

In Case 1 of Example 1, the deletion error has been corrected and the pattern has been classified as a submedian. But in Case 2, the output string derived is an unwanted string. That is, the pattern it described does not represent a legitimate chromosome pattern. Actually, unwanted strings are the excessive strings generated by the pattern grammar which is usually constructed heuristically by the designer. In this case, the minimum-distance error-correcting parser cannot avoid the possibility of selecting an unwanted pattern as its answer.

Stochastic language can be used to control the unwanted strings by assigning appropriate probability to each production
rule such that very small values of probability would be associated to the unwanted strings [8]. Also different (wanted)
strings could be associated with different values of probability
according to their frequencies of occurrence in practical cases.
A detailed discussion on methods of inferring production probabilities from a given grammar and sample information has been
presented in [7]. Using the approach of stochastic languages,
Case 3 can be solved by choosing the most likely pattern between the two.

In addition to the grammar error discussed above, the randomness of sentnece error, i.e., substitution error, deletion error,
and insertion error discussed in previous sections, can also be
taken into consideration [9].

In the following, we will discuss the use of probabilities
for substitution error, deletion error, and insertion error of
a terminal symbol. Let P^S, P^I, and P^D, be the error probability
associated with transformation T_S, T_I, and T_D, respectively. We
may denote them as:

(1) $xay \xrightarrow{\quad T_S, P^S_{ab} \quad} xby$, where $P^S_{ab} = p(b|a)$ is substitution
error probability.

(2) $xay \xrightarrow{\quad T_D, P^D_a \quad} xy$, where $P^D_a = p(\lambda|a)$ is deletion error
probability.

(3) $xay \xrightarrow{\quad T_I, P^I_{a\alpha} \quad} xa\alpha y$, where $P^I_{a\alpha} = p(\alpha a|a)$ is insertion err-
or probability. Furthermore,

$$\sum_{b \in \Sigma} p(b|a) + p(\lambda|a) + \sum_{\alpha \in \Sigma^*} p(\alpha a|a) = 1$$

If x and y are strings in Σ^*, $x = a_1, a_2, \ldots, a_n$ where a_i
$\in \Sigma$. We may partition y into n substrings $\alpha_1, \alpha_2, \ldots \alpha_n$ where
$\alpha_i \in \Sigma^*$, $i = 1, 2, \ldots, n$. We say y is the result of noise de-
formation of x with probability $p(y|x)$ if

$$p(y|x) = \sum_{\substack{\alpha_i}} \{ \sum_{i=1}^{n} p(\alpha_i|a_i) \}$$

all partition of y

Suppose that $G_S = (N, \Sigma, P_S, S)$ is a stochastic pattern grammar and each terminal is associated with some of the error probabilities. The maximum-likelihood error-correcting parser should be designed to assign the noisy string y to pattern class C_i such that for $x \in L(G_S)$, $P(y|x,C_i)P(x|C_i)P(C_i)$ attains its maximum value.

Before the discussion of the parsing algorithm, we first infer the stochastic CFG $G_S = (N, \Sigma, P_S, S)$ with terminal error probabilities as follows:

Algorithm 2. Let $\overline{G}_S = (\overline{N}, \Sigma, \overline{P}_S, S)$ be a stochastic CFG with error probabilities.

Step 1. For each production in P_S, substitute all terminal $a \in \Sigma$ by a new non-terminal E_a and add to $\overline{P}_S$ with probability assignment the same as that in P_S.

Step 2. Add to $\overline{P}_S$ the production rules

a. $S' \xrightarrow{P_{S_1}} S$

b. $S' \xrightarrow{P_{S_2}} SH$ where $P_{S_1} + P_{S_2} = 1$

c. $H \xrightarrow{P_{h_1}} HI$

d. $H \xrightarrow{P_{h_2}} I$ where $P_{h_1} + P_{h_2} = 1$

Step 3. Add to $\overline{P}_S$ the productions

a. $E_a \xrightarrow{p(a|a)} a$

b. $E_a \xrightarrow{p(b|a)} b$ for all b in Σ, $b \neq a$

c. $E_a \xrightarrow{p(\lambda|a)} \lambda$

d. $E_a \dfrac{p(\alpha a | a)}{} \to Ha$

Step 4.   For all $a \in \Sigma$ add to $\overline{P}_S$ the productions

$$I \xrightarrow{\ P_{I_a}\ } a \quad \text{where} \quad \sum_{a \in \Sigma_S} P_{I_a} = 1$$

Again, a modified Earley's parser is used as a maximum-likelihood error-correcting parser with a provision added to keep the
record of the probability associated with each item in the
parse list.   In this parsing algorithm, whenever items in a
parse list are identical, it adds the probabilities together
when their corresponding production is a terminal error production, and chooses the item associated with the maximum probability, otherwise.

    Algorithm 3:   Maximum-likelihood error-correcting parsing
algorithm.

    Input: A stochastic CFG $\overline{G} = (\overline{N}, \Sigma, \overline{P}, S)$ and a string
$y = a_1, a_2, \ldots a_n$ in Σ.
    Output: The parse lists $I_0, I_1, \ldots I_n$ for y.
    Method: Step 1.   Let $j = 0$, $i = 0$.   Add $[S' \to \cdot S, 0, p]$
and $[S' \to \cdot SH, 0, q]$ to I_0.

            Step 2.   If $[A \to \alpha \cdot B\beta, 0, q]$ is in I_j and $B \overset{R}{\to} \gamma$ is
in $\overline{P}$, then add item $[B \to \cdot \gamma, j, p]$ to I_j if it is not already in
I_j.

            Step 3.   If $[A \to \alpha \cdot B\beta, h, q]$ is in I_i, and $[B \to \gamma \cdot, i,
p]$ is in I_j, then add item $[A \to \alpha B \cdot \beta, h, r]$ to I_j, where $r = pq$.
Store with this item two pointers.   The first points to item
$[A \to \alpha \cdot B\beta, h, q]$ in I_i; the second to $[B \to \gamma \cdot, i, p]$ in I_j.   If
$[A \to \alpha B \cdot \beta, h, r']$ is already in I_j and if $A \to \alpha B\beta$ is an error production rule, then $r' = r' + r$, and do not add $[A \to \alpha B \cdot \beta, h, r]$
to I_j.   Otherwise, if $r' \geq r$, then do not add $[A \to \alpha B \cdot \beta, h, r]$
to I_j; if $r' < r$, then delete $[A \to \alpha B \cdot \beta, h, r']$ from I_j.

Step 4.   Repeat step 2 and 3 until no new item can be added to I_j.

Step 5. $j = j + 1$, if $j > n$, stop. Otherwise, go to step 6.

Step 6.   For each item $[A \rightarrow \alpha \cdot a\beta, i, p]$ in I_{j-1}, such that $a = a_j$, add $[A \rightarrow \alpha a \cdot \beta, i, p]$ to I_j. Along with this item, add a pointer to item $[A \rightarrow \alpha \cdot a\beta, i, p]$ in I_{j-1}. Go to step 2.

From these parse lists $I_0, I_1, \ldots, I_n$, we can extract a parse for y that is the most probable one among all the derivations of y. The algorithm that construct a parse π for x according to parse lists is almost identical to that of minimum-distance error-correcting parser and is given in step 2 of the appendix.

Example 2.   The chromosome patterns in Example 1 is again used to illustrate how this parsing algorithm classify a pattern from a given noisy string. Now the grammar G_{M_S} and G_{S_S} are inferred with probabilities and error probabilities are also added. $\bar{G}_{M_S}$ and $\bar{G}_{S_S}$ are given in Table 1 and Table 2 where we assume:
$p(d|d) = .95$; $p(b|d) = .03$; $p(a|d) = 0.15$; $p(\alpha d|d) = .005$; $p(b|b) = .80$; $p(d|b) = .15$; $p(a|b) = .04$; $p(\alpha b|b) = .01$. A block diagram of the maximum-likelihood pattern recognition system is shown in Figure 3 in which Parser M is designed for parsing $\bar{G}_{M_S}$ and Parser S is designed for parsing $\bar{G}_{S_S}$. The input string y parsed by both parsers will generate two parses, parse M and Parse S, with two associated probabilities, $P_M = p(y|x_M, C_M)p(x_M|C_M)$ and $P_S = p(y|x_S, C_S)p(x_S|C_S)$. Where x_M, $x_M \in \Sigma_M^*$. is the output string that is the most probable one among all the strings in $L(G_M)$, and x_S is among all the strings in $L(\bar{G}_S)$. Multiplying by the a priori probability $p(C_M)$ and $p(C_S)$, respectively, and passing through the selector, the class with higher value of probability will be selected. In this example we assume $P(C_M) = 1/3$, $p(C_S) = 2/3$.

The input strings in Case 1, Case 2, and Case 3, in Example 1 are now parsed by the maximum-likelihood error-correcting parser and it gives the following results:

<u>Case 1.</u>   Input string y = cbbabbdbbabcbabbdbbbabb

x_M = cbbabbdbbabbcbbabbdbbabb

P_M = .68 x 10^{-10}

$p(y|x_M, C_M)p(x_M|C_M)p(C_M)$ = .23 x 10^{-10}

x_S = cbbabbbdbbabcbabbdbbbabb

P_S = 4.21 x 10^{-10}

$p(y|x_S, C_S)p(x_S|C_S)p(C_S)$ = 2.81 x 10^{-10}

Therefore, the string x_S is selected, which corresponds to a submedian chromosome as shown in Figure 2(b).

<u>Case 2.</u>   Input string y = cbabdbbbabcbabdbbab

x_M = cbabbdbbabcbabbdbbab

P_M = 30.48 x 10^{-10}

$p(y|x_M, C_M)p(x_M|C_M)p(C_M)$ = 10.2 x 10^{-10}

x_S = cbabdbbabbcbbabbdbab

P_S = .24 x 10^{-10}

$p(y|x_S, C_S(p(x_S|C_S)p(C)$ = .16 x 10^{-10}

Therefore, the string x_M is selected which corresponds to a median chromosome as shown in Figure 2(a).

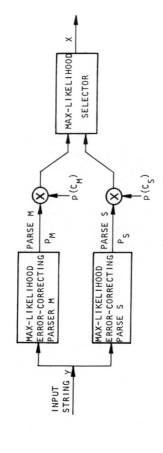

Figure 3

Block Diagram of Max-Likelihood Pattern Recognition System

465

<u>Case 3.</u> Input string: cbabdbbabcbbabbdbbab

x_M = cbabbdbbabcbabbdbbab

P_M = 131.7 x 10^{-10}

$p(y|x_M,C_M)p(x_M|C_M)p(C_M)$ = 43.9 x 10^{-10}

x_S = cbabdbbabbcbbabbdbab

P_S = 130.1 x 10^{-10}

$p(y|x_S,C_S)p(x_S|C_S)p(C_S)$ = 86.7 x 10^{-10}

Therefore, the string x_S is selected which corresponds to a submedian chromosome.

The results of case 1 in both examples are the same. In Case 2 the result from Example 2 gives a median chromosome. Thus, the dangers of deciding an unwanted pattern as that in Example 1 is avoided. In case 3 although x_M, x_S are almost equally probable with respect to both grammars, due to the fact that submedian chromosomes usually occur twice as many times as median chromosomes, i.e., $p(C_S) = 2p(C_M)$, the recognition system decides that the input string represents a submedian chromosome.

Usually, certain types of errors may occur more often than others. Statistics on types of errors will give larger values of probability to errors that occur more often. Thus, maximum-likelihood error-correcting parsers automatically gain the capability of controlling specific errors under consideration. For example, in median chromosome patterns, if there is a very high tendency of inserting b's in front of a terminal b, the unwanted pattern as shown in Figure 4 will be highly probable. In

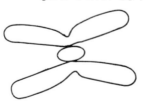

Figure 4: An Unwanted Median Chromosome Where Insertion of b's is More Likely to Occur

this case, $p(\alpha b|b)$ and P_{I_b} will have higher values such that the parse will contain more insertion error productions.

Table 3

An example of Eliminating Insertion Error.

	Input String y	Pattern	Output String X_M	Probability $p(y|X_M,C_M)$ $\cdot p(X_M|C_M)$
Case (a)	cbabbdbbab cbabbdbbab		the same as input	$.82 \times 10^{-6}$
Case (b)	cbbabbdbbabb cbbabbdbbabb		the same as input	$.43 \times 10^{-8}$
Case (c)	cbbbabbdbbabbb cbbbabbdbbabbb		cbabbdbbab cbabbdbbab	$.01 \times 10^{-8}$

Table 3 gives three median chromosome patterns, wanted or un-wanted, to illustrate how this parsing scheme can handle such situations. Here the probability associated with each produc-tion rule is the same as that in Table 1. The error probabili-ties are assigned as $p(\alpha b|b) = .4$, $p(b|b) = .6$ and $p_{I_b} = 1.0$.

IV. TRANSITION NETWORK GRAMMAR - INTRODUCTION

Transition Networks (TN) have been proposed by Woods as models for language analysis [19]. It has been found that transition network grammars are powerful and practical to model natural languages [12, 20]. It achieves some of the objectives of a transformational grammar and is efficient in representation and parsing. A basic transition network (BTN) is a directed graph with labeled states and arcs, a distinguished state called the

start state and a distinguished set of states called final states. It looks essentially like a nondeterministic finite state
transition diagram, except that the labels on the arcs may be
state names as well as input symbols. The interpretation of an
arc with a state name as its label is that the state at the end
of the arc will be saved on a pushdown store and the control
will jump (without advancing the input pointer) to the state
that is the arc label. When a final state is encountered, the
pushdown store may be "popped" by transferring control to the
state which is named on the top of the stack. An attempt to
pop an empty stack when the last input symbol has just been processed is the criterion for acceptance of the input string.

The TN described above is a generalized pushdown automaton
and is equivalent to a context-free grammar. However, a TN
could be augmented into a more powerful machine by adding facilities to each arc, including arbitrary conditions which must
be satisfied in order for the arc to be followed and a set of
register setting actions. Actually, an augmented transition
network (ATN) is similar to a two-pushdown-store automaton
which has been shown to be as powerful as a Turing machine.
The power of an ATN is determined by the facilities added to
the arcs.

A TN can be described as a generalized pushdown automaton
consisting of a finite set of finite-state machines and a finite set of pushdown stores. Formally, a TN can be defined as a
6-tuple.

$$TN = (\Sigma, Q, A, Q_0, Q_f, q_0)$$

Σ is a finite set of input symbols,

Q is a finite set of states,

$Q_0 \subseteq Q$ is the set of initial states of the
finite state machines,

$Q_f \subseteq Q$ is the set of final states of the
finite state machines,

$q_0 \in Q_0$ is the initial state of the TN

A is a finite set of arcs. Associated with each state there
are several arcs for transitions and actions. The arcs can be
categorized into five types:

1. CAT arc: (CAT C). A transition is made from the present state to the state at the **end** of the arc consuming an input symbol which is in the syntactic class labeled on the arc. The consumed symbol may be saved in a hold list when a HOLD action is required on the arc. This is done for future tests of context relationship.

2. PUSH arc: (PUSH q_0'): $q_0' \in Q_0$. The destination state of the arc is saved in the pushdown store and the state is transferred to the state shown on the arc which is the initial state of a finite-state machine.

3. POP arc: (POP) The state is transferred to the state shown on the top of the pushdown store. And the stack is popped one element up.

4. VIR arc: (VIR C). A transition from the present state to the state at the end of the arc is made by testing for the symbol shown on the VIR arc in the hold list.

5. JUMP arc: (JUMP) A transition from the present state to the state at the end of the arc is made if the conditions specified on the arc are satisfied. The transition does not consume any of the input string. This is a means of making a transition from one state to another without advancing the input pointer.

The input string is accepted if the input head is pointing beyond the last symbol of the string when popping the empty pushdown store with empty hold list.

Example 3. The set of directed graphs showin in Figure 5 is a BTN for simple sentences consisting of a noun phrase and a verb. A noun phrase can be a determinant followed by a common noun or just a proper noun.

A CAT arc represents a transition that can be taken of the word being scanned in the input string is a member of the syntactic category indicated on the arc. In taking such a transition, the pointer to the input string is advanced one symbol. A state with a pop arc means it is a final state. If a substring w causes a sequence of transitions from some initial state X to a final state Y, then w is said to be accepted by state X. The arc represents a transition that can be taken if a substring is accepted by the state indicated as the label of the PUSH arc. The transition of the arc (PUSH NP/) will be followed if the input pointer scans a substring accepted by the state NP/. After the transition, the input pointer is advanced beyond the accepted substring.

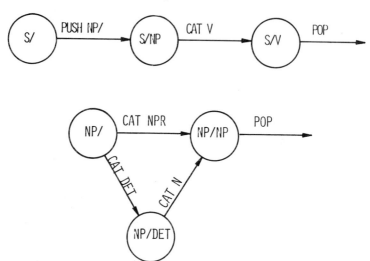

Figure 5:   The BTN for EXAMPLE 3

Example 4. The language $L = \{a^n b^n c^n \mid n \geq 1\}$ is known to be expressed as the following:

$G = (N, \Sigma, P, S)$

$N = \{S, B, C\}$

$\Sigma = \{a, b, c\}$

P: (1) $S \rightarrow aBC$ (4) $aB \rightarrow ab$ (7) $cC \rightarrow cc$

    (2) $S \rightarrow aSBC$ (5) $bB \rightarrow bb$

    (3) $CB \rightarrow BC$ (6) $bC \rightarrow bc$

From the view point of transformational grammars, productions (1) and (2) represent the deep structure (base) of the language. All the other productions are the transformations. The form of the strings generated through productions (1) and (2) is ...(a(a(abc)bc)bc). The parentheses are added to make the deep structure clear. Compare to the final form of the language (i.e, the surface structure) aaa...bb...ccc..., all the b's except the first one generated are out of place. That is, there are word order inversions between deep and surface structures of the language. The deep structure characterized in production (1) and (2) can be easily represented by a BTN shown in Figure 6.

Those b's that are out of places in the surface structure are going to be held in a stack. The stack is designed to temporarily hold pieces of the input sentence which are out of places. The hold list will be checked later by VIR arcs to place the pieces into their proper position in the deep structure. Two additional arcs are added to Figure 6 completing the ATN (see Figure 7) which analyzes L.

There are conditions and register setting actions required on arcs 4, 7, and 8. Initially, all the registers are off. Registers 1 and 2 are set after transitions are made through arcs 4 and 8 respectively. Transitions can be made through arcs 4 and 7 only when registers 1 and 2 are off respectively. With the aid of these registers, the network is prevented from accepting the language $\{a^n(bc)^n | n > 1\}$.

The language accepted by a TN can be parsed by Earley's Algorithm with minor modifications. It is easy to see the arcs of PUSH, CAT and POP are analogous to the operators, predictor, scanner and completer, respectively in Earley's Algorithm. The hold list can be constructed whenever required by the hold action. The VIR arcs can be handled in a way very much like that of CAT arcs. Instead of scanning the input tape, the parser checks the hold list to make state transitions without advancing the input pointer.

V.   RELATIONSHIPS BETWEEN TNG AND CHOMSKY'S HIERARCHY

It is interesting to compare the acceptors of phrase structure grammars with the transition networks. Note that a TN consists of a finite set of finite-state machines and pushdown stores. Consider a TN with only one network which is a set of states with CAT and POP arcs. This appears exactly like a finite-state automaton which accepts type 3 languages. If we consider a BTN with a set of finite-state machines and a push-

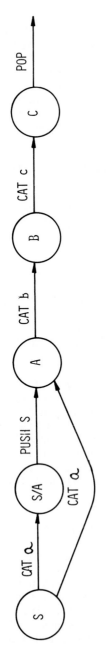

Figure 6: The BTN for EXAMPLE 4

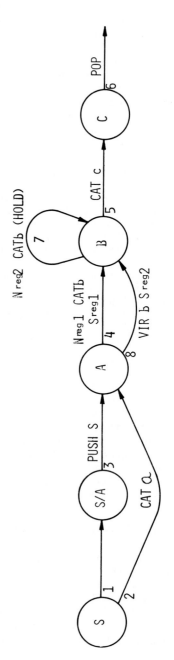

Figure 7: The Final ATN for EXAMPLE 4

472

down store, the BTN appears to be the same as the acceptor of a context-free language. With the aid of register-setting actions on the arcs and the checking action of the VIR arcs, the ATN could achieve the power of a Turing machine. Suppose that there is a bound on the summing size of all the stores of an ATN such that the size is less or equal to the rest length of the input string not yet scanned by the input pointer. Then the ATN appears to be like a linear-bounded automaton which accepts context-sensitive languages (CSL). It is then clear that an ATN is equivalent to a Turing machine. All the acceptors accepting different classes of languages can be derived from special cases of augmented transition networks. The conversion of a type 3 grammar to a finite automaton is quite straight-forward. Hence it is easy to construct a simple TN for a type 3 grammar. Constructing a BTN and a pushdown automaton from a CFG is a little different. It is necessary to convert first the CFG to its Greibach Normal Form, in order to obtain the pushdown automaton. It is, however, rather straightforward to convert a CFG to its BTN. The procedure is stated below.

Let $G = (N, \Sigma, P, S)$ be any CFG.

1. For $A \rightarrow \{\beta_1, \beta_2, \ldots \beta_t\}$ in P, $A \varepsilon N$, if there exists a β_i $(1 \leq i \leq t)$ such that $\beta_i \varepsilon \{(N \cup \Sigma)^* - \Sigma\}$ then let A be the name of the initial state of a subnetwork in BTN. A has t branches.

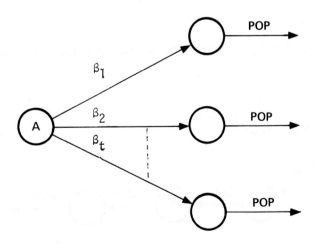

2. Let $\beta_i = x_1, x_2, \ldots, x_n$, $x_j \in (N \cup \Sigma)$ $\begin{array}{l} 1 < j < n \text{ each} \\ 1 < i < t \end{array}$

branch β_i is constructed as follows:

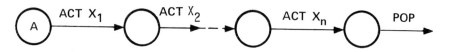

where ACT = CAT if $x_j \in N$ and x_j is not a subnetwork in BTN.

ACT = CAT if $x_j \in \Sigma$

ACT = PUSH if $x_j \in N$ and x_j is a subnetwork in BTN.

3. In each subnetwork, two arc sets are merged into one if they are identical, where an arc set is a state with one or more arcs coming out from it. And two arc sets are "unioned" if the two states are the destinations of the same set of arcs.

Example 5: $G = (\{S, T, E\}, \{a, *, +\}, P, S)$

where P: $S \rightarrow \{T, T+S\}$

$T \rightarrow \{E, E*T\}$

$E \rightarrow a$

According to step 1, E is not a subnetwork, S and T are subnetworks

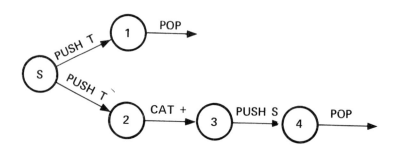

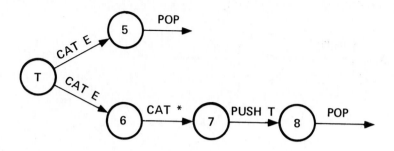

According to step 3, states 1 and 2 can be unioned

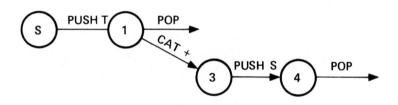

or states 1 and 4 can be merged.

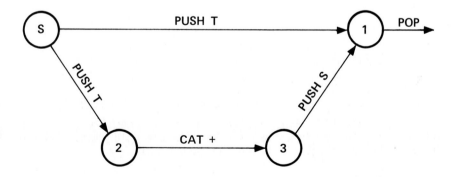

Similarly, states 5 and 6 can be unioned or states 5 and 8 can be merged. The resulting TN is shown in Figure 8.

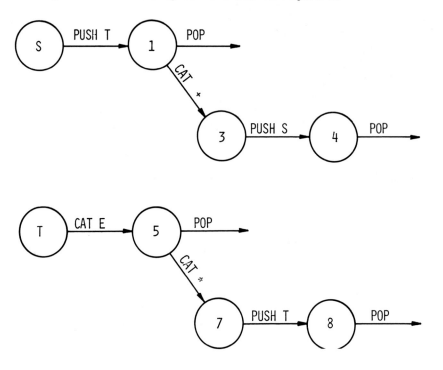

Figure 8: The TN for EXAMPLE 5

The procedure to convert a CSG to an ATN is rather flexible. The reason that an ATN can accept CSL is the additional facility of the hold list to remember the necessary context for the re-writing rules. It is straightforward that as long as the neces-sary information is held in the list, the designer is free to "program" his ATN. Consider Example 4, the CSL is $L = \{a^n b^n c^n \mid n \geq 1\}$. After the generation of $a^n b^n$ in the subnetwork Y/, $a^n b^n c^n$ is easy to produce if the count n is remembered. Thus in network Y/, the consumed bs' are held in the hold list. Then in network S/, a "c" is generated for each b held.

VI. STOCHASTIC TRANSITION NETWORKS

A stochastic TN is a TN with probability distributions defined over its arcs. It is defined as a 7-tuple STN = $(\Sigma, Q, A, D, Q_0, Q_f, q_0)$. Σ, Q, A, Q_0, Q_f, and q_0 are the same as those of TN.
D is a set of probability distributions over the set of arcs A*.
In an augmented transition network, it is important to note that all the augmented arcs, that are added to achieve the transformations in transformational grammars are virtual ones since the transitions through these augmented arcs are made only to aid the recovery of deep structures from their corresponding surface structures. Therefore, in assigning probability distributions to the arcs, the augmented arcs are considered nonexistent.
The probability of a sentence generated by a STN is the product of the probabilities on the arcs which are the path of generation. Let L(TN) be the language accepted by the non-stochastic version of a STN. Let $\Pi_x = r_1 r_2, \ldots, r_n$ be the sequence of arch numbers followed when a sentence is generated by the TN. Let P_{r_i} be the probability of arch r_i in the STN. The language accepted by the STN is defined as

$$L(STN) = \{(x, P(x)) | x \in L(TN), P(x) = \prod_{r_i \in \Pi_x} P_{r_i}\}$$

A stochastic transition network is a finite set of stochastic finite-state machines and pushdown stores. The STN with only one stochastic finite-state machine without any pushdown store is a stochastic finite-state automaton. The languages accepted by the STN are stochastic finite-state languages. The properties of stochastic languages studied in reference 5 are also true for the STN. The STN with a finite set of stochastic finite-state machines with only one pushdown store is a stochastic pushdown automaton. The language accepted by such a STN is a stochastic context-free language [5]. It turns out that a general STN is a stochastic Turing machine. A stochastic linear bounded automaton can be obtained by placing a bound on the summing size of the stores.

Example 6: A stochastic augmented transition network is constructed to accept the language

$$L = \{a^n b^n c^n, (0.5)^n | n \geq 1\}$$

---

*In order that the generated language will be consistent, the total probability of all the arcs associated with each state should be equal to one.

$$STN = (\Sigma, Q, A, D, \{S_0\}, \{S_4\}, S_0),$$

where

$$\Sigma = \{a, b, c\}$$

$$Q = \{S_0, S_1, S_2, S_3, S_4\}$$

and (A, D)

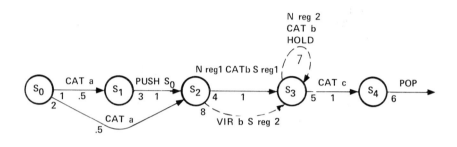

Here arcs 7 and 8 have been shown by dotted arcs to stress the fact that they are augmented arcs. Note that there are no probability assignment over these augmented arcs.

VII. ERROR-CORRECTING SYNTAX ANALYSIS FOR TNG

Earley's algorithm has the advantage that for an ambiguous language it finds every possible parse of the input sentence. However, there are many situations that not all parses are of interest. In the application such as error-correcting, the expanded grammar is large in size and highly ambiguous. The space and time needed for implementing Earley's algorithm sometimes become practically intolerable. Persoon and Fu [17] have proposed a sequential version of Earley's algorithm. The idea is to perform only part of the possible operations on a state at one time. As long as we can reach the final state, we conclude that the input string will be accepted. Otherwise, we have to trace out other paths from the beginning. This has been shown to be useful in improving the parsing efficiency. Woods, in his experimental parser [20], saves a list of alternative paths. At each point, the parser chooses a path to go and suspends all other possible paths in the alternative list. When the dead end of the path followed is confronted or other reasons which cause the parser to suspend the present path, the parser goes to the list for another path. The order of items in the list

determines the path priority to be followed by the parser.   The
local context and the parsing history of the sentence up to a
certain point are considered to be the variables of a function.
The function value becomes an index of ordering the suspended
paths.   With the aid of the list, the parser is able to save
the work completed during the previous process, and always
follows the most probable path.   In the case of stochastic TN,
the probability distribution over the arcs should be used as an
important information for ordering the alternative paths.   In
Example 7, the Earley's algorithm for a TN will be executed for
cases with and without an alternative list.

   Example 7:   Consider the transition network grammar shown
in Figure 9, and the input string aaaba.

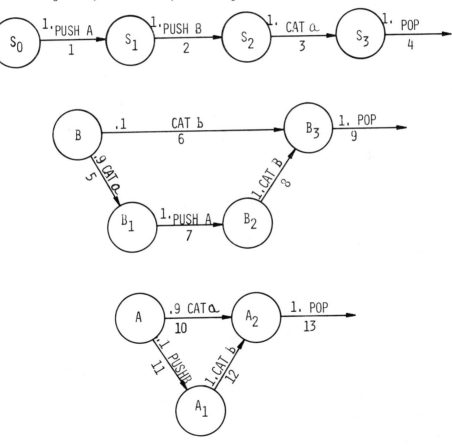

Figure 9:   The TN for EXAMPLE 7

The following is a step-by-step simulation of the Earley's parser for the input string.

1.   Nondeterministic Case

C_0 $<S_0, 0, 0>$ C_1 $<A_2, 0, 10>$

      $<A, 0, 1>$ $<B_1, 0, 5>$

      $<B, 0, 11>$ $<S_1, 0, 1>$

                                             $<A, 1, 7>$

                                             $<B, 1, 2>$

                                             $<B, 1, 11>$

C_2 $<A_2, 1, 10>$ C_3 $<A_2, 2, 10>$

      $<B_1, 1, 5>$ $<B_1, 2, 5>$

      $<B_2, 0, 7>$ $<B_2, 1, 7>$

      $<A, 2, 7>$ $<A, 3, 7>$

      $<B, 2, 11>$ $<B, 3, 11>$

C_4 $<B_3, 1, 8>$ C_5 $<S_3, 0, 3>$

      $<B_3, 3, 6>$ $<S_0, 0, 0>$

      $<S_2, 0, 2>$

      $<A_1, 1, 11>$

      $<A_1, 3, 11>$

                $n = 5$, $<S_0, 0, 0>$ ε C_5 $\Rightarrow$ aaaba ε L(TN)

2. Stochastic Case (with alternative list)

The arcs are ordered according to the probability distribution. When an item is added to the state sets, its position in the state sets is saved in the A list.

		A LIST
C_0, 1 $<S_0$, 0, 0>	C_1, 1 $<A_2$, 0, 10>	1 0,1'
		2 0,2
2 $<A$, 0, 1>	2 $<S_1$, 0, 1>	3 1,1'
		4 1,2'
	3 $<B$, 1, 2>	5 1,3
		6 2,1
C_2, 1 $<B_1$, 1, 5>	C_3, 1 $<A_2$, 2, 10>	7 2,2
		8 3,1
2 $<A$, 2, 7>	2 $<B_2$, 1, 7>	9 3,2'
		10 4,1
C_4, 1 $<B_3$, 1, 8>	C_5, 1 $<S_3$, 0, 3>	11 4,2
		12 5,1
2 $<S_2$, 0, 2>	2 $<S_0$, 0, 0>	13 5,2

$n = 5$ $<S_0$, 0, 0> ε C_5 => aaaba ε $L(TN)$

If the step of recognition is **incremented** by 1 when a state item is added, the resulting numbers of steps for the two procedures are listed below:

nondeterministic 26
stochastic with A LIST 13

Following Aho's and Peterson's algorithm of adding error productions to a context-free grammar, a straightforward way of constructing an error-correcting model for transition network grammars can be carried out. Given a basic transition network with n state, $TN = (\Sigma, Q, A, Q_0, Q_f, q_0)$, construct a new transition network TN' by adding new arcs to TN as follows:

Step 1. For each CAT arc like 'CAT a' from state q_i to state q_j, i,j = 1,...,n, i $\neq$ j, in TN, add to TN arcs.

a. 'CAT b' from state q_i to state q_j, for every b ε Σ - {a},

b. 'CAT c' from state q_i to state q_i, for
    every c ε Σ, or simply denoted as CAT Σ,

c. 'JUMP' from state q_i to state q_j.

Step 2. Construct a new subnetwork q_0' as follows:

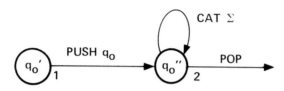

The error correcting model for TN is TN' = $(\Sigma,Q',A',Q_0',Q_f',q_0')$,
where Q' = Q ∪ {q_0', q_0''}, A' includes A and all arcs added by
the above procedure, Q_0' = Q_0 ∪ {q_0'}, Q_f' = Q_f ∪ {q_0''}. All the
arcs added by the above procedure except arcs 1 and 2 in Step 2
are called error arcs. The transition through an error arc
will introduce a syntax error. In TN', the arc 'CAT B' introduces a replacement error. 'JUMP' introduces a deletion error.
The arc 'CAT Σ' introduces one insertion error. To place one
or more insertion errors at the end of a sentence, we add 'CAT
c' at the final state of the subnetwork q_0'.

Example 8: A series of experiments have been performed
on the voice-chess language [15]. Its lexicon and BNF grammar
are shown in Table 4 and Table 5. A transition network grammar
constructed using the algorithm described in Section V is shown
in Figure 10. Furthermore, errors of replacement for each CAT
arc are assumed. A set of probability distribution over the
arcs is arbitrarily assigned. The resulting expanded transition
network for error-correction is shown in Figure 11.

The set of sentences is prepared by a generator traversing
through every possible path of the expanded transition network.
Along with each sentence generated, there is a list of arc
numbers representing the traversed path and a probability value
weighting the sentence in the language. The weighting value is
the product of the probabilities on the arcs of the path. There
are 2,418 sentences generated. The total weight is one. Among
the sentences, there are correct ones weighting 0.60445 (i.e.,
60.445% of the set), and noisy ones weighting 0.39555 (i.e.,
39.555% of the set). There are 2.7196% of the set that have

zero distance from correct sentences. That is, given X_i, X_j ϵ L, where L is the correct set of the language if X_i is deformed and appeared as X_j, the X_j is a noisy form of X_i.[1] But X_j itself is actually syntactically correct. Then the noisy form of X_i has zero distance from X_j ϵ L. In this case, it is impossible to recover X_i from X_j.

The noisy language is fed into parsers implementing Earley's algorithm with and without alternative list. The number of parsing steps is incremented by one for each test taken in transition through the arcs. Since only substitution error is assumed, the parsers accept every such Y_j ϵ Σ^* that exists X_L ϵ L and $|X_L| = |Y_j|$ where $|X_L|$ is the length of sentence X_L. The number of paths through the expanded transition network for an input string Y_j is usually very large. For the error-correcting parser, only the "best" path is needed. In the Earley's algorithm, each state item has to keep an index. If the minimum-distance criterion is used, it indicates the number of correct terminals have been encountered up to the point. When a new state item is going to be added to a state set, the parser has to check through that set. Should any state in the set be the same as the added state, the parser further checks to see their indices. Only the state item with higher index will be kept in the set. In the case that the maximum-likelihood criterion is used, the index indicates the weight of the parsing path up to the point. The weight value can be the product of the probabilities of arcs traveled. When the input string is accepted, its parsing path is compared to its generating path. If the two are identical, the string is correctly recovered. If they are different, the string is mis-recovered.

Both stochastic and nondeterministic cases are tested. For the parser without the alternative list, the nondeterministic case is tested using the minimum-distance criterion and the stochastic case using the maximum-likelihood criterion. For the parser with alternative list, the error-correcting criterion is mainly the minimum-distance. The nondeterministic case is implemented using a purely randomized strategy based on the assumption of selecting arcs with equal probabilities. The stochastic case is implemented with the arcs ordered according to the probability information. The parser always follows the most probable path, it automatically satisfies the maximum-likelihood criterion. The percentage distribution of the source input and the corrected results for different sentence lengths is tabulated in Table 6. The correct percentage in terms of sentence

484   K. S. FU

length is shown and plotted in Table 7 and Figure 12, respectively. The average parsing steps vs. sentence length is shown in Table 8 and plotted in Figure 13.

It is noted that the error-correcting parsers employing probability information give better results both in correctly recovered sentences and in average parsing steps. By employing an alternative list, the number of parsing steps is greatly reduced. Though, there is some trade-offs for the correctly recovered sentences, it is, however, very small when compared with the reduction in average parsing steps. Furthermore, the error-correcting parser with alternative list results in an average number of parsing steps which is close to the average parsing steps of the nonerror-correcting parser. That is, without too much additional cost, the error-correcting parser with alternative list can recover most of the noisy sentences.

APPENDIX

Input: The covering grammar G' = (N', Σ', P', S) string
x = $a_1 a_2 \ldots a_n$ in Σ*

STEP 1:   CONSTRUCT PARSE LIST $I_0, I_1 \ldots I_n$ FOR x.

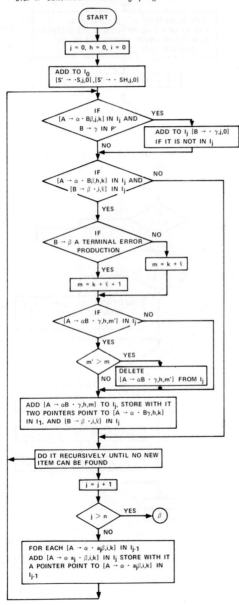

STEP 2:   FROM $I_0, I_1, ..., I_n$ FIND PARSE π.

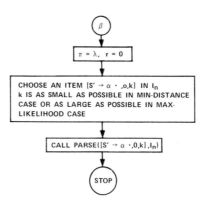

β

$\pi = \lambda, \quad r = 0$

CHOOSE AN ITEM $[S' \rightarrow \alpha \cdot , o, k]$ IN I_n
k IS AS SMALL AS POSSIBLE IN MIN-DISTANCE
CASE OR AS LARGE AS POSSIBLE IN MAX-
LIKELIHOOD CASE

CALL PARSE($[S' \rightarrow \alpha \cdot, 0, k], I_n$)

STOP

SUBROUTINE PARSE ($[A \rightarrow \alpha \cdot \beta, i, \ell], I_j$)

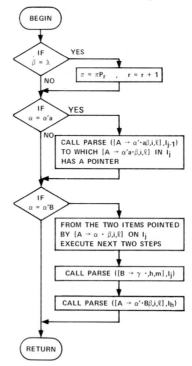

BEGIN

IF
$\beta = \lambda$ — YES → $\pi = \pi P_r$, $r = r + 1$

NO

IF
$\alpha = \alpha' a$ — YES → CALL PARSE ($[A \rightarrow \alpha' \cdot a\beta, i, \ell], I_{j-1}$)
TO WHICH $[A \rightarrow \alpha' a \cdot \beta, i, \ell]$ IN I_j
HAS A POINTER

NO

IF
$\alpha = \alpha' B$ → FROM THE TWO ITEMS POINTED
BY $[A \rightarrow \alpha \cdot \beta, i, \ell]$ ON I_j
EXECUTE NEXT TWO STEPS

CALL PARSE ($[B \rightarrow \gamma \cdot, h, m], I_j$)

CALL PARSE ($[A \rightarrow \alpha' \cdot B\beta, i, \ell], I_h$)

RETURN

Table 4

The Lexicon of the Voice-Chess Language

Words	Abbreviations	Words	Abbreviations
Bishop	B	Mate	M
Bishop's	B	Moves-to	-
Captures	X	On	/
Castle	C	One	1
Castles	C		
Check	CH	Pawn	P
Eight	8	Queen	Q
En-passant	E	Queen's	Q
Five	5	Rook	R
Four	4	Rook's	R
Goes-to	-	Seven	7
		Side	S
King	K	Six	6
King's	K		
Knight	N	Takes	X
Knight's	N	Three	3
		To	-
		Two	2

Table 5

The BNF Grammar of the Voice-Chess Language

```
1.  <moved>  :: = <regular-move>|<capture>|<castle>
2.  <castle> :: = <castle-word> ON <uniroyal> SIDE
                  |<castle-word><uniroyal> SIDE
                  |<castle-word>
3.  <regular-move>  :: = <man-spec><move-word><square>
4.  <capture> :: = <man-spec><capture-word>
                   PAWN EN-PASSANT
                  | <man-spec><capture-word><man-spec>
5.  <castle-word> :: = CASTLE|CASTLES
6.  <move-word> :: = TO|MOVES- TO|GOES-TO
7.  <CAPTURE-WORD>:: = TAKES CAPTURES
8.  <man-spec> :: = <uniroyal><unipiece> PAWN
                   |<uniroyal><piece>
                   |<uniroyal>PAWN
                   |<unipiece>PAWN
                   |<man>
9.  <square> :: = <uniroyal><piece><rank>| <nopawn><rank>
10. <man> :: = KING|QUEEN|BISHOP|KNIGHT|ROOK|PAWN
11. <uniroyal> :: = KING|QUEEN|KING'S|QUEEN'S
12. <unipiece> :: = BISHOP|KNIGHT|ROOK
                  |BISHOP'S|KNIGHT'S|ROOK'S
13. <nopawn> :: = KING|QUEEN|BISHOP|KNIGHT|ROOK
14. <piece> :: = BISHOP|KNIGHT|ROOK
15. <rank> :: = ONE|TWO|THREE|FOUR|FIVE|SIX|SEVEN|EIGHT
```

Table 6

Percentage Distribution of the Source Input and the Corrected Results

Length	1	2	3	4	5	6	7	Total
SOURCE	2.0	0	6.813	27.323	34.549	25.019	4.297	100
non-error-correcting parse	1.8	0	4.967	17.927	20.400	13.296	2.055	64.445
without a list — nondeterministic error correcting	2.0	0	6.659	24.501	28.640	22.509	4.283	88.590
without a list — stochastic error correcting	2.0	0	6.639	25.06	29.924	23.400	4.283	91.308
with a list — nondeterministic error correcting	2.0	0	6.681	23.730	25.827	19.141	3.872	81.251
with a list — stochastic error correcting	2.0	0	6.697	25.280	29.460	21.352	4.58	88.947

Table 7

Corrected Percentages in Terms of Sentence Length

		1	2	3	4	5	6	7
	non-error-correcting	90		72.9	65.6	59.1	53.1	46.7
without a list	nondeterministic error-correcting	100		97.7	89.7	83.0	90.0	99.7
	stochastic error-correcting	100		97.4	91.7	86.6	93.6	99.7
with a list	nondeterministic error-correcting	100		98.1	86.9	74.9	76.5	90.1
	stochastic error-correcting	100		98.3	92.6	85.4	85.4	96.8

Table 8

Average Parsing Steps

	1	2	3	4	5	6	7	Total
NEC	8		10.9	14.2	19.9	23.7	26.9	11.49
NSE-C	19.1		73.1	107.3	130	142.6	148.1	121.66
SE-C	19.1		73.1	106.7	129.2	141.2	147.1	120.83
A	4		9.53	14.1	22.15	25.34	31.6	19.93
NSE-C	5.7		9.1	12.9	17.6	19.9	25.5	16.44

REFERENCES

1. Aho, A. V. and Peterson, T. G., "A Minimum Distance Error-Correcting Parser for Context-Free Language," *SIAM Journal of Computing, Vol. 1,* December 1972.

2. Chou, S. M. and Fu, K.S., "Transition Network Grammars for Syntactic Pattern Recognition," *Proceedings Conference on Computer Graphics, Pattern Recognition and Data Structure,* May 14-16, 1975, Los Angeles, California.

3. Earley, J., "An Efficient Context-Free Parsing Algorithm," *Comm. ACM,* February 1970.

4. Fu, K.S., "Stochastic Automata, Stochastic Languages and Pattern Recognition," *Journal of Cybernetics, Vol 1, No. 3,* 1971.

5. Fu, K.S., and Huang, T., "Stochastic Grammars and Languages," *International Journal of Computer and Informational Sciences, Vol 1, No. 2,* 1972.

6. Fu, K.S., "On Syntactic Pattern Recognition and Stochastic Languages," in *Frontiers of Pattern Recognition,* ed. by S. Watanabe, Academic Press, 1972.

7. Fu, K. S., "Stochastic Languages for Picture Analysis," *Computer Graphics and Image Process, Vol. 2,* 1973.

8. Fu, K. S., *Syntactic Methods in Pattern Recognition,* Academic Press, 1974.

9. Fung, L. W. and Fu, K. S., "Stochastic Syntactic Decoding for Pattern Classification," *IEEE Trans. on Computers, Vol. C-24, No. 6,* 1975.

10. Hopcroft, John E. and Ullman, Jeffrey, D., *Formal Languages and Their Relation to Automata,* Addison-Wesley, 1969.

11. Joshi, A. K., "Remarks on Some Aspects of Language Structure and Their Relevance to Pattern Analysis," *Pattern Recognition, Vol. 5, No. 4,* 1973.

12. Kaplan, Ronald M., "Augmented Transition Networks as Psychological Models of Sentence Comprehension," *Artificial Intelligence, 3,* 1972.

13. Lee, H. C. and Fu, K. S., "A Stochastic Syntax Analysis Procedure and Application of Pattern Classification," *IEEE Trans. on Computers, Vol. C-21, No. 7,* 1972.

14. Lu, S. Y. and Fu, K. S., "Error-Correcting Syntax Analysis for Recognition of Noisy and Distorted Patterns," *Proc. International Computer Symposium 1975,* August 20-22, 1975, Taipei, Republic of China.

15. Neely, R. B., "On the Use of Syntax and Semantics in a Speech Understanding System," Ph.D. Thesis, Dept. of Computer Science, Carnegie-Mellon University, May 1973.

16. Pavlidis, T., "Functional Approximation for Syntactic Pattern Recognition," US-Hungary Seminar on Pattern Recognition, June 10-14, 1975, Budapest, Hungary.

17. Persoon, E., and Fu, K.S., "Sequential Decision Procedures with Prespecified Error Probabilities and Their Applications," TR-EE 74-30, August 1974, School of Electrical Engineering, Purdue University, West Lafayette, Ind. 47907.

18. Thomason, M. G. and Gonzalez, R. G., "Syntactic Recognition of Imperfectly Specified Patterns," *IEEE Trans. on Computers, Vol. C-24, No. 1,* 1975.

19. Woods, W. A., "Transition Network Grammars for Natural Language Analysis," *CACM,* Oct. 1970.

20. Woods, W. A., "An Experimental Parsing System for Transition Network Grammars," BBN Report No. 2362, May 1972.

Index